BEASTARS

Volume 12

Story & Art by
Paru Itagaki

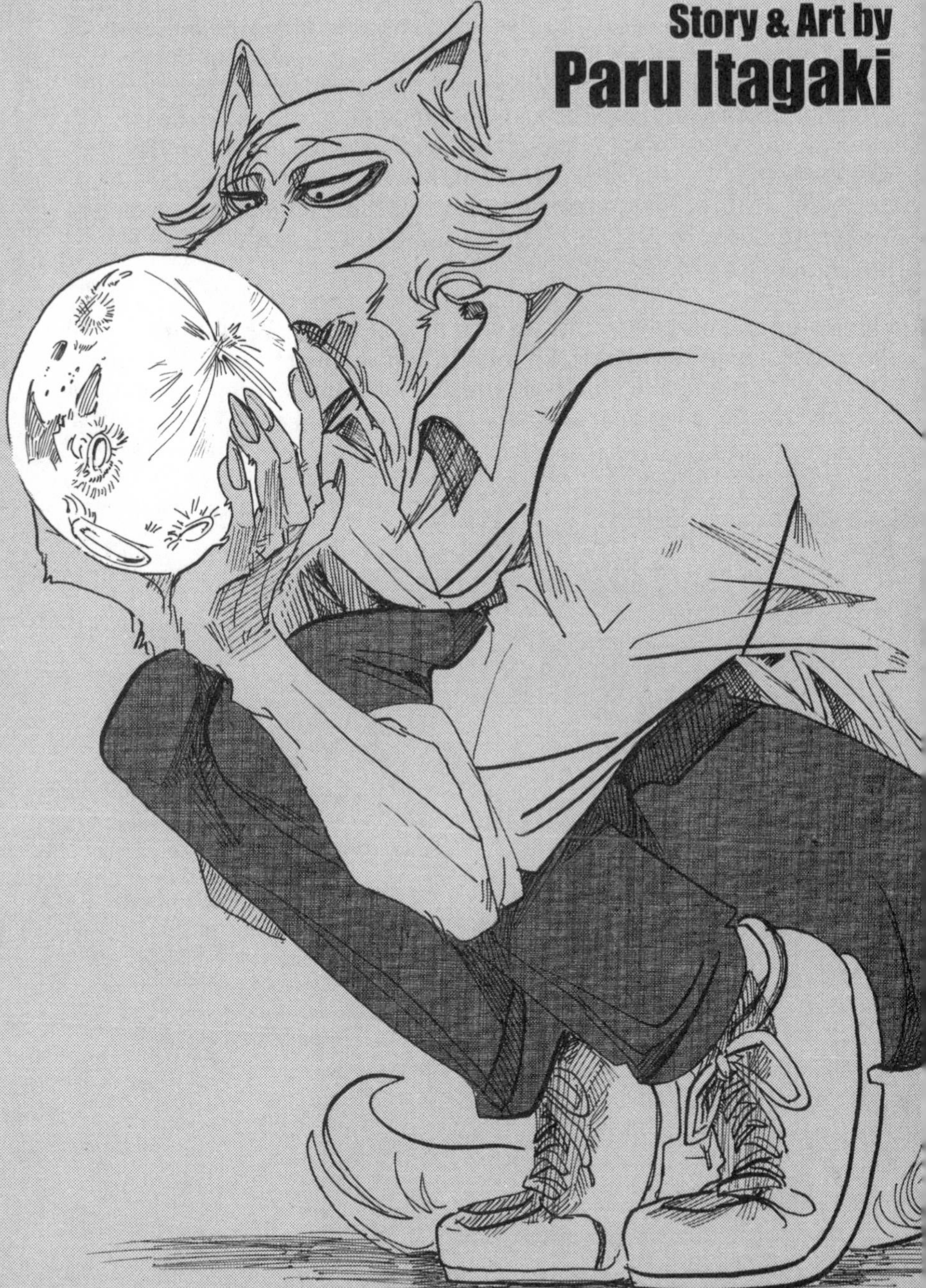

STORY & CAST OF CHARACTERS

Cherryton Academy is an integrated boarding school for a diverse group of carnivores and herbivores. Recently Tem, an alpaca member of the Drama Club, was slain and devoured on campus. Since then tensions between predators and prey have been running high...

On New Year's Eve, Legoshi battles Riz, the brown bear who murdered Tem. Riz has come into his full strength, having prepared for their showdown by ceasing to take the legally mandated medications that atrophy his muscles. Legoshi is losing the fight, even though he is motivated by a desire for justice and is willing to put his life on the line to defend his herbivore friends. Meanwhile, as Louis abdicates his leadership of the Shishi-gumi lion gang, his most faithful gang member Ibuki gets killed. Then Louis offers his right leg to Legoshi to give him the strength to overcome Riz.

Carnivores and herbivores. Those who devour and those who are devoured. Opposites attract. Riz admits defeat when he witnesses the true bond of friendship between Legoshi and Louis. The fight is over. But then the police appear and haul Riz and Legoshi away!

Legoshi

★Gray wolf ♂
★High school second-year
★Member of the Drama Club production crew
★Physically powerful yet emotionally sensitive
★Struggles with his identity as a carnivore

B
E
A
S
T
A
R
S

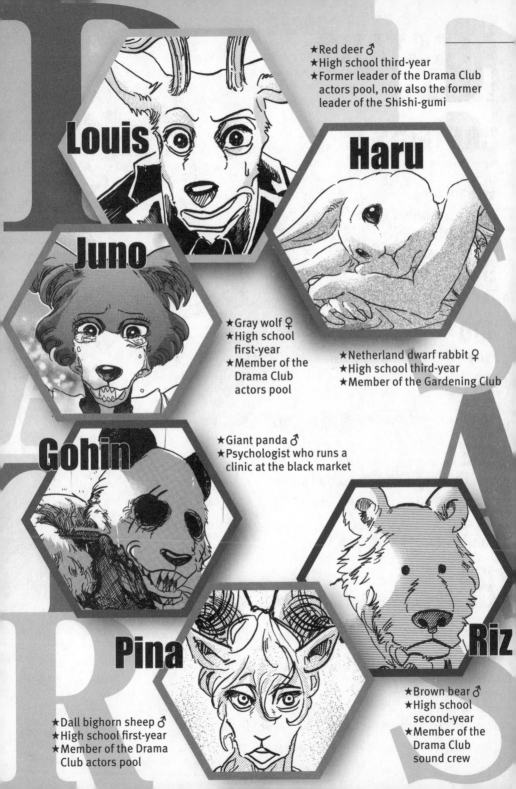

Louis

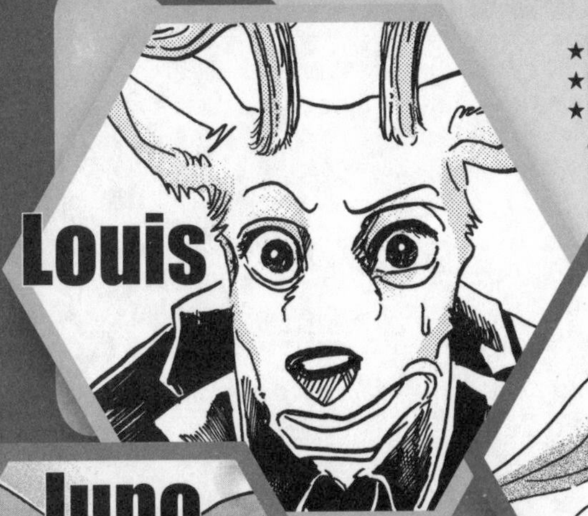

★Red deer ♂
★High school third-year
★Former leader of the Drama Club actors pool, now also the former leader of the Shishi-gumi

Haru

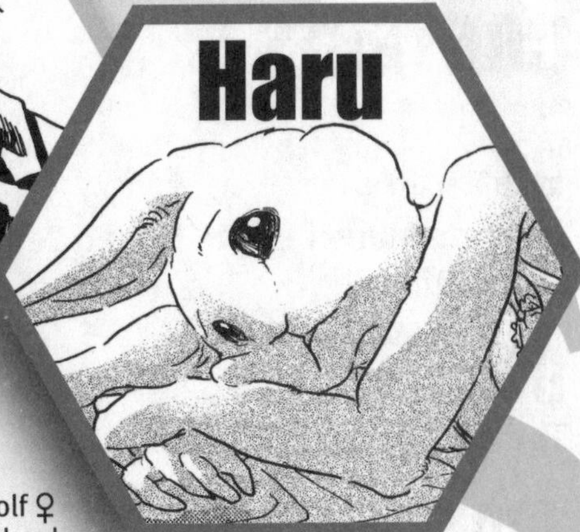

★Netherland dwarf rabbit ♀
★High school third-year
★Member of the Gardening Club

Juno

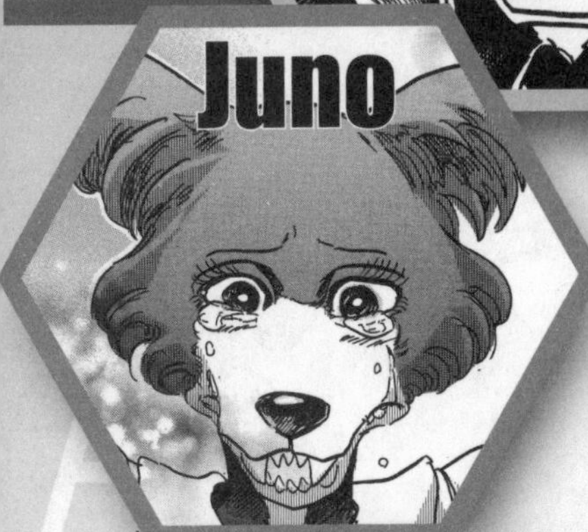

★Gray wolf ♀
★High school first-year
★Member of the Drama Club actors pool

Gohin

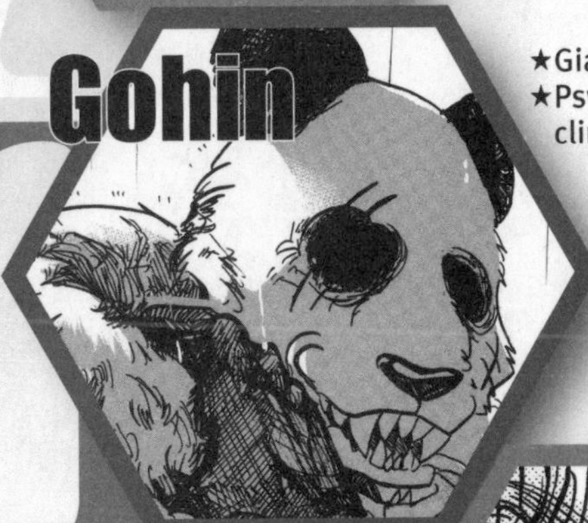

★Giant panda ♂
★Psychologist who runs a clinic at the black market

Riz

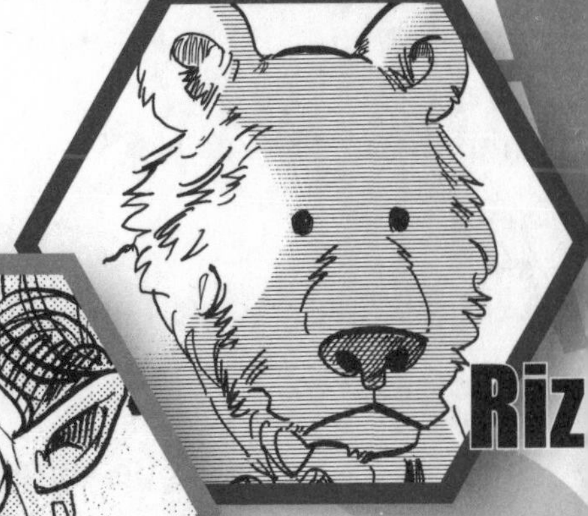

★Brown bear ♂
★High school second-year
★Member of the Drama Club sound crew

Pina

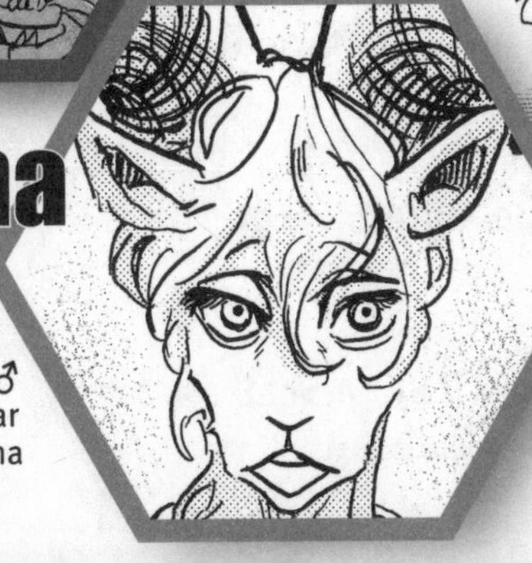

★Dall bighorn sheep ♂
★High school first-year
★Member of the Drama Club actors pool

BEASTARS
Volume 12

CONTENTS

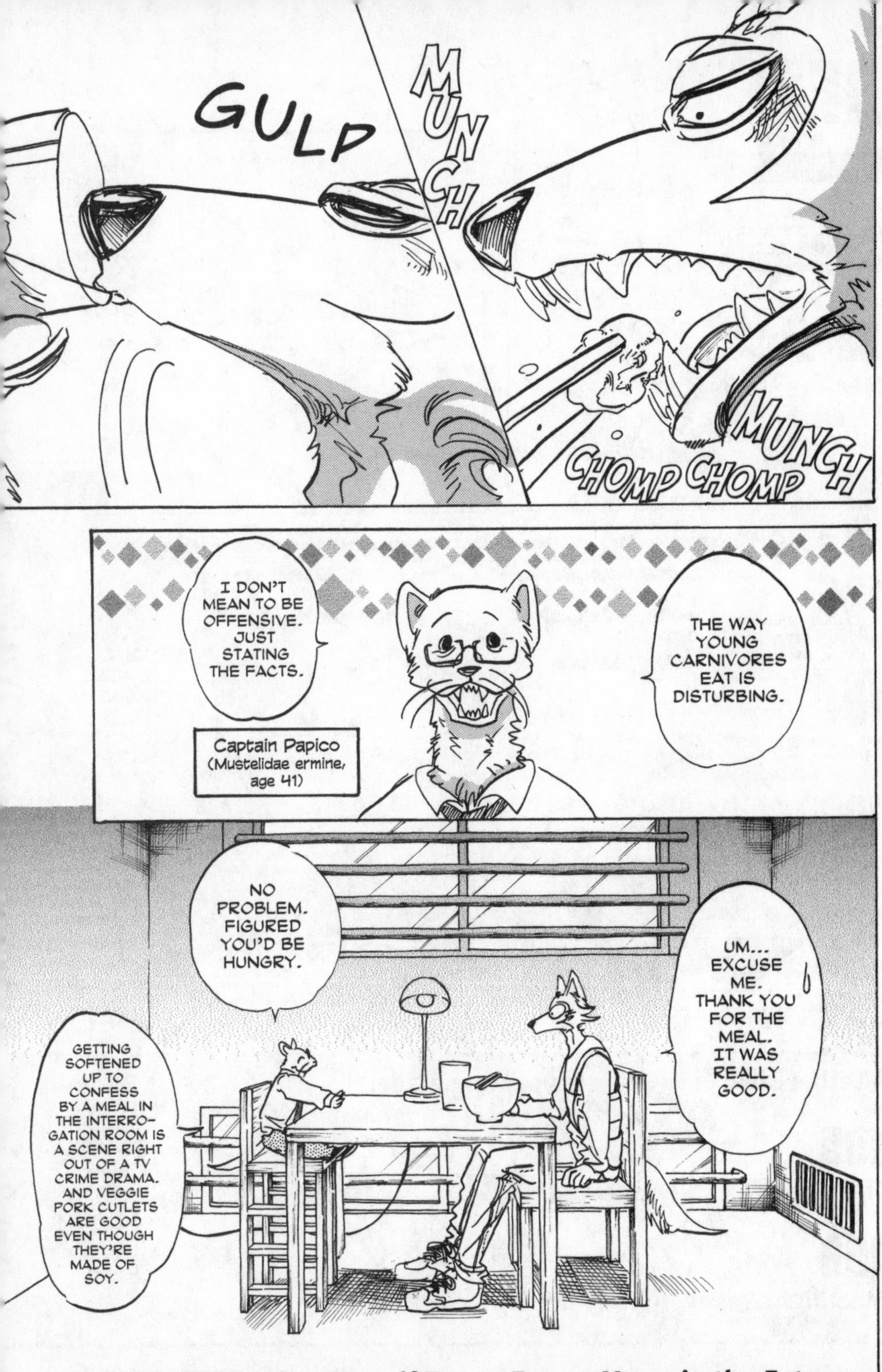
MUNCH
MUNCH
CHOMP CHOMP
GULP
THE WAY YOUNG CARNIVORES EAT IS DISTURBING.
I DON'T MEAN TO BE OFFENSIVE. JUST STATING THE FACTS.
Captain Papico (Mustelidae ermine, age 41)
UM... EXCUSE ME. THANK YOU FOR THE MEAL. IT WAS REALLY GOOD.
NO PROBLEM. FIGURED YOU'D BE HUNGRY.
GETTING SOFTENED UP TO CONFESS BY A MEAL IN THE INTERRO-GATION ROOM IS A SCENE RIGHT OUT OF A TV CRIME DRAMA. AND VEGGIE PORK CUTLETS ARE GOOD EVEN THOUGH THEY'RE MADE OF SOY.

Chapter 98: Meeting Myself Eye to Eye 20 Years in the Future

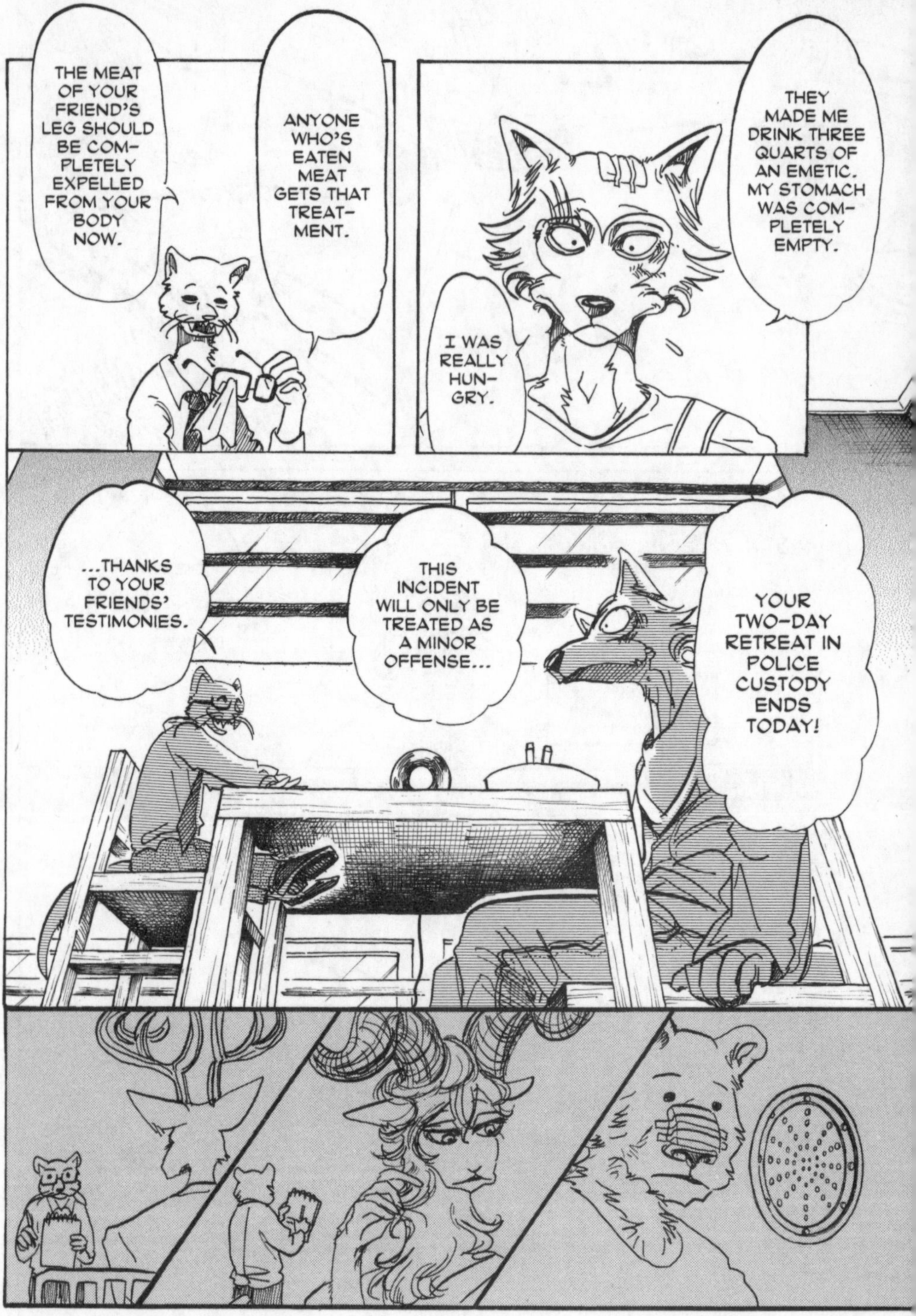

THEY MADE ME DRINK THREE QUARTS OF AN EMETIC. MY STOMACH WAS COMPLETELY EMPTY.
I WAS REALLY HUNGRY.
ANYONE WHO'S EATEN MEAT GETS THAT TREATMENT.
THE MEAT OF YOUR FRIEND'S LEG SHOULD BE COMPLETELY EXPELLED FROM YOUR BODY NOW.
YOUR TWO-DAY RETREAT IN POLICE CUSTODY ENDS TODAY!
THIS INCIDENT WILL ONLY BE TREATED AS A MINOR OFFENSE...
...THANKS TO YOUR FRIENDS' TESTIMONIES.

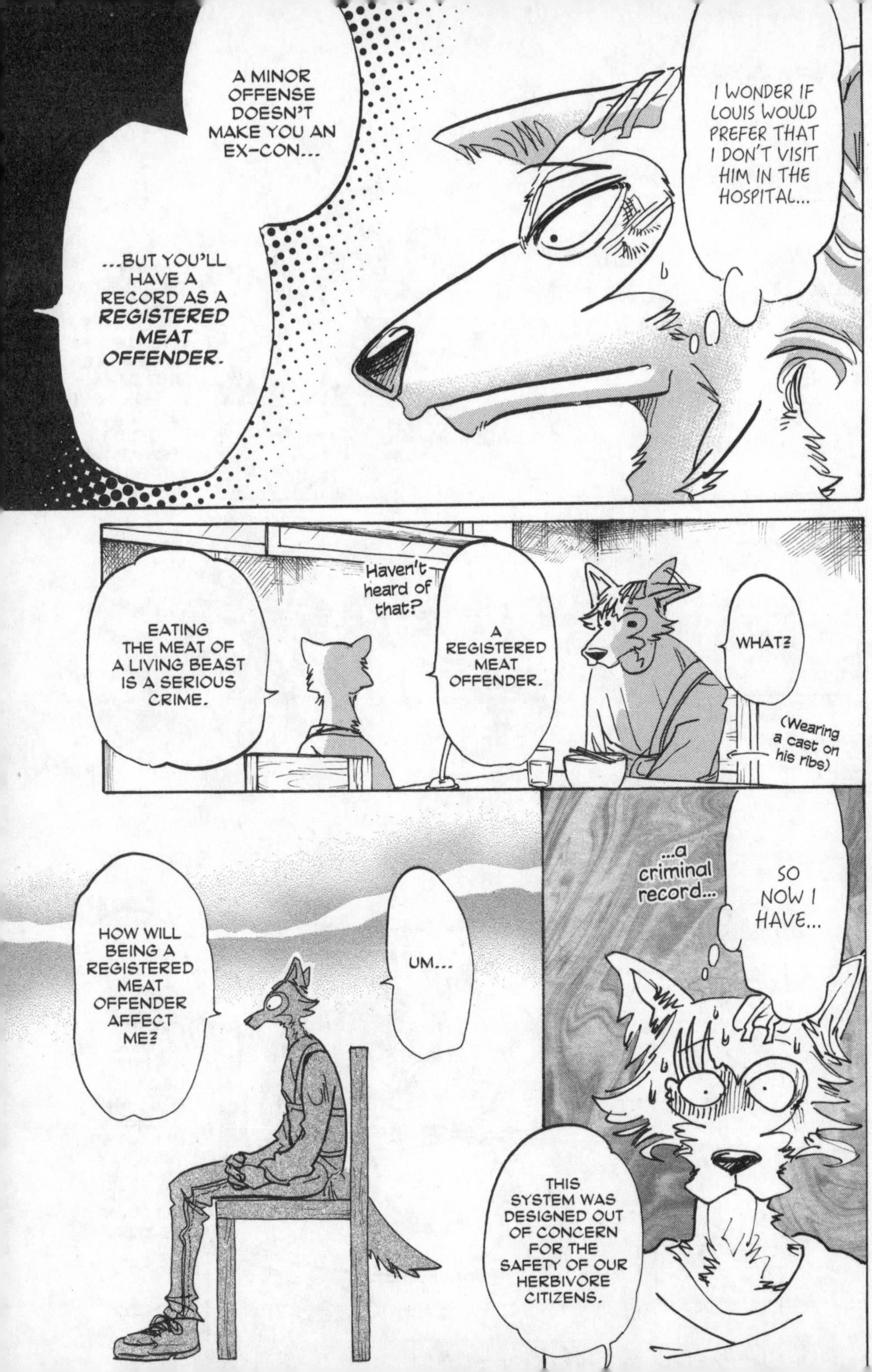
I WONDER IF LOUIS WOULD PREFER THAT I DON'T VISIT HIM IN THE HOSPITAL...
A MINOR OFFENSE DOESN'T MAKE YOU AN EX-CON...
...BUT YOU'LL HAVE A RECORD AS A *REGISTERED MEAT OFFENDER.*
WHAT?
(Wearing a cast on his ribs)
A REGISTERED MEAT OFFENDER.
Haven't heard of that?
EATING THE MEAT OF A LIVING BEAST IS A SERIOUS CRIME.
SO NOW I HAVE...
...a criminal record...
UM...
HOW WILL BEING A REGISTERED MEAT OFFENDER AFFECT ME?
THIS SYSTEM WAS DESIGNED OUT OF CONCERN FOR THE SAFETY OF OUR HERBIVORE CITIZENS.

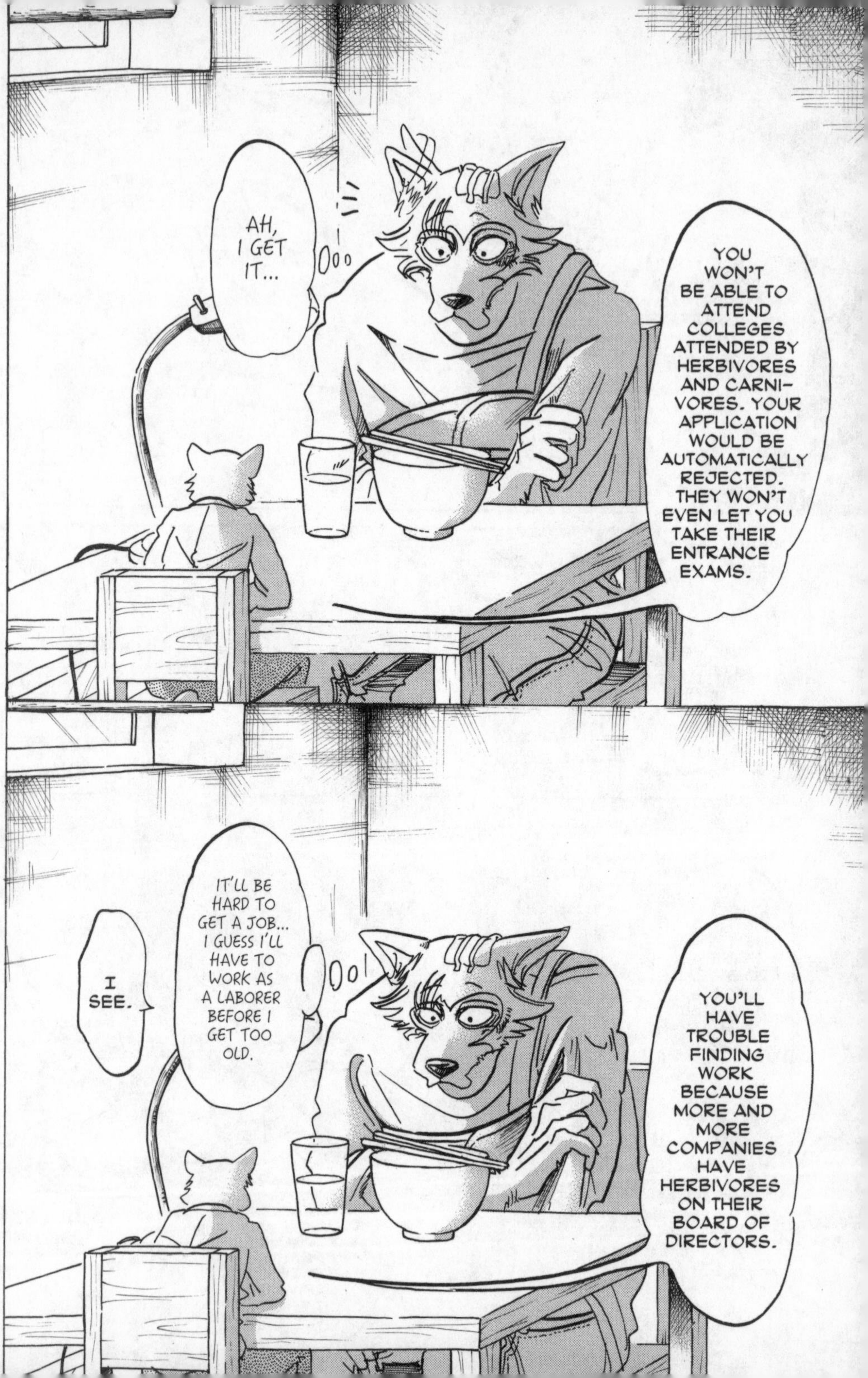
YOU WON'T BE ABLE TO ATTEND COLLEGES ATTENDED BY HERBIVORES AND CARNI-VORES. YOUR APPLICATION WOULD BE AUTOMATICALLY REJECTED. THEY WON'T EVEN LET YOU TAKE THEIR ENTRANCE EXAMS.
AH, I GET IT...
YOU'LL HAVE TROUBLE FINDING WORK BECAUSE MORE AND MORE COMPANIES HAVE HERBIVORES ON THEIR BOARD OF DIRECTORS.
IT'LL BE HARD TO GET A JOB... I GUESS I'LL HAVE TO WORK AS A LABORER BEFORE I GET TOO OLD.
I SEE.

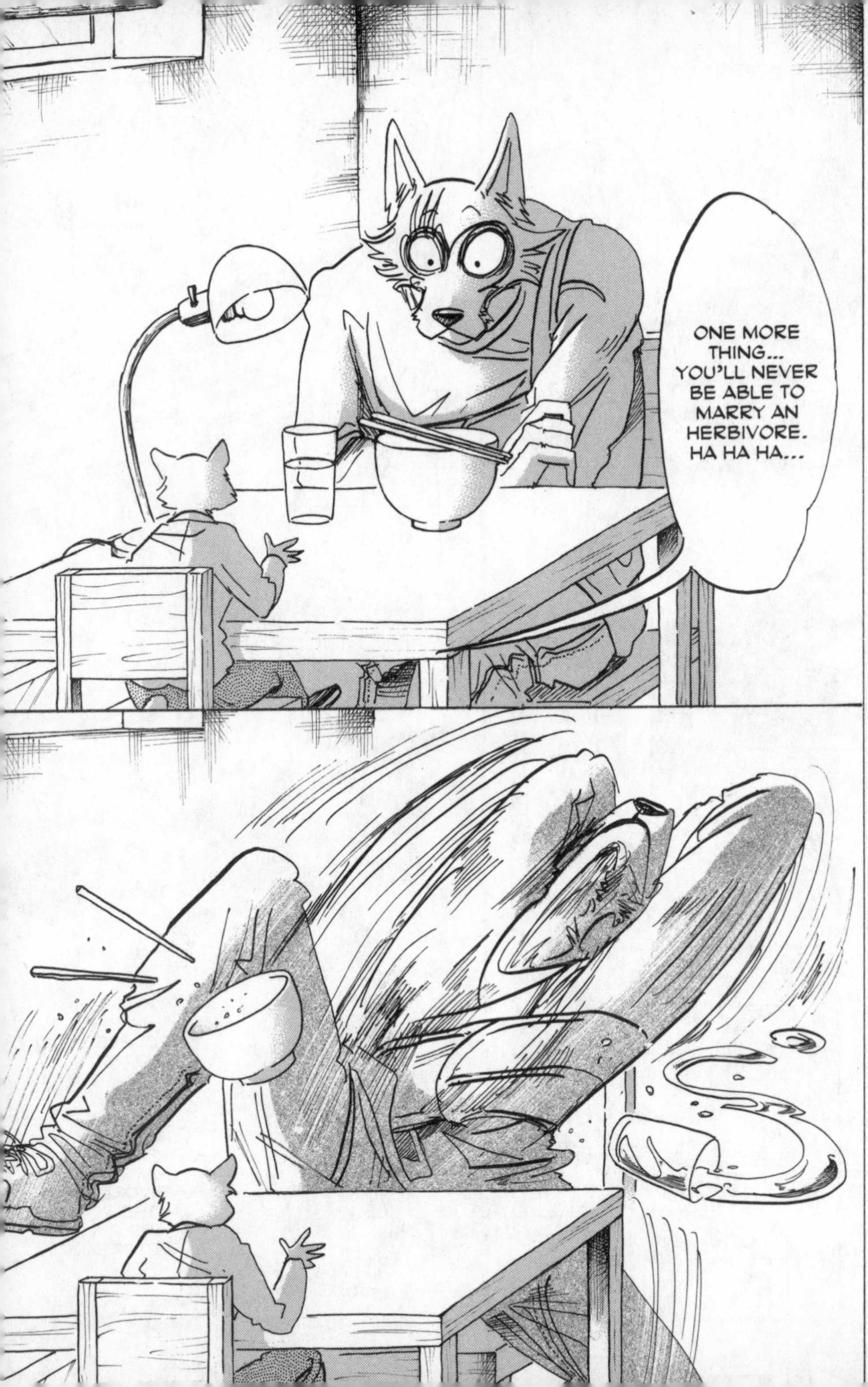
ONE MORE THING... YOU'LL NEVER BE ABLE TO MARRY AN HERBIVORE. HA HA HA...

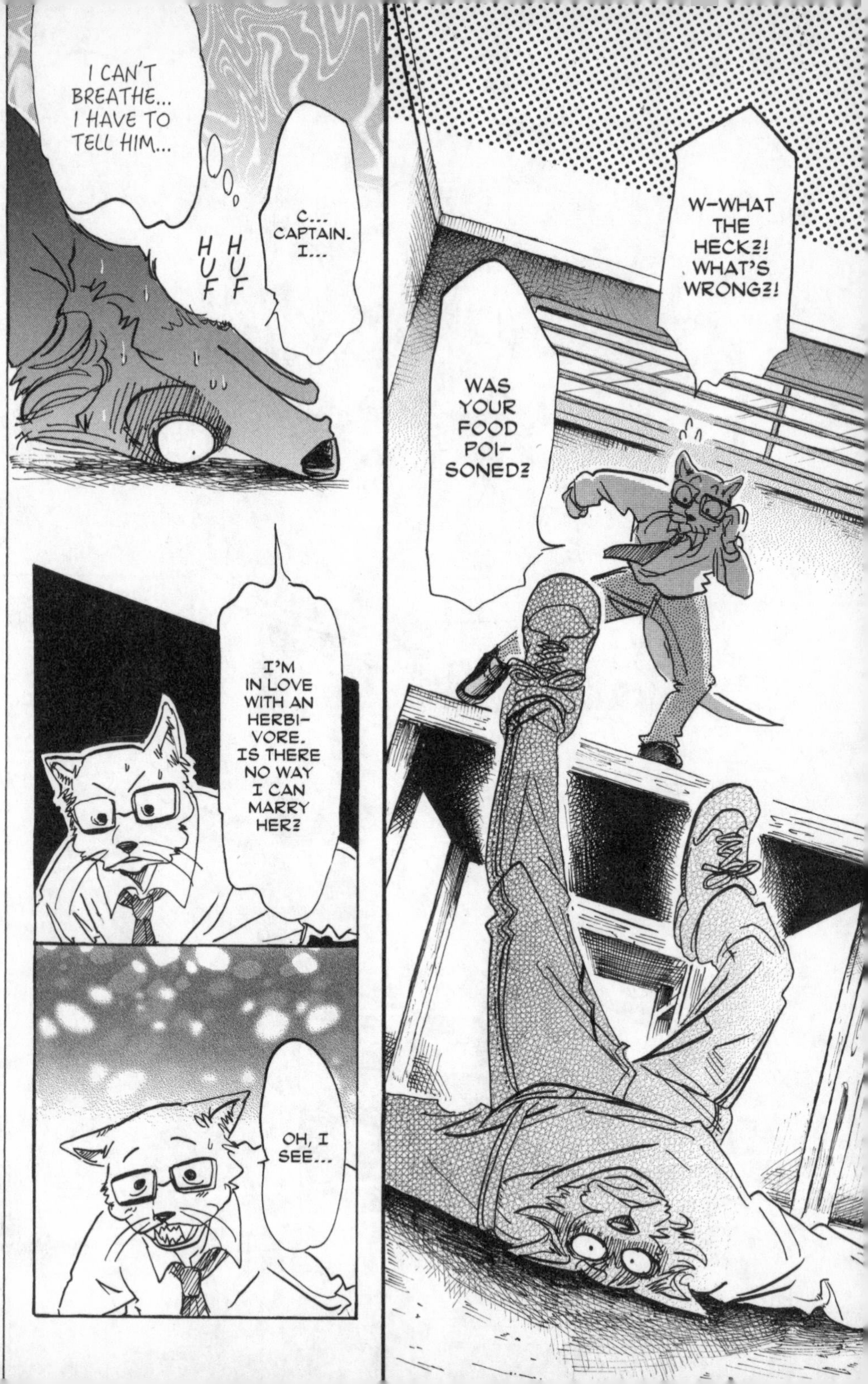
W-WHAT THE HECK?! WHAT'S WRONG?!
WAS YOUR FOOD POI-SONED?
I CAN'T BREATHE... I HAVE TO TELL HIM...
HUF HUF
C... CAPTAIN. I...
I'M IN LOVE WITH AN HERBI-VORE. IS THERE NO WAY I CAN MARRY HER?
OH, I SEE...

WELL, WELL... A HOPELESS TEENAGE ROMANTIC, EH?

WHEN YOU GROW UP, YOU'LL LOOK BACK FONDLY ON YOUR BITTERSWEET INTERSPECIES RELATIONSHIPS.

...

THE RECIDIVISM RATE OF MINORS WHO HAVE EATEN LIVING MEAT IS EXTREMELY HIGH...

MAKE SURE TO AVOID TRIGGERS SO YOU DON'T GET WITHDRAWAL SYMPTOMS!

THANK YOU FOR LOOKING OUT FOR ME.

I UNDERSTAND WHY I WOULD HAVE A CRIMINAL RECORD, BUT...

I PROMISE I'LL BE CAREFUL.

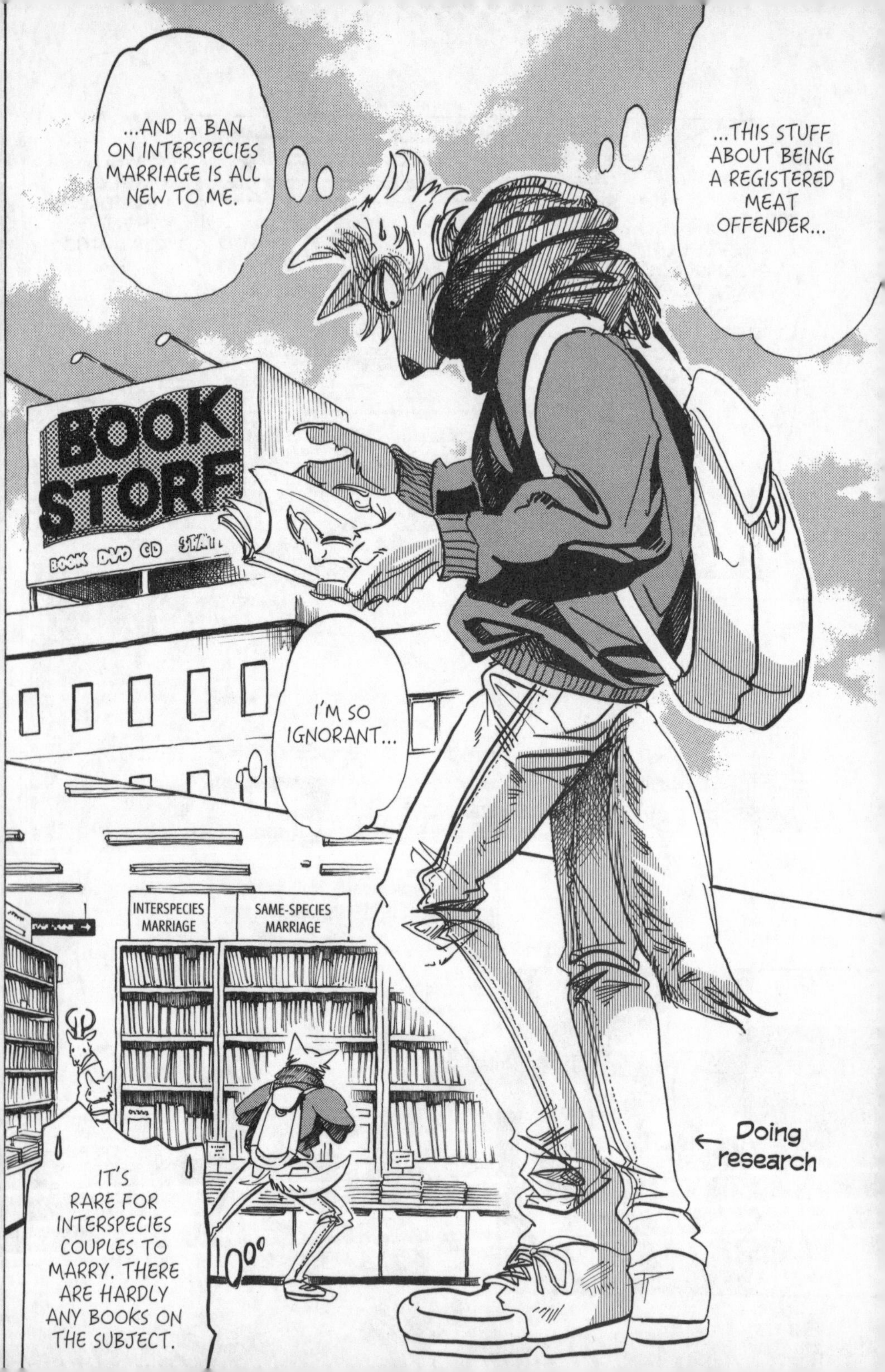
...THIS STUFF ABOUT BEING A REGISTERED MEAT OFFENDER...
...AND A BAN ON INTERSPECIES MARRIAGE IS ALL NEW TO ME.
BOOK
BOOK DVD CD
I'M SO IGNORANT...
← Doing research
SAME-SPECIES MARRIAGE
INTERSPECIES MARRIAGE
IT'S RARE FOR INTERSPECIES COUPLES TO MARRY. THERE ARE HARDLY ANY BOOKS ON THE SUBJECT.

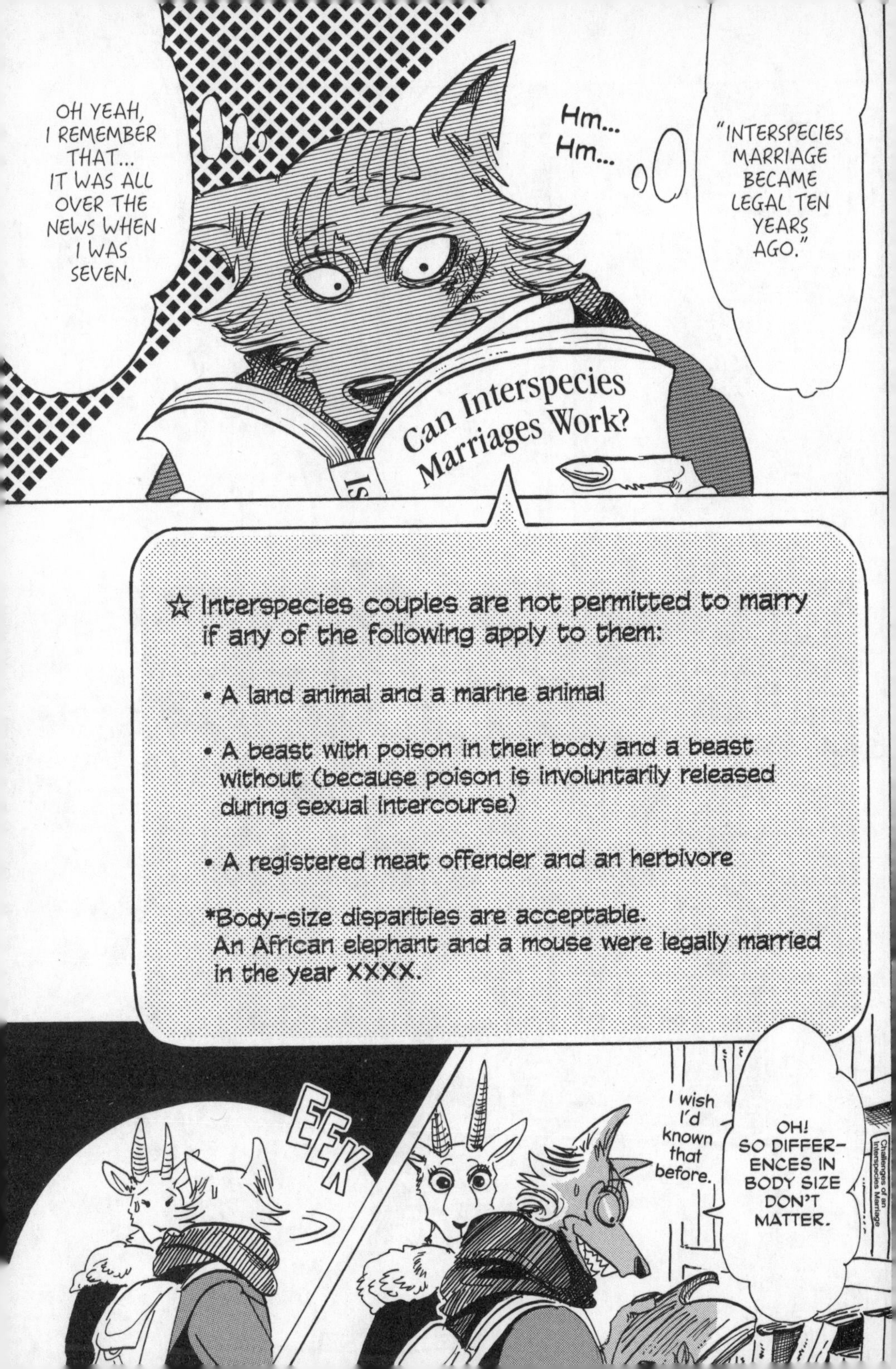
"INTERSPECIES MARRIAGE BECAME LEGAL TEN YEARS AGO."
Hm... Hm...
OH YEAH, I REMEMBER THAT... IT WAS ALL OVER THE NEWS WHEN I WAS SEVEN.
Can Interspecies Marriages Work?
☆ Interspecies couples are not permitted to marry if any of the following apply to them:
• A land animal and a marine animal
• A beast with poison in their body and a beast without (because poison is involuntarily released during sexual intercourse)
• A registered meat offender and an herbivore
*Body-size disparities are acceptable. An African elephant and a mouse were legally married in the year XXXX.
OH! SO DIFFERENCES IN BODY SIZE DON'T MATTER.
I wish I'd known that before.
Challenges of an Interspecies Marriage
EEK

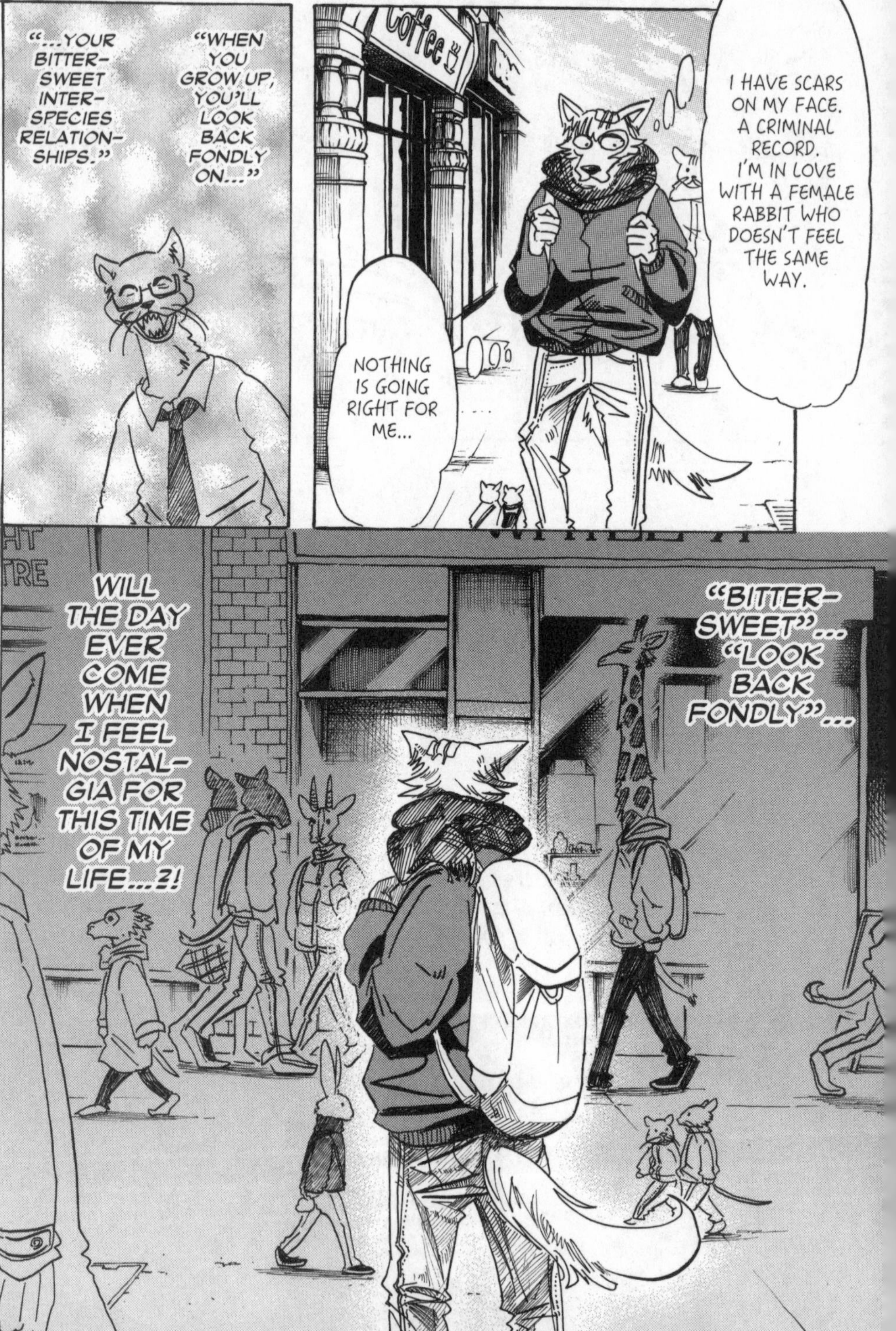
Coffee
I HAVE SCARS ON MY FACE. A CRIMINAL RECORD. I'M IN LOVE WITH A FEMALE RABBIT WHO DOESN'T FEEL THE SAME WAY.
NOTHING IS GOING RIGHT FOR ME...
"WHEN YOU GROW UP, YOU'LL LOOK BACK FONDLY ON..."
"...YOUR BITTER-SWEET INTER-SPECIES RELATION-SHIPS."
"BITTER-SWEET"... "LOOK BACK FONDLY"...
WILL THE DAY EVER COME WHEN I FEEL NOSTAL-GIA FOR THIS TIME OF MY LIFE...?!

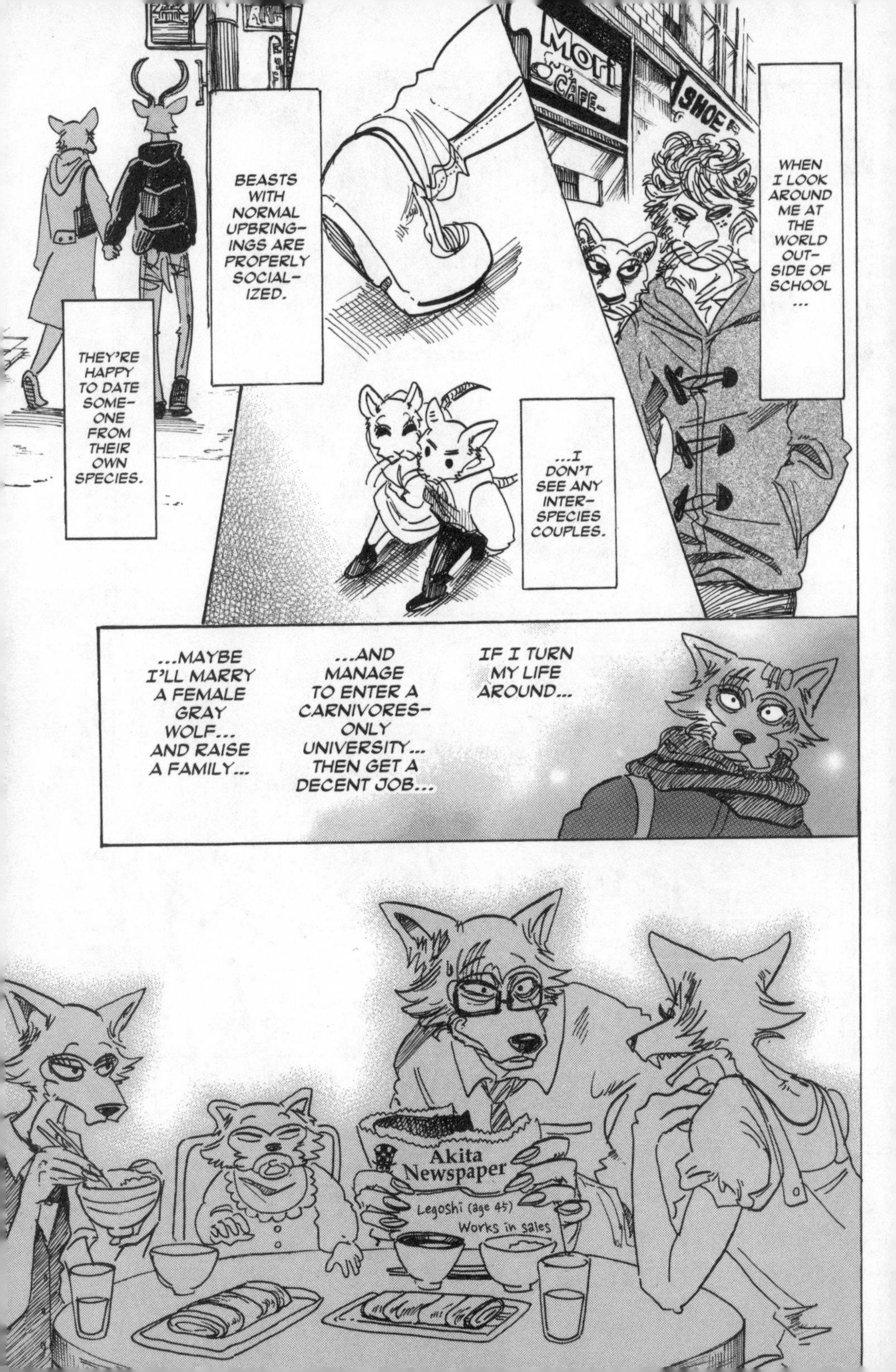
WHEN I LOOK AROUND ME AT THE WORLD OUT-SIDE OF SCHOOL...
Mori
CAFE
SHOE
...I DON'T SEE ANY INTER-SPECIES COUPLES.
BEASTS WITH NORMAL UPBRING-INGS ARE PROPERLY SOCIAL-IZED.
THEY'RE HAPPY TO DATE SOME-ONE FROM THEIR OWN SPECIES.
IF I TURN MY LIFE AROUND...
...AND MANAGE TO ENTER A CARNIVORES-ONLY UNIVERSITY... THEN GET A DECENT JOB...
...MAYBE I'LL MARRY A FEMALE GRAY WOLF... AND RAISE A FAMILY...
Akita Newspaper
Legoshi (age 45)
Works in sales

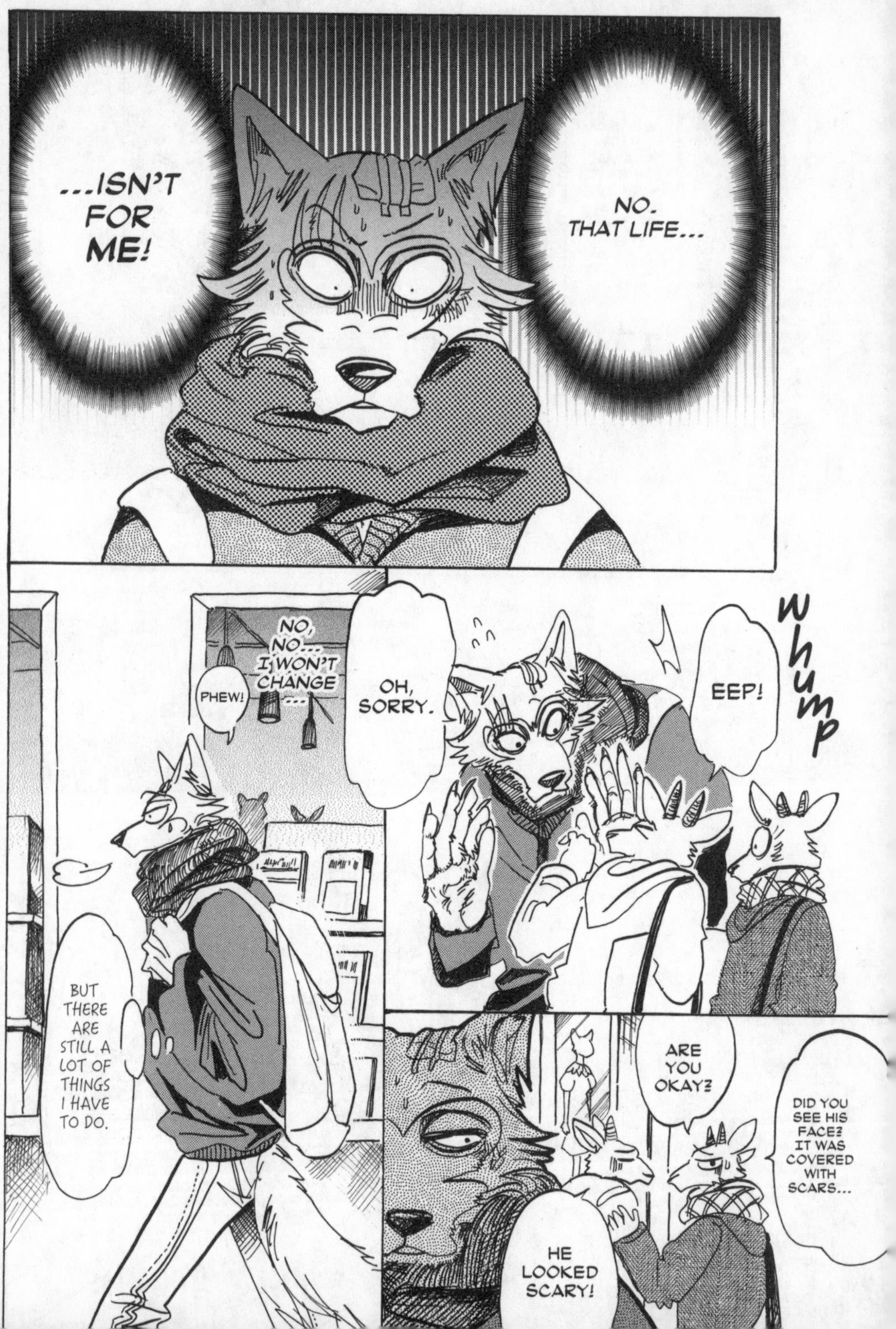
NO. THAT LIFE...
...ISN'T FOR ME!
WHUMP
EEP!
OH, SORRY.
DID YOU SEE HIS FACE? IT WAS COVERED WITH SCARS...
ARE YOU OKAY?
HE LOOKED SCARY!
NO, NO... I WON'T CHANGE...
PHEW!
BUT THERE ARE STILL A LOT OF THINGS I HAVE TO DO.

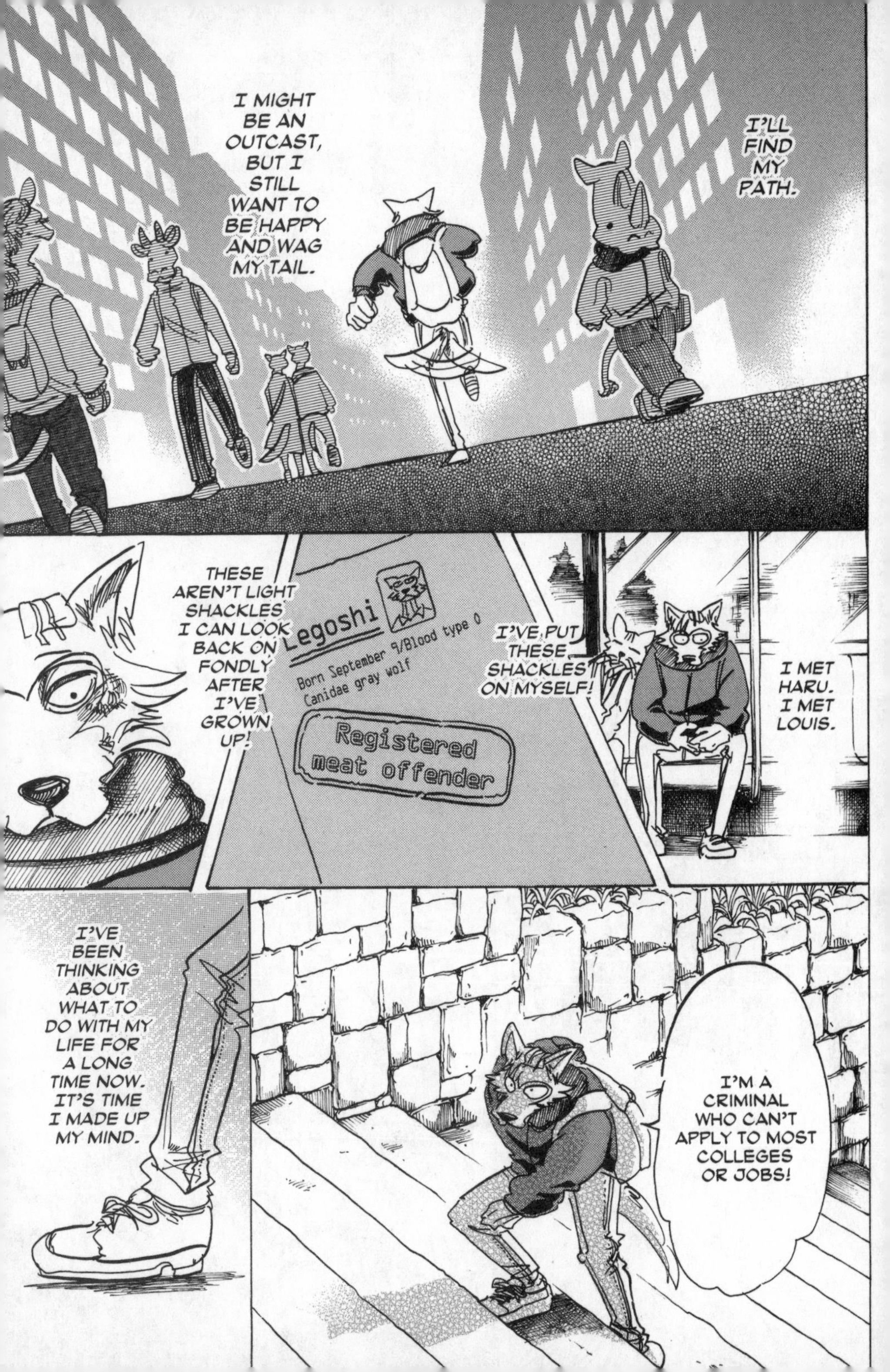
I'LL FIND MY PATH.
I MIGHT BE AN OUTCAST, BUT I STILL WANT TO BE HAPPY AND WAG MY TAIL.
I MET HARU. I MET LOUIS.
I'VE PUT THESE SHACKLES ON MYSELF!
Legoshi
Born September 9/Blood type O
Canidae gray wolf
Registered meat offender
THESE AREN'T LIGHT SHACKLES I CAN LOOK BACK ON FONDLY AFTER I'VE GROWN UP!
I'M A CRIMINAL WHO CAN'T APPLY TO MOST COLLEGES OR JOBS!
I'VE BEEN THINKING ABOUT WHAT TO DO WITH MY LIFE FOR A LONG TIME NOW. IT'S TIME I MADE UP MY MIND.

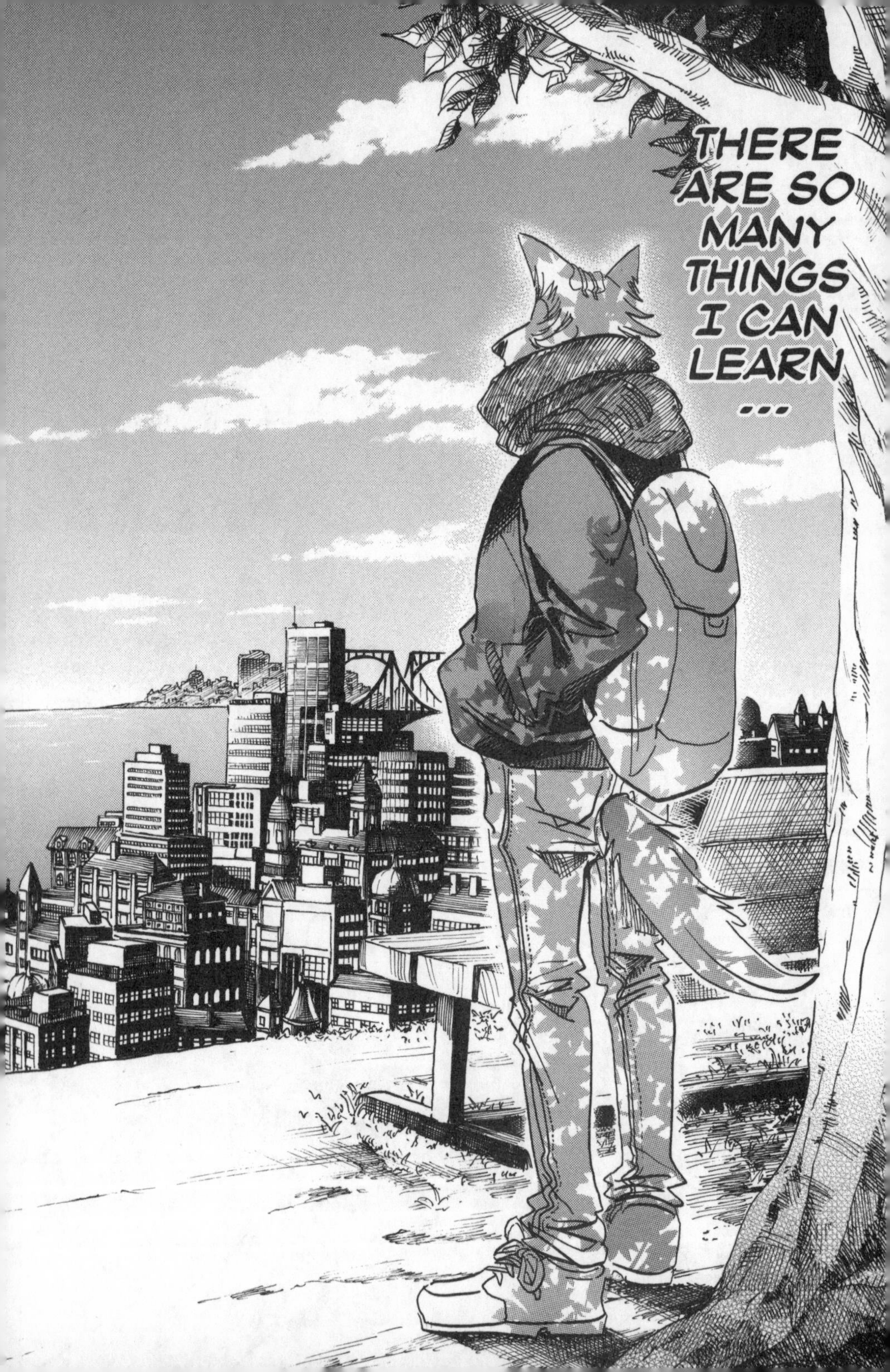
THERE ARE SO MANY THINGS I CAN LEARN...

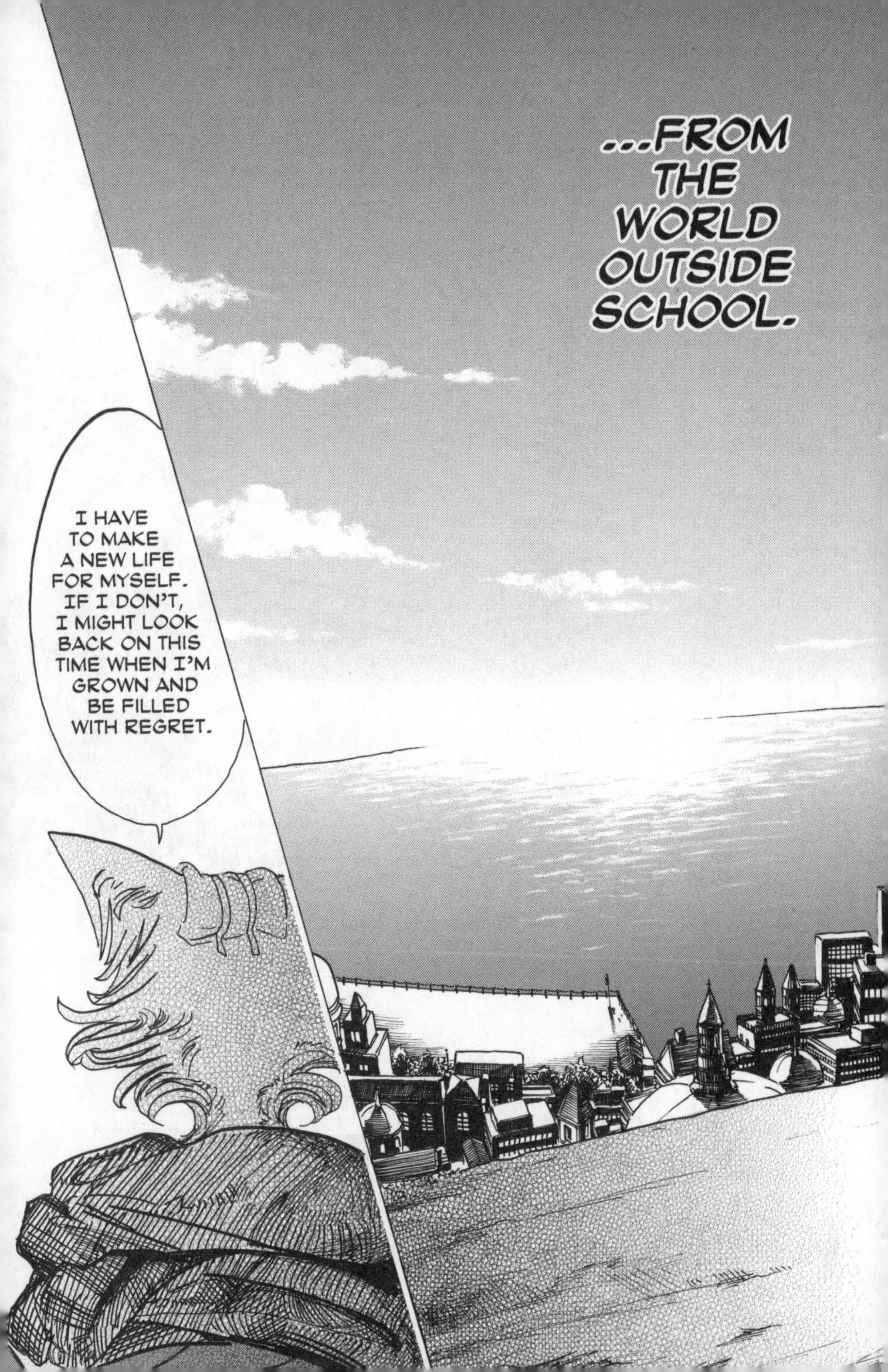
...FROM THE WORLD OUTSIDE SCHOOL.
I HAVE TO MAKE A NEW LIFE FOR MYSELF. IF I DON'T, I MIGHT LOOK BACK ON THIS TIME WHEN I'M GROWN AND BE FILLED WITH REGRET.

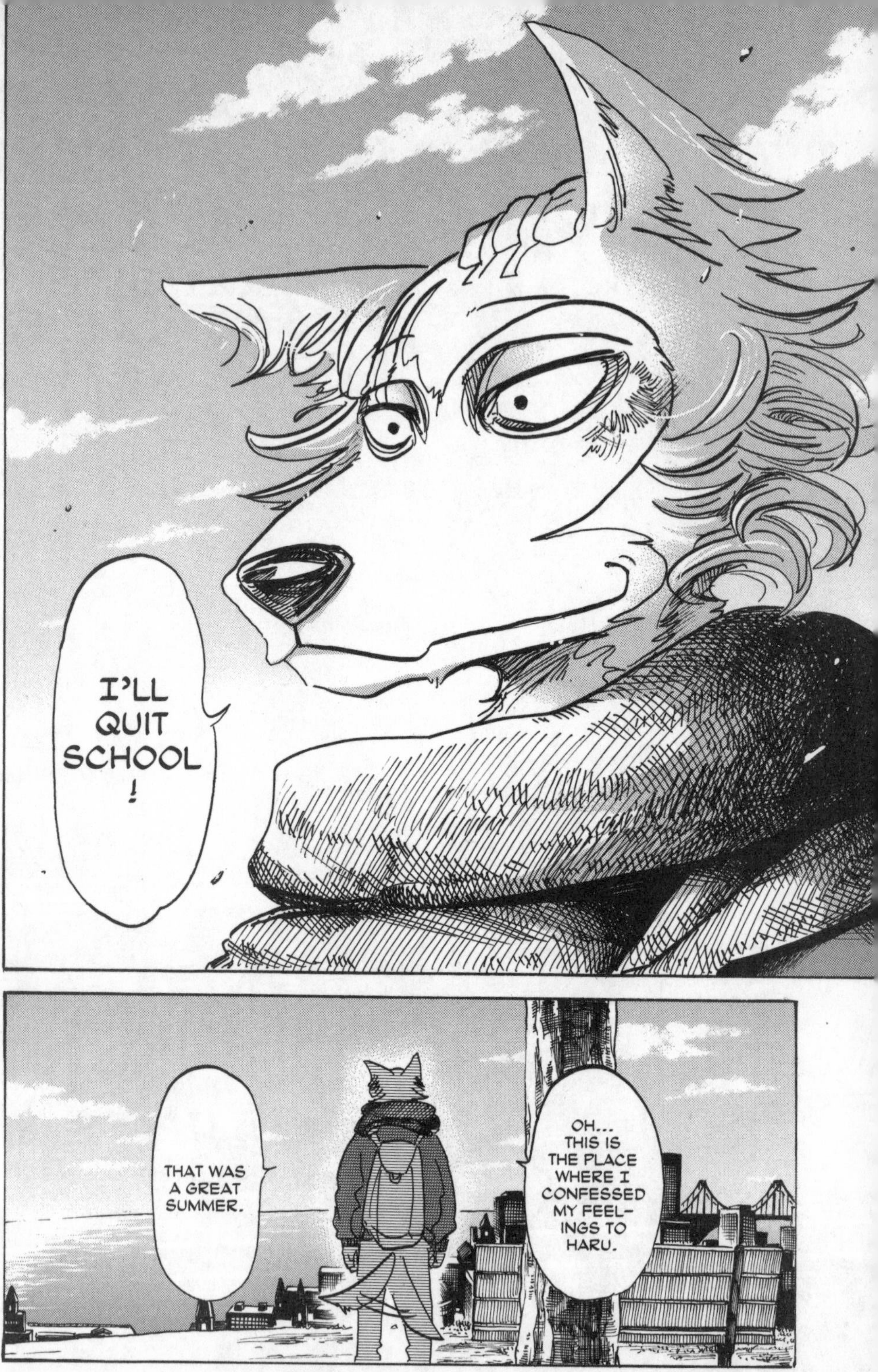
I'LL QUIT SCHOOL!
OH... THIS IS THE PLACE WHERE I CONFESSED MY FEEL-INGS TO HARU.
THAT WAS A GREAT SUMMER.

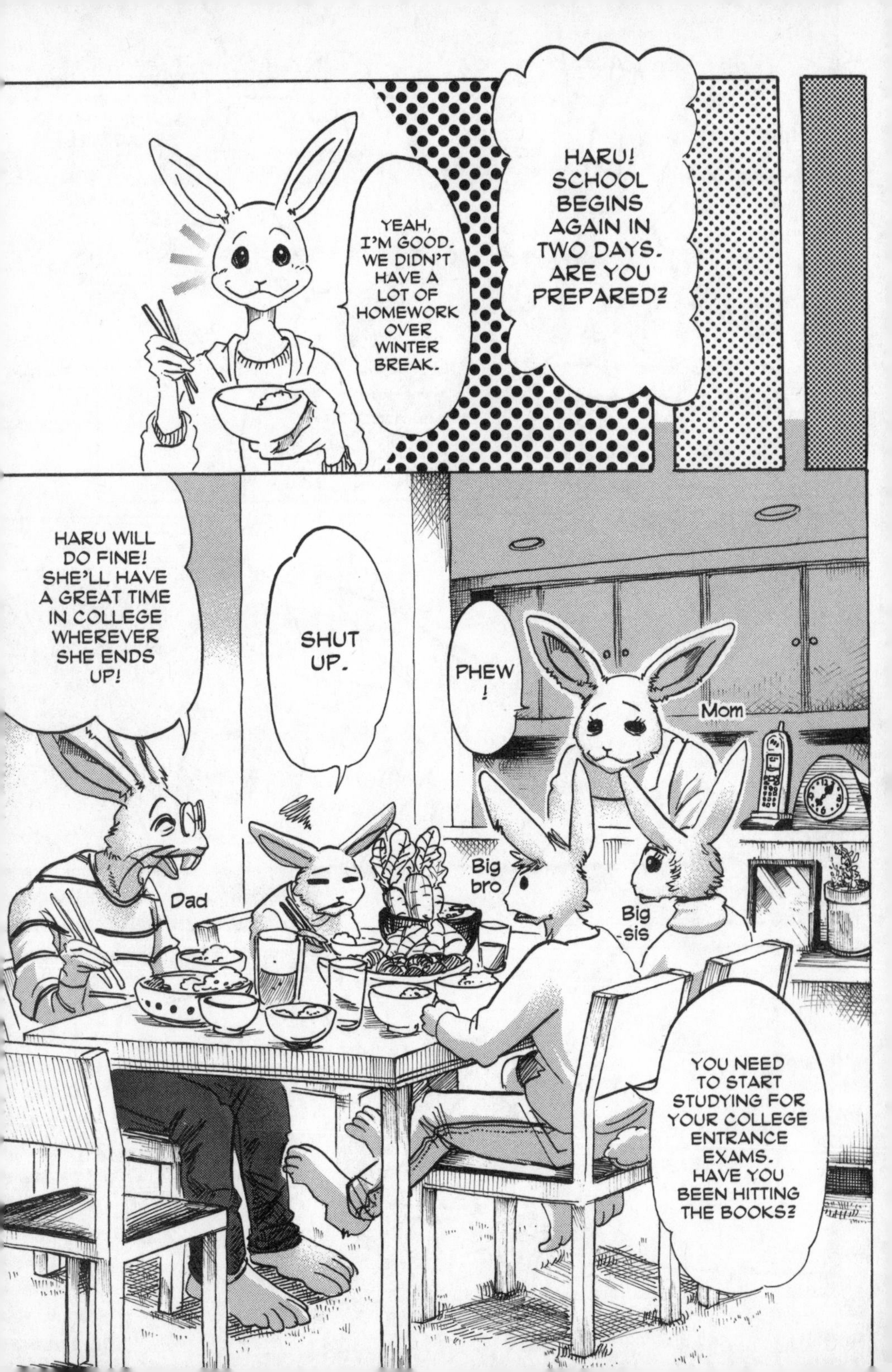
HARU! SCHOOL BEGINS AGAIN IN TWO DAYS. ARE YOU PREPARED?
YEAH, I'M GOOD. WE DIDN'T HAVE A LOT OF HOMEWORK OVER WINTER BREAK.
Mom
PHEW!
SHUT UP.
HARU WILL DO FINE! SHE'LL HAVE A GREAT TIME IN COLLEGE WHEREVER SHE ENDS UP!
Big sis
Big bro
Dad
YOU NEED TO START STUDYING FOR YOUR COLLEGE ENTRANCE EXAMS. HAVE YOU BEEN HITTING THE BOOKS?

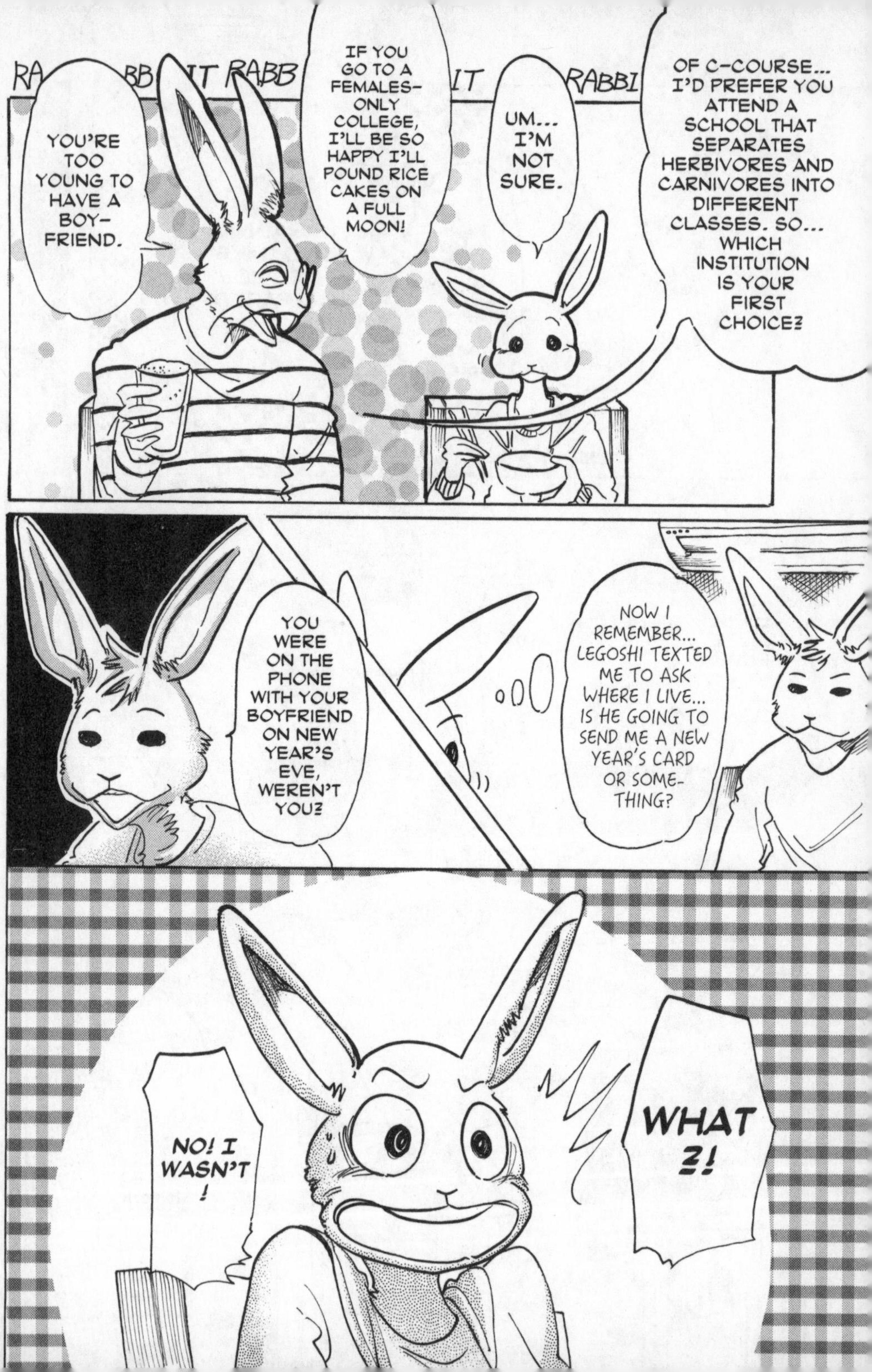
RA BB IT RABB IT RABBI
OF C-COURSE... I'D PREFER YOU ATTEND A SCHOOL THAT SEPARATES HERBIVORES AND CARNIVORES INTO DIFFERENT CLASSES. SO... WHICH INSTITUTION IS YOUR FIRST CHOICE?
UM... I'M NOT SURE.
IF YOU GO TO A FEMALES-ONLY COLLEGE, I'LL BE SO HAPPY I'LL POUND RICE CAKES ON A FULL MOON!
YOU'RE TOO YOUNG TO HAVE A BOY-FRIEND.
NOW I REMEMBER... LEGOSHI TEXTED ME TO ASK WHERE I LIVE... IS HE GOING TO SEND ME A NEW YEAR'S CARD OR SOME-THING?
YOU WERE ON THE PHONE WITH YOUR BOYFRIEND ON NEW YEAR'S EVE, WEREN'T YOU?
WHAT?!
NO! I WASN'T!

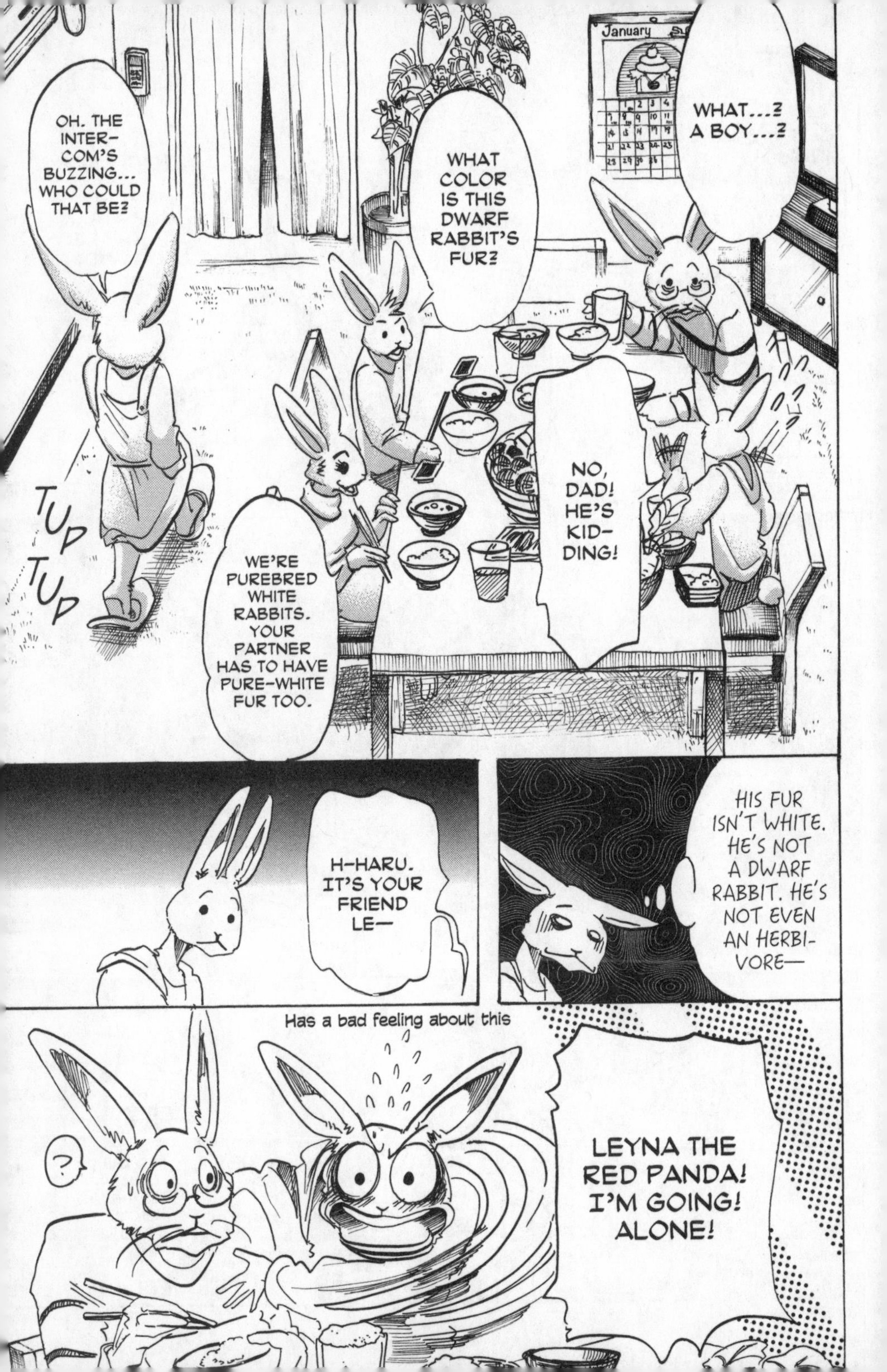
January
WHAT...? A BOY...?
WHAT COLOR IS THIS DWARF RABBIT'S FUR?
OH. THE INTERCOM'S BUZZING... WHO COULD THAT BE?
NO, DAD! HE'S KIDDING!
WE'RE PUREBRED WHITE RABBITS. YOUR PARTNER HAS TO HAVE PURE-WHITE FUR TOO.
TUP TUP
HIS FUR ISN'T WHITE. HE'S NOT A DWARF RABBIT. HE'S NOT EVEN AN HERBIVORE—
H-HARU. IT'S YOUR FRIEND LE—
LEYNA THE RED PANDA! I'M GOING! ALONE!
Has a bad feeling about this
?

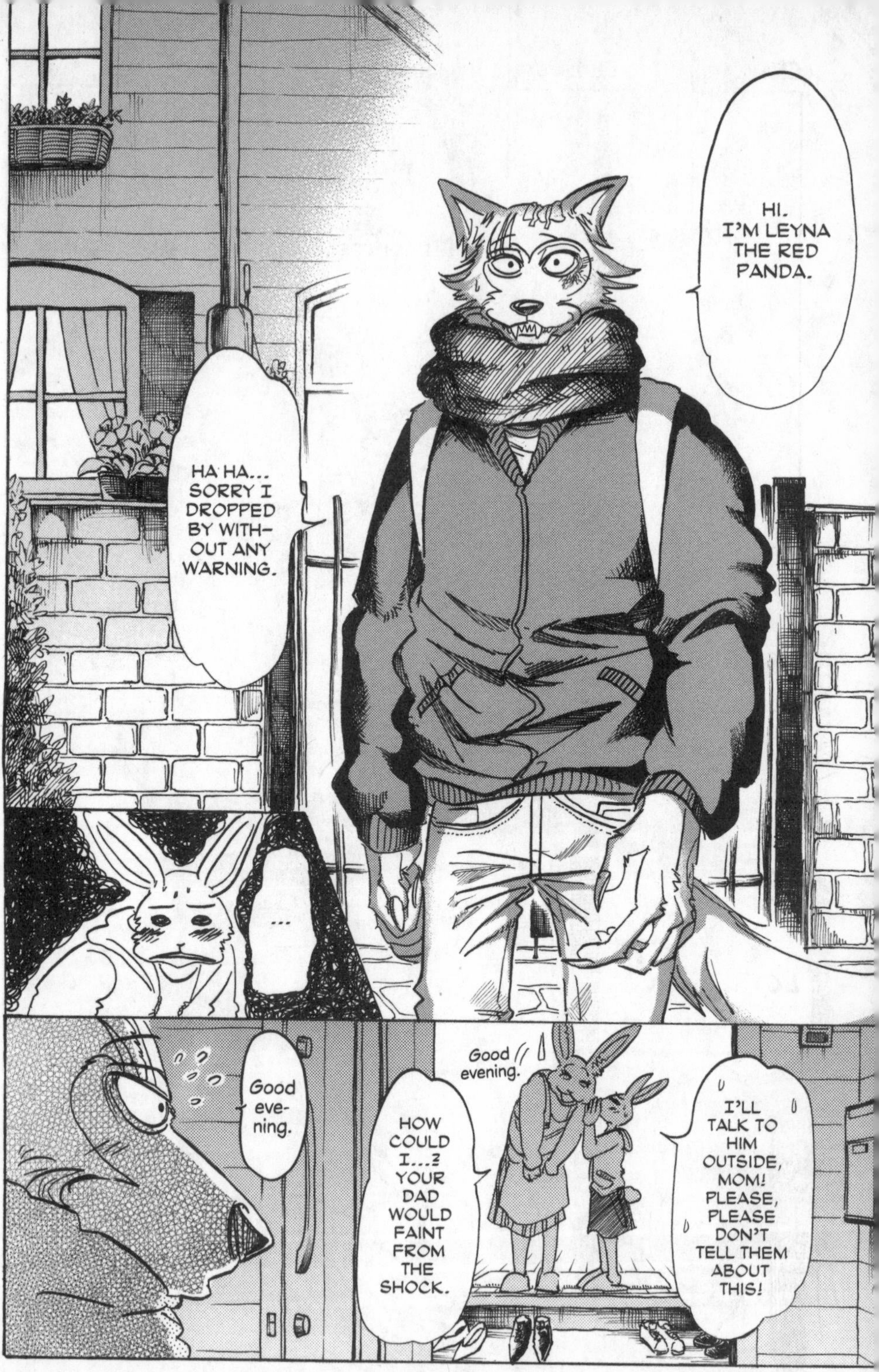
HI. I'M LEYNA THE RED PANDA.
HA HA... SORRY I DROPPED BY WITHOUT ANY WARNING.
...
I'LL TALK TO HIM OUTSIDE, MOM! PLEASE, PLEASE DON'T TELL THEM ABOUT THIS!
Good evening.
HOW COULD I...? YOUR DAD WOULD FAINT FROM THE SHOCK.
Good evening.

Chapter 99: The Blue-Furred Big Shot

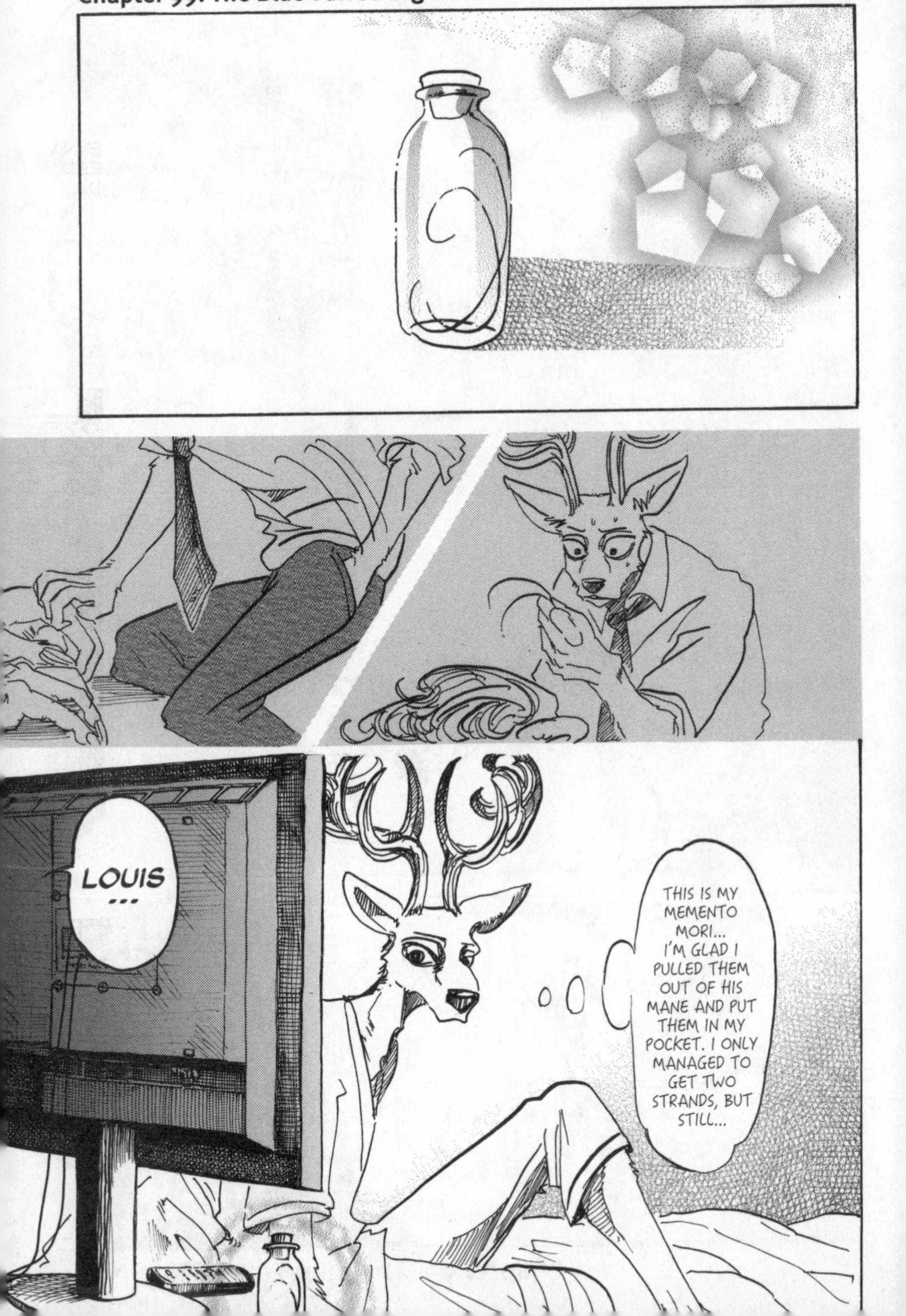
THIS IS MY MEMENTO MORI... I'M GLAD I PULLED THEM OUT OF HIS MANE AND PUT THEM IN MY POCKET. I ONLY MANAGED TO GET TWO STRANDS, BUT STILL...
LOUIS...

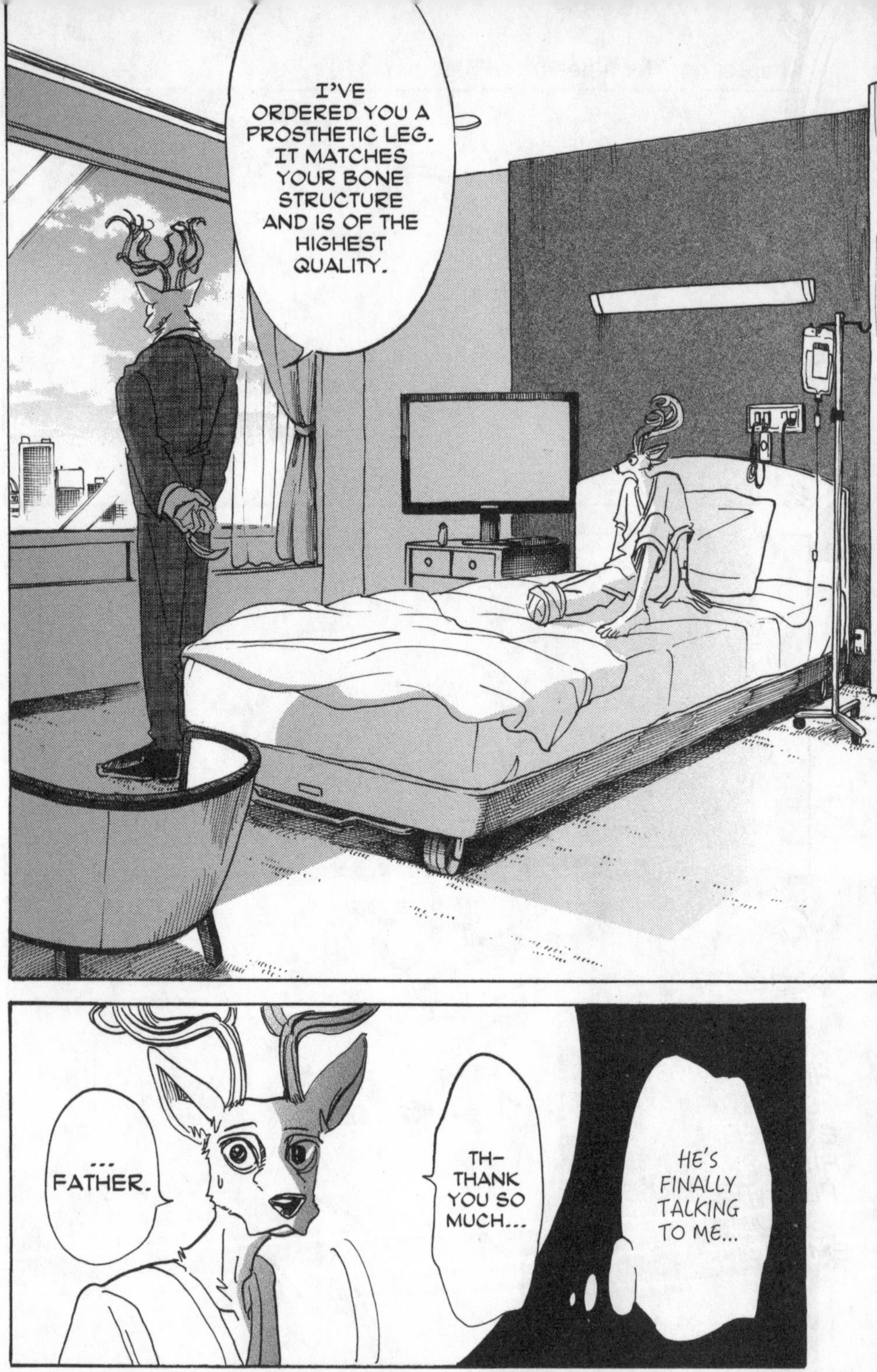
I'VE ORDERED YOU A PROSTHETIC LEG. IT MATCHES YOUR BONE STRUCTURE AND IS OF THE HIGHEST QUALITY.
HE'S FINALLY TALKING TO ME...
TH- THANK YOU SO MUCH...
... FATHER.

Chapter 99: The Blue-Furred Big Shot

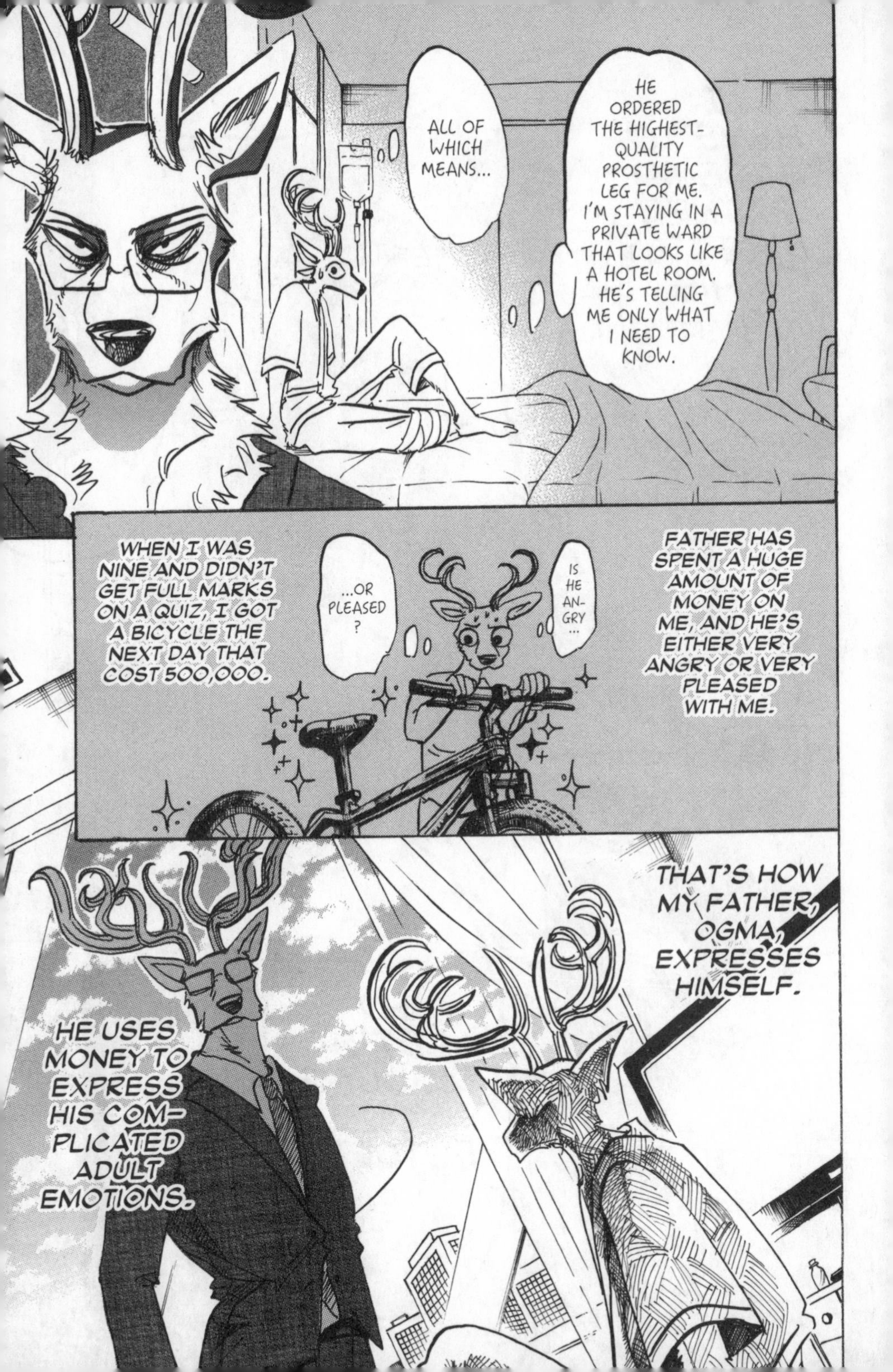
HE ORDERED THE HIGHEST-QUALITY PROSTHETIC LEG FOR ME. I'M STAYING IN A PRIVATE WARD THAT LOOKS LIKE A HOTEL ROOM. HE'S TELLING ME ONLY WHAT I NEED TO KNOW.
ALL OF WHICH MEANS...
FATHER HAS SPENT A HUGE AMOUNT OF MONEY ON ME, AND HE'S EITHER VERY ANGRY OR VERY PLEASED WITH ME.
IS HE ANGRY...
...OR PLEASED?
WHEN I WAS NINE AND DIDN'T GET FULL MARKS ON A QUIZ, I GOT A BICYCLE THE NEXT DAY THAT COST 500,000.
THAT'S HOW MY FATHER, OGMA, EXPRESSES HIMSELF.
HE USES MONEY TO EXPRESS HIS COMPLICATED ADULT EMOTIONS.

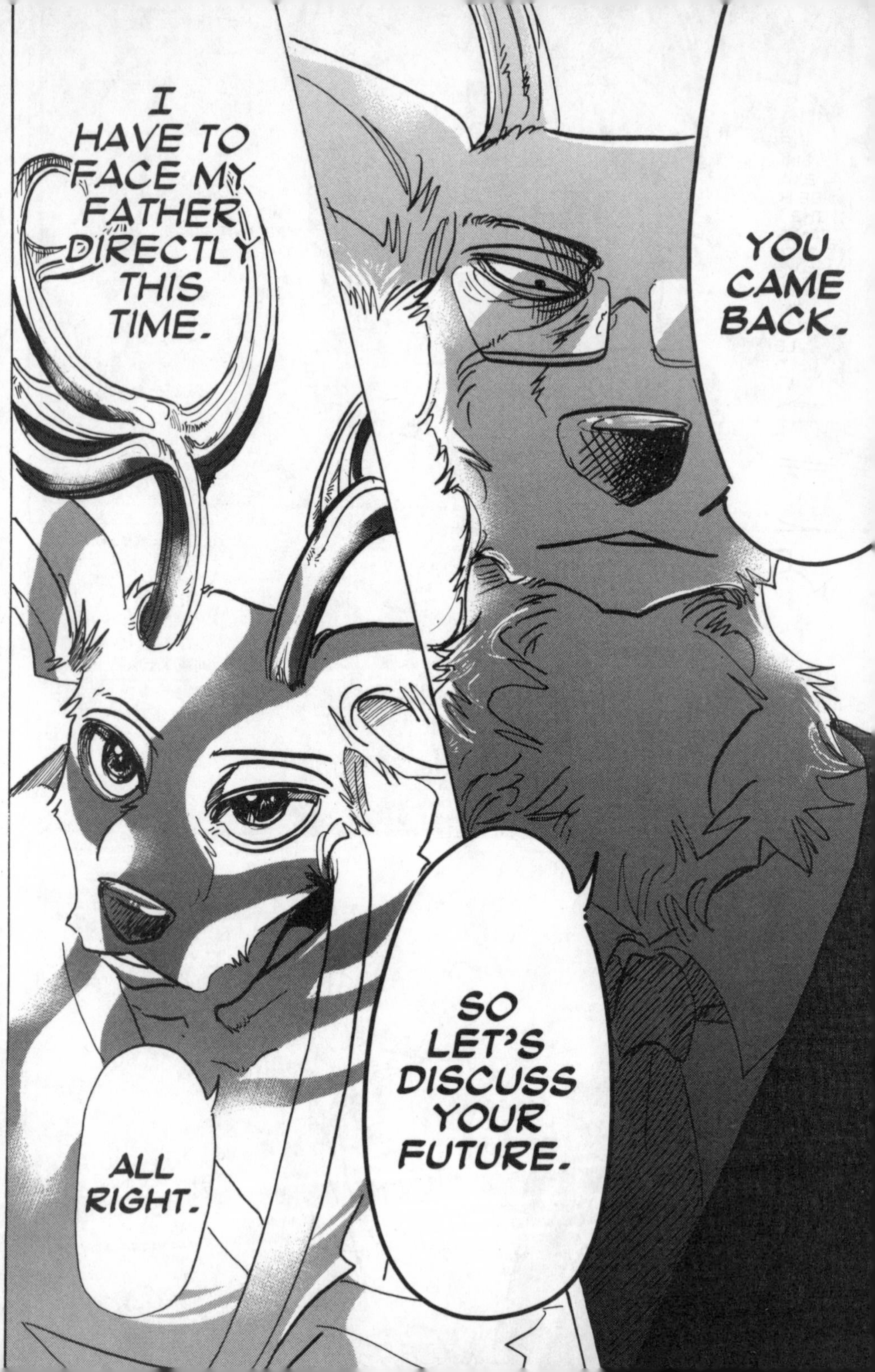
YOU CAME BACK.
SO LET'S DISCUSS YOUR FUTURE.
I HAVE TO FACE MY FATHER DIRECTLY THIS TIME.
ALL RIGHT.

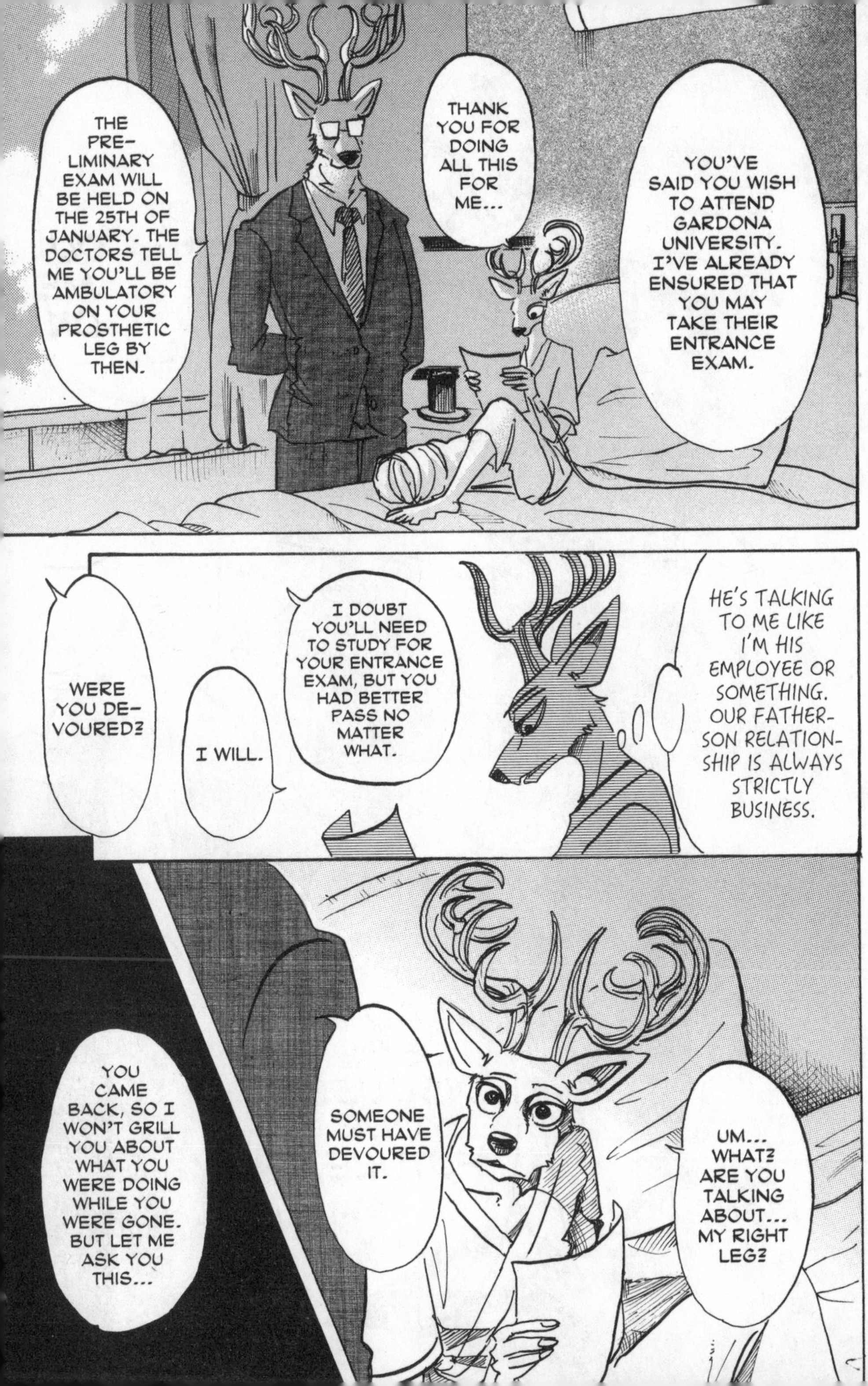

YOU'VE SAID YOU WISH TO ATTEND GARDONA UNIVERSITY. I'VE ALREADY ENSURED THAT YOU MAY TAKE THEIR ENTRANCE EXAM.
THANK YOU FOR DOING ALL THIS FOR ME...
THE PRE-LIMINARY EXAM WILL BE HELD ON THE 25TH OF JANUARY. THE DOCTORS TELL ME YOU'LL BE AMBULATORY ON YOUR PROSTHETIC LEG BY THEN.
HE'S TALKING TO ME LIKE I'M HIS EMPLOYEE OR SOMETHING. OUR FATHER-SON RELATION-SHIP IS ALWAYS STRICTLY BUSINESS.
I DOUBT YOU'LL NEED TO STUDY FOR YOUR ENTRANCE EXAM, BUT YOU HAD BETTER PASS NO MATTER WHAT.
I WILL.
WERE YOU DE-VOURED?
UM... WHAT? ARE YOU TALKING ABOUT... MY RIGHT LEG?
SOMEONE MUST HAVE DEVOURED IT.
YOU CAME BACK, SO I WON'T GRILL YOU ABOUT WHAT YOU WERE DOING WHILE YOU WERE GONE. BUT LET ME ASK YOU THIS...

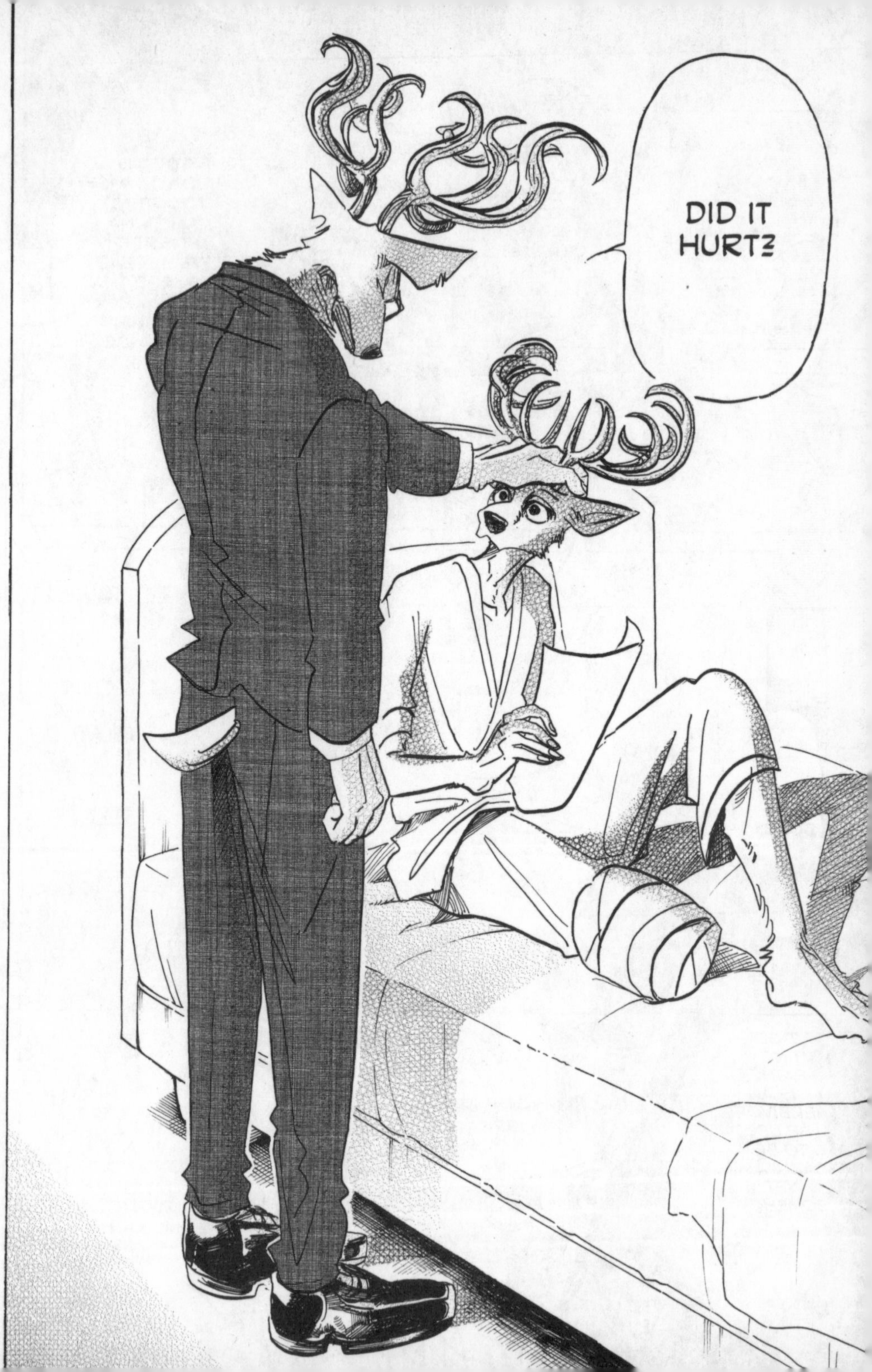
DID IT HURT?

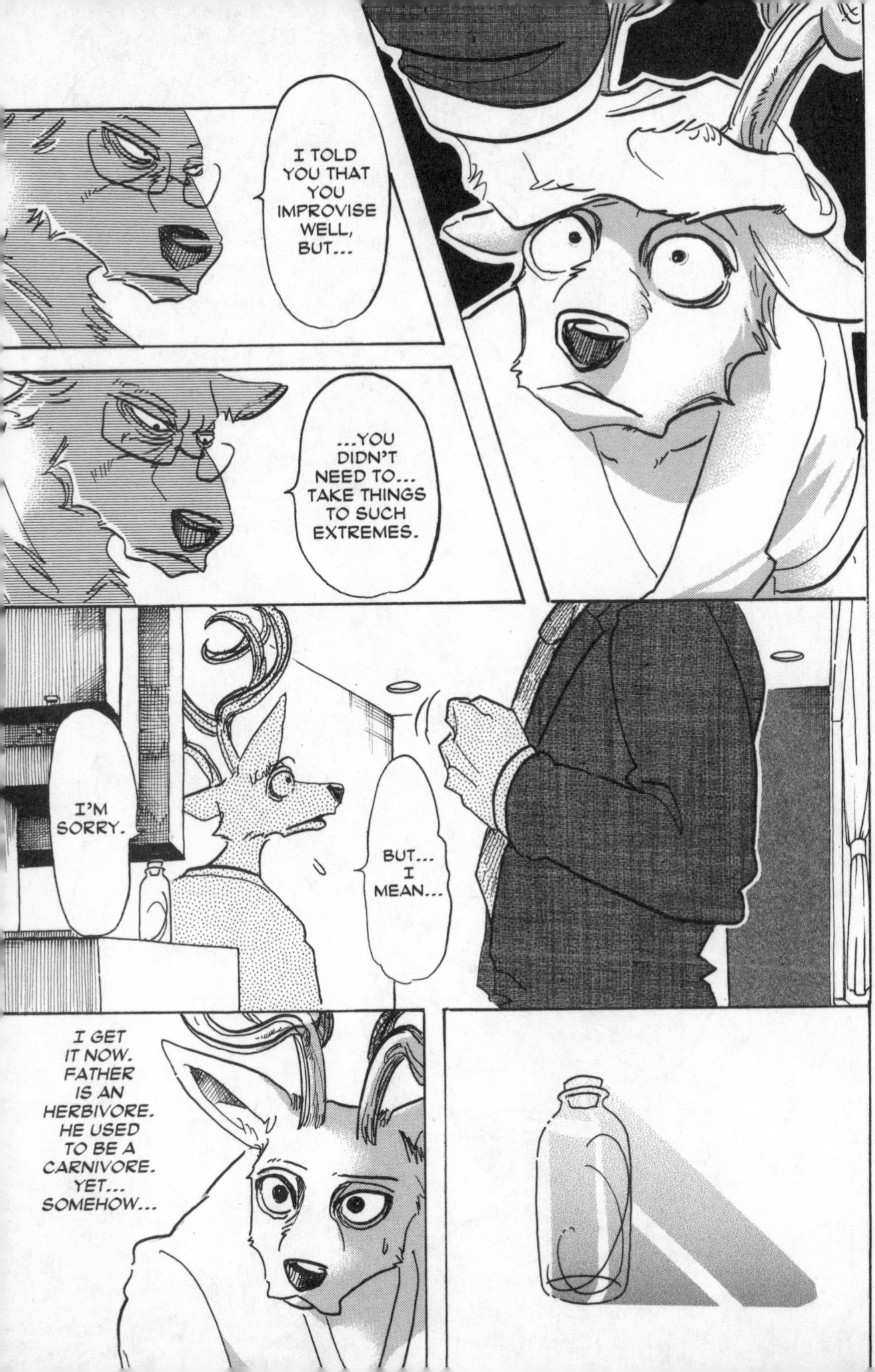
I TOLD YOU THAT YOU IMPROVISE WELL, BUT...
...YOU DIDN'T NEED TO... TAKE THINGS TO SUCH EXTREMES.
BUT... I MEAN...
I'M SORRY.
I GET IT NOW. FATHER IS AN HERBIVORE. HE USED TO BE A CARNIVORE. YET... SOMEHOW...

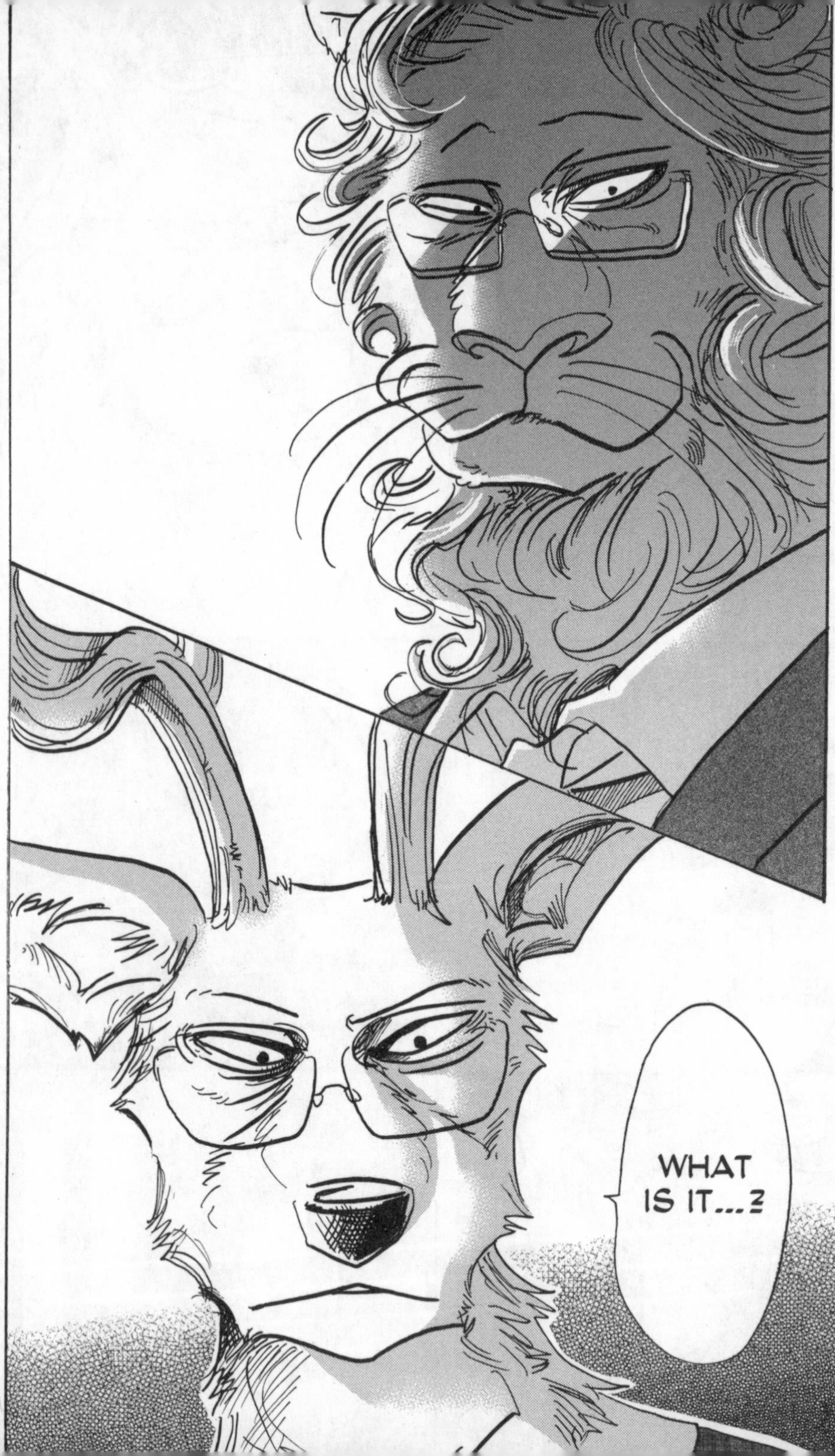
WHAT IS IT...?

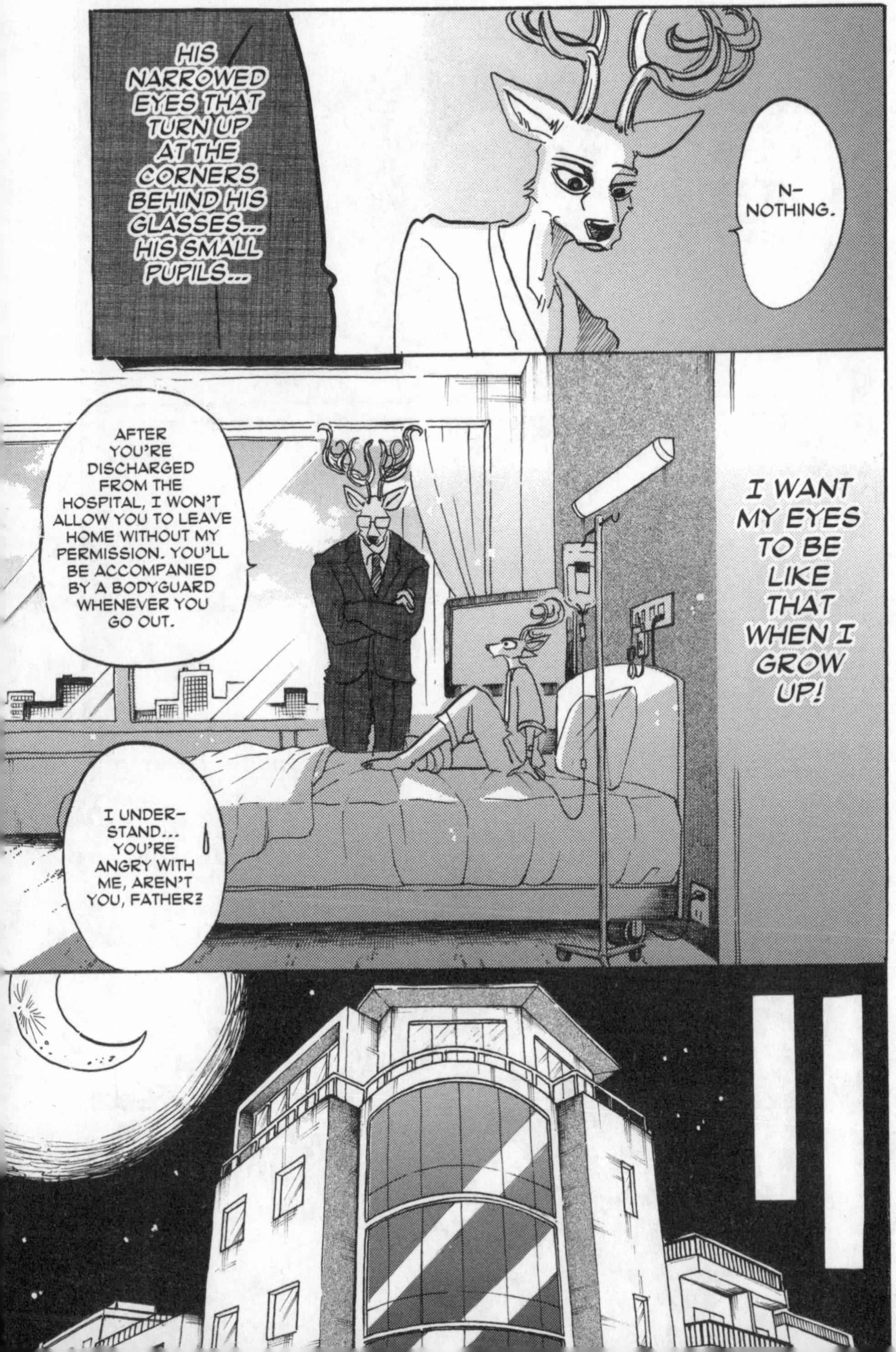
N-NOTHING.
HIS NARROWED EYES THAT TURN UP AT THE CORNERS BEHIND HIS GLASSES... HIS SMALL PUPILS...
I WANT MY EYES TO BE LIKE THAT WHEN I GROW UP!
AFTER YOU'RE DISCHARGED FROM THE HOSPITAL, I WON'T ALLOW YOU TO LEAVE HOME WITHOUT MY PERMISSION. YOU'LL BE ACCOMPANIED BY A BODYGUARD WHENEVER YOU GO OUT.
I UNDER-STAND... YOU'RE ANGRY WITH ME, AREN'T YOU, FATHER?

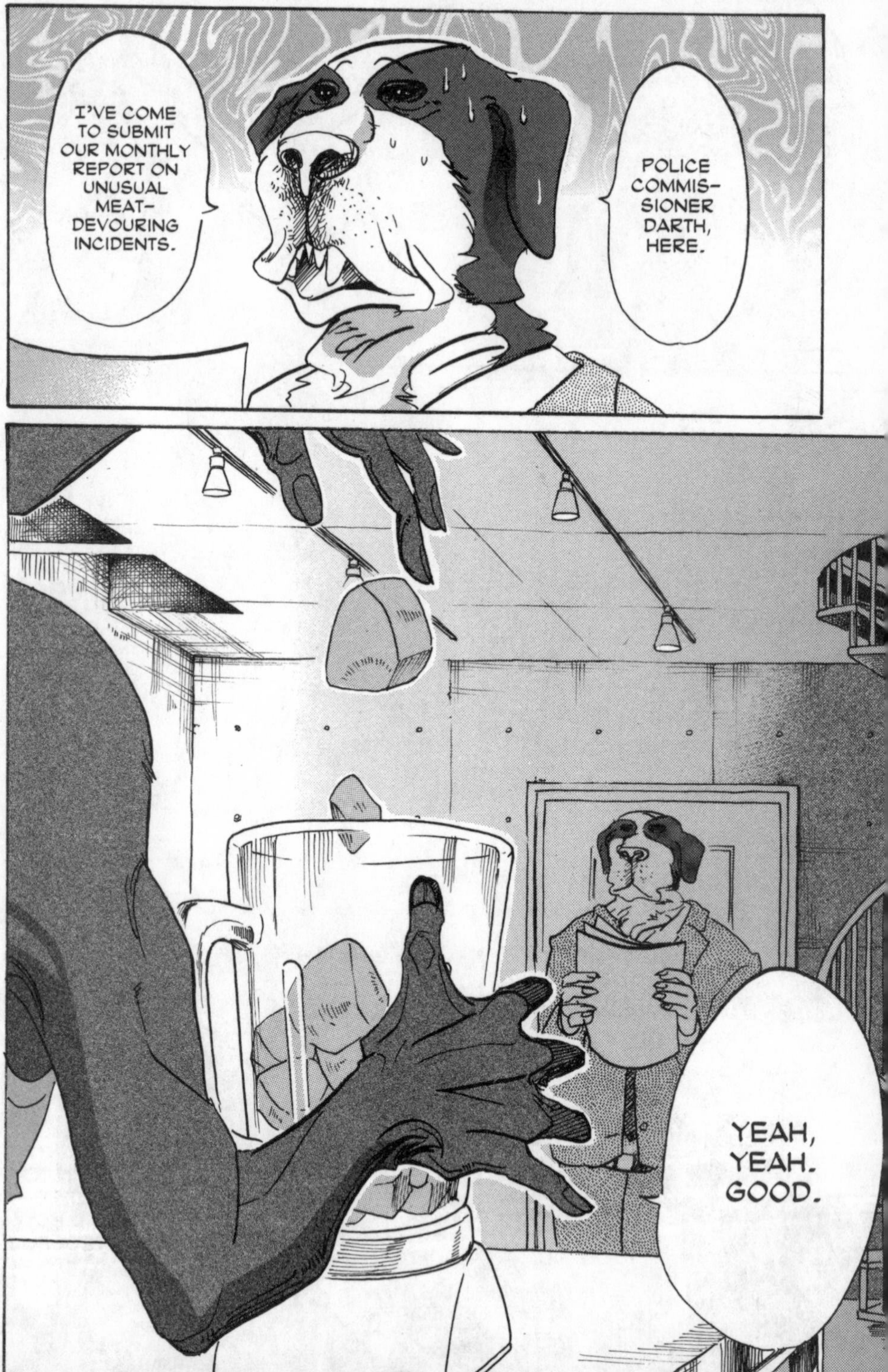
POLICE COMMIS-SIONER DARTH, HERE.
I'VE COME TO SUBMIT OUR MONTHLY REPORT ON UNUSUAL MEAT-DEVOURING INCIDENTS.
YEAH, YEAH. GOOD.

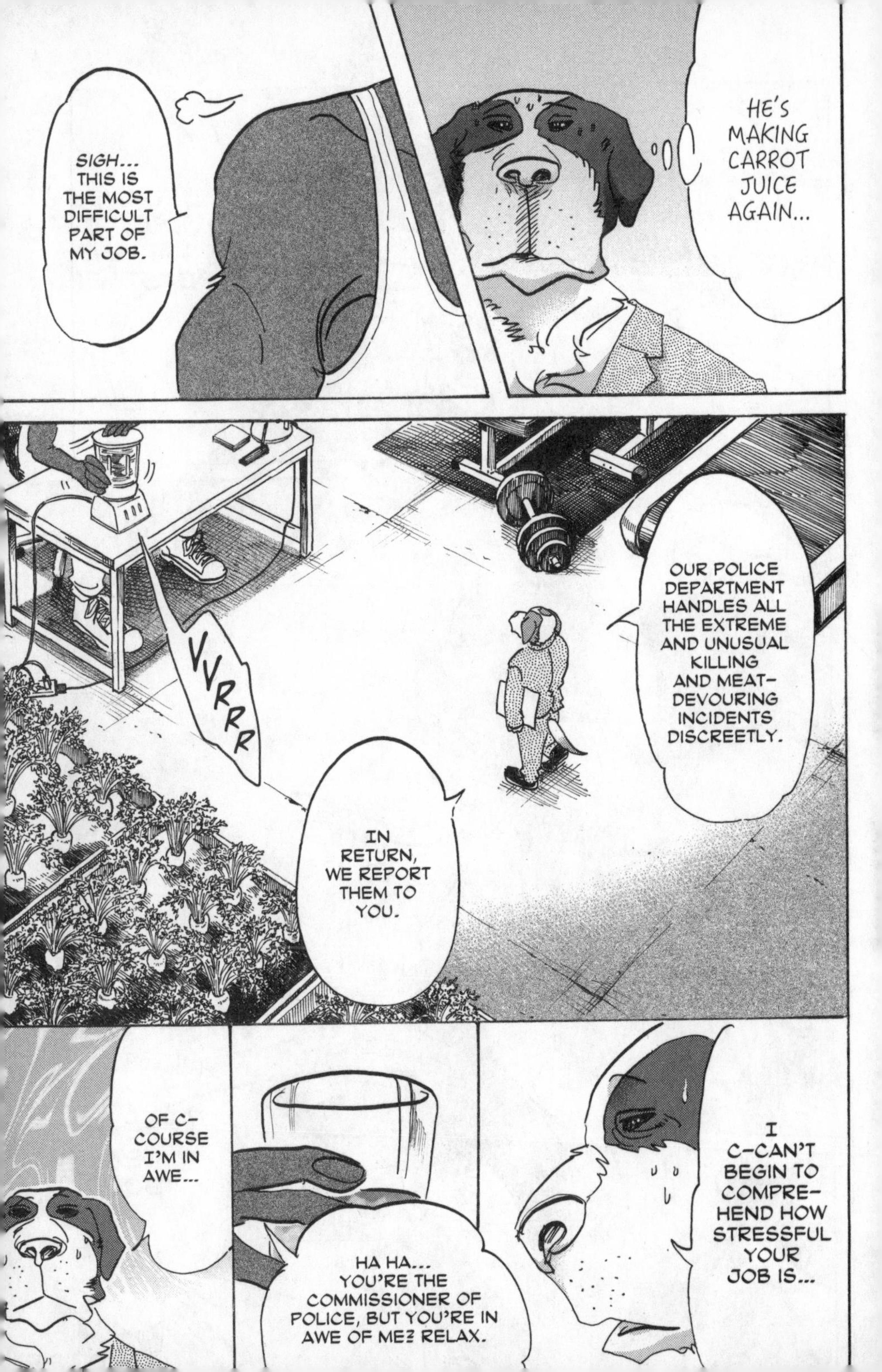
HE'S MAKING CARROT JUICE AGAIN...
SIGH... THIS IS THE MOST DIFFICULT PART OF MY JOB.
OUR POLICE DEPARTMENT HANDLES ALL THE EXTREME AND UNUSUAL KILLING AND MEAT-DEVOURING INCIDENTS DISCREETLY.
VVRRR
IN RETURN, WE REPORT THEM TO YOU.
I C-CAN'T BEGIN TO COMPRE-HEND HOW STRESSFUL YOUR JOB IS...
HA HA... YOU'RE THE COMMISSIONER OF POLICE, BUT YOU'RE IN AWE OF ME? RELAX.
OF C-COURSE I'M IN AWE...

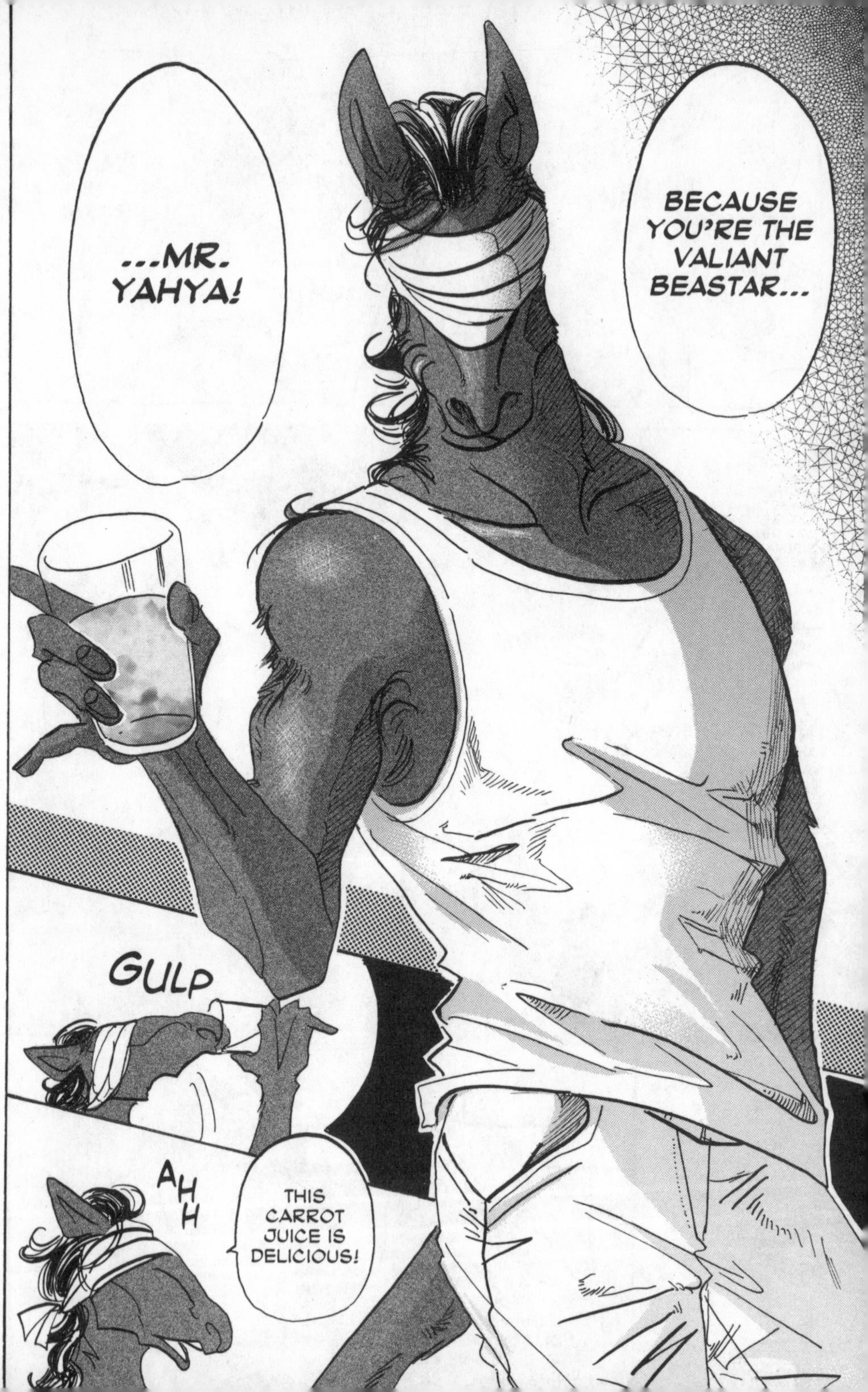
BECAUSE YOU'RE THE VALIANT BEASTAR...
...MR. YAHYA!
GULP
THIS CARROT JUICE IS DELICIOUS!
AHH

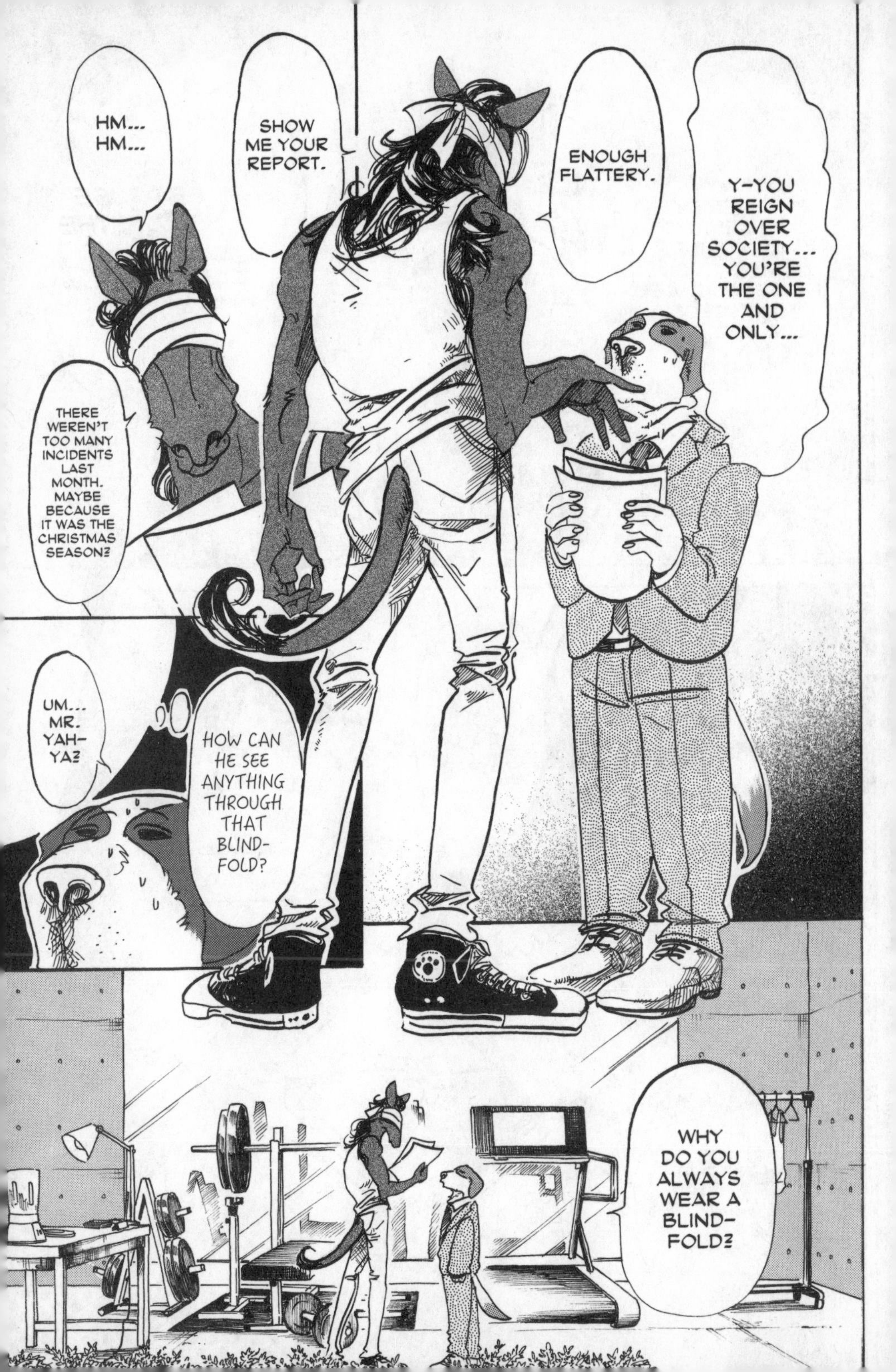
Y-YOU REIGN OVER SOCIETY... YOU'RE THE ONE AND ONLY...
ENOUGH FLATTERY.
SHOW ME YOUR REPORT.
HM... HM...
THERE WEREN'T TOO MANY INCIDENTS LAST MONTH. MAYBE BECAUSE IT WAS THE CHRISTMAS SEASON?
UM... MR. YAH-YA?
HOW CAN HE SEE ANYTHING THROUGH THAT BLIND-FOLD?
WHY DO YOU ALWAYS WEAR A BLIND-FOLD?

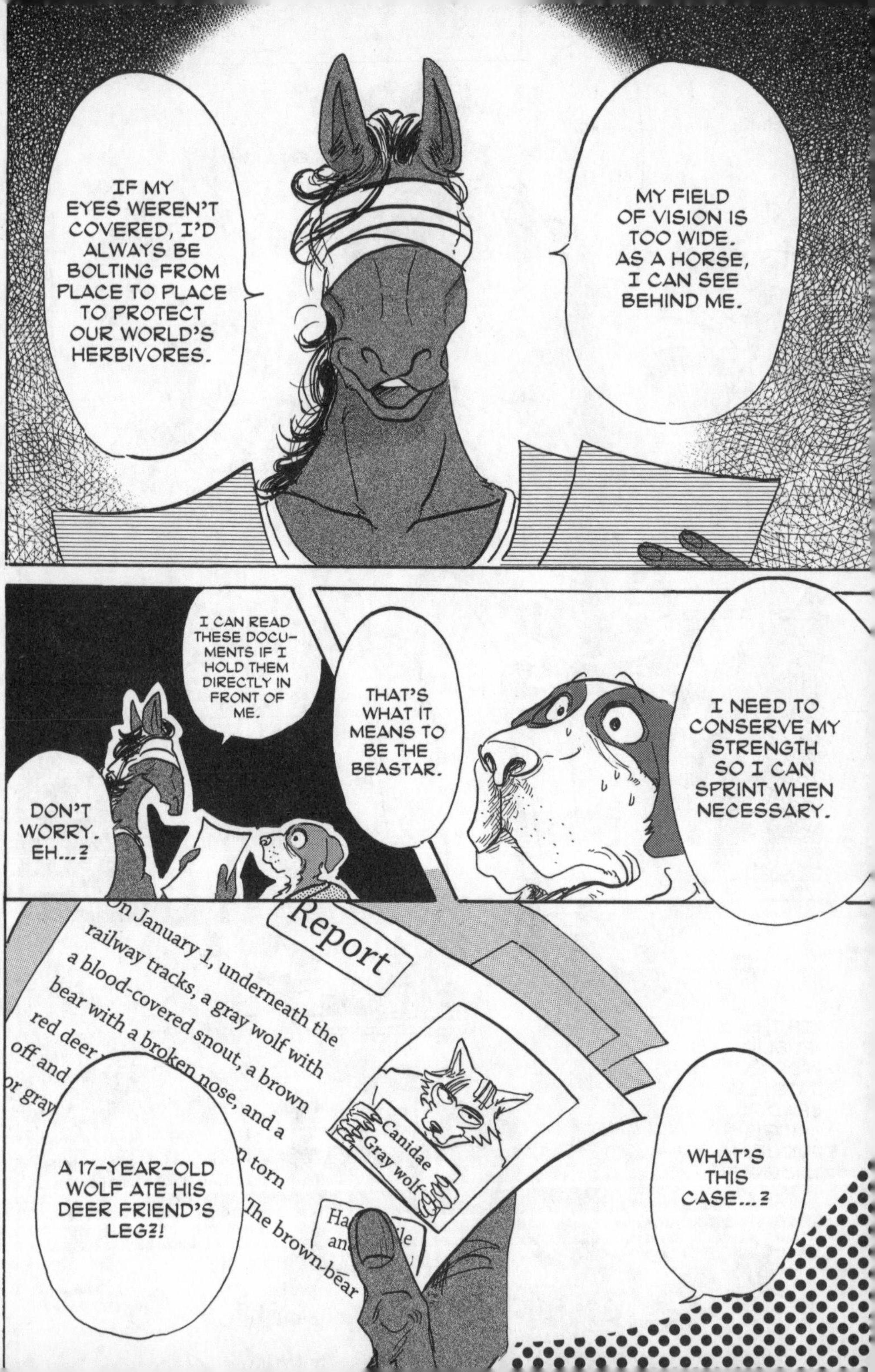
MY FIELD OF VISION IS TOO WIDE. AS A HORSE, I CAN SEE BEHIND ME.
IF MY EYES WEREN'T COVERED, I'D ALWAYS BE BOLTING FROM PLACE TO PLACE TO PROTECT OUR WORLD'S HERBIVORES.
I NEED TO CONSERVE MY STRENGTH SO I CAN SPRINT WHEN NECESSARY.
THAT'S WHAT IT MEANS TO BE THE BEASTAR.
I CAN READ THESE DOCUMENTS IF I HOLD THEM DIRECTLY IN FRONT OF ME.
DON'T WORRY. EH...?
Report
On January 1, underneath the railway tracks, a gray wolf with a blood-covered snout, a brown bear with a broken nose, and a
red deer
off and
or gray
n torn
The brown-bear
Canidae Gray wolf
WHAT'S THIS CASE...?
A 17-YEAR-OLD WOLF ATE HIS DEER FRIEND'S LEG?!

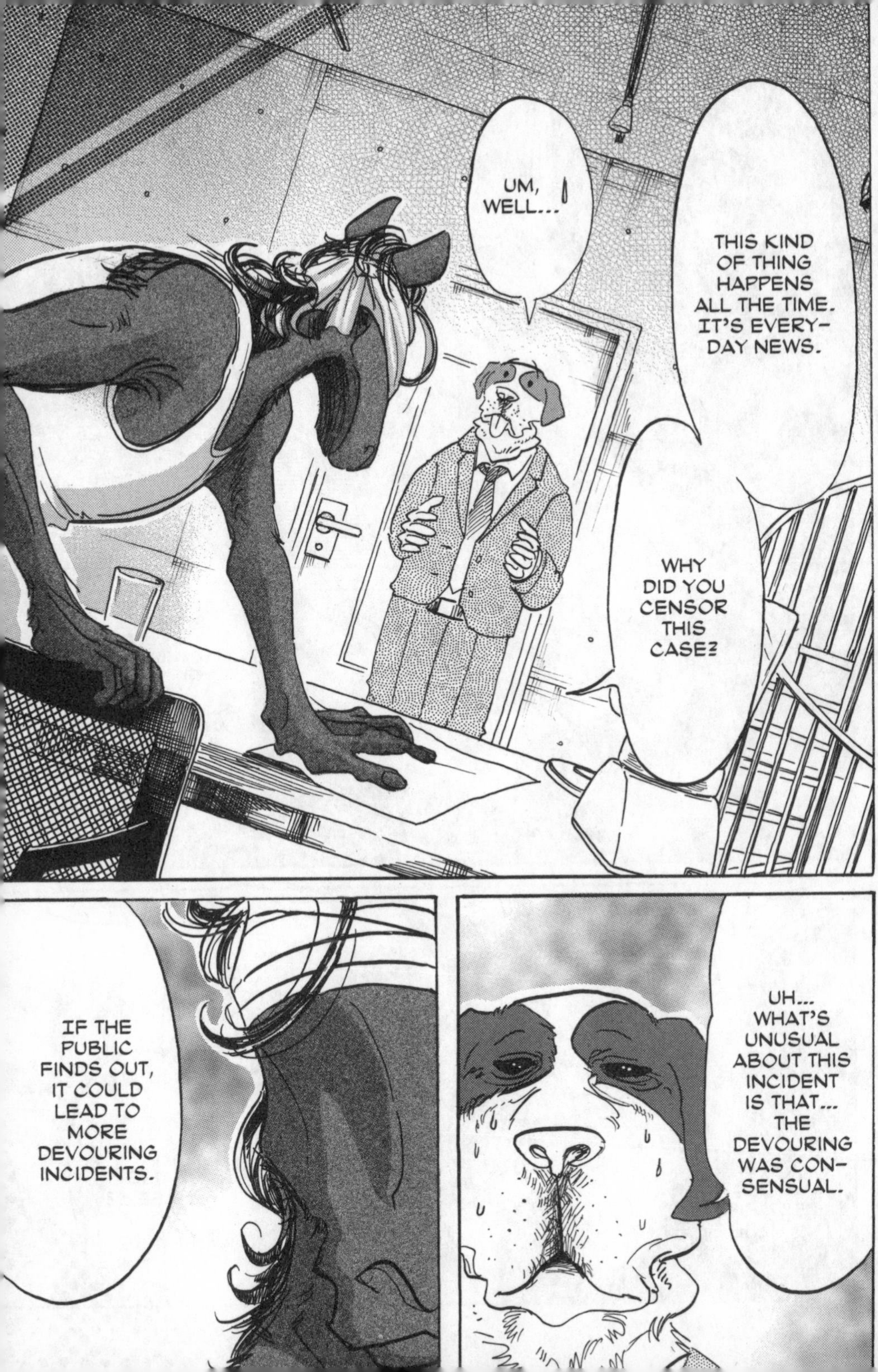
THIS KIND OF THING HAPPENS ALL THE TIME. IT'S EVERY-DAY NEWS.
WHY DID YOU CENSOR THIS CASE?
UM, WELL...
UH... WHAT'S UNUSUAL ABOUT THIS INCIDENT IS THAT... THE DEVOURING WAS CON-SENSUAL.
IF THE PUBLIC FINDS OUT, IT COULD LEAD TO MORE DEVOURING INCIDENTS.

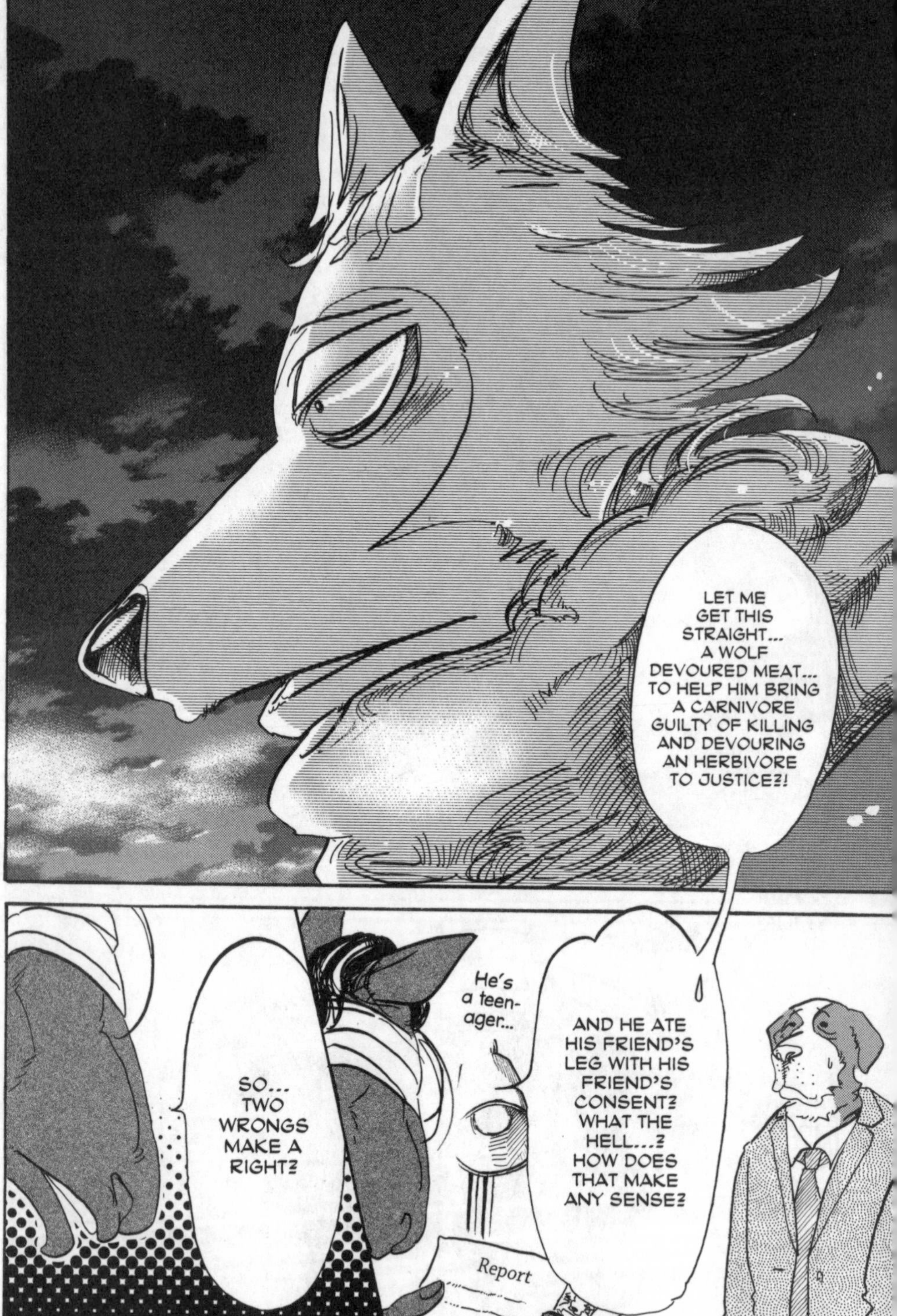
LET ME GET THIS STRAIGHT... A WOLF DEVOURED MEAT... TO HELP HIM BRING A CARNIVORE GUILTY OF KILLING AND DEVOURING AN HERBIVORE TO JUSTICE?!
AND HE ATE HIS FRIEND'S LEG WITH HIS FRIEND'S CONSENT? WHAT THE HELL...? HOW DOES THAT MAKE ANY SENSE?
He's a teen-ager...
SO... TWO WRONGS MAKE A RIGHT?
Report

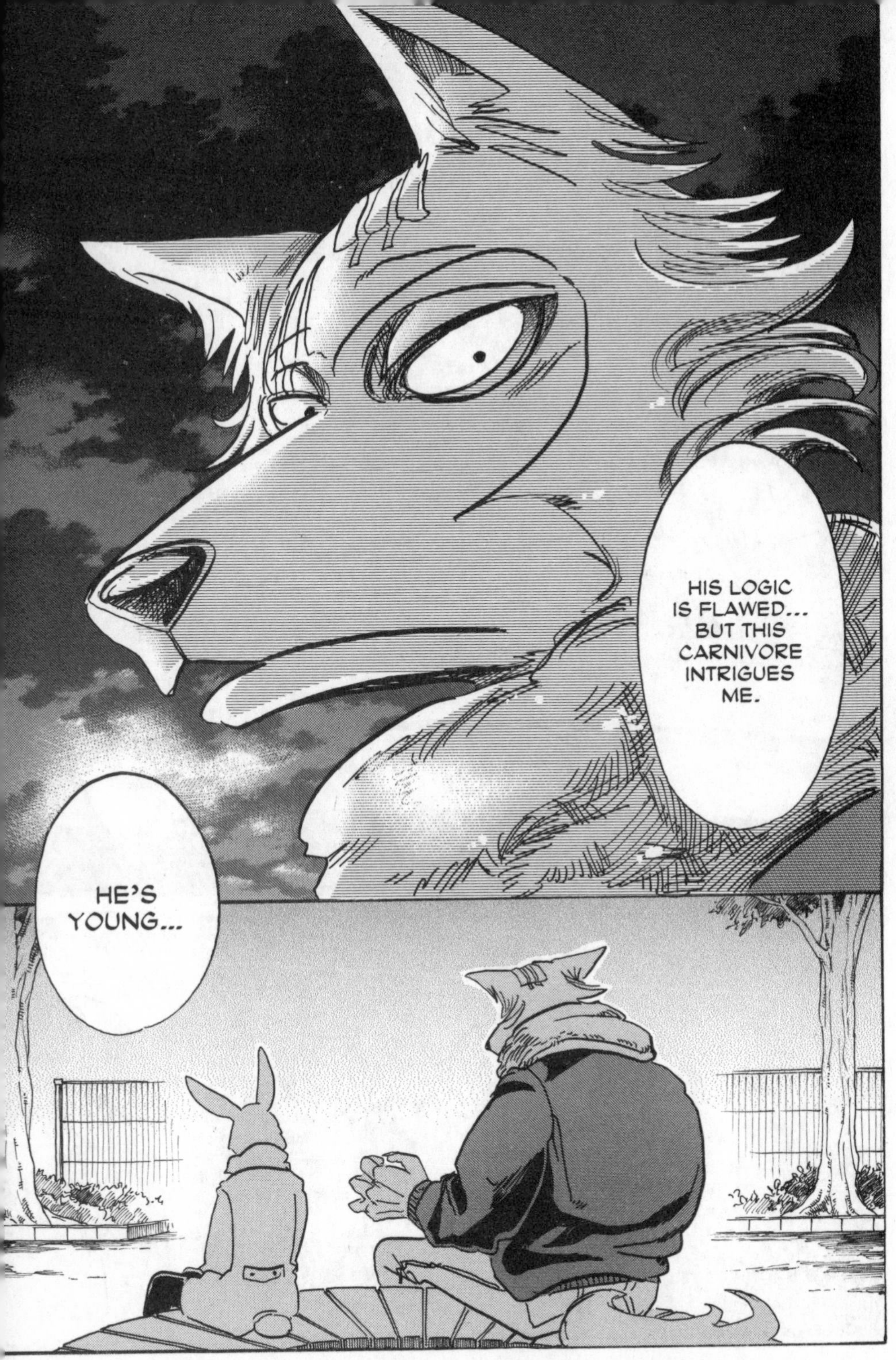
HIS LOGIC IS FLAWED... BUT THIS CARNIVORE INTRIGUES ME.
HE'S YOUNG...

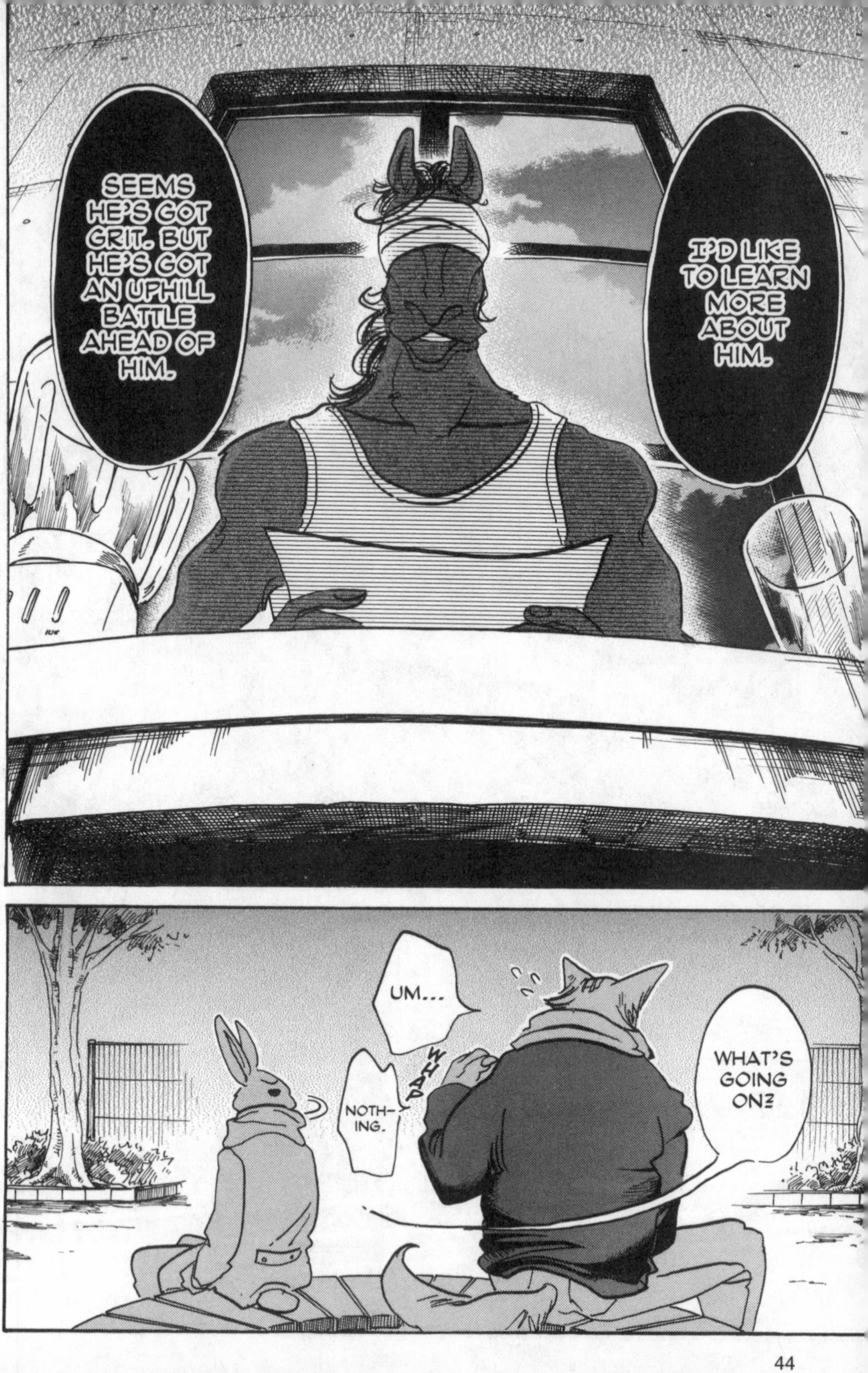
I'D LIKE TO LEARN MORE ABOUT HIM.
SEEMS HE'S GOT GRIT. BUT HE'S GOT AN UPHILL BATTLE AHEAD OF HIM.
WHAT'S GOING ON?
UM...
WHAP
NOTH-ING.

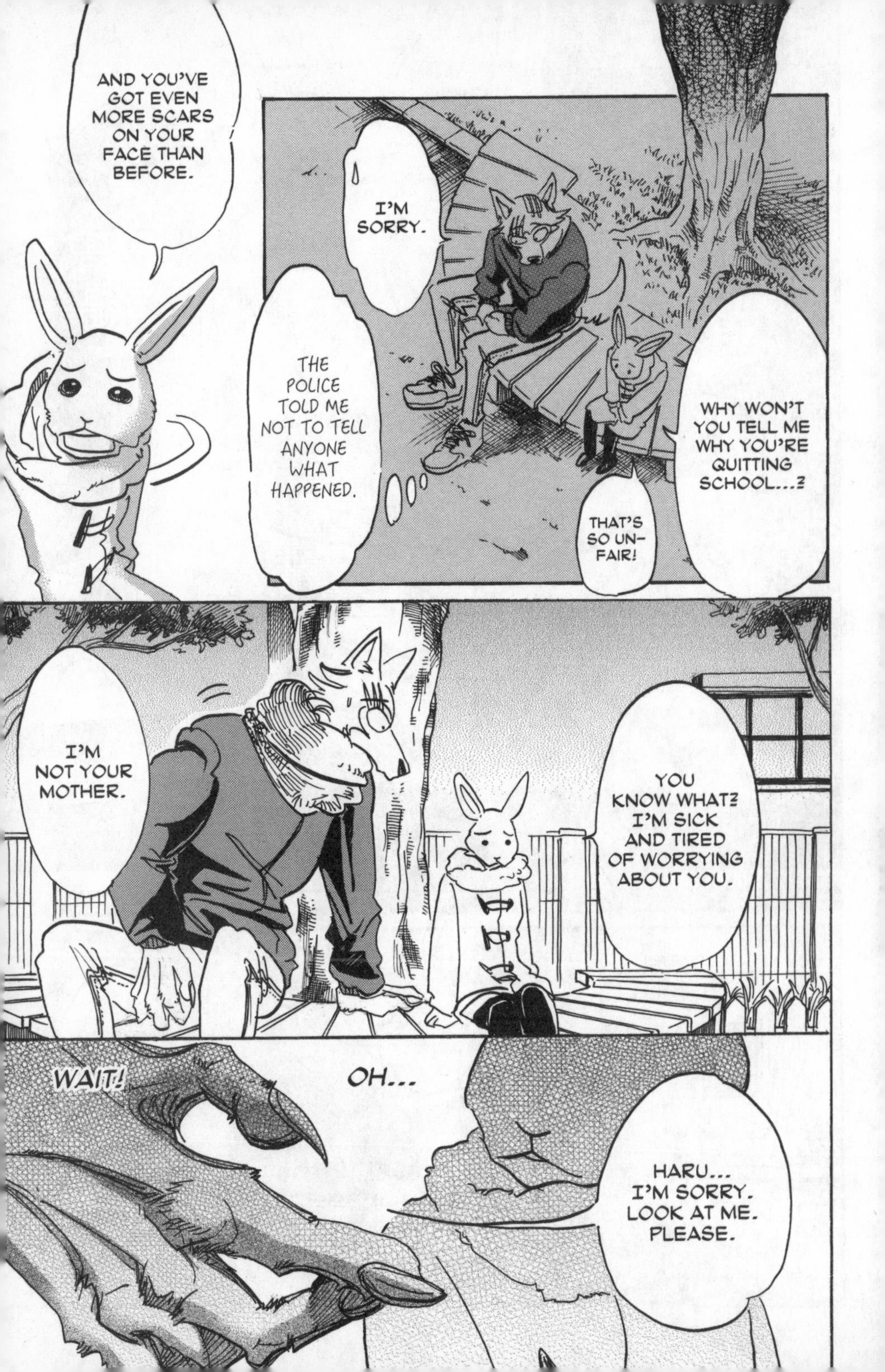
WHY WON'T YOU TELL ME WHY YOU'RE QUITTING SCHOOL...?
THAT'S SO UN-FAIR!
I'M SORRY.
THE POLICE TOLD ME NOT TO TELL ANYONE WHAT HAPPENED.
AND YOU'VE GOT EVEN MORE SCARS ON YOUR FACE THAN BEFORE.
YOU KNOW WHAT? I'M SICK AND TIRED OF WORRYING ABOUT YOU.
I'M NOT YOUR MOTHER.
WAIT!
OH...
HARU... I'M SORRY. LOOK AT ME. PLEASE.

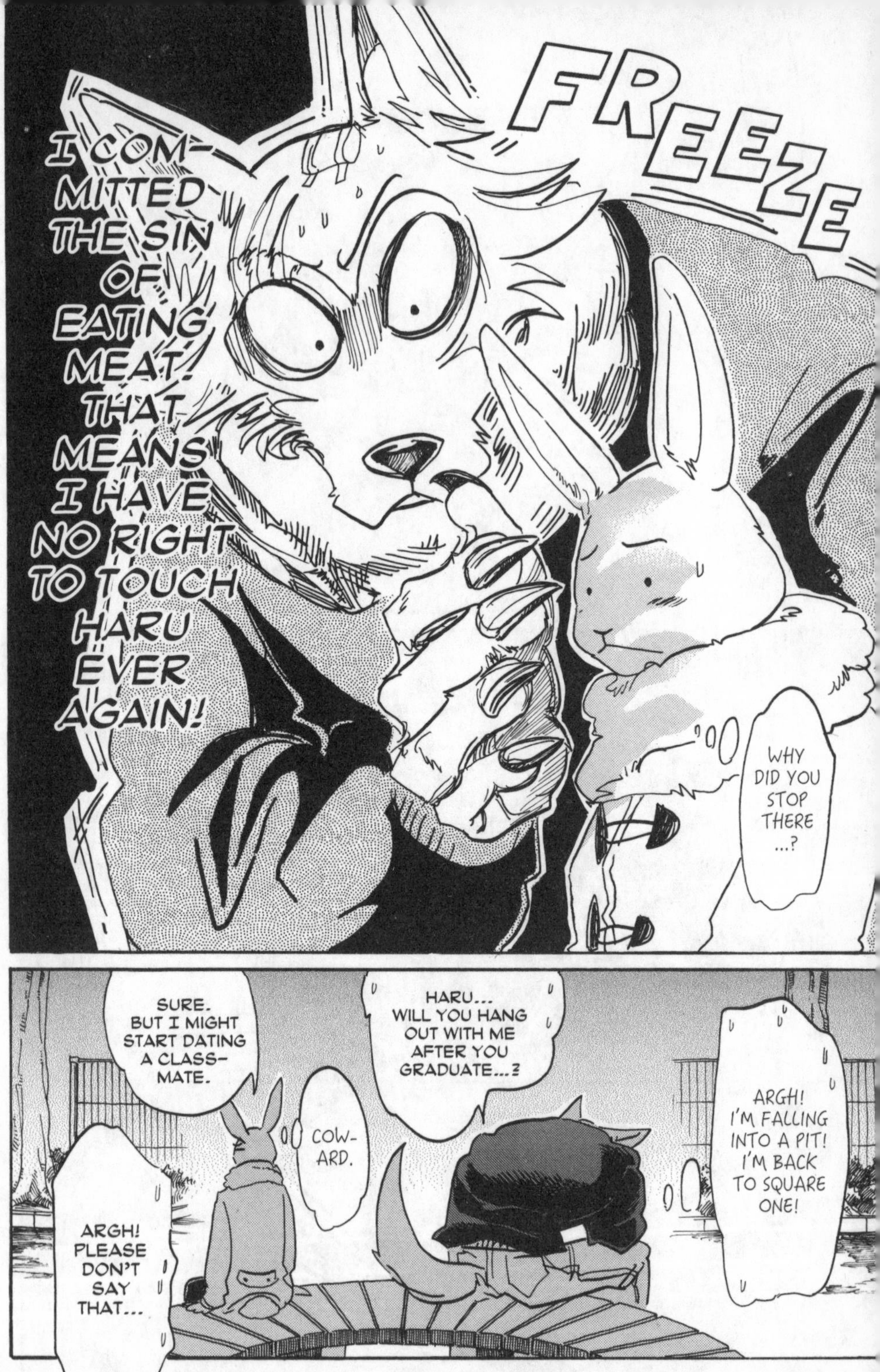
FREEZE
I COMMITTED THE SIN OF EATING MEAT. THAT MEANS I HAVE NO RIGHT TO TOUCH HARU EVER AGAIN!
WHY DID YOU STOP THERE ...?
HARU... WILL YOU HANG OUT WITH ME AFTER YOU GRADUATE...?
SURE. BUT I MIGHT START DATING A CLASSMATE.
COWARD.
ARGH! PLEASE DON'T SAY THAT...
ARGH! I'M FALLING INTO A PIT! I'M BACK TO SQUARE ONE!

A family of purebred Netherland dwarf rabbits

Father

Older sister

Older brother

Mother

Haru

Chapter 100: When the Train Is Packed

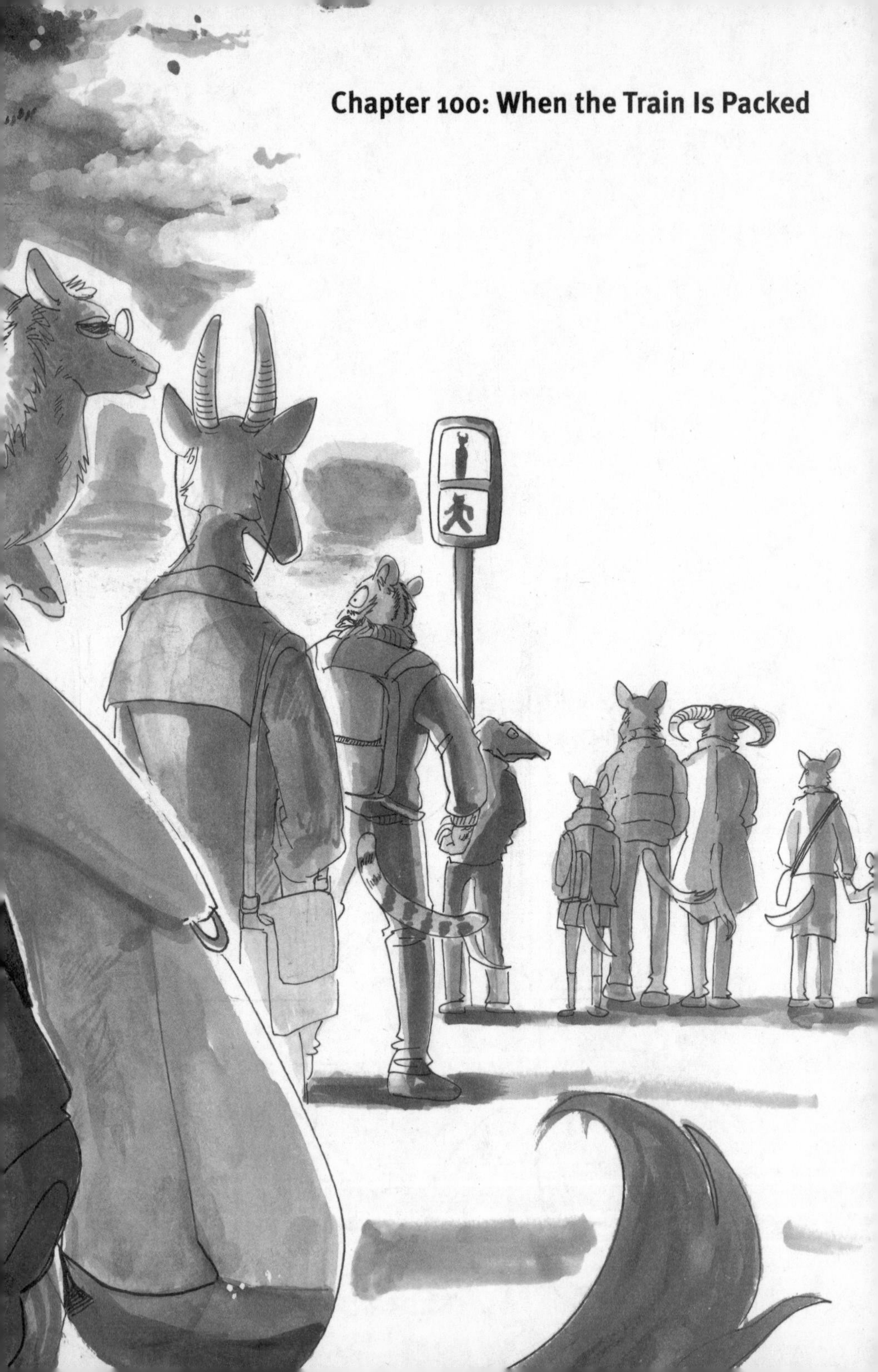

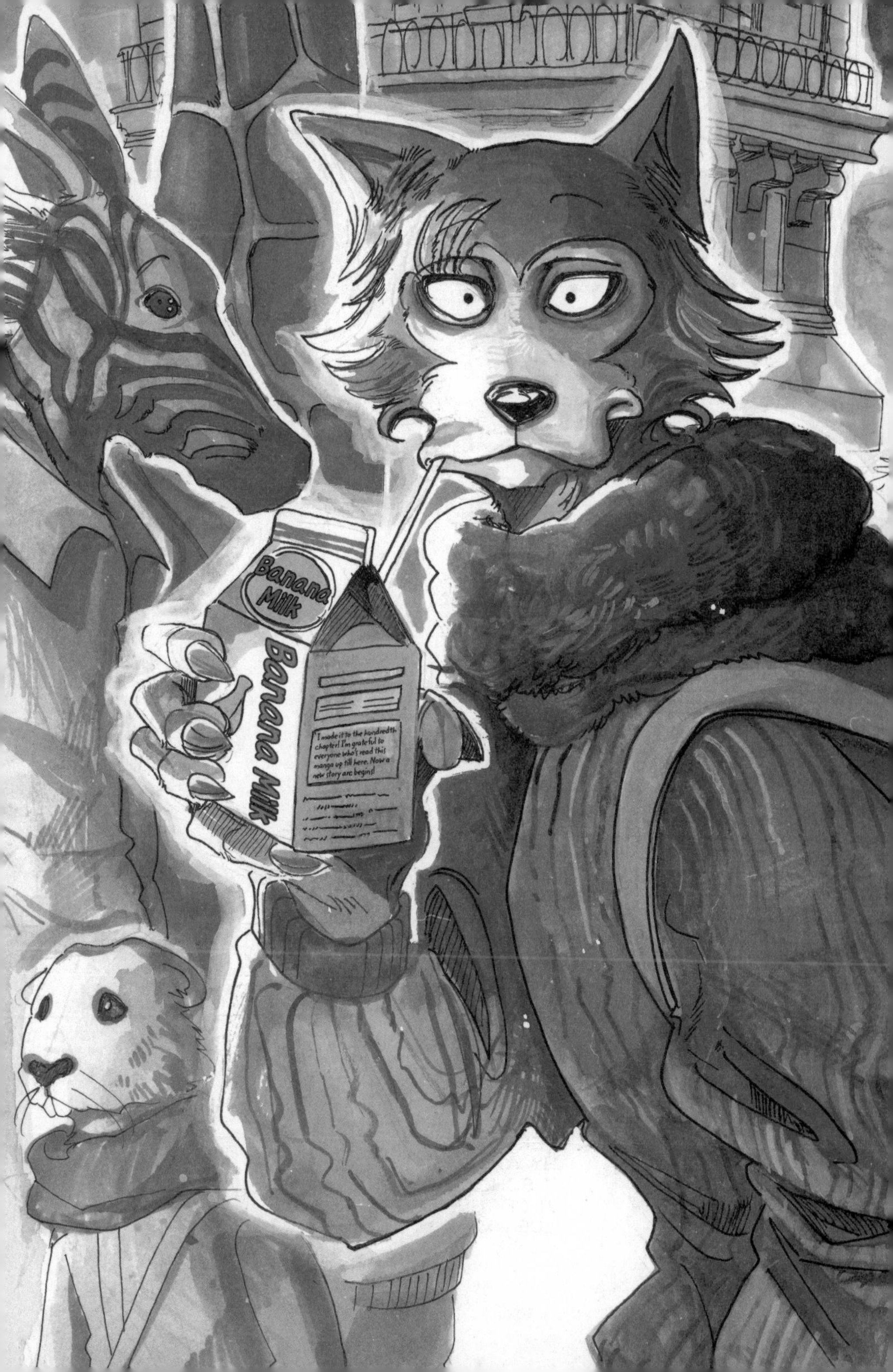
Banana Milk
Banana Milk
"I made it to the hundredth chapter! I'm grateful to everyone who's read this manga up till here. Now a new story arc begins!

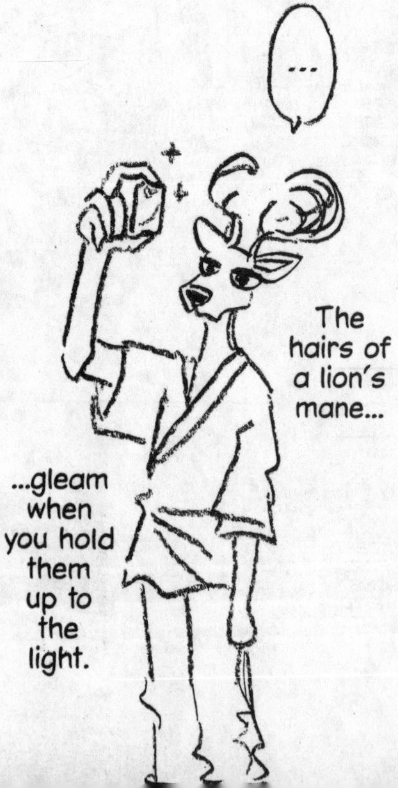
...
The hairs of a lion's mane...
...gleam when you hold them up to the light.

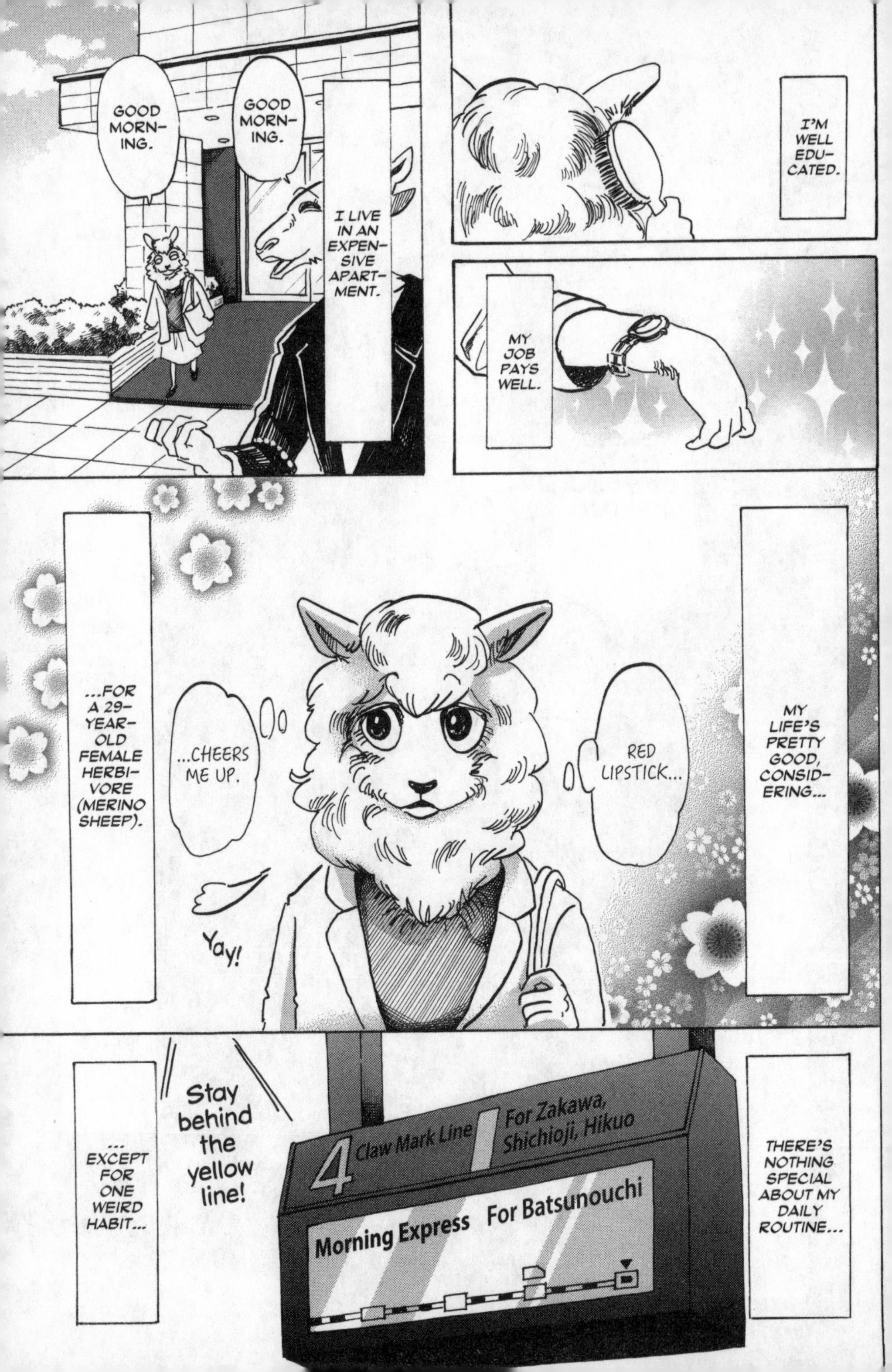
I'M WELL EDUCATED.
MY JOB PAYS WELL.
I LIVE IN AN EXPENSIVE APARTMENT.
GOOD MORNING.
GOOD MORNING.
MY LIFE'S PRETTY GOOD, CONSIDERING...
RED LIPSTICK...
...CHEERS ME UP.
...FOR A 29-YEAR-OLD FEMALE HERBIVORE (MERINO SHEEP).
Yay!
THERE'S NOTHING SPECIAL ABOUT MY DAILY ROUTINE...
4 Claw Mark Line
For Zakawa, Shichioji, Hikuo
Morning Express For Batsunouchi
Stay behind the yellow line!
...EXCEPT FOR ONE WEIRD HABIT...

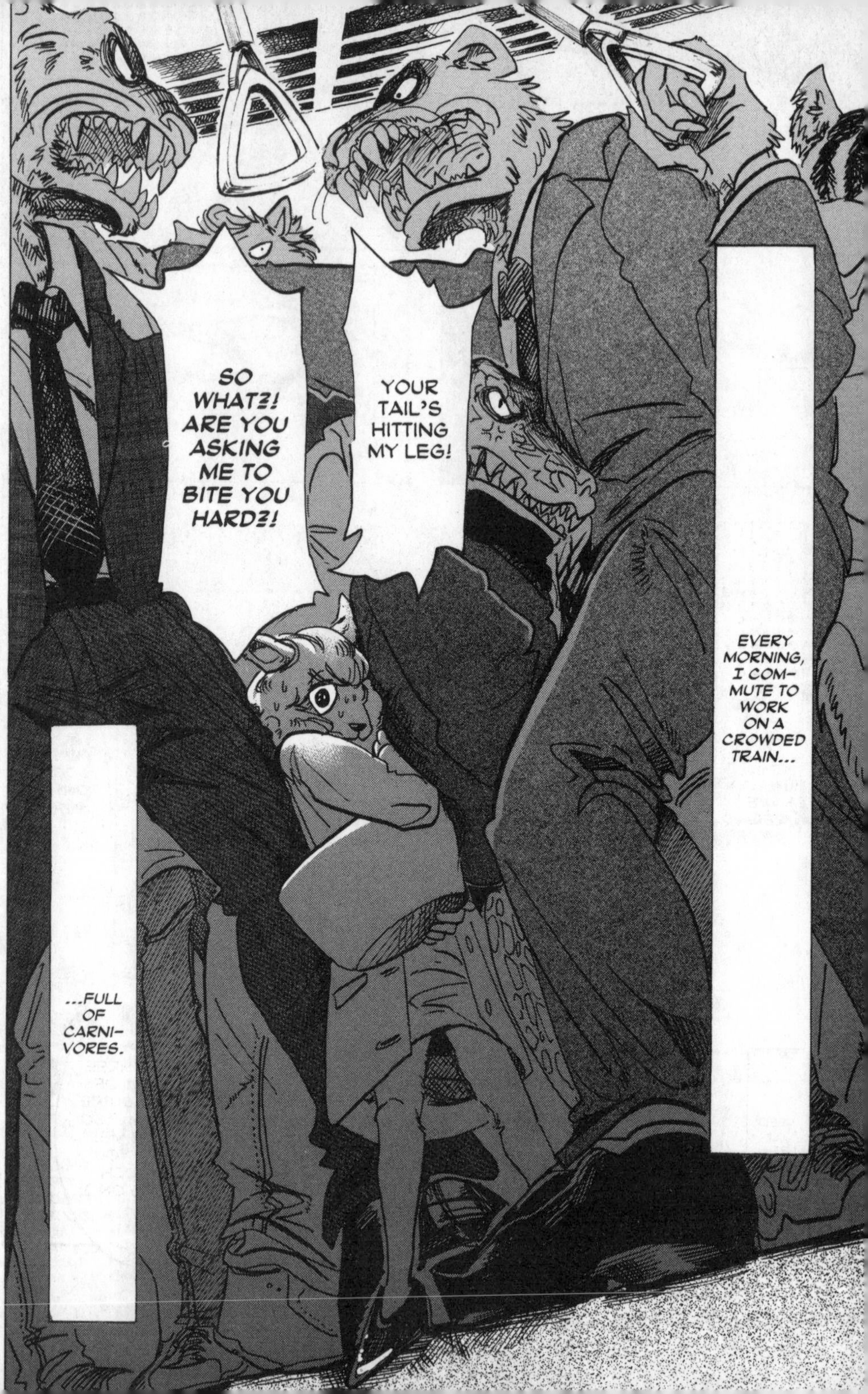
YOUR TAIL'S HITTING MY LEG!
SO WHAT?! ARE YOU ASKING ME TO BITE YOU HARD?!
EVERY MORNING, I COMMUTE TO WORK ON A CROWDED TRAIN...
...FULL OF CARNIVORES.

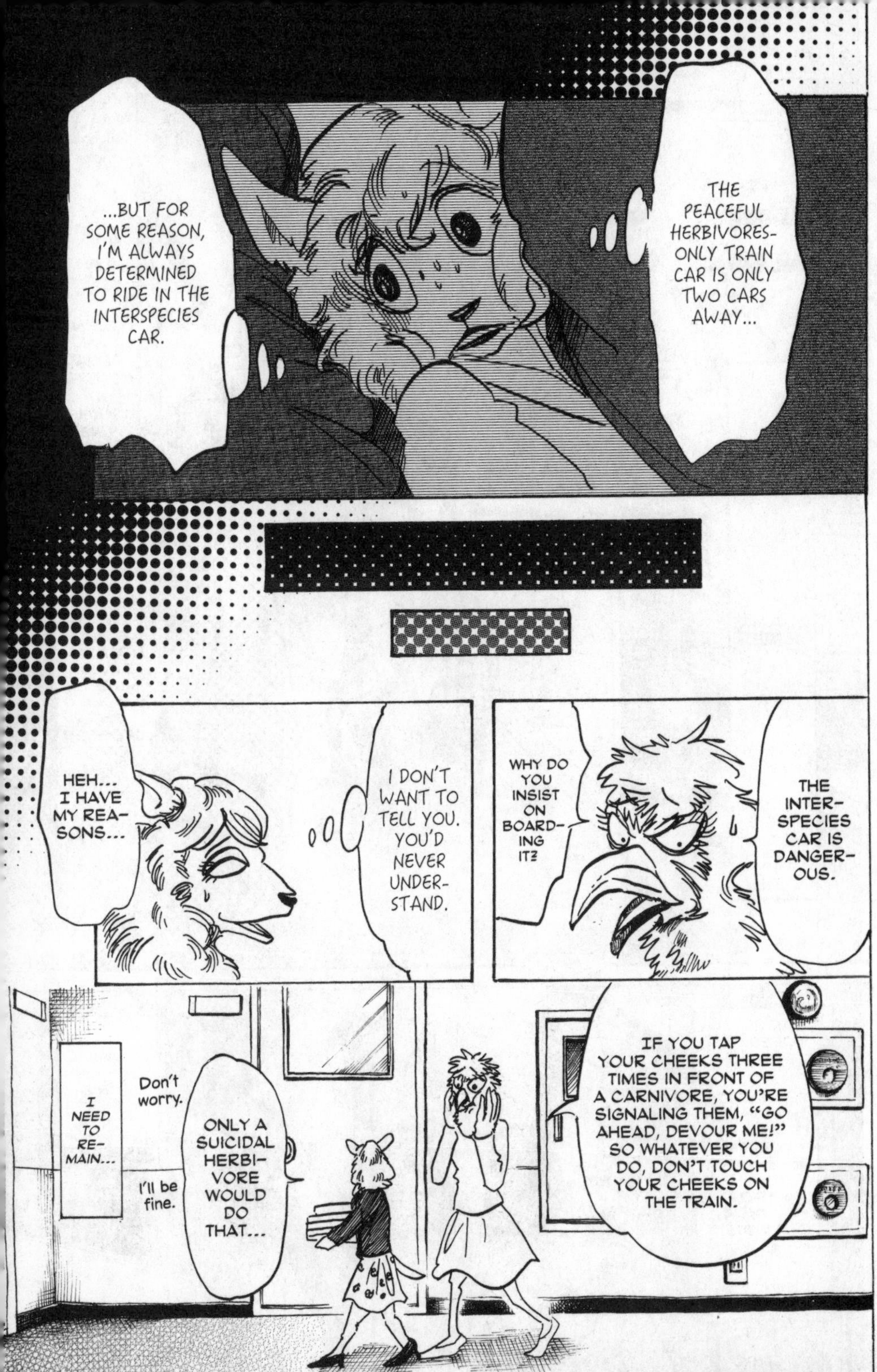
THE PEACEFUL HERBIVORES-ONLY TRAIN CAR IS ONLY TWO CARS AWAY...
...BUT FOR SOME REASON, I'M ALWAYS DETERMINED TO RIDE IN THE INTERSPECIES CAR.
THE INTER-SPECIES CAR IS DANGER-OUS.
WHY DO YOU INSIST ON BOARD-ING IT?
I DON'T WANT TO TELL YOU. YOU'D NEVER UNDER-STAND.
HEH... I HAVE MY REA-SONS...
IF YOU TAP YOUR CHEEKS THREE TIMES IN FRONT OF A CARNIVORE, YOU'RE SIGNALING THEM, "GO AHEAD, DEVOUR ME!" SO WHATEVER YOU DO, DON'T TOUCH YOUR CHEEKS ON THE TRAIN.
ONLY A SUICIDAL HERBI-VORE WOULD DO THAT...
Don't worry.
I'll be fine.
I NEED TO RE-MAIN...

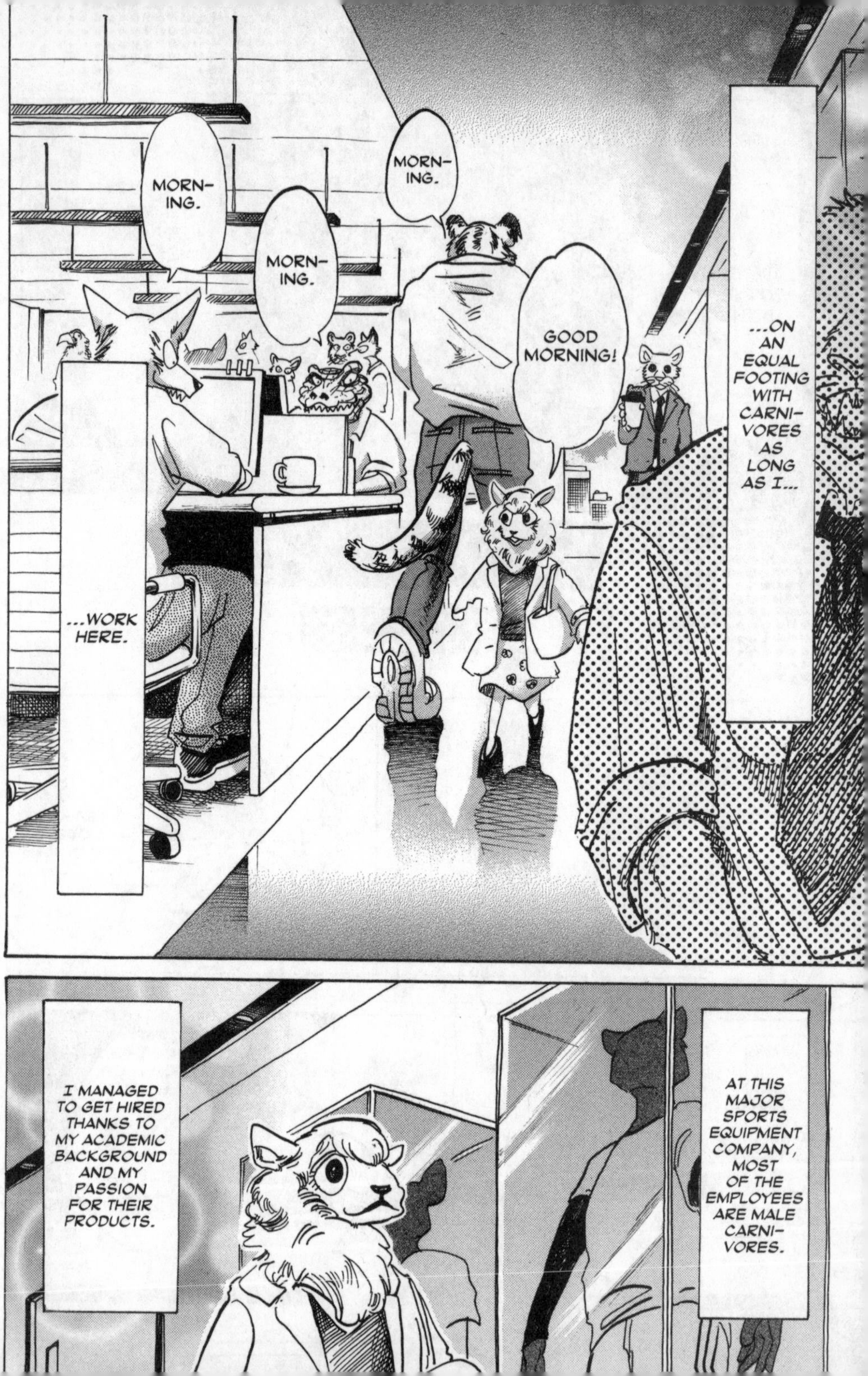
...ON AN EQUAL FOOTING WITH CARNIVORES AS LONG AS I...
GOOD MORNING!
MORNING.
MORNING.
MORNING.
...WORK HERE.
AT THIS MAJOR SPORTS EQUIPMENT COMPANY, MOST OF THE EMPLOYEES ARE MALE CARNIVORES.
I MANAGED TO GET HIRED THANKS TO MY ACADEMIC BACKGROUND AND MY PASSION FOR THEIR PRODUCTS.

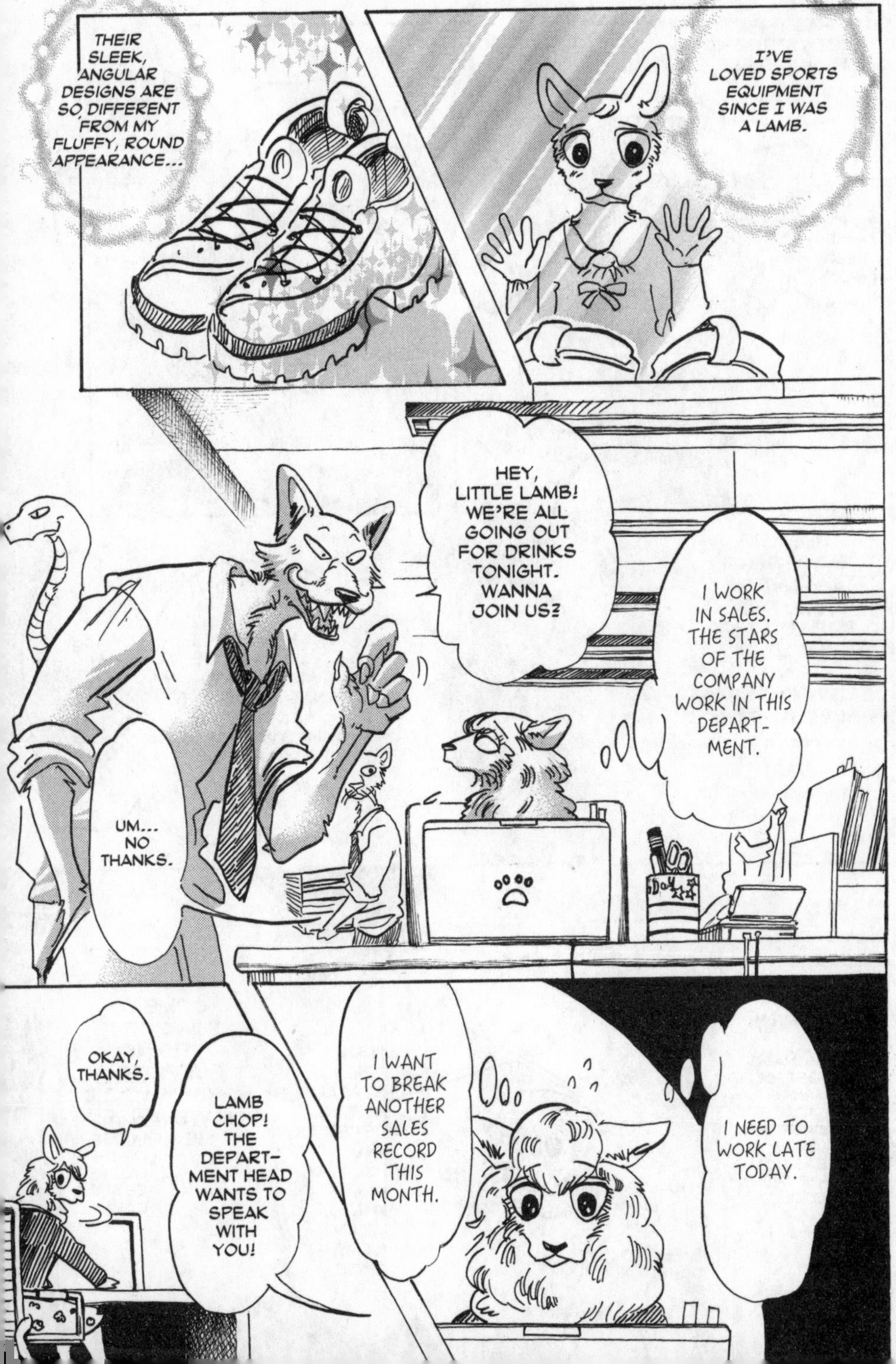
I'VE LOVED SPORTS EQUIPMENT SINCE I WAS A LAMB.
THEIR SLEEK, ANGULAR DESIGNS ARE SO DIFFERENT FROM MY FLUFFY, ROUND APPEARANCE...
I WORK IN SALES. THE STARS OF THE COMPANY WORK IN THIS DEPARTMENT.
HEY, LITTLE LAMB! WE'RE ALL GOING OUT FOR DRINKS TONIGHT. WANNA JOIN US?
UM... NO THANKS.
I NEED TO WORK LATE TODAY.
I WANT TO BREAK ANOTHER SALES RECORD THIS MONTH.
LAMB CHOP! THE DEPARTMENT HEAD WANTS TO SPEAK WITH YOU!
OKAY, THANKS.

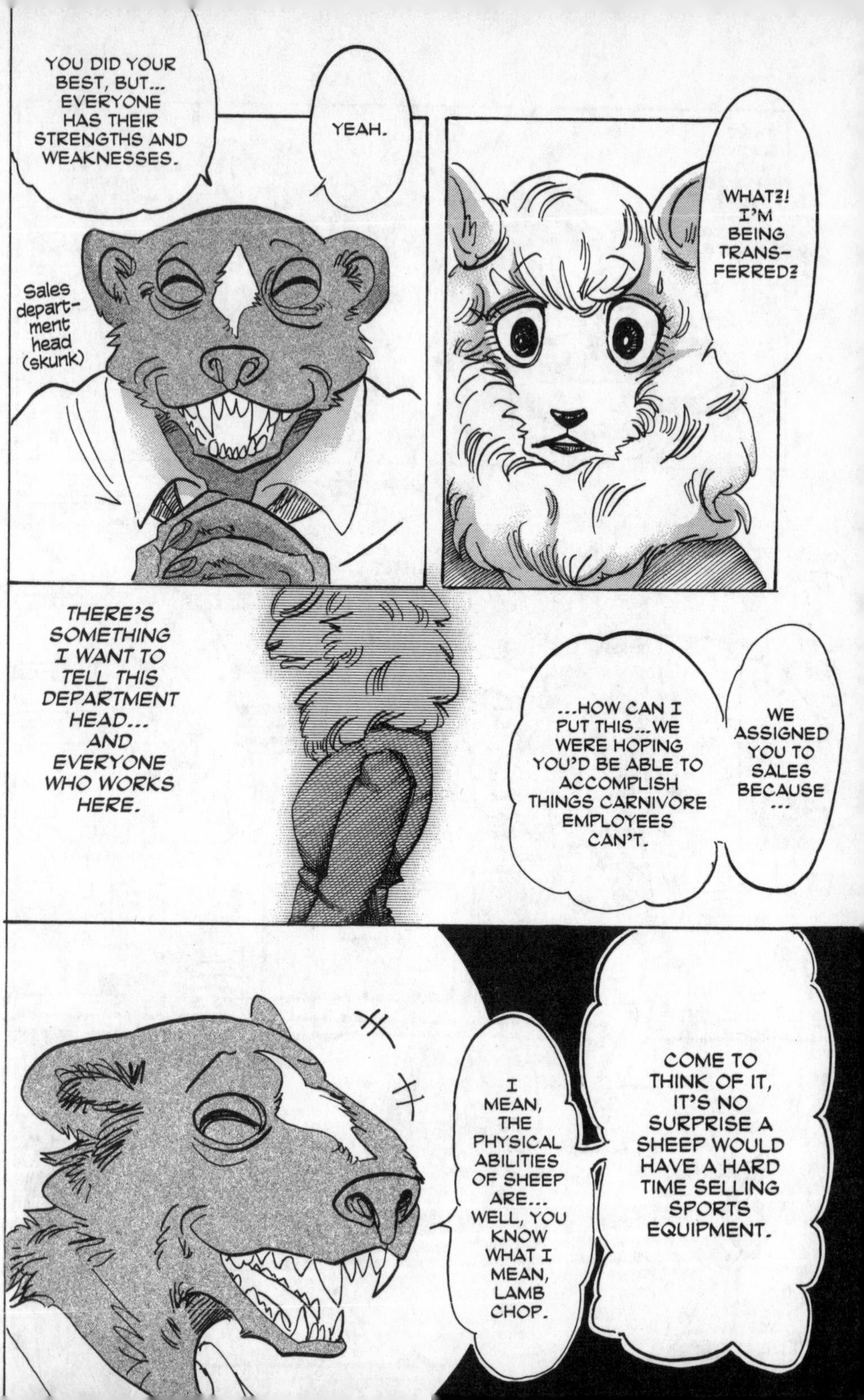
WHAT?! I'M BEING TRANS-FERRED?
YEAH.
YOU DID YOUR BEST, BUT... EVERYONE HAS THEIR STRENGTHS AND WEAKNESSES.
Sales department head (skunk)
WE ASSIGNED YOU TO SALES BECAUSE...
...HOW CAN I PUT THIS...WE WERE HOPING YOU'D BE ABLE TO ACCOMPLISH THINGS CARNIVORE EMPLOYEES CAN'T.
THERE'S SOMETHING I WANT TO TELL THIS DEPARTMENT HEAD... AND EVERYONE WHO WORKS HERE.
COME TO THINK OF IT, IT'S NO SURPRISE A SHEEP WOULD HAVE A HARD TIME SELLING SPORTS EQUIPMENT.
I MEAN, THE PHYSICAL ABILITIES OF SHEEP ARE... WELL, YOU KNOW WHAT I MEAN, LAMB CHOP.

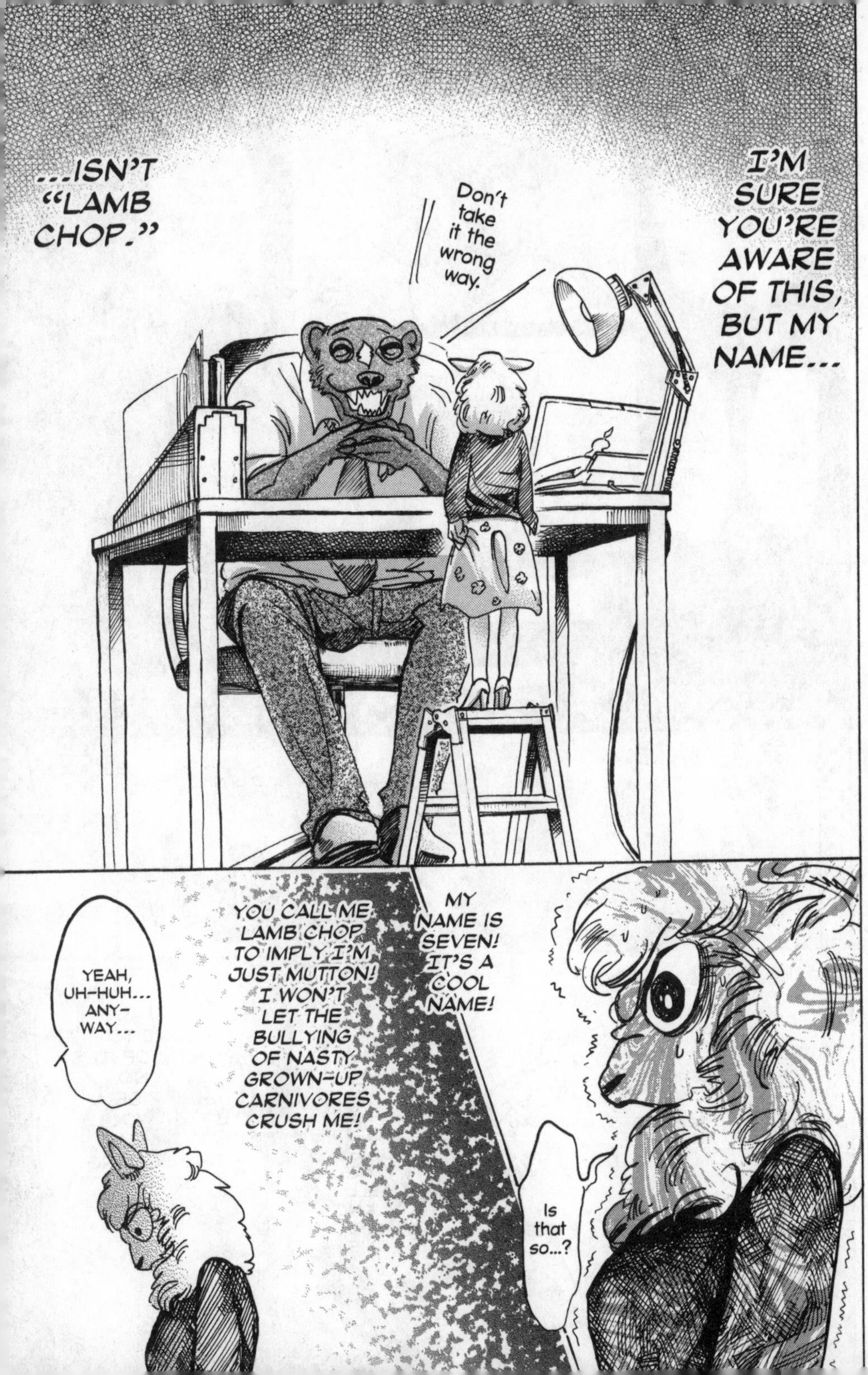

I'M SURE YOU'RE AWARE OF THIS, BUT MY NAME...
Don't take it the wrong way.
...ISN'T "LAMB CHOP."
MY NAME IS SEVEN! IT'S A COOL NAME!
Is that so...?
YOU CALL ME LAMB CHOP TO IMPLY I'M JUST MUTTON! I WON'T LET THE BULLYING OF NASTY GROWN-UP CARNIVORES CRUSH ME!
YEAH, UH-HUH... ANY-WAY...

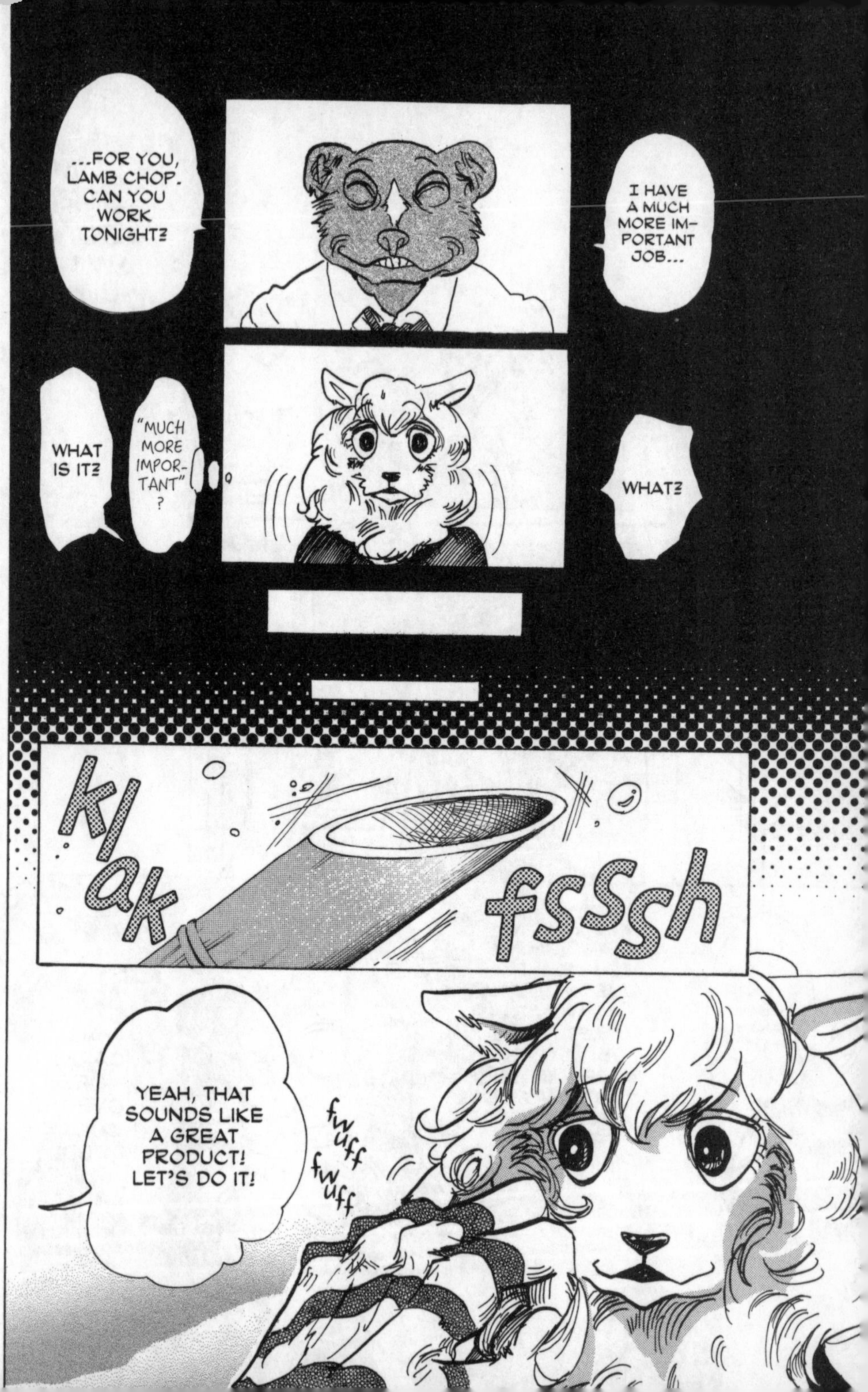

I HAVE A MUCH MORE IM-PORTANT JOB...
...FOR YOU, LAMB CHOP. CAN YOU WORK TONIGHT?
WHAT?
"MUCH MORE IMPOR-TANT"?
WHAT IS IT?
fsssh
klak
fwuff fwuff
YEAH, THAT SOUNDS LIKE A GREAT PRODUCT! LET'S DO IT!

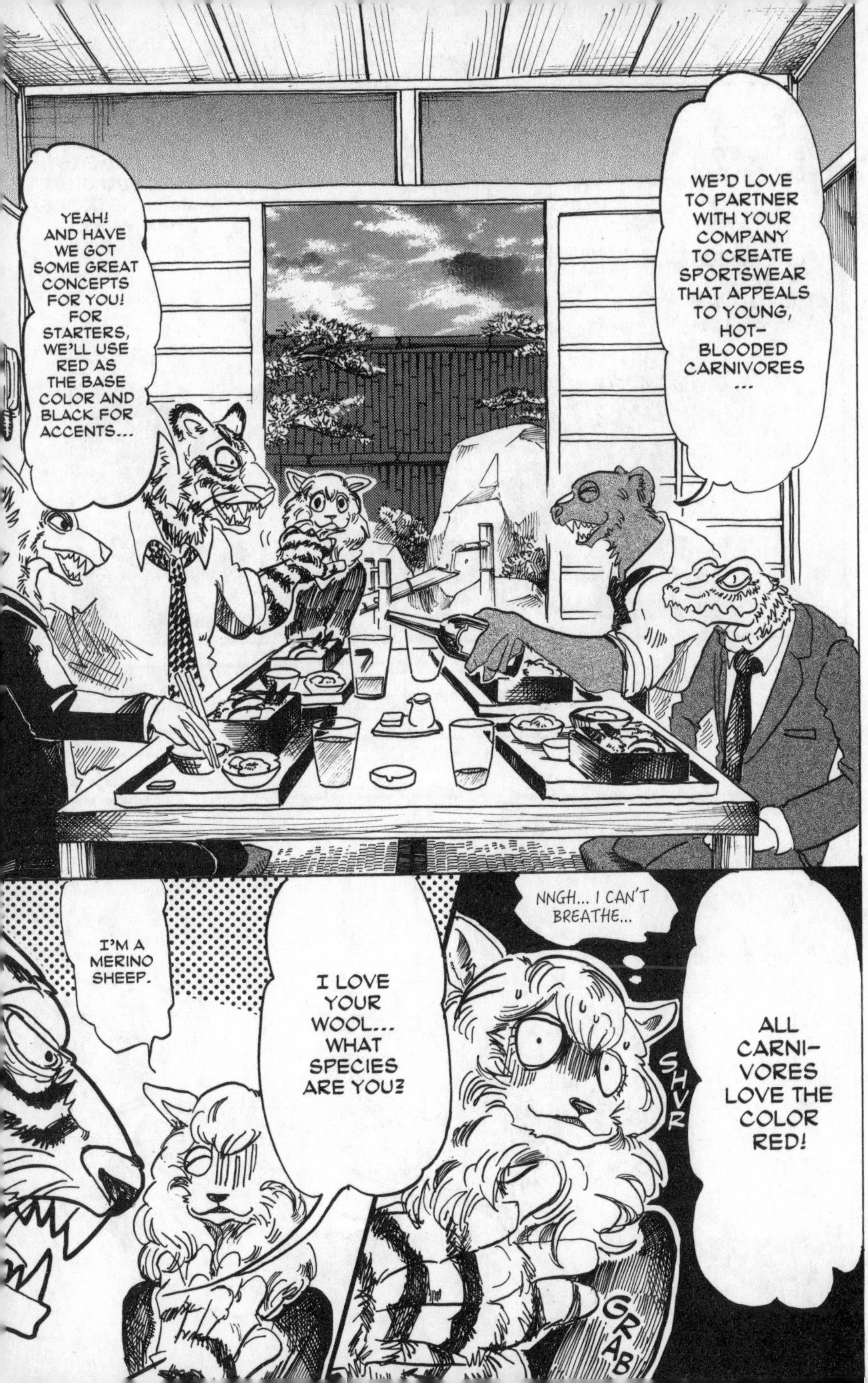
WE'D LOVE TO PARTNER WITH YOUR COMPANY TO CREATE SPORTSWEAR THAT APPEALS TO YOUNG, HOT-BLOODED CARNIVORES...
YEAH! AND HAVE WE GOT SOME GREAT CONCEPTS FOR YOU! FOR STARTERS, WE'LL USE RED AS THE BASE COLOR AND BLACK FOR ACCENTS...
ALL CARNI-VORES LOVE THE COLOR RED!
NNGH... I CAN'T BREATHE...
SHVR
GRAB
I LOVE YOUR WOOL... WHAT SPECIES ARE YOU?
I'M A MERINO SHEEP.

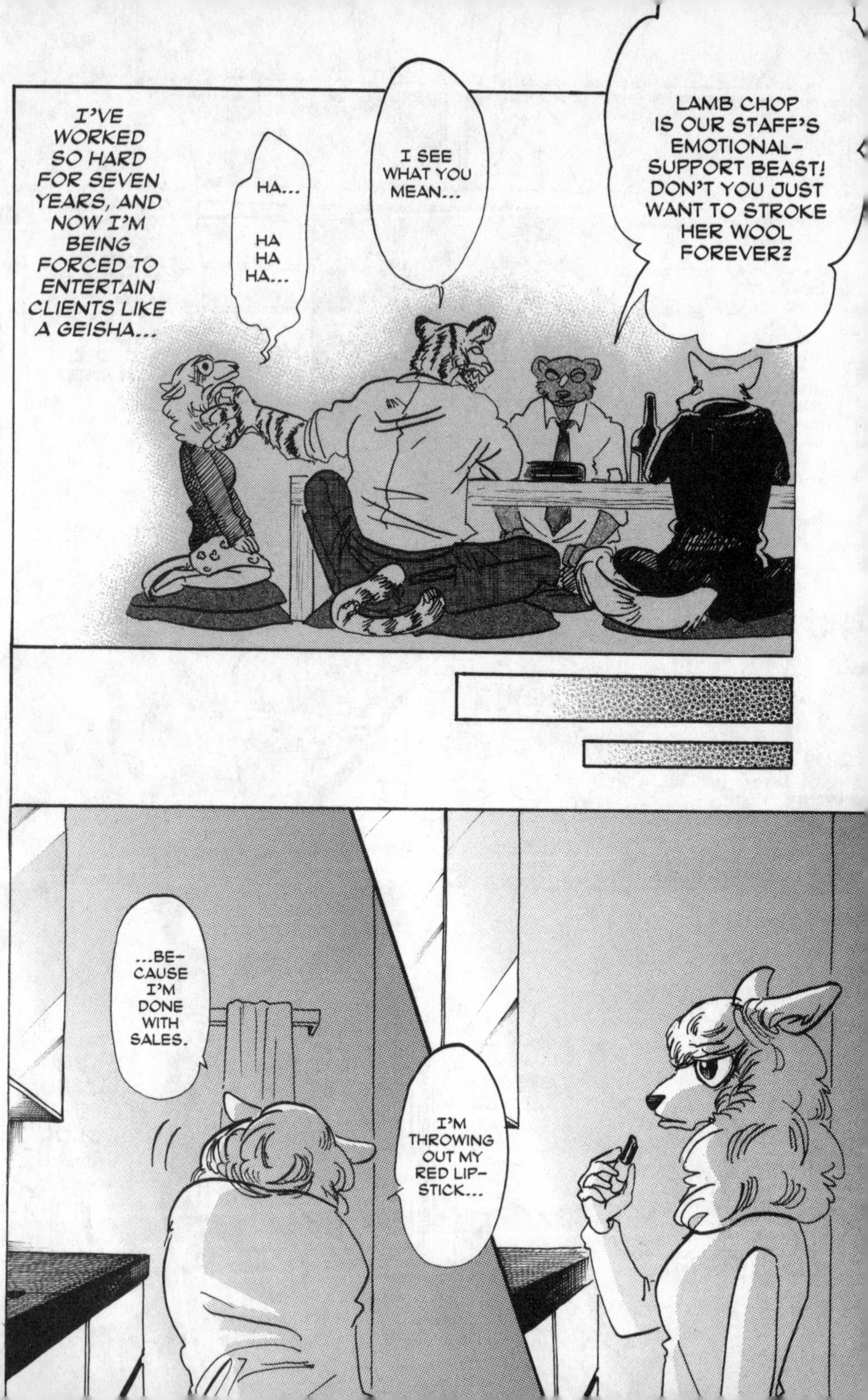
LAMB CHOP IS OUR STAFF'S EMOTIONAL-SUPPORT BEAST! DON'T YOU JUST WANT TO STROKE HER WOOL FOREVER?
I SEE WHAT YOU MEAN...
HA... HA HA HA...
I'VE WORKED SO HARD FOR SEVEN YEARS, AND NOW I'M BEING FORCED TO ENTERTAIN CLIENTS LIKE A GEISHA...
I'M THROWING OUT MY RED LIP-STICK...
...BE-CAUSE I'M DONE WITH SALES.

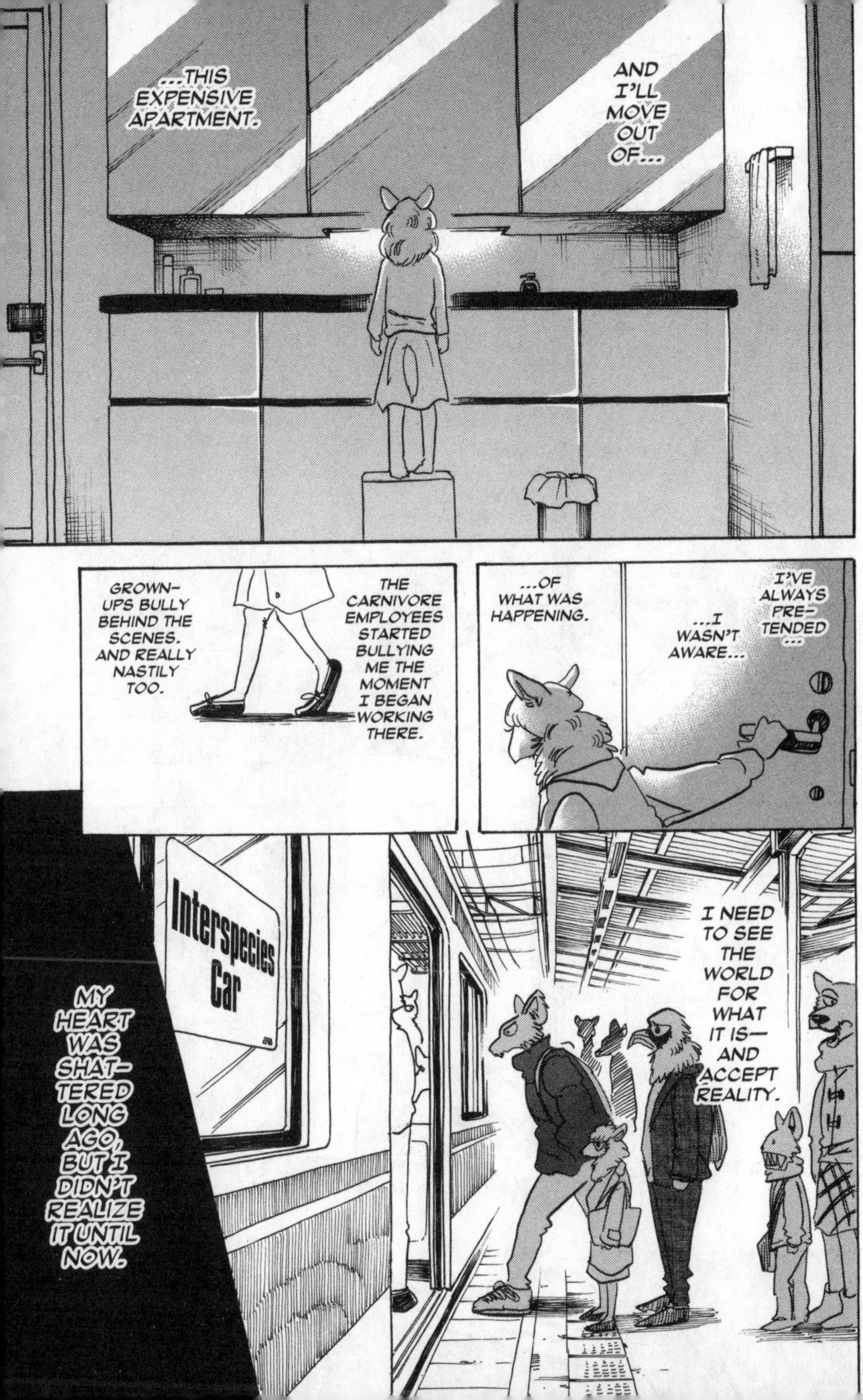
AND I'LL MOVE OUT OF...
...THIS EXPENSIVE APARTMENT.
I'VE ALWAYS PRETENDED...
...I WASN'T AWARE...
...OF WHAT WAS HAPPENING.
THE CARNIVORE EMPLOYEES STARTED BULLYING ME THE MOMENT I BEGAN WORKING THERE.
GROWN-UPS BULLY BEHIND THE SCENES. AND REALLY NASTILY TOO.
I NEED TO SEE THE WORLD FOR WHAT IT IS—AND ACCEPT REALITY.
Interspecies Car
MY HEART WAS SHATTERED LONG AGO, BUT I DIDN'T REALIZE IT UNTIL NOW.

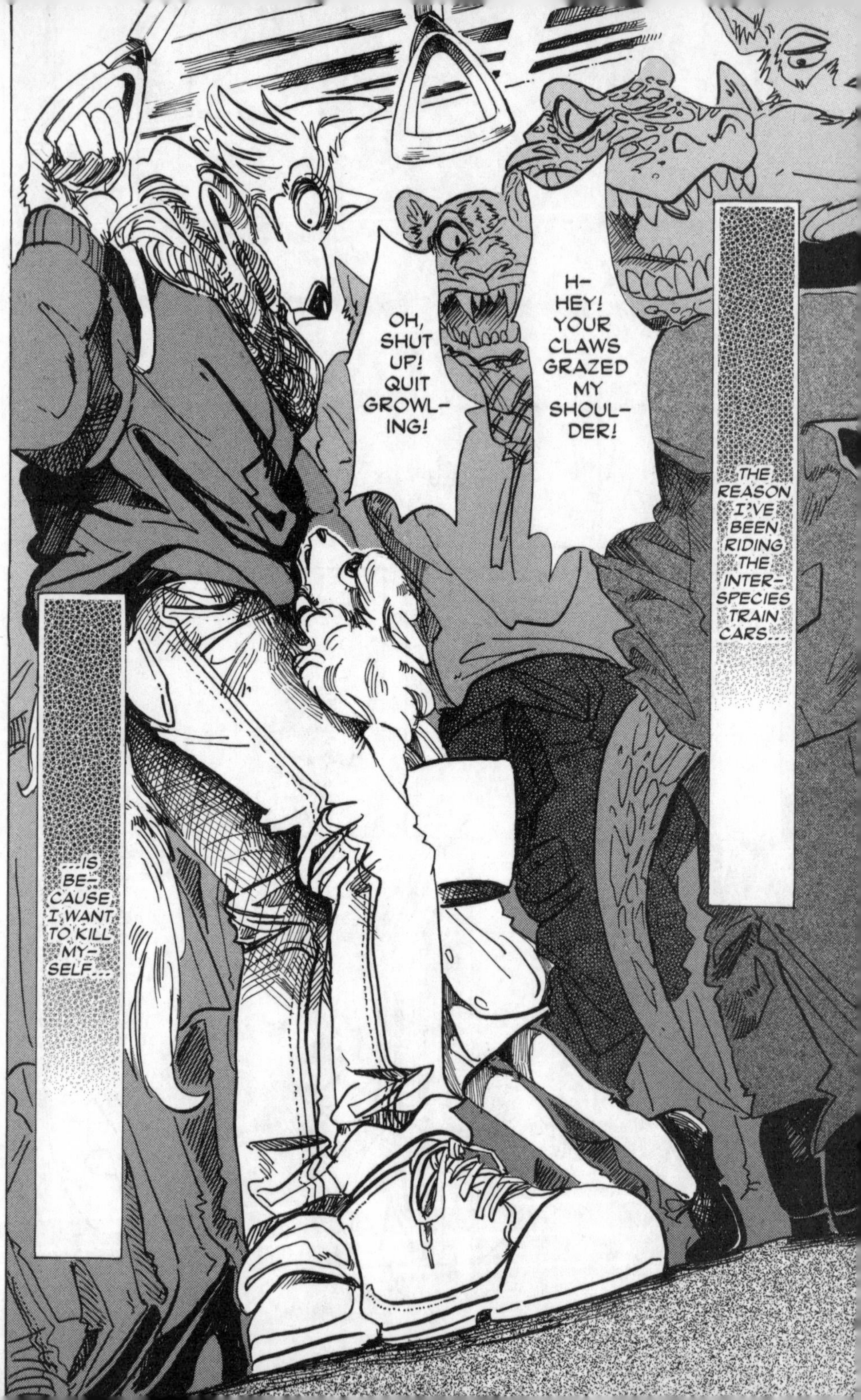
THE REASON I'VE BEEN RIDING THE INTER-SPECIES TRAIN CARS...
H-HEY! YOUR CLAWS GRAZED MY SHOULDER!
OH, SHUT UP! QUIT GROWLING!
...IS BECAUSE I WANT TO KILL MYSELF...

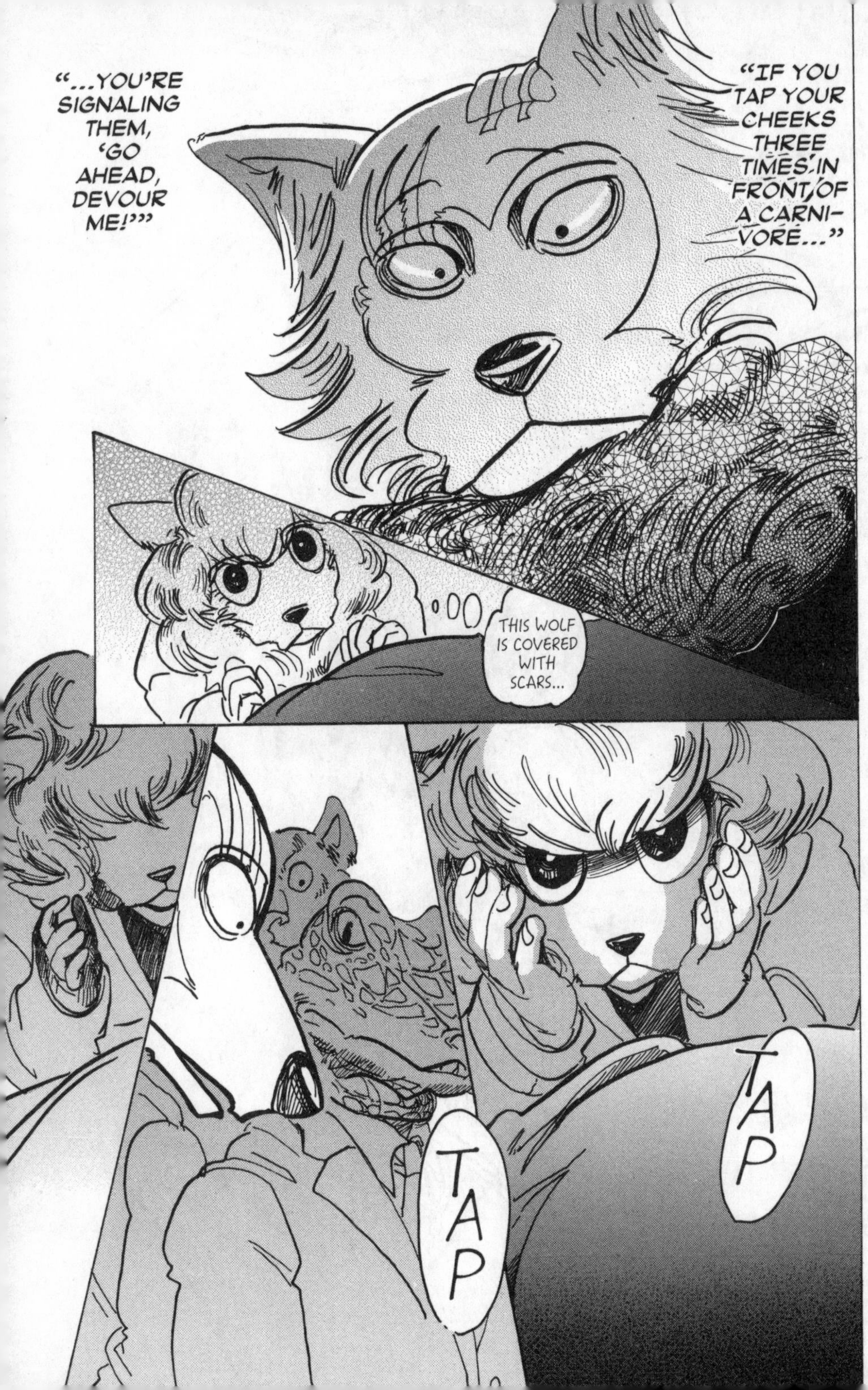
"IF YOU TAP YOUR CHEEKS THREE TIMES IN FRONT OF A CARNI-VORE..."
"...YOU'RE SIGNALING THEM, 'GO AHEAD, DEVOUR ME!'"
THIS WOLF IS COVERED WITH SCARS...
TAP
TAP

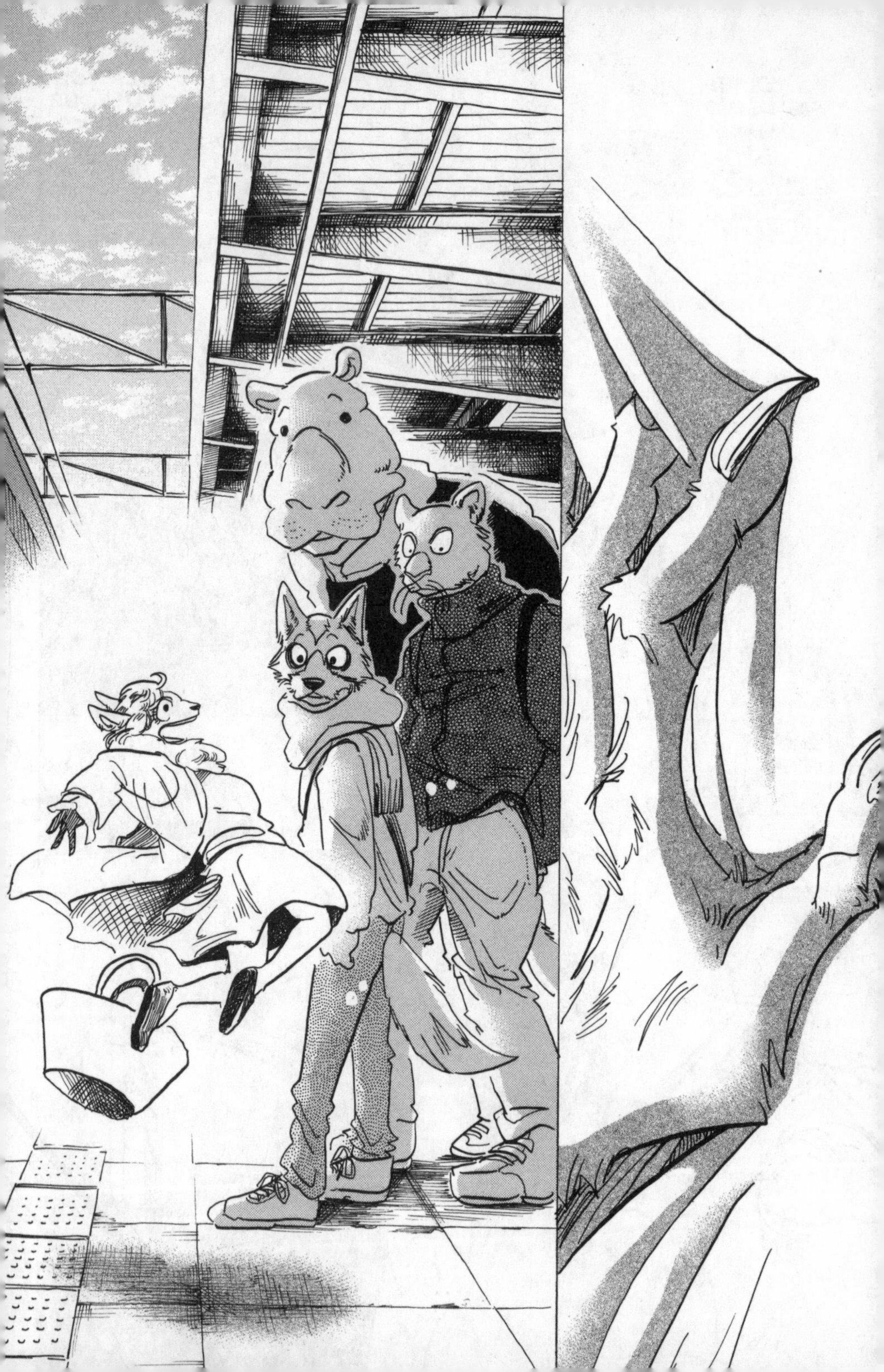

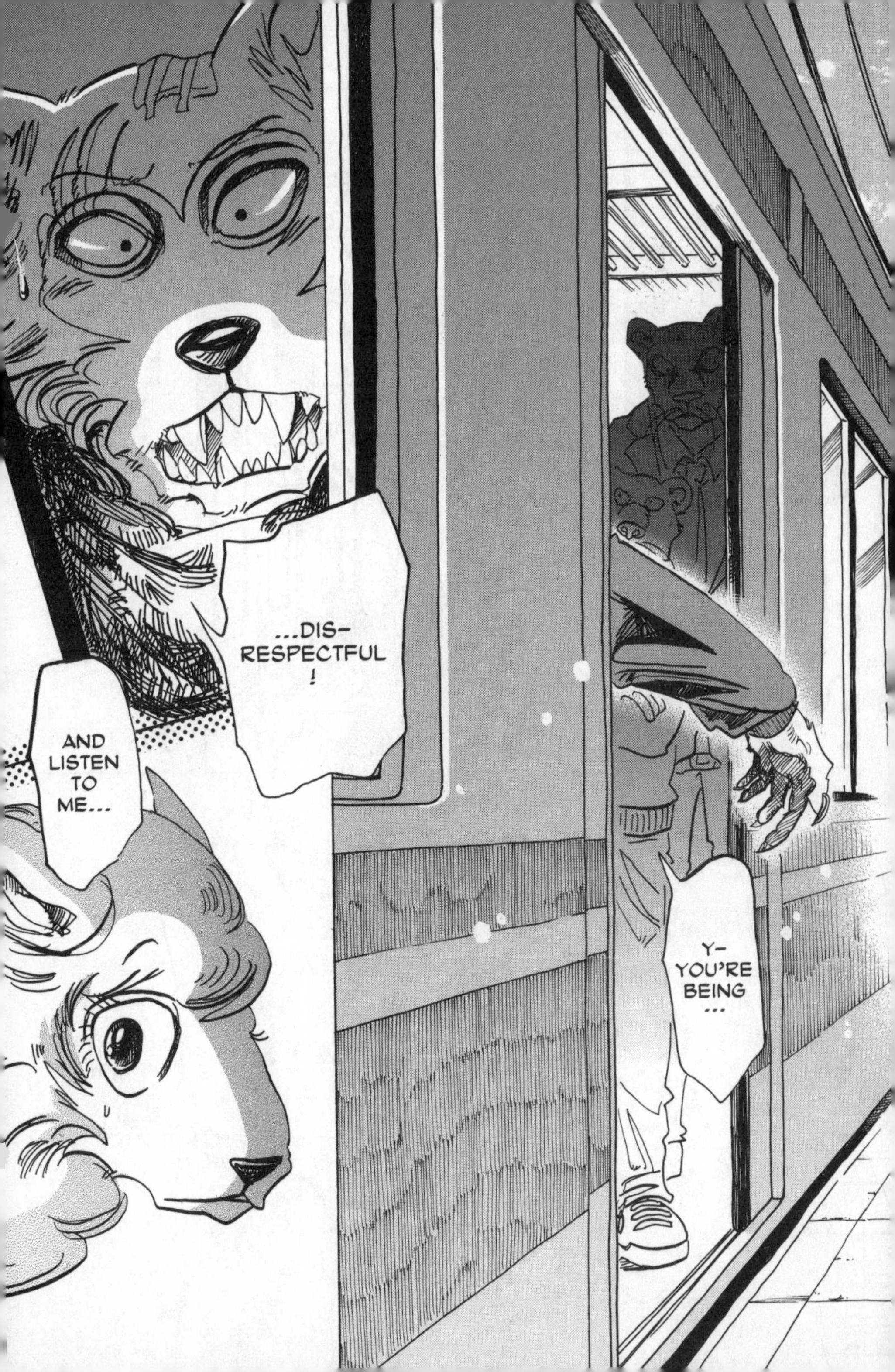
Y-YOU'RE BEING...
...DIS-RESPECTFUL!
AND LISTEN TO ME...

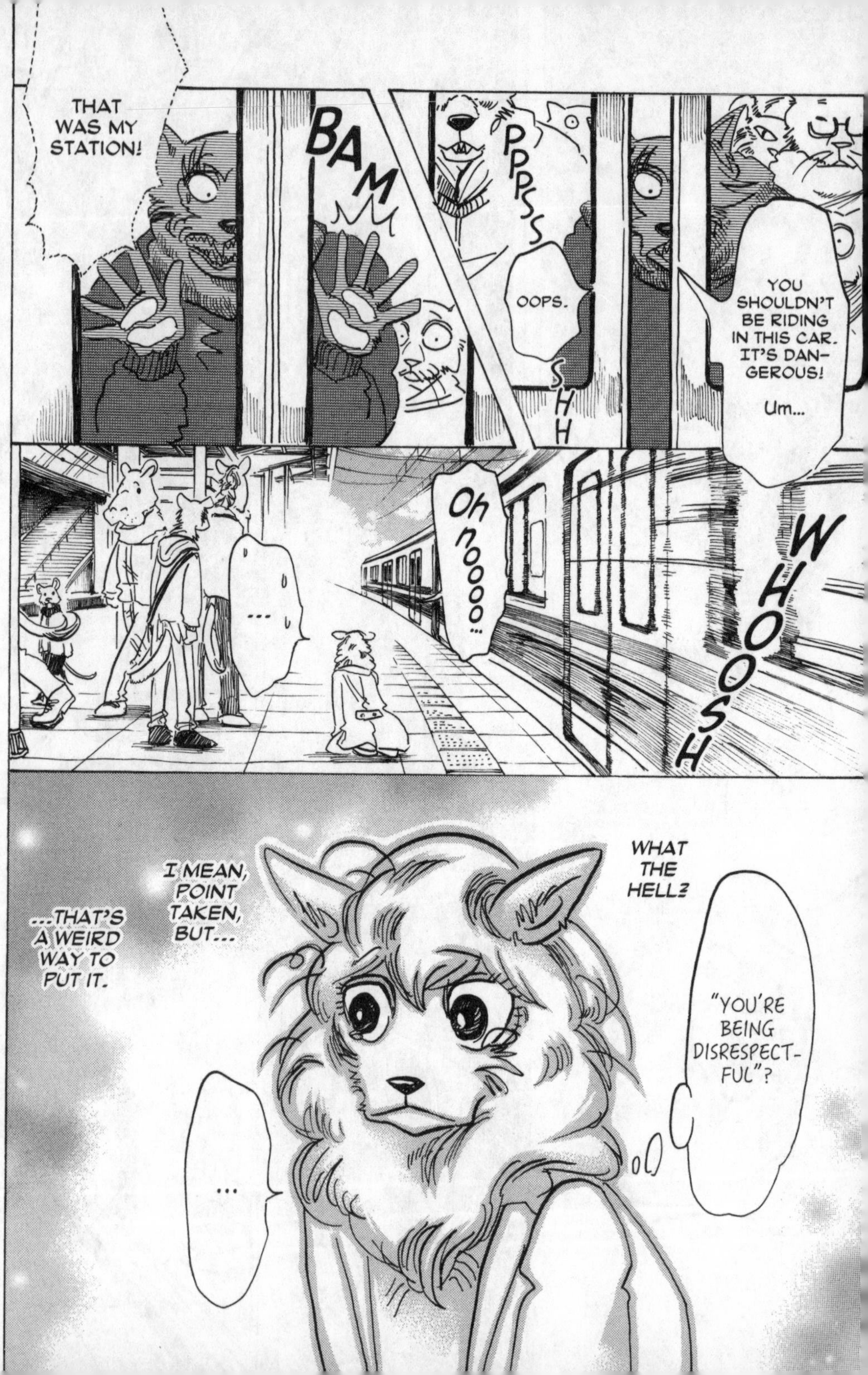
YOU SHOULDN'T BE RIDING IN THIS CAR. IT'S DANGEROUS!
Um...
PPPSSSHH
OOPS.
BAM
THAT WAS MY STATION!
WHOOOSH
Oh nooooo...
...
WHAT THE HELL?
"YOU'RE BEING DISRESPECTFUL"?
I MEAN, POINT TAKEN, BUT...
...THAT'S A WEIRD WAY TO PUT IT.
...

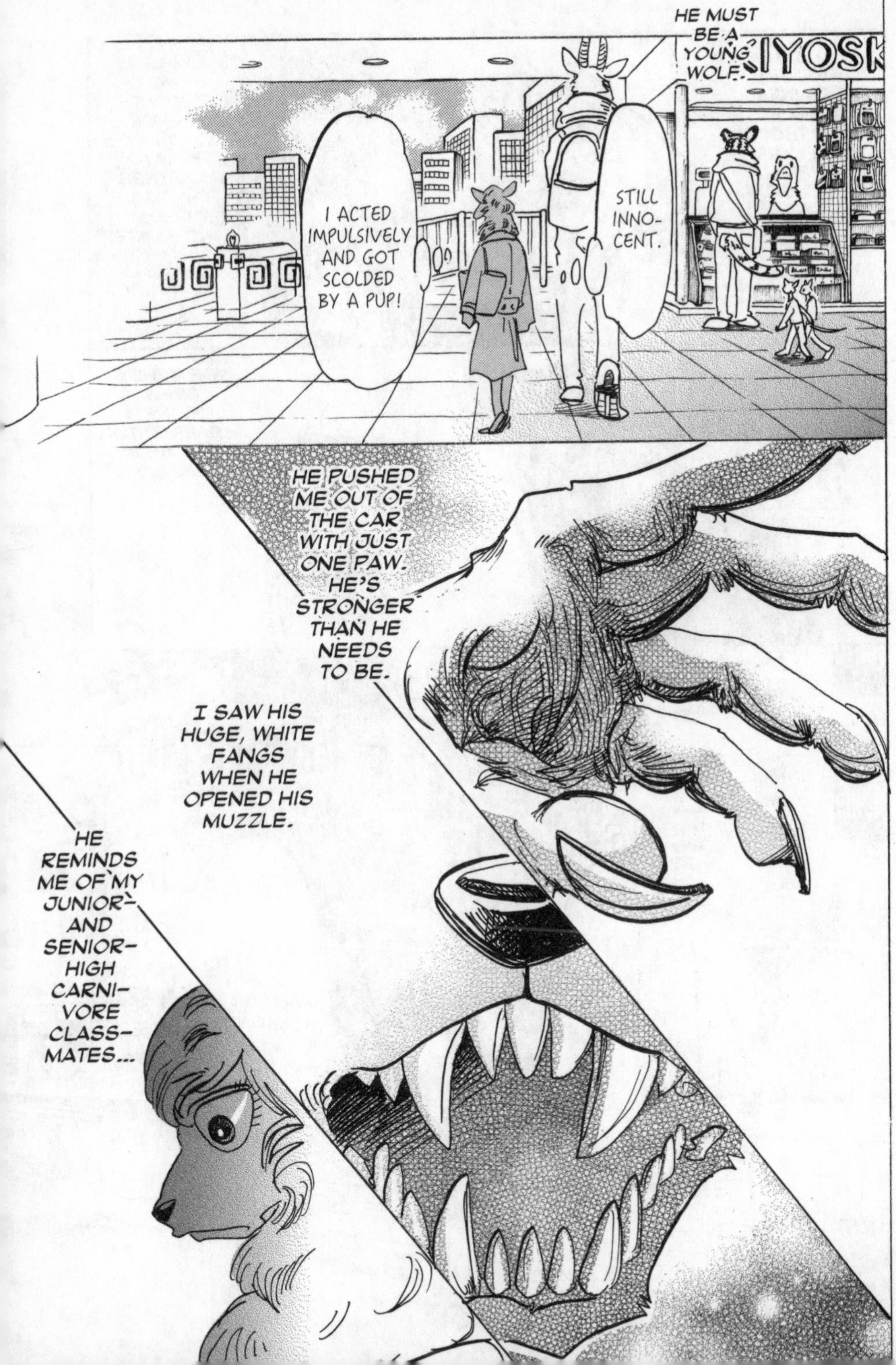
HE MUST BE A YOUNG WOLF.
STILL INNO-CENT.
I ACTED IMPULSIVELY AND GOT SCOLDED BY A PUP!
IYOSK
HE PUSHED ME OUT OF THE CAR WITH JUST ONE PAW. HE'S STRONGER THAN HE NEEDS TO BE.
I SAW HIS HUGE, WHITE FANGS WHEN HE OPENED HIS MUZZLE.
HE REMINDS ME OF MY JUNIOR- AND SENIOR-HIGH CARNI-VORE CLASS-MATES...

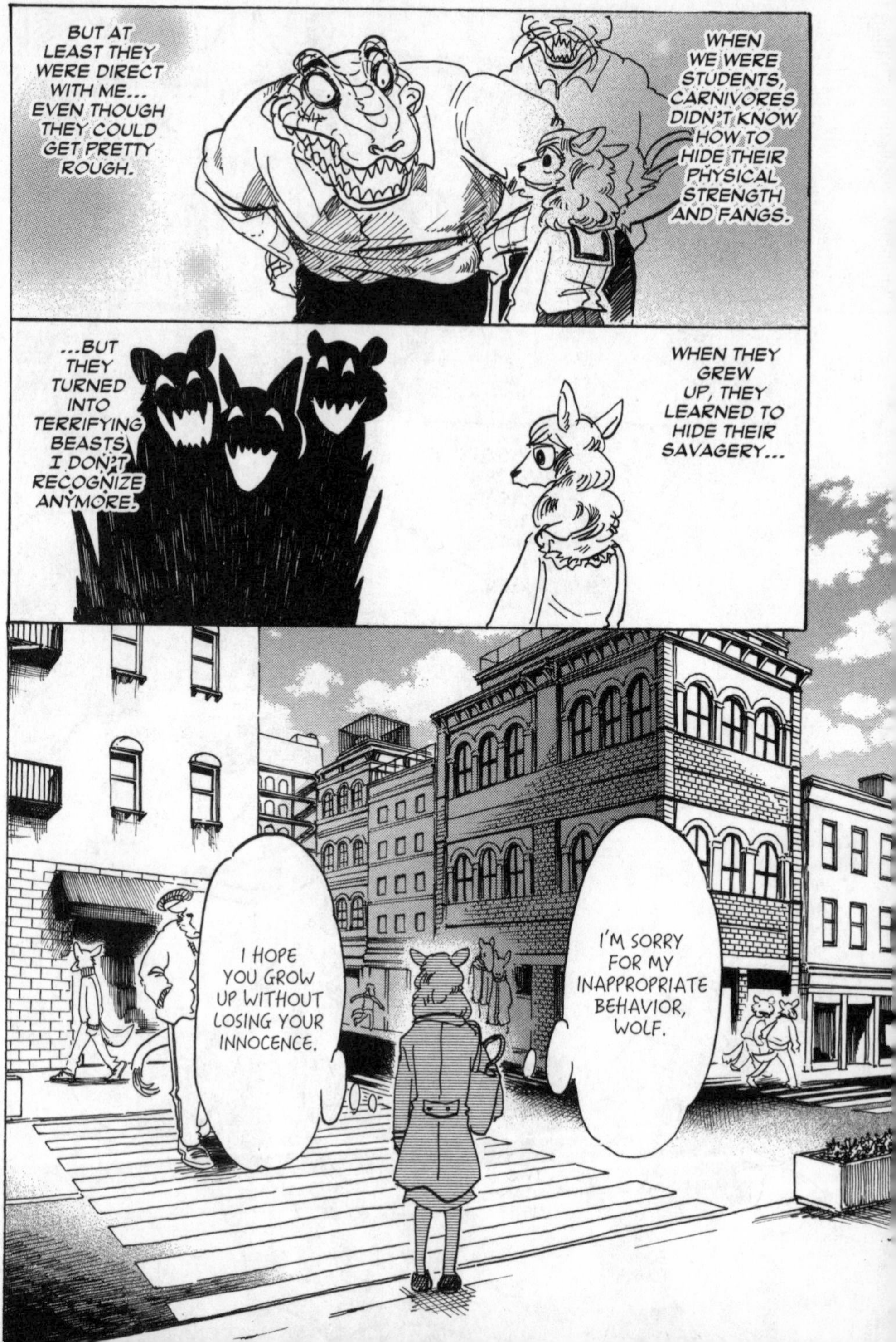
WHEN WE WERE STUDENTS, CARNIVORES DIDN'T KNOW HOW TO HIDE THEIR PHYSICAL STRENGTH AND FANGS.
BUT AT LEAST THEY WERE DIRECT WITH ME... EVEN THOUGH THEY COULD GET PRETTY ROUGH.
WHEN THEY GREW UP, THEY LEARNED TO HIDE THEIR SAVAGERY...
...BUT THEY TURNED INTO TERRIFYING BEASTS I DON'T RECOGNIZE ANYMORE.
I'M SORRY FOR MY INAPPROPRIATE BEHAVIOR, WOLF.
I HOPE YOU GROW UP WITHOUT LOSING YOUR INNOCENCE.

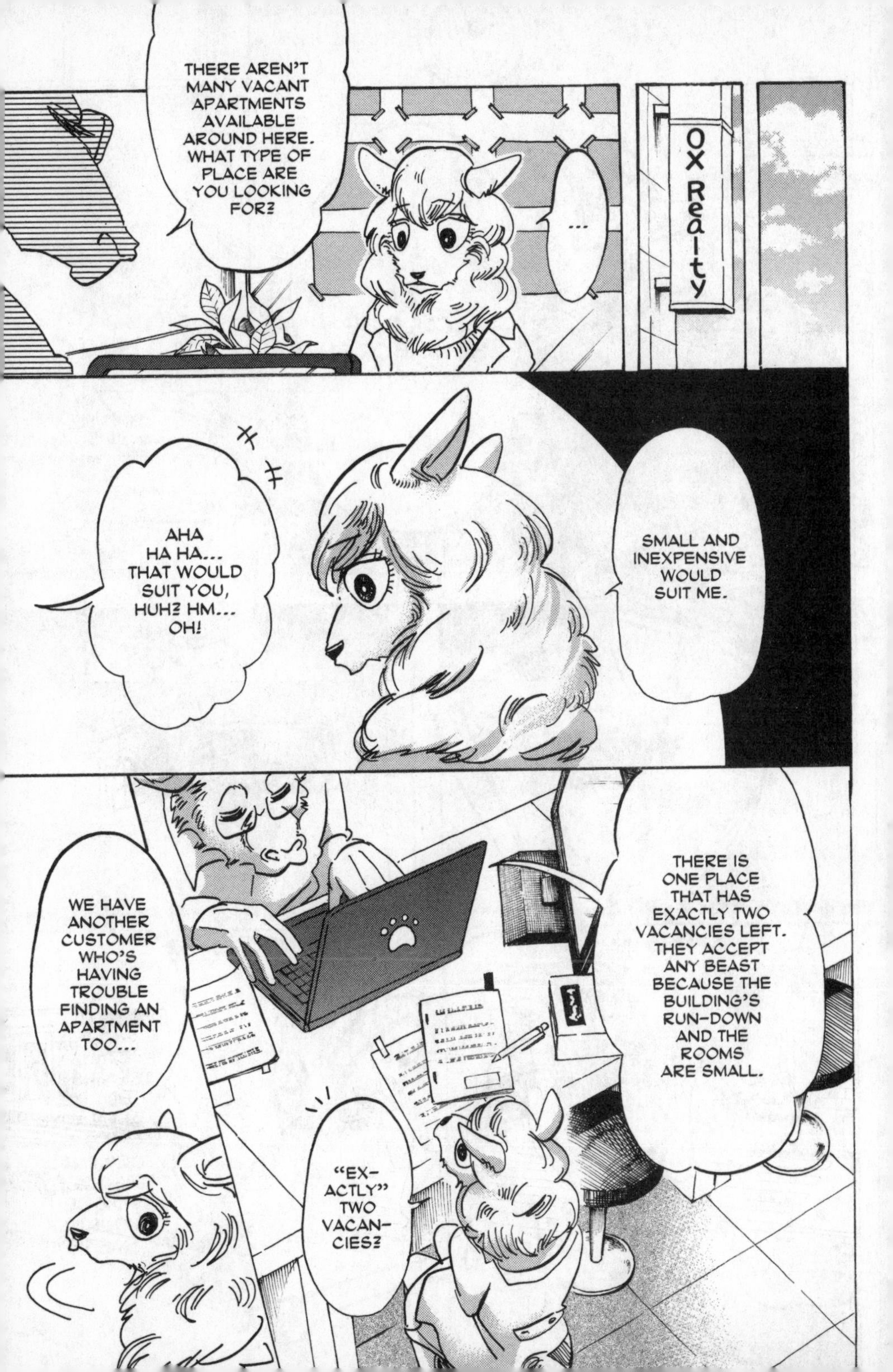
THERE AREN'T MANY VACANT APARTMENTS AVAILABLE AROUND HERE. WHAT TYPE OF PLACE ARE YOU LOOKING FOR?
...
OX Realty
SMALL AND INEXPENSIVE WOULD SUIT ME.
AHA HA HA... THAT WOULD SUIT YOU, HUH? HM... OH!
THERE IS ONE PLACE THAT HAS EXACTLY TWO VACANCIES LEFT. THEY ACCEPT ANY BEAST BECAUSE THE BUILDING'S RUN-DOWN AND THE ROOMS ARE SMALL.
"EX-ACTLY" TWO VACAN-CIES?
WE HAVE ANOTHER CUSTOMER WHO'S HAVING TROUBLE FINDING AN APARTMENT TOO...

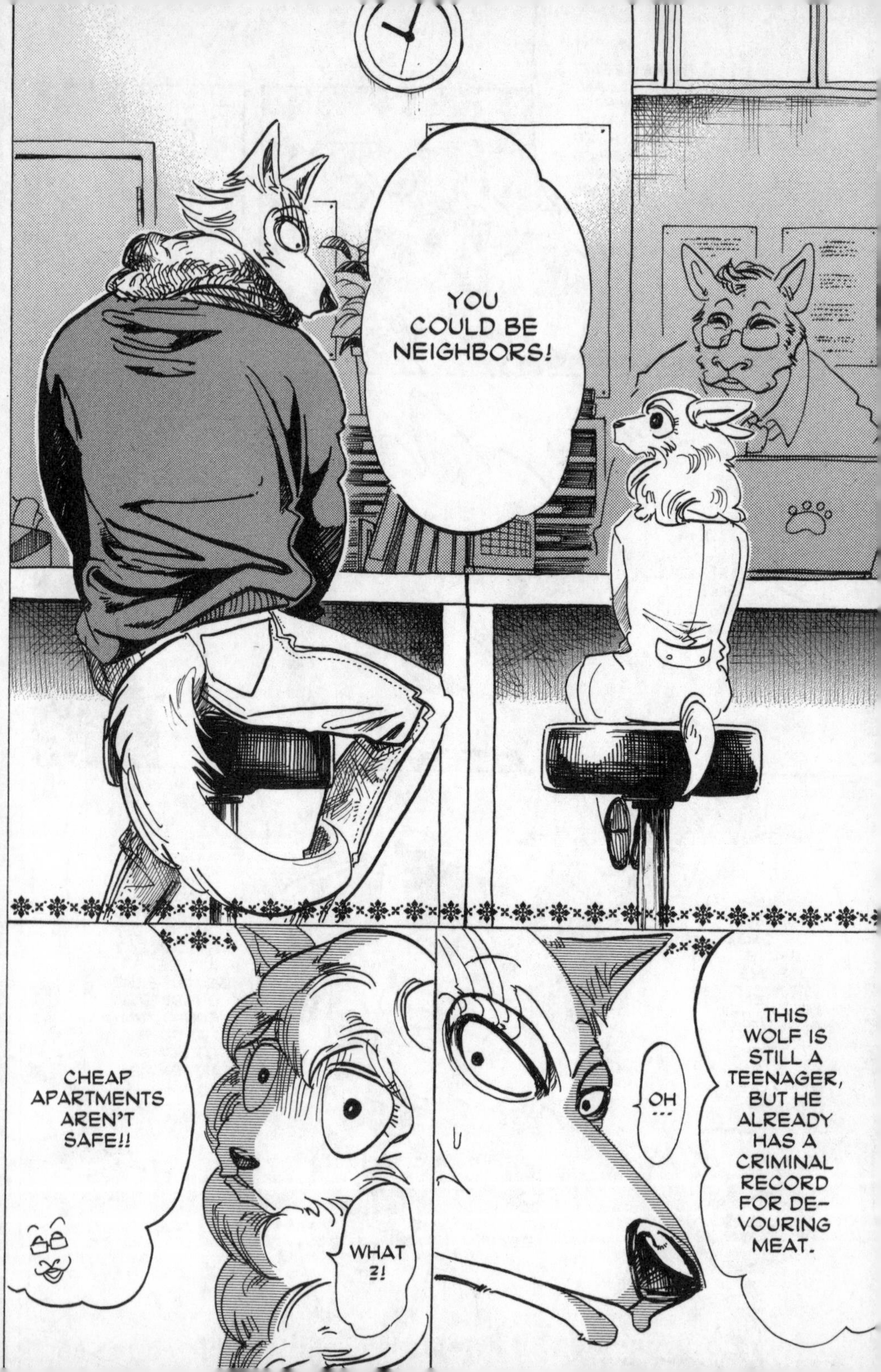
YOU COULD BE NEIGHBORS!
THIS WOLF IS STILL A TEENAGER, BUT HE ALREADY HAS A CRIMINAL RECORD FOR DE-VOURING MEAT.
OH...
WHAT?!
CHEAP APARTMENTS AREN'T SAFE!!

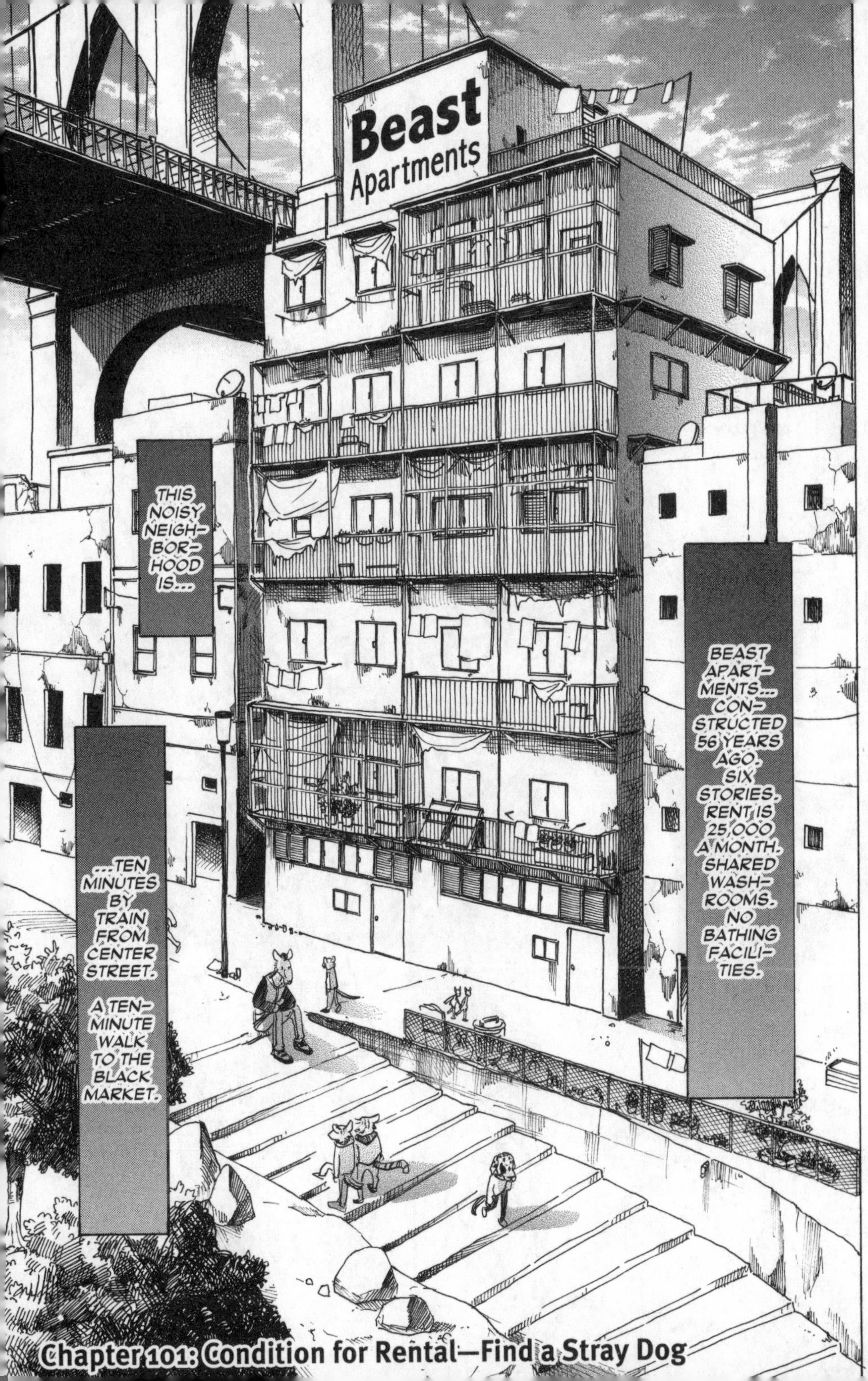
Beast
Apartments
THIS NOISY NEIGHBORHOOD IS...
...TEN MINUTES BY TRAIN FROM CENTER STREET.
A TEN-MINUTE WALK TO THE BLACK MARKET.
BEAST APARTMENTS... CONSTRUCTED 56 YEARS AGO. SIX STORIES. RENT IS 25,000 A MONTH. SHARED WASHROOMS. NO BATHING FACILITIES.

Chapter 101: Condition for Rental—Find a Stray Dog

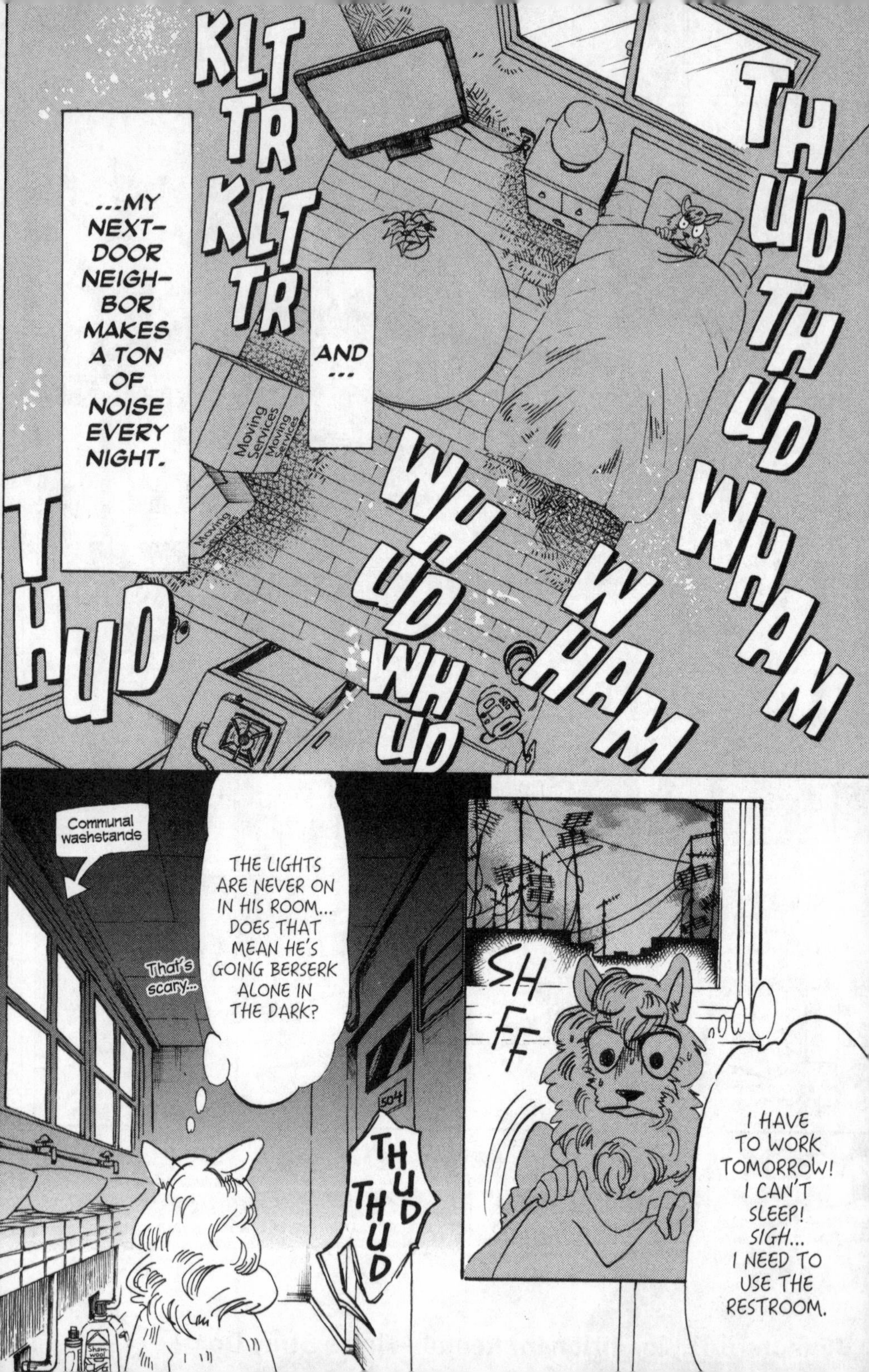
THUD THUD WHAM
WHAM
AND...
WHUD WHUD
Moving Services
Moving Services
KLT TR KLT TR
...MY NEXT-DOOR NEIGHBOR MAKES A TON OF NOISE EVERY NIGHT.
THUD
SHFF
I HAVE TO WORK TOMORROW! I CAN'T SLEEP! SIGH... I NEED TO USE THE RESTROOM.
THE LIGHTS ARE NEVER ON IN HIS ROOM... DOES THAT MEAN HE'S GOING BERSERK ALONE IN THE DARK?
That's scary...
Communal washstands
504
THUD THUD

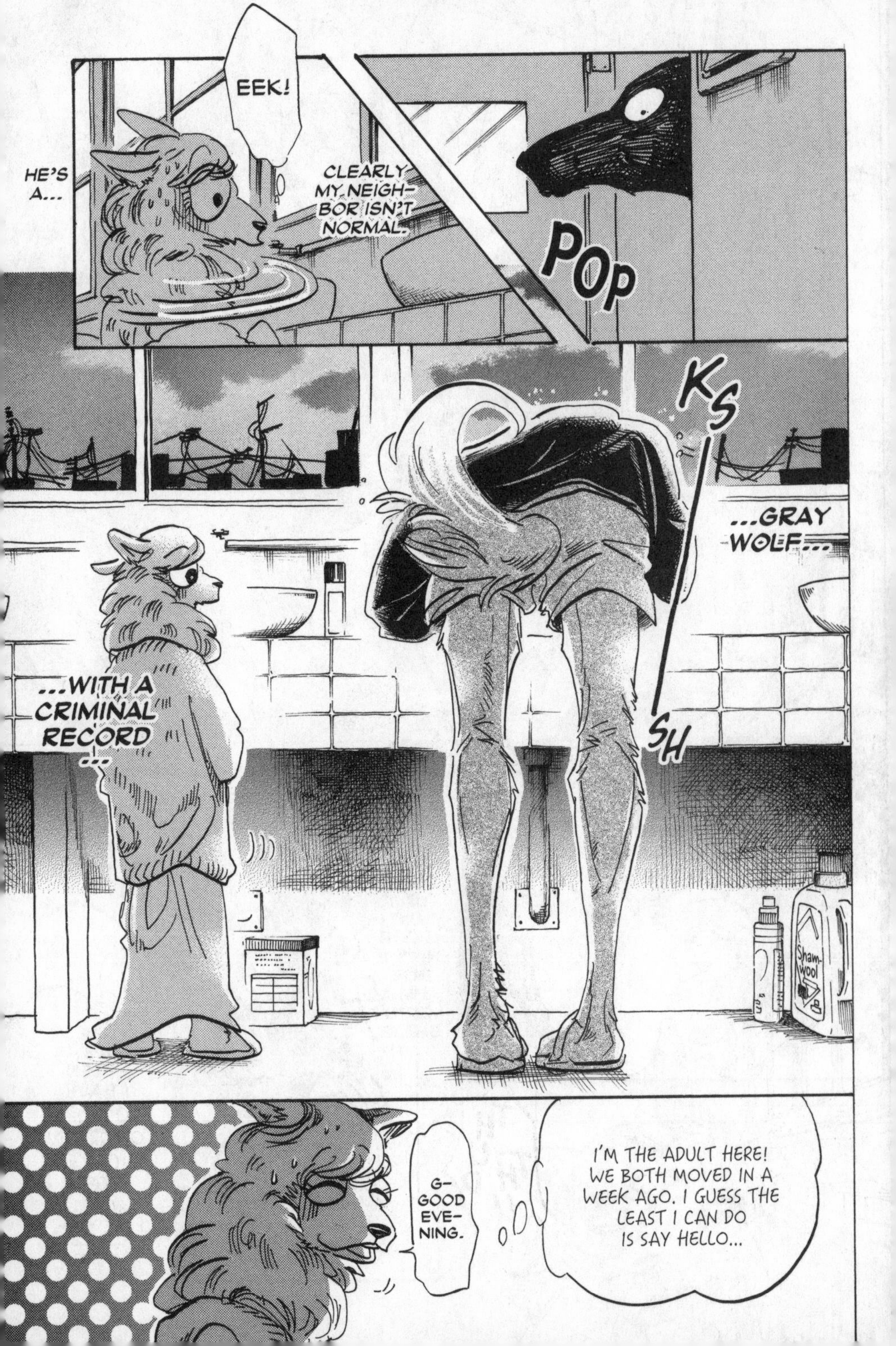
POP
EEK!
CLEARLY MY NEIGHBOR ISN'T NORMAL.
HE'S A...
KSSH
...GRAY WOLF...
...WITH A CRIMINAL RECORD...
I'M THE ADULT HERE! WE BOTH MOVED IN A WEEK AGO. I GUESS THE LEAST I CAN DO IS SAY HELLO...
G-GOOD EVENING.

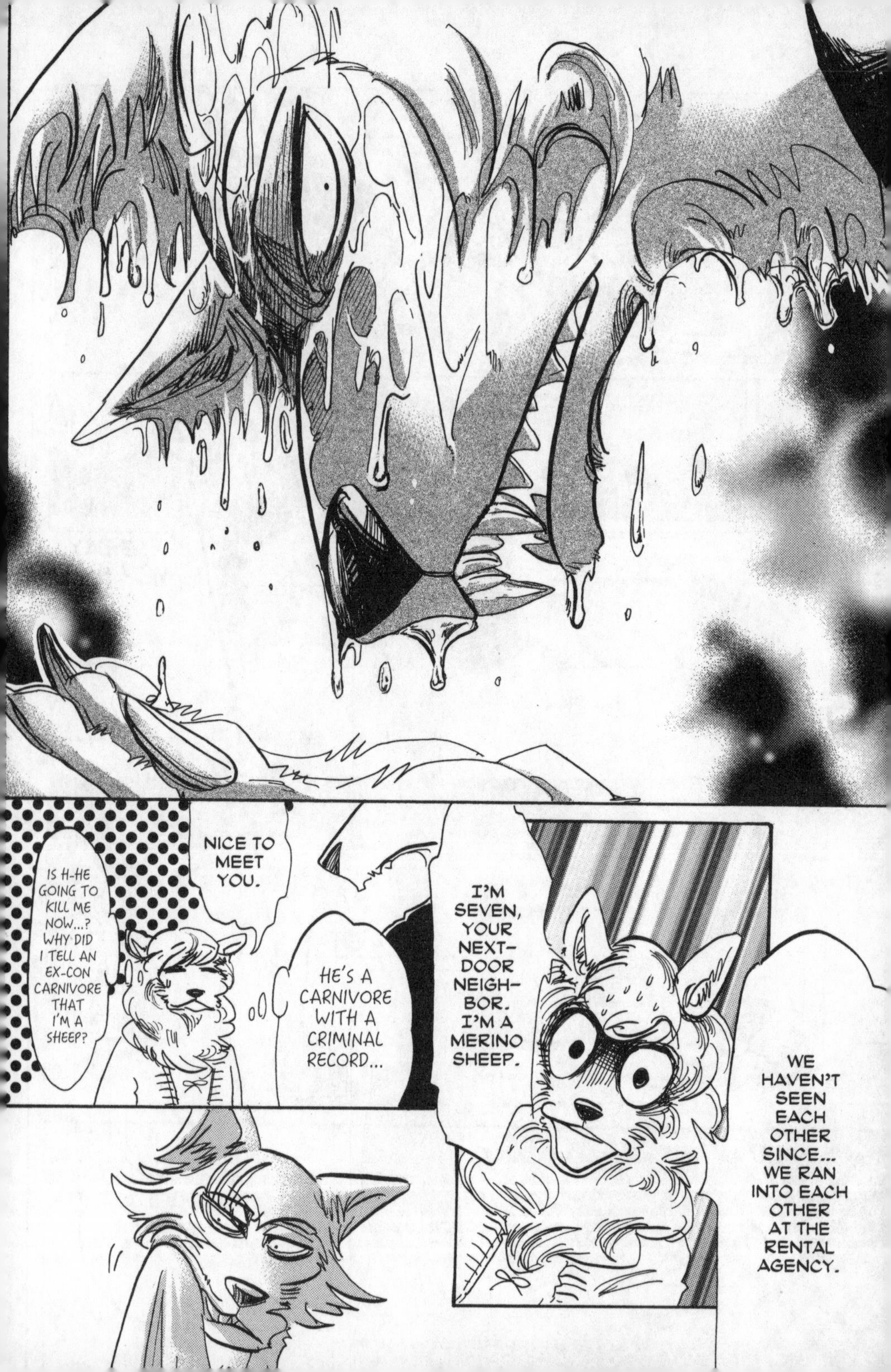
I'M SEVEN, YOUR NEXT-DOOR NEIGHBOR. I'M A MERINO SHEEP.
NICE TO MEET YOU.
HE'S A CARNIVORE WITH A CRIMINAL RECORD...
IS H-HE GOING TO KILL ME NOW...? WHY DID I TELL AN EX-CON CARNIVORE THAT I'M A SHEEP?
WE HAVEN'T SEEN EACH OTHER SINCE... WE RAN INTO EACH OTHER AT THE RENTAL AGENCY.

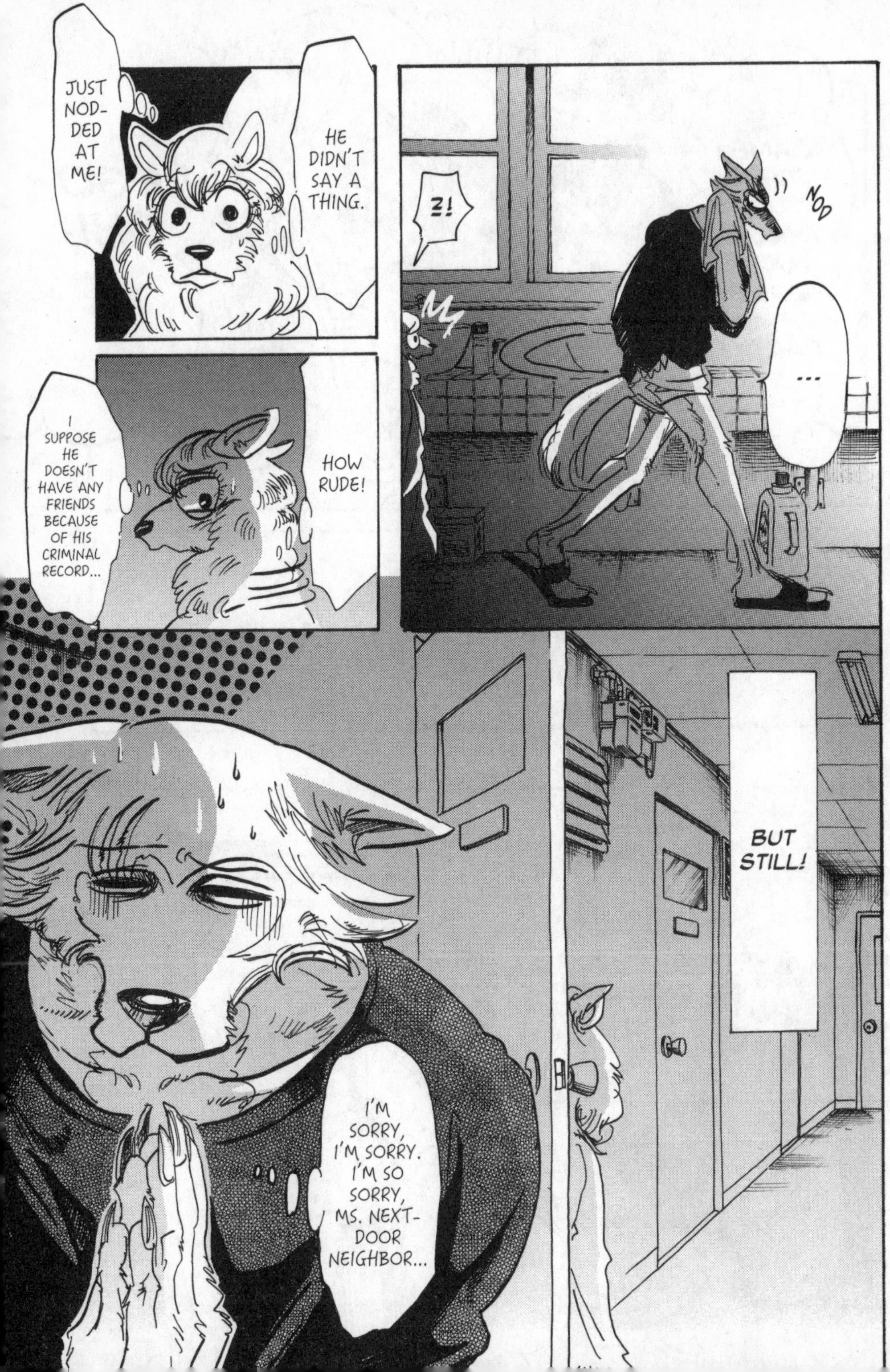

Z!
NOD
...
HE DIDN'T SAY A THING.
JUST NOD-DED AT ME!
HOW RUDE!
I SUPPOSE HE DOESN'T HAVE ANY FRIENDS BECAUSE OF HIS CRIMINAL RECORD...
BUT STILL!
I'M SORRY, I'M SORRY. I'M SO SORRY, MS. NEXT-DOOR NEIGHBOR...

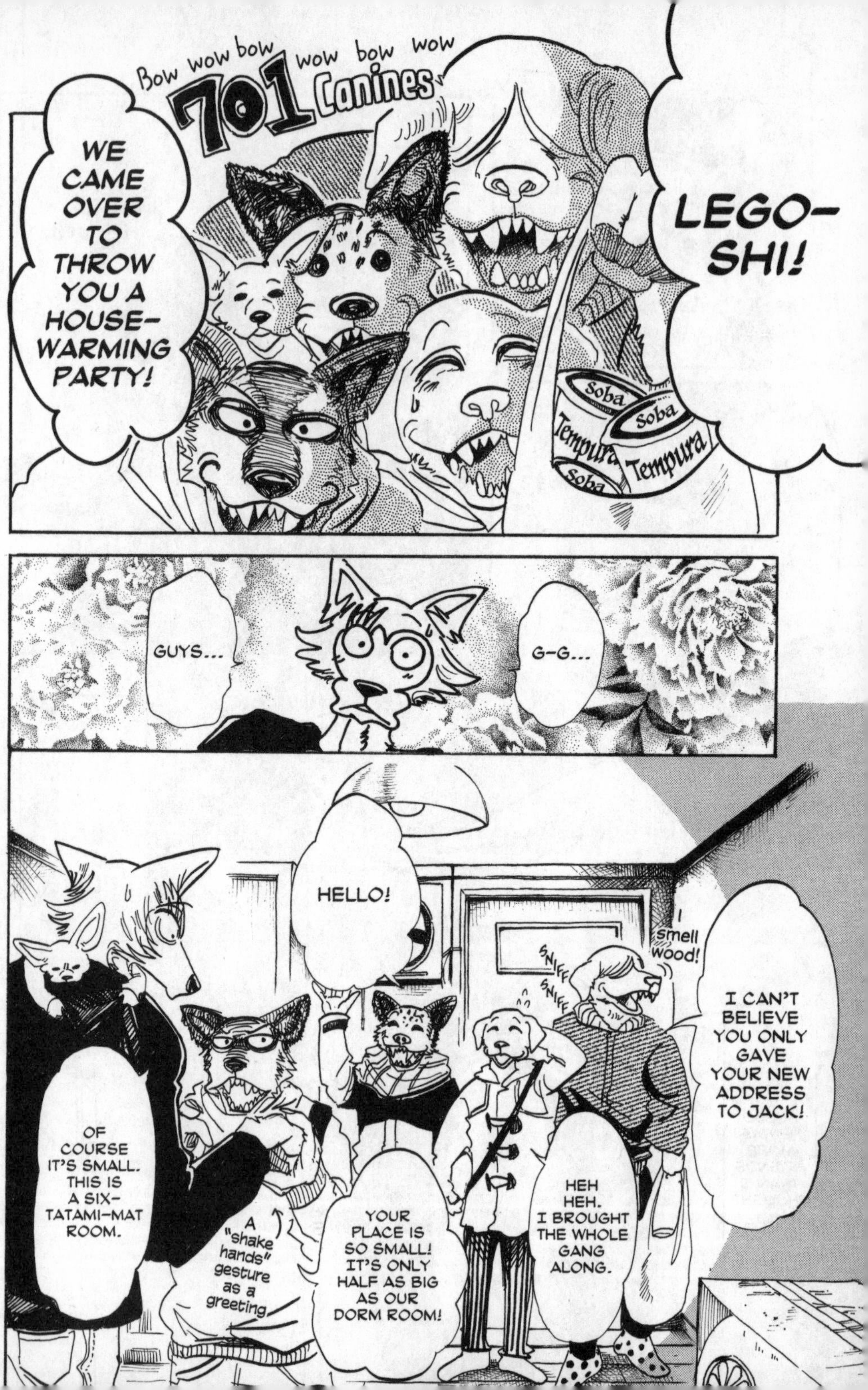

Bow wow bow wow bow wow
701 Canines
LEGO-SHI!
WE CAME OVER TO THROW YOU A HOUSE-WARMING PARTY!
Soba
Tempura
Soba
Tempura
Soba
G-G...
GUYS...
I smell wood!
SNIFF SNIFF
I CAN'T BELIEVE YOU ONLY GAVE YOUR NEW ADDRESS TO JACK!
HELLO!
HEH HEH. I BROUGHT THE WHOLE GANG ALONG.
YOUR PLACE IS SO SMALL! IT'S ONLY HALF AS BIG AS OUR DORM ROOM!
A "shake hands" gesture as a greeting
OF COURSE IT'S SMALL. THIS IS A SIX-TATAMI-MAT ROOM.

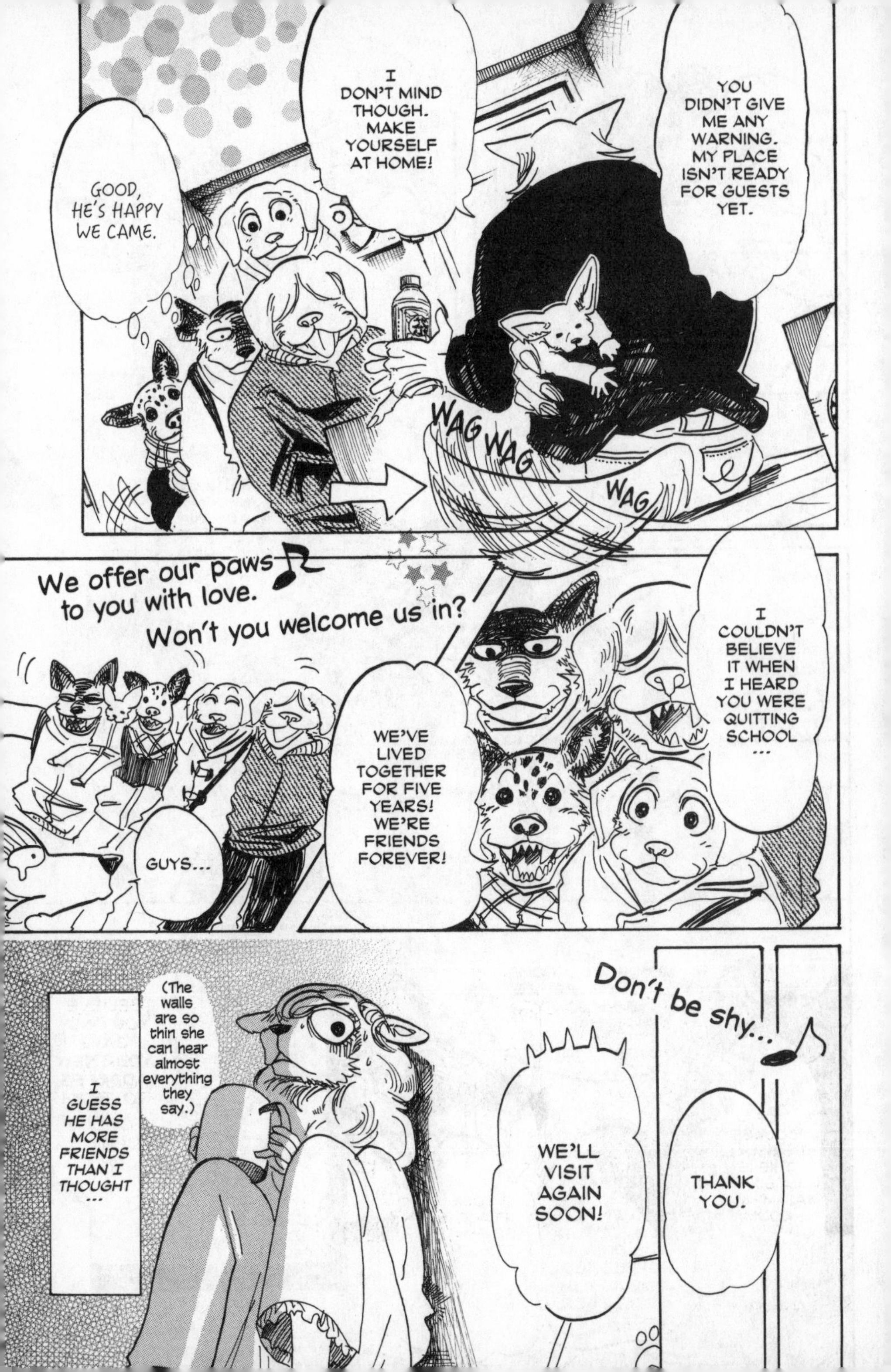
YOU DIDN'T GIVE ME ANY WARNING. MY PLACE ISN'T READY FOR GUESTS YET.
I DON'T MIND THOUGH. MAKE YOURSELF AT HOME!
GOOD, HE'S HAPPY WE CAME.
WAG WAG WAG
I COULDN'T BELIEVE IT WHEN I HEARD YOU WERE QUITTING SCHOOL...
WE'VE LIVED TOGETHER FOR FIVE YEARS! WE'RE FRIENDS FOREVER!
We offer our paws to you with love.
Won't you welcome us in?
GUYS...
Don't be shy...
THANK YOU.
WE'LL VISIT AGAIN SOON!
(The walls are so thin she can hear almost everything they say.)
I GUESS HE HAS MORE FRIENDS THAN I THOUGHT...

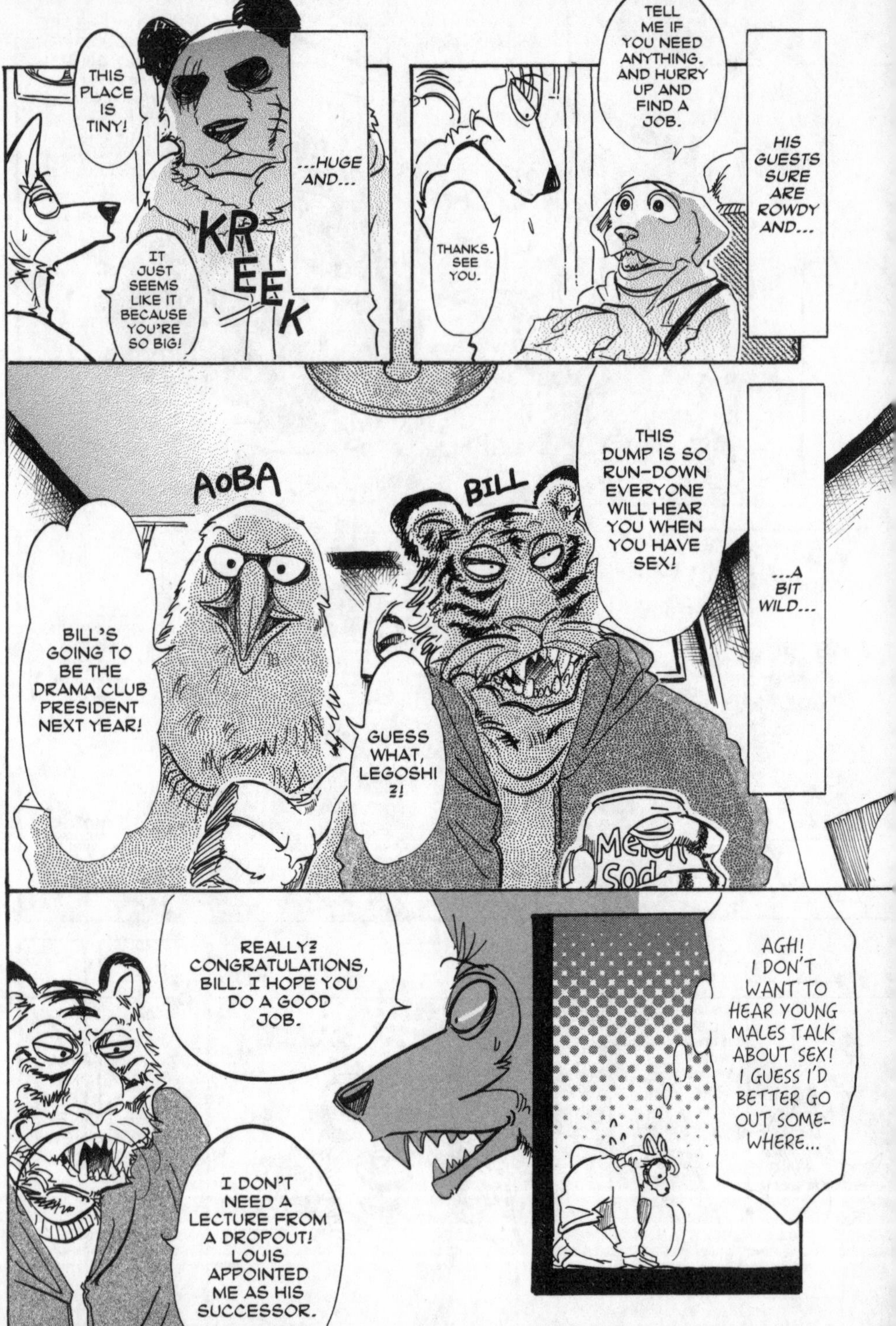
HIS GUESTS SURE ARE ROWDY AND...
TELL ME IF YOU NEED ANYTHING. AND HURRY UP AND FIND A JOB.
THANKS. SEE YOU.
...HUGE AND...
THIS PLACE IS TINY!
KREEK
IT JUST SEEMS LIKE IT BECAUSE YOU'RE SO BIG!
...A BIT WILD...
THIS DUMP IS SO RUN-DOWN EVERYONE WILL HEAR YOU WHEN YOU HAVE SEX!
BILL
AOBA
GUESS WHAT, LEGOSHI?!
BILL'S GOING TO BE THE DRAMA CLUB PRESIDENT NEXT YEAR!
AGH! I DON'T WANT TO HEAR YOUNG MALES TALK ABOUT SEX! I GUESS I'D BETTER GO OUT SOME-WHERE...
REALLY? CONGRATULATIONS, BILL. I HOPE YOU DO A GOOD JOB.
I DON'T NEED A LECTURE FROM A DROPOUT! LOUIS APPOINTED ME AS HIS SUCCESSOR.

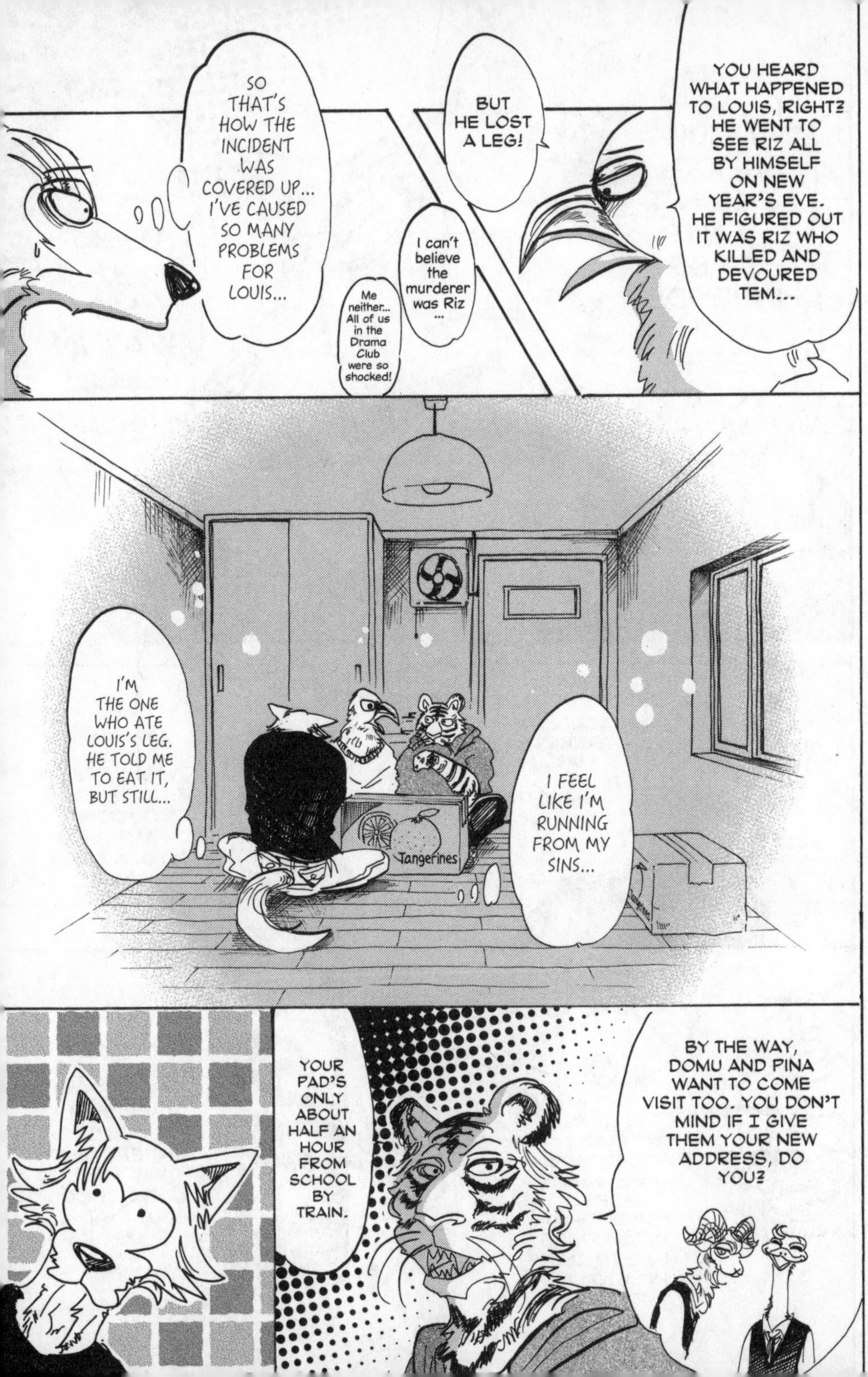
YOU HEARD WHAT HAPPENED TO LOUIS, RIGHT? HE WENT TO SEE RIZ ALL BY HIMSELF ON NEW YEAR'S EVE. HE FIGURED OUT IT WAS RIZ WHO KILLED AND DEVOURED TEM...
BUT HE LOST A LEG!
I can't believe the murderer was Riz...
Me neither... All of us in the Drama Club were so shocked!
SO THAT'S HOW THE INCIDENT WAS COVERED UP... I'VE CAUSED SO MANY PROBLEMS FOR LOUIS...
I'M THE ONE WHO ATE LOUIS'S LEG. HE TOLD ME TO EAT IT, BUT STILL...
I FEEL LIKE I'M RUNNING FROM MY SINS...
Tangerines
BY THE WAY, DOMU AND PINA WANT TO COME VISIT TOO. YOU DON'T MIND IF I GIVE THEM YOUR NEW ADDRESS, DO YOU?
YOUR PAD'S ONLY ABOUT HALF AN HOUR FROM SCHOOL BY TRAIN.

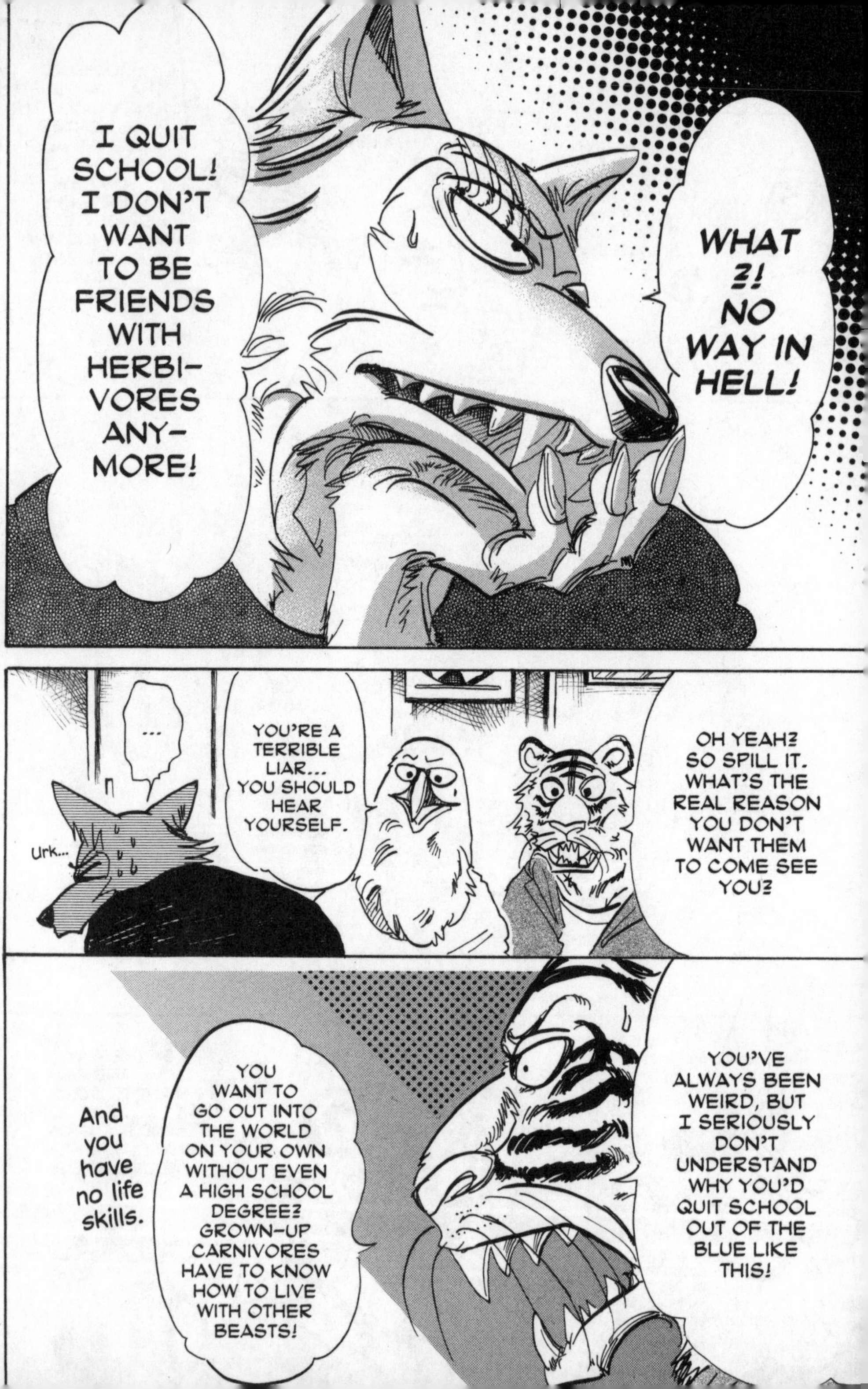
WHAT?! NO WAY IN HELL!
I QUIT SCHOOL! I DON'T WANT TO BE FRIENDS WITH HERBIVORES ANYMORE!
OH YEAH? SO SPILL IT. WHAT'S THE REAL REASON YOU DON'T WANT THEM TO COME SEE YOU?
YOU'RE A TERRIBLE LIAR... YOU SHOULD HEAR YOURSELF.
...
Urk...
YOU'VE ALWAYS BEEN WEIRD, BUT I SERIOUSLY DON'T UNDERSTAND WHY YOU'D QUIT SCHOOL OUT OF THE BLUE LIKE THIS!
YOU WANT TO GO OUT INTO THE WORLD ON YOUR OWN WITHOUT EVEN A HIGH SCHOOL DEGREE? GROWN-UP CARNIVORES HAVE TO KNOW HOW TO LIVE WITH OTHER BEASTS!
And you have no life skills.

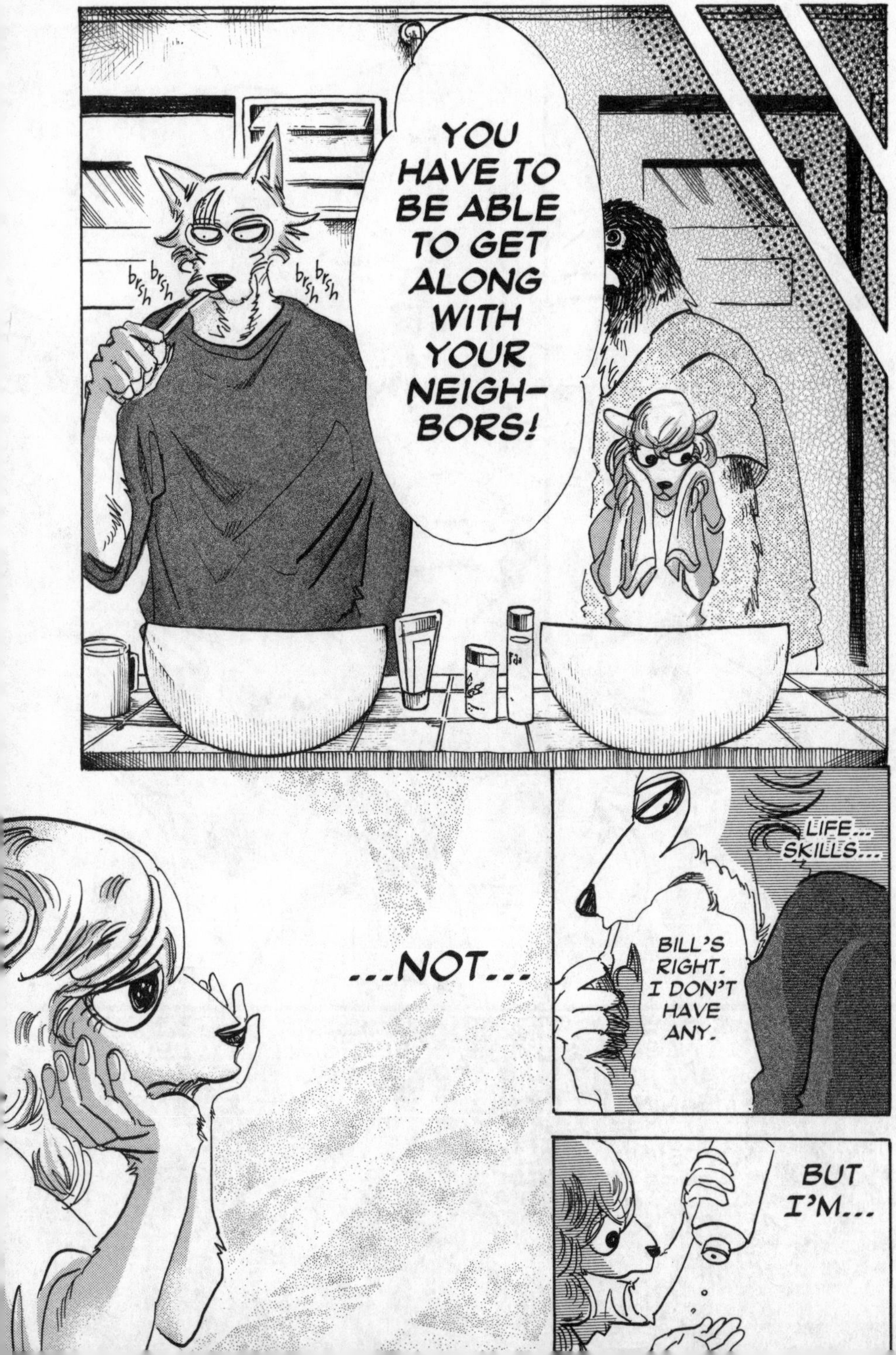
YOU HAVE TO BE ABLE TO GET ALONG WITH YOUR NEIGH-BORS!
brsh brsh
brsh brsh
LIFE... SKILLS...
BILL'S RIGHT. I DON'T HAVE ANY.
BUT I'M...
...NOT...

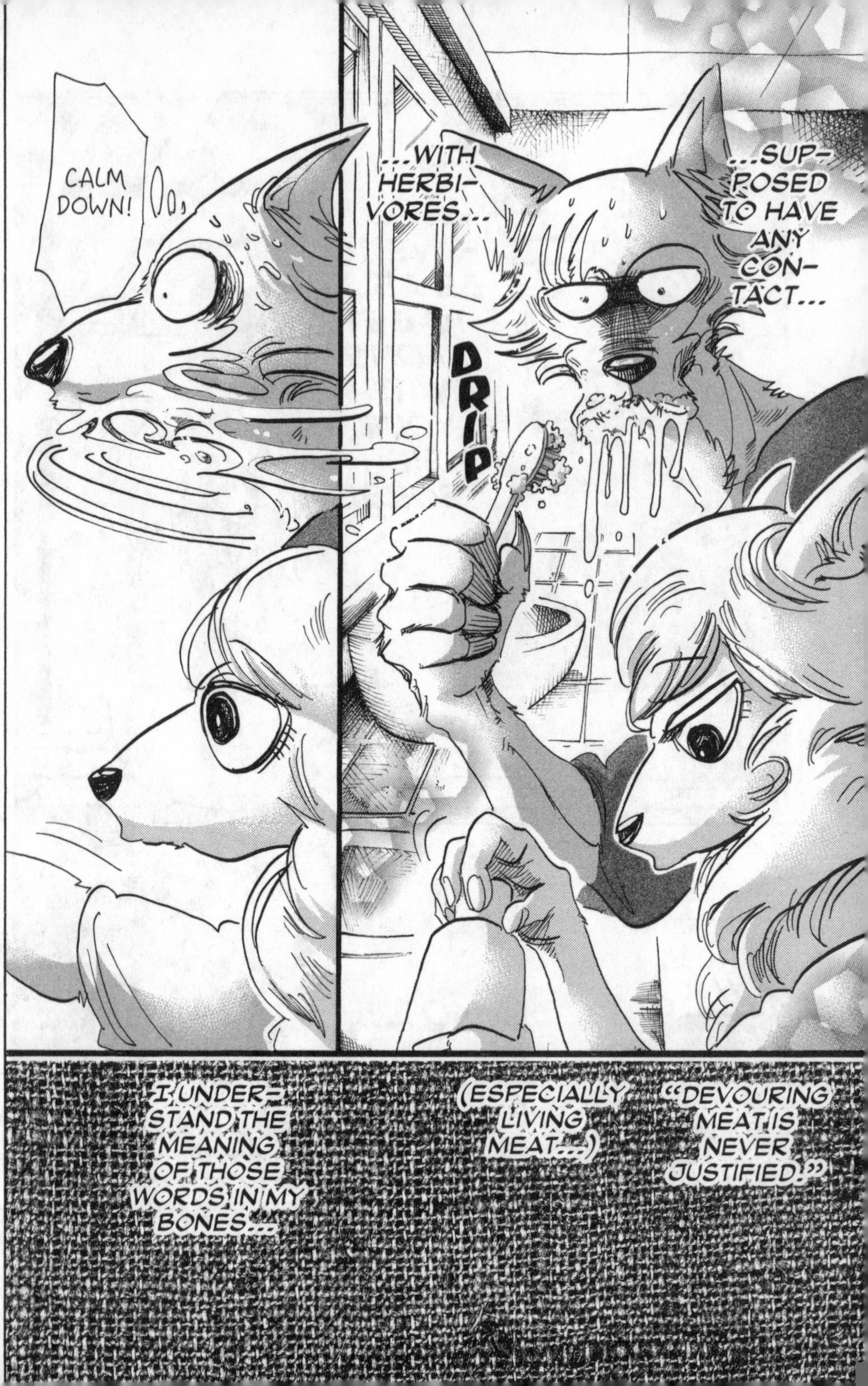
...SUPPOSED TO HAVE ANY CONTACT...
...WITH HERBIVORES...
DRIP
CALM DOWN!
"DEVOURING MEAT IS NEVER JUSTIFIED."
(ESPECIALLY LIVING MEAT...)
I UNDERSTAND THE MEANING OF THOSE WORDS IN MY BONES...

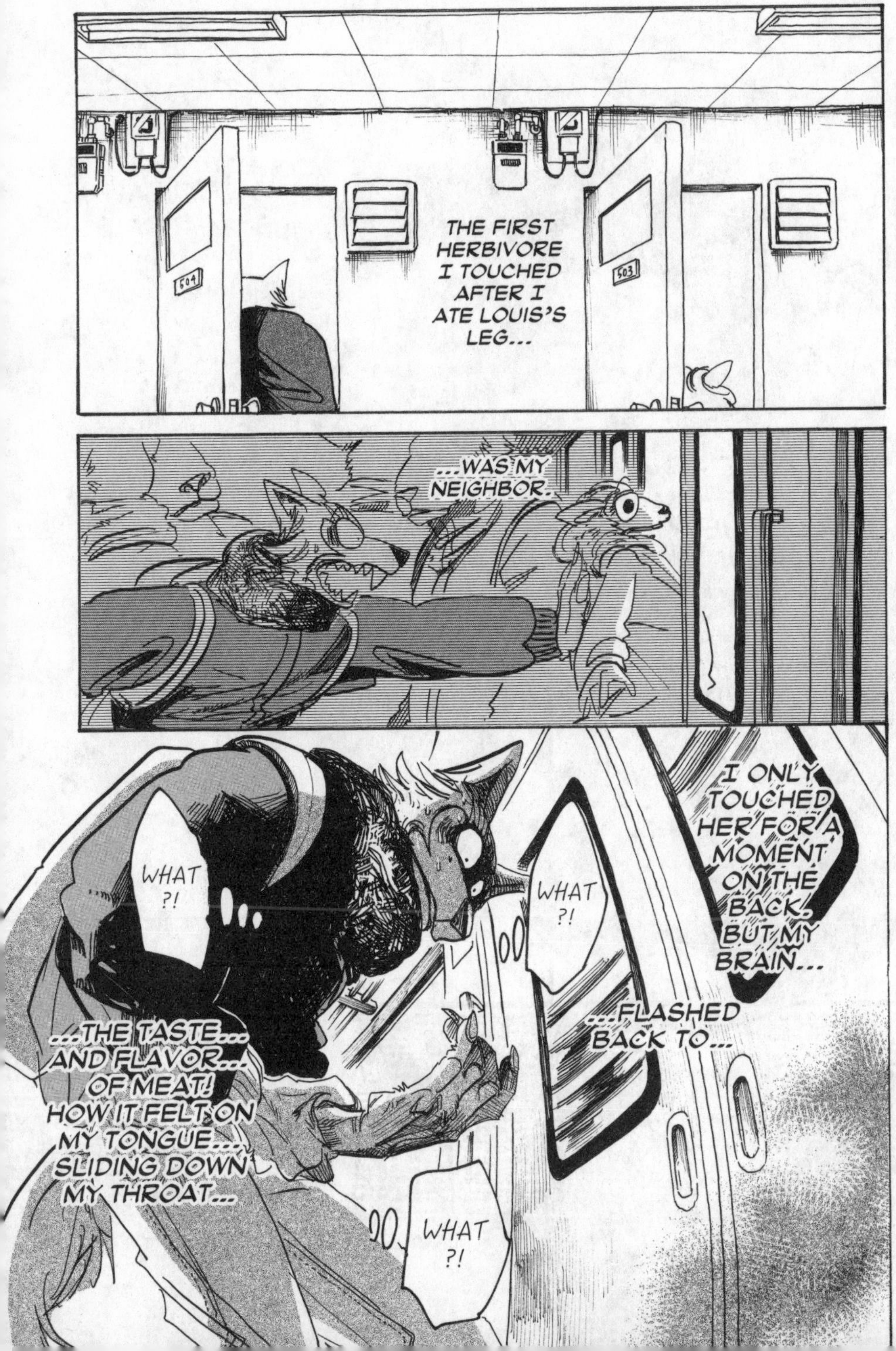
THE FIRST HERBIVORE I TOUCHED AFTER I ATE LOUIS'S LEG...
...WAS MY NEIGHBOR.
I ONLY TOUCHED HER FOR A MOMENT ON THE BACK. BUT MY BRAIN...
WHAT ?!
WHAT ?!
...FLASHED BACK TO...
...THE TASTE... AND FLAVOR... OF MEAT! HOW IT FELT ON MY TONGUE... SLIDING DOWN MY THROAT...
WHAT ?!

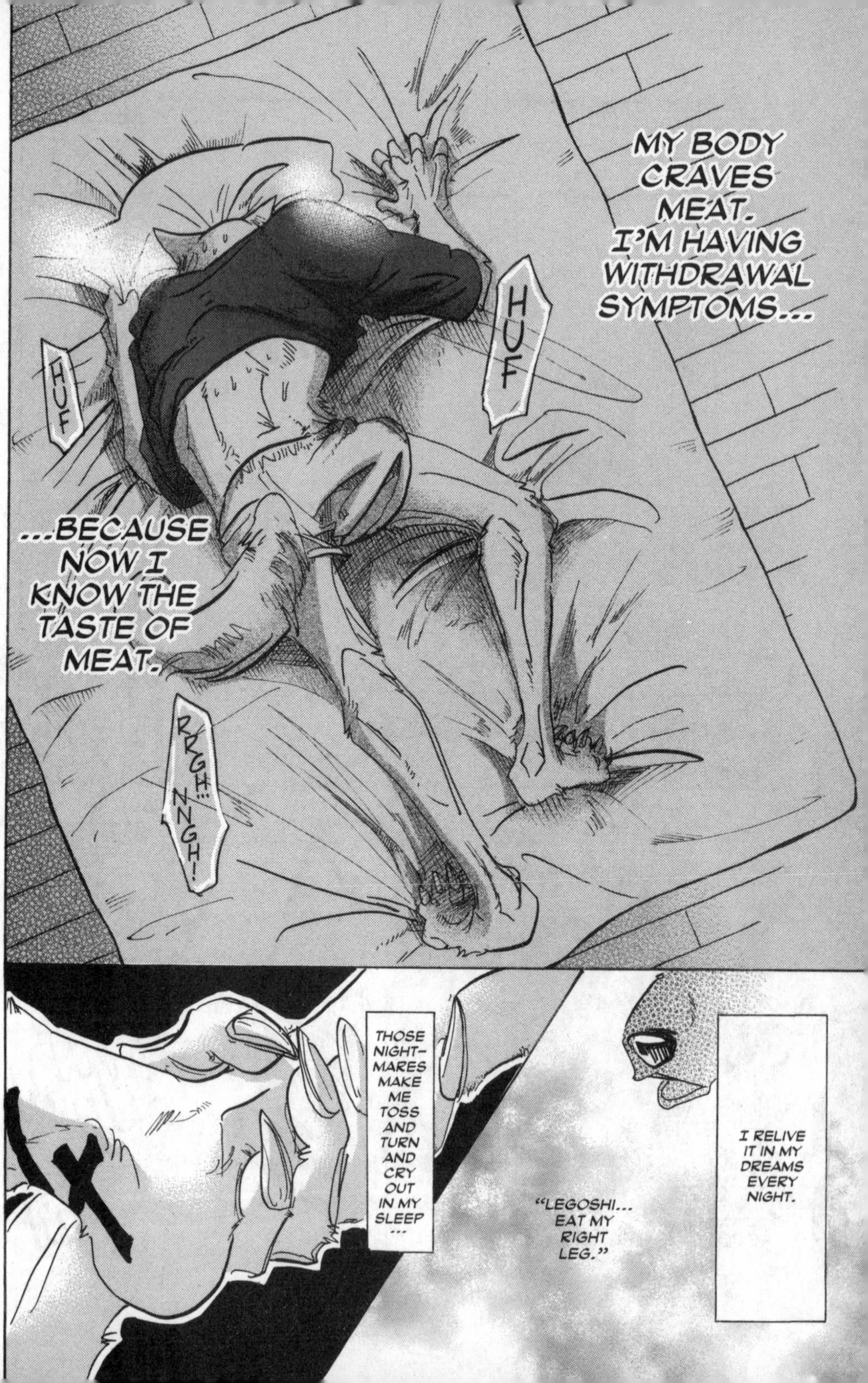
MY BODY CRAVES MEAT. I'M HAVING WITHDRAWAL SYMPTOMS...
HUF
HUF
...BECAUSE NOW I KNOW THE TASTE OF MEAT.
RRGH!! NNGH!
I RELIVE IT IN MY DREAMS EVERY NIGHT.
"LEGOSHI... EAT MY RIGHT LEG."
THOSE NIGHT-MARES MAKE ME TOSS AND TURN AND CRY OUT IN MY SLEEP...

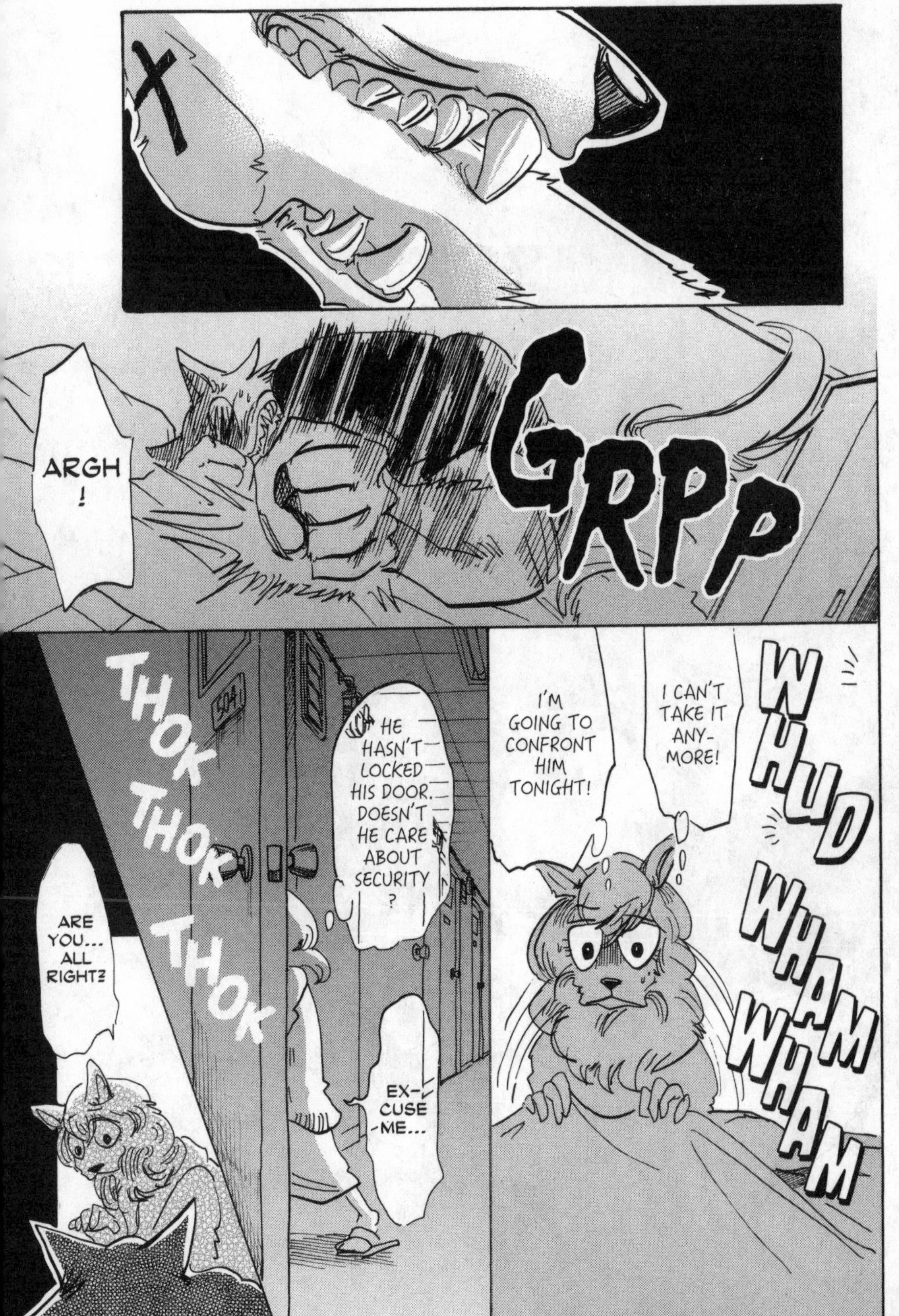
GRPP
ARGH!
WHUD
WHAM WHAM
I CAN'T TAKE IT ANYMORE!
I'M GOING TO CONFRONT HIM TONIGHT!
THOK THOK THOK
HE HASN'T LOCKED HIS DOOR. DOESN'T HE CARE ABOUT SECURITY?
EX-CUSE ME...
ARE YOU... ALL RIGHT?

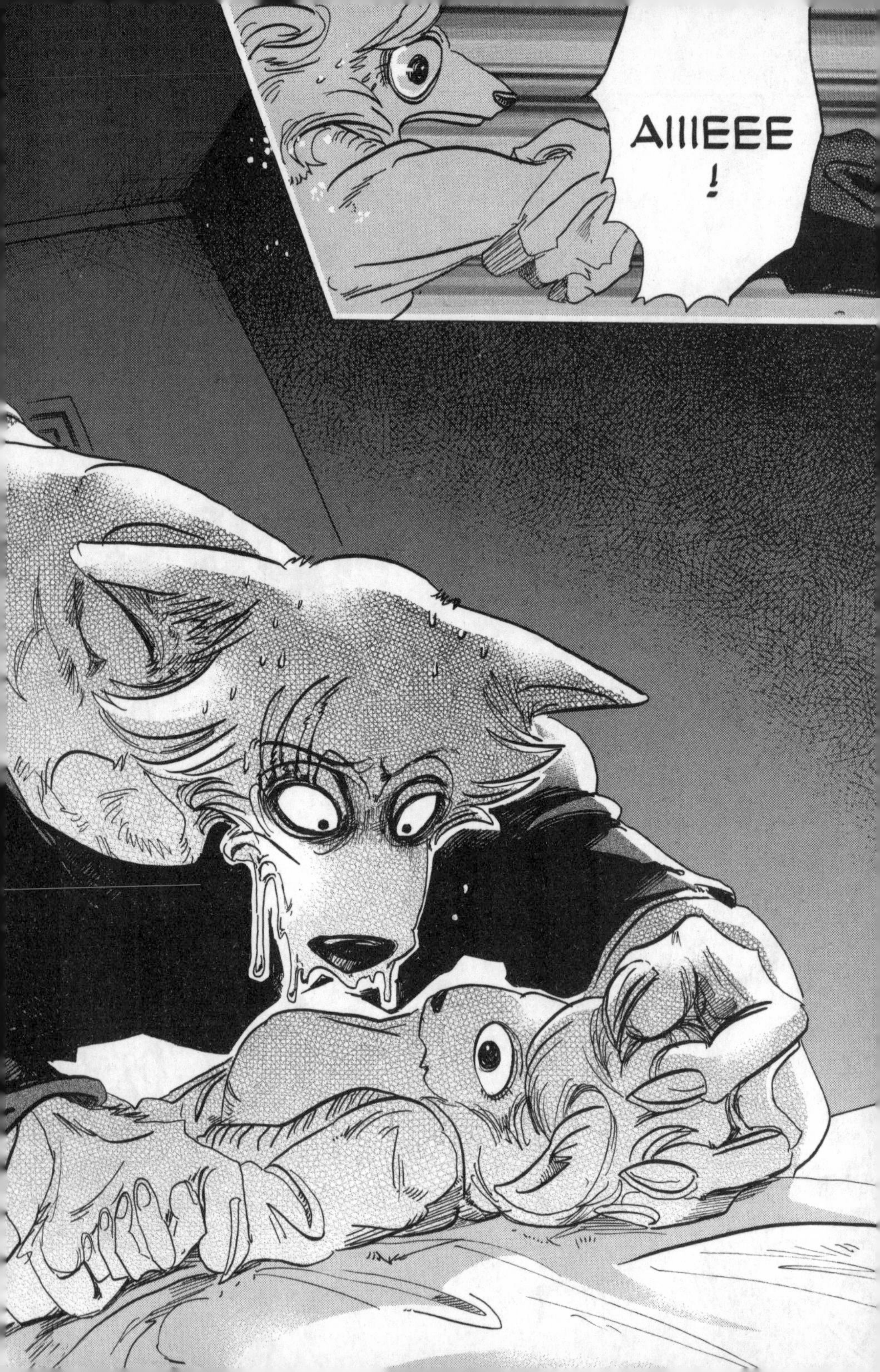
AIIIEEE
!

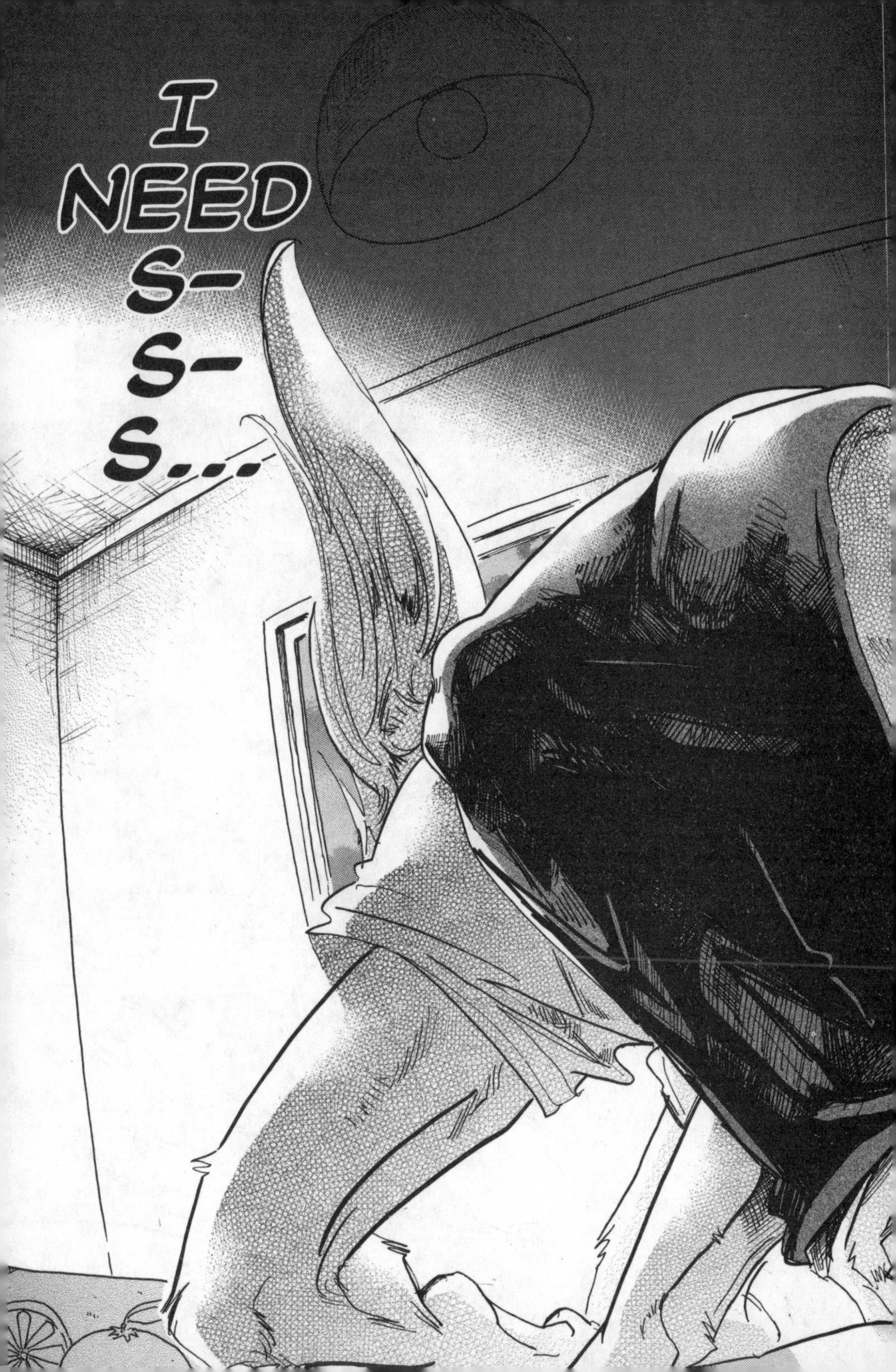
I NEED S-S-S...

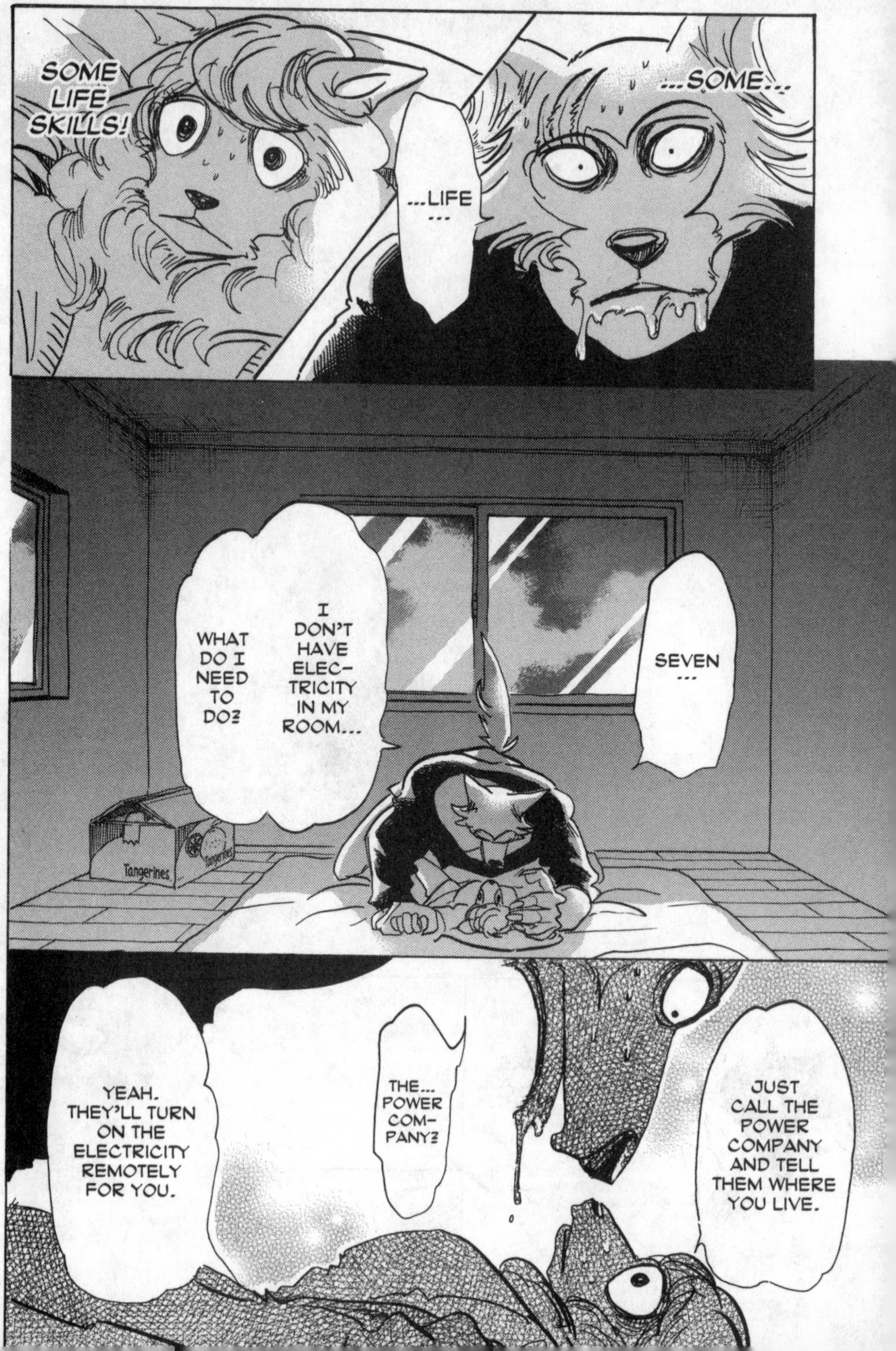
...SOME...
...LIFE ...
SOME LIFE SKILLS!
SEVEN ...
I DON'T HAVE ELEC-TRICITY IN MY ROOM...
WHAT DO I NEED TO DO?
Tangerines
JUST CALL THE POWER COMPANY AND TELL THEM WHERE YOU LIVE.
THE... POWER COM-PANY?
YEAH. THEY'LL TURN ON THE ELECTRICITY REMOTELY FOR YOU.

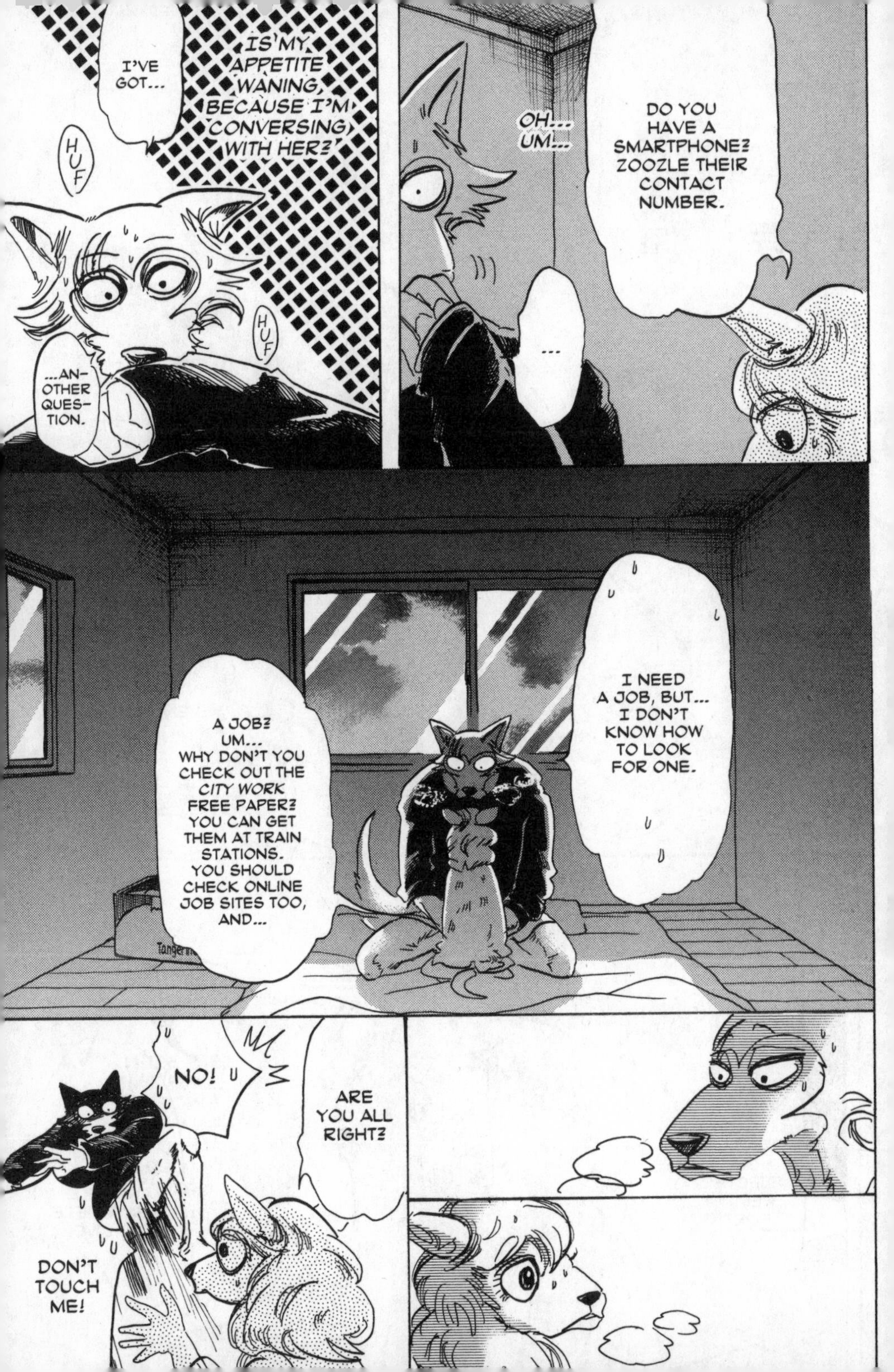
DO YOU HAVE A SMARTPHONE? ZOOZLE THEIR CONTACT NUMBER.
OH... UM...
...
IS MY APPETITE WANING, BECAUSE I'M CONVERSING WITH HER?
I'VE GOT...
HUF
HUF
...ANOTHER QUESTION.
I NEED A JOB, BUT... I DON'T KNOW HOW TO LOOK FOR ONE.
A JOB? UM... WHY DON'T YOU CHECK OUT THE *CITY WORK* FREE PAPER? YOU CAN GET THEM AT TRAIN STATIONS. YOU SHOULD CHECK ONLINE JOB SITES TOO, AND...
ARE YOU ALL RIGHT?
NO!
DON'T TOUCH ME!

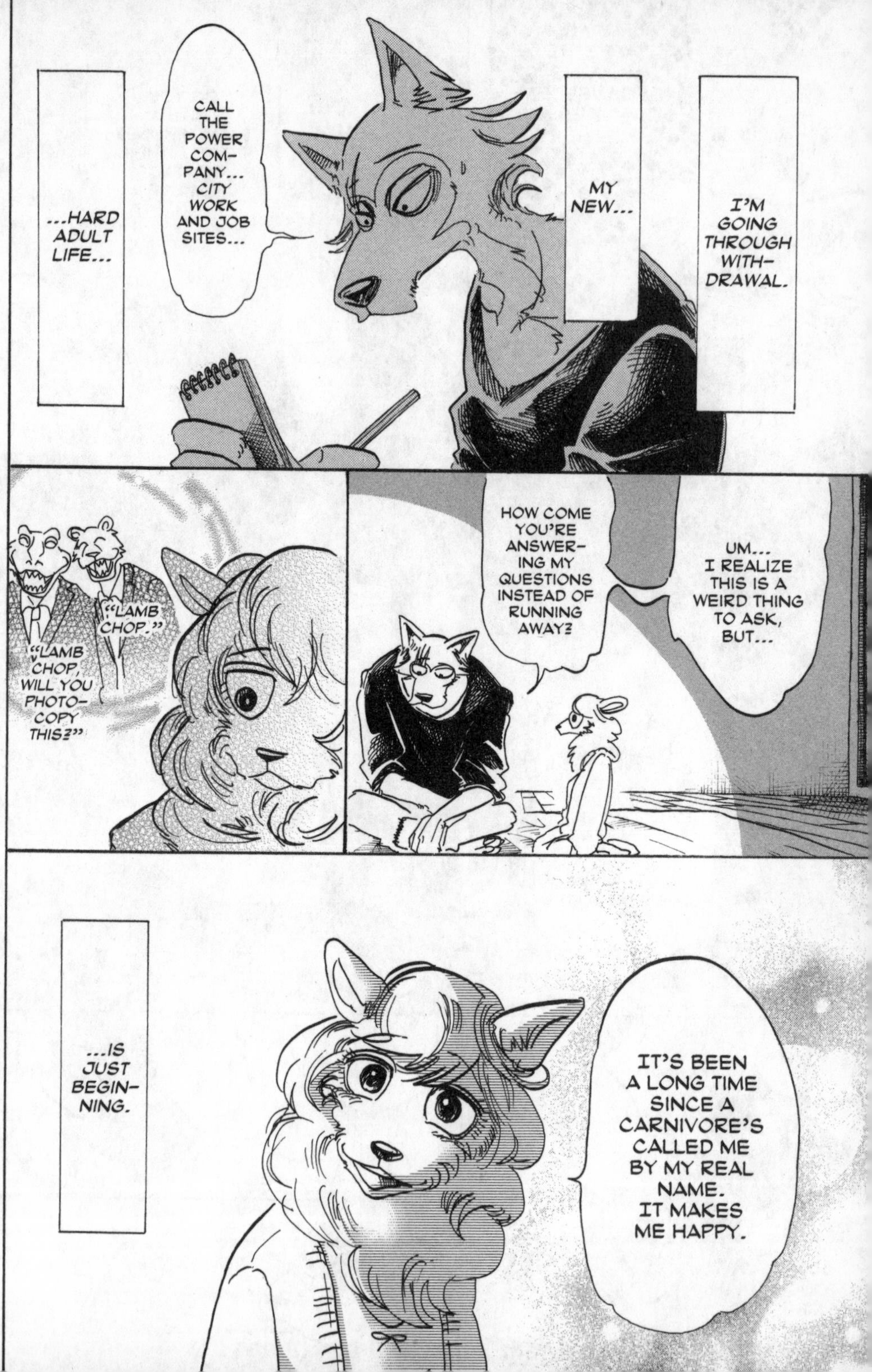
I'M GOING THROUGH WITH-DRAWAL.
MY NEW...
CALL THE POWER COM-PANY... CITY WORK AND JOB SITES...
...HARD ADULT LIFE...
UM... I REALIZE THIS IS A WEIRD THING TO ASK, BUT...
HOW COME YOU'RE ANSWER-ING MY QUESTIONS INSTEAD OF RUNNING AWAY?
"LAMB CHOP."
"LAMB CHOP, WILL YOU PHOTO-COPY THIS?"
IT'S BEEN A LONG TIME SINCE A CARNIVORE'S CALLED ME BY MY REAL NAME. IT MAKES ME HAPPY.
...IS JUST BEGIN-NING.

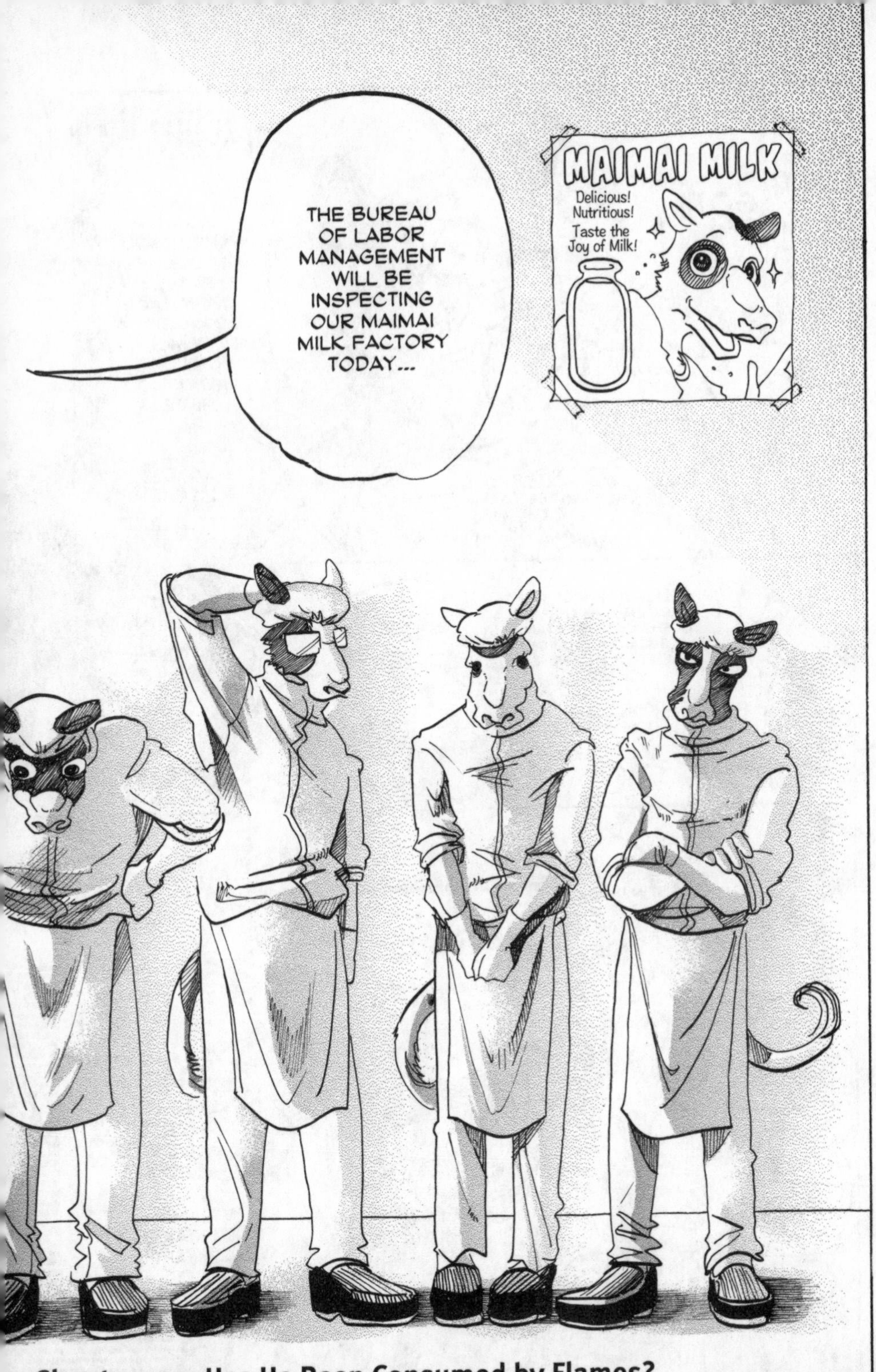
THE BUREAU OF LABOR MANAGEMENT WILL BE INSPECTING OUR MAIMAI MILK FACTORY TODAY...
MAIMAI MILK
Delicious! Nutritious! Taste the Joy of Milk!

Chapter 102: Has He Been Consumed by Flames?

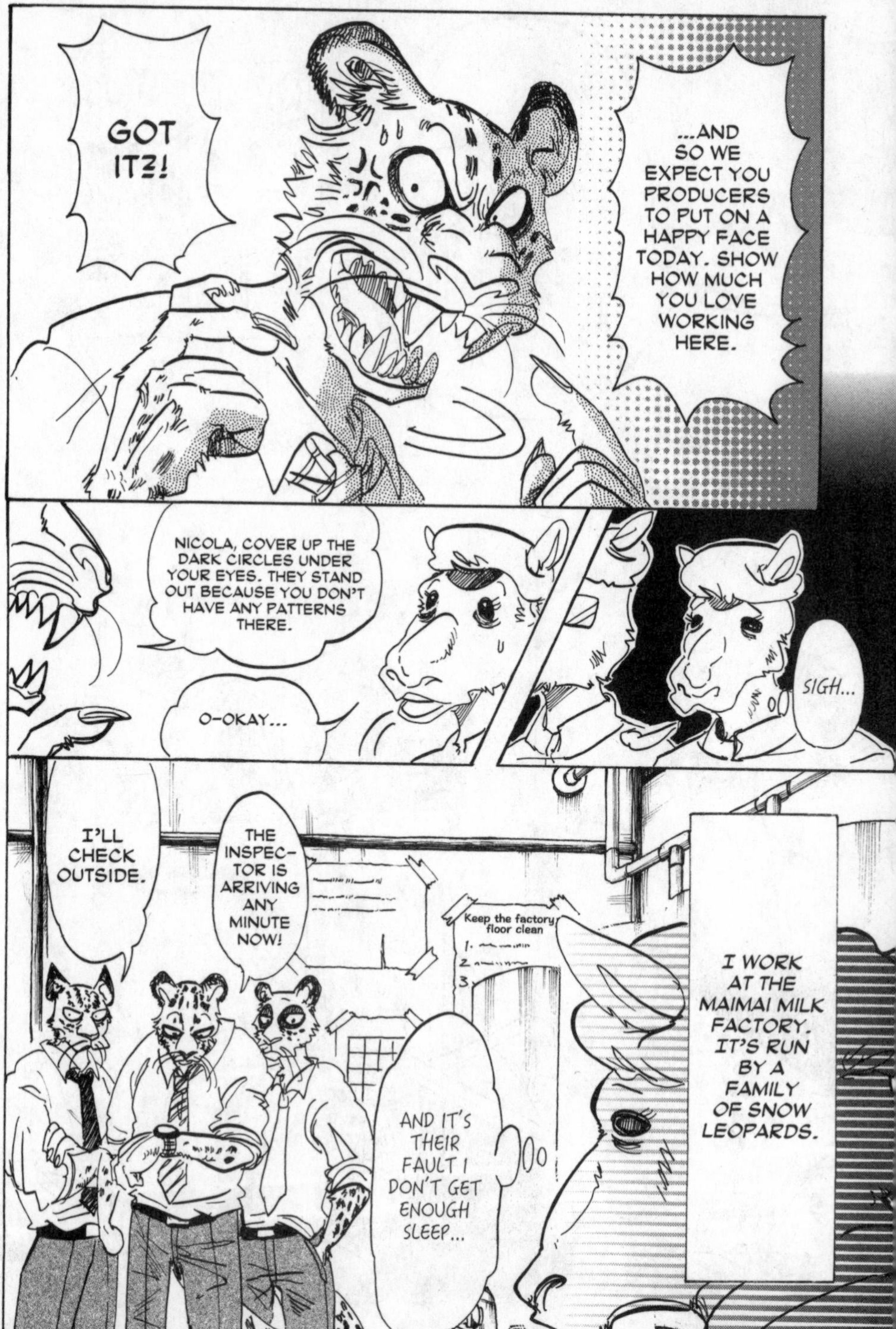
...AND SO WE EXPECT YOU PRODUCERS TO PUT ON A HAPPY FACE TODAY. SHOW HOW MUCH YOU LOVE WORKING HERE.
GOT IT~!
SIGH...
NICOLA, COVER UP THE DARK CIRCLES UNDER YOUR EYES. THEY STAND OUT BECAUSE YOU DON'T HAVE ANY PATTERNS THERE.
O-OKAY...
I WORK AT THE MAIMAI MILK FACTORY. IT'S RUN BY A FAMILY OF SNOW LEOPARDS.
AND IT'S THEIR FAULT I DON'T GET ENOUGH SLEEP...
Keep the factory floor clean
1.
2.
3.
THE INSPECTOR IS ARRIVING ANY MINUTE NOW!
I'LL CHECK OUTSIDE.

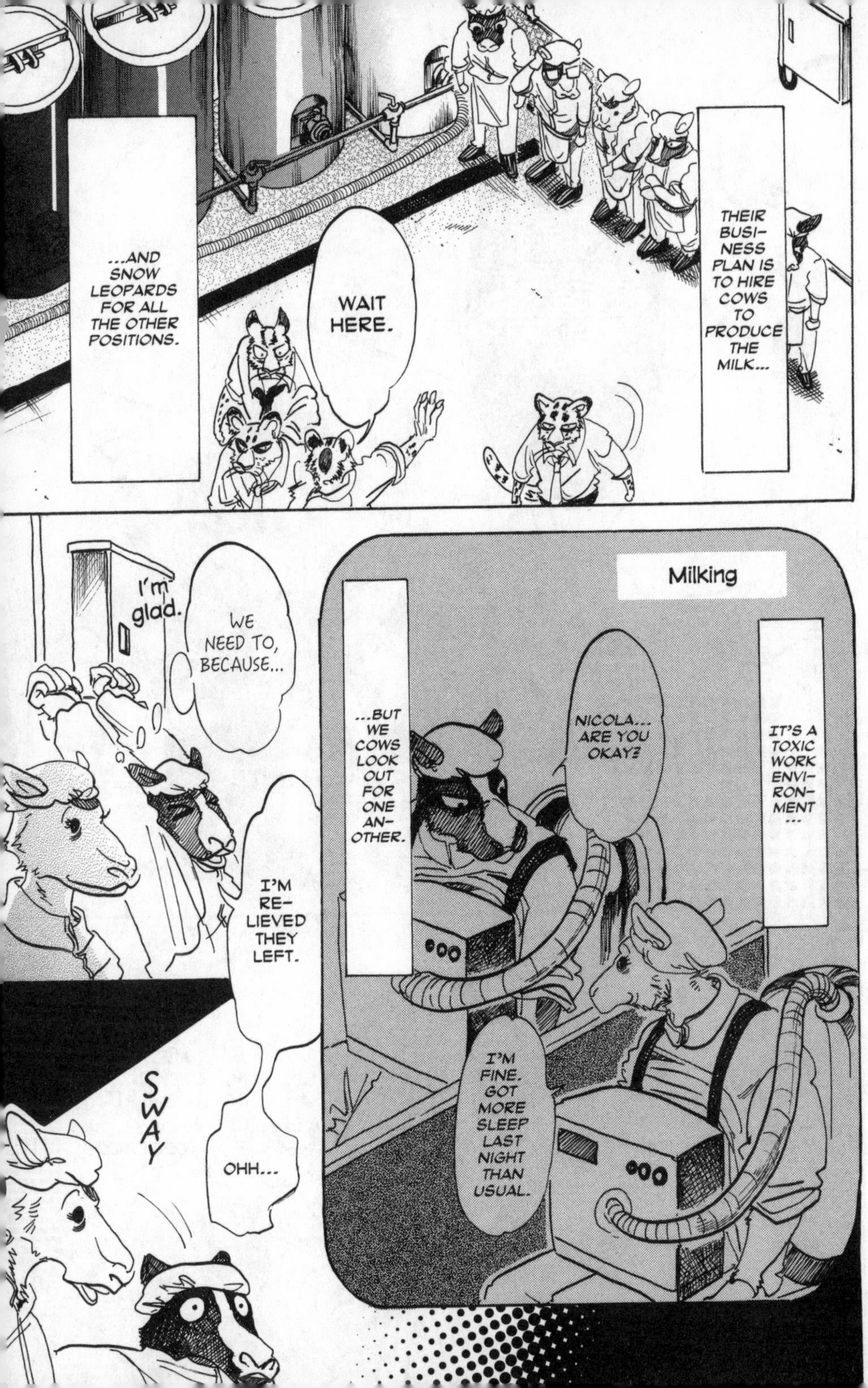
THEIR BUSINESS PLAN IS TO HIRE COWS TO PRODUCE THE MILK...
WAIT HERE.
...AND SNOW LEOPARDS FOR ALL THE OTHER POSITIONS.
Milking
IT'S A TOXIC WORK ENVIRONMENT...
NICOLA... ARE YOU OKAY?
...BUT WE COWS LOOK OUT FOR ONE ANOTHER.
I'M FINE. GOT MORE SLEEP LAST NIGHT THAN USUAL.
WE NEED TO, BECAUSE...
I'm glad.
I'M RELIEVED THEY LEFT.
SWAY
OHH...

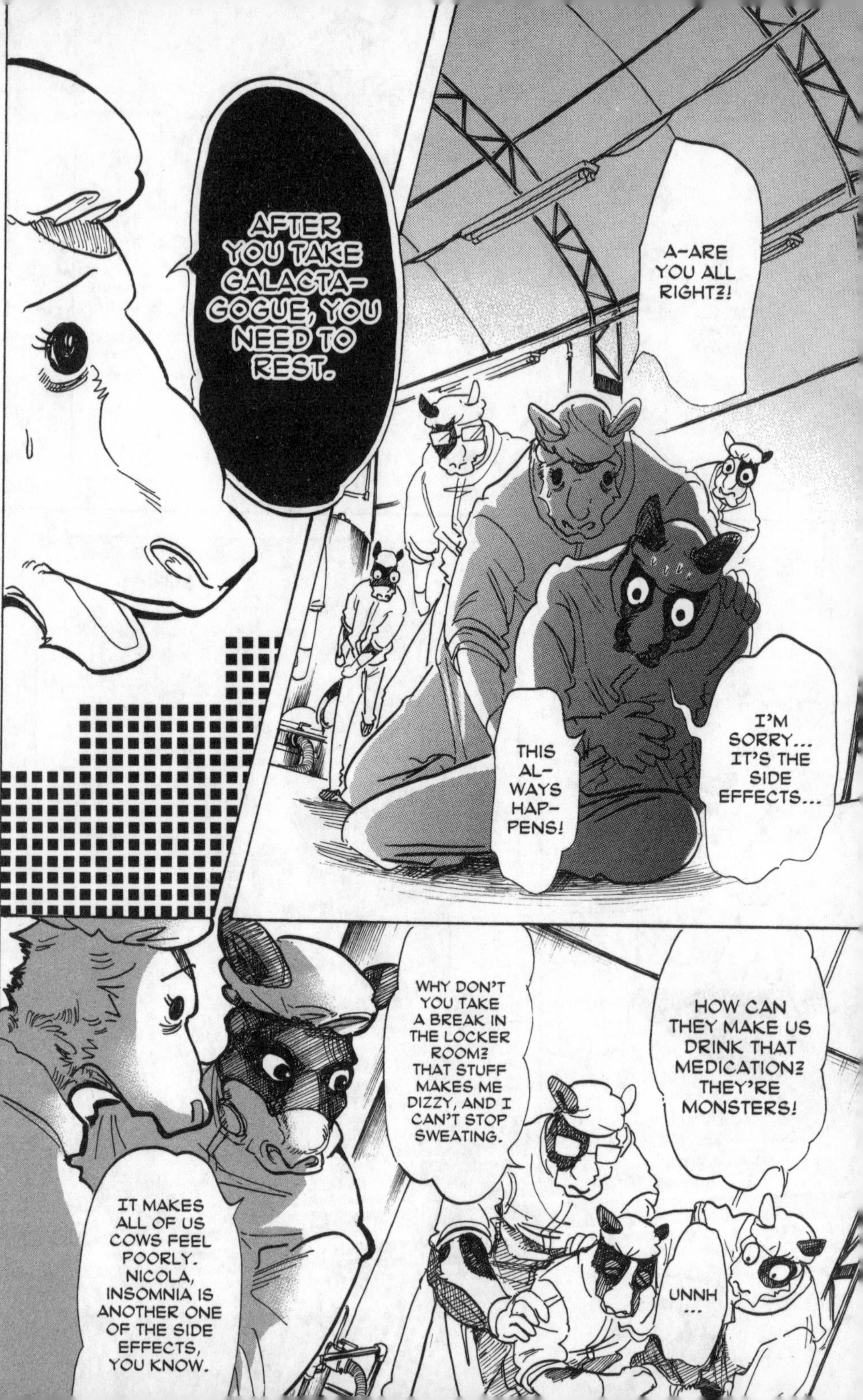
A-ARE YOU ALL RIGHT?!
I'M SORRY... IT'S THE SIDE EFFECTS...
THIS AL-WAYS HAP-PENS!
AFTER YOU TAKE GALACTA-GOGUE, YOU NEED TO REST.
HOW CAN THEY MAKE US DRINK THAT MEDICATION? THEY'RE MONSTERS!
WHY DON'T YOU TAKE A BREAK IN THE LOCKER ROOM? THAT STUFF MAKES ME DIZZY, AND I CAN'T STOP SWEATING.
UNNH ...
IT MAKES ALL OF US COWS FEEL POORLY. NICOLA, INSOMNIA IS ANOTHER ONE OF THE SIDE EFFECTS, YOU KNOW.

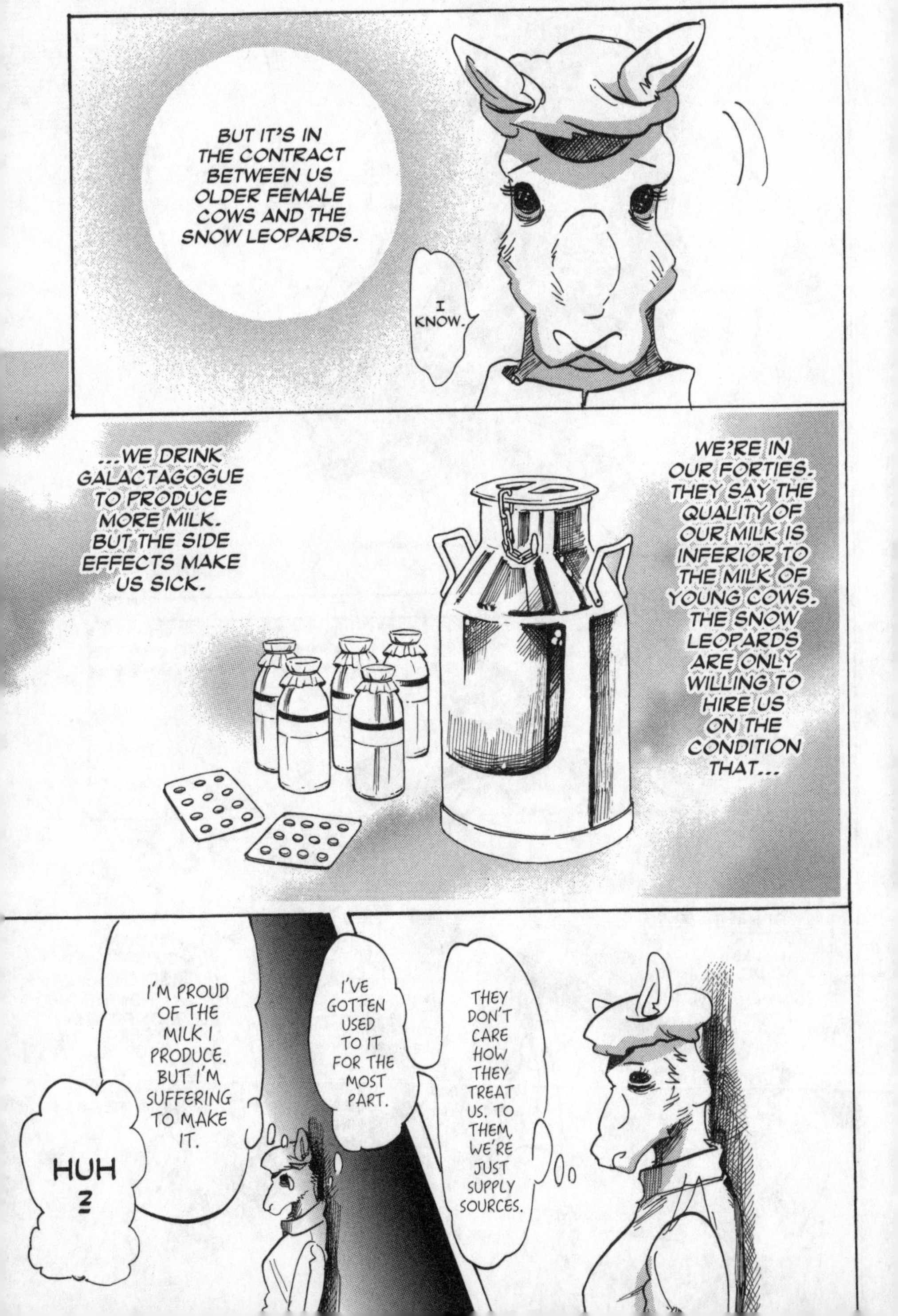
I KNOW.
BUT IT'S IN THE CONTRACT BETWEEN US OLDER FEMALE COWS AND THE SNOW LEOPARDS.
WE'RE IN OUR FORTIES. THEY SAY THE QUALITY OF OUR MILK IS INFERIOR TO THE MILK OF YOUNG COWS. THE SNOW LEOPARDS ARE ONLY WILLING TO HIRE US ON THE CONDITION THAT...
...WE DRINK GALACTAGOGUE TO PRODUCE MORE MILK. BUT THE SIDE EFFECTS MAKE US SICK.
THEY DON'T CARE HOW THEY TREAT US. TO THEM, WE'RE JUST SUPPLY SOURCES.
I'VE GOTTEN USED TO IT FOR THE MOST PART.
I'M PROUD OF THE MILK I PRODUCE. BUT I'M SUFFERING TO MAKE IT.
HUH?

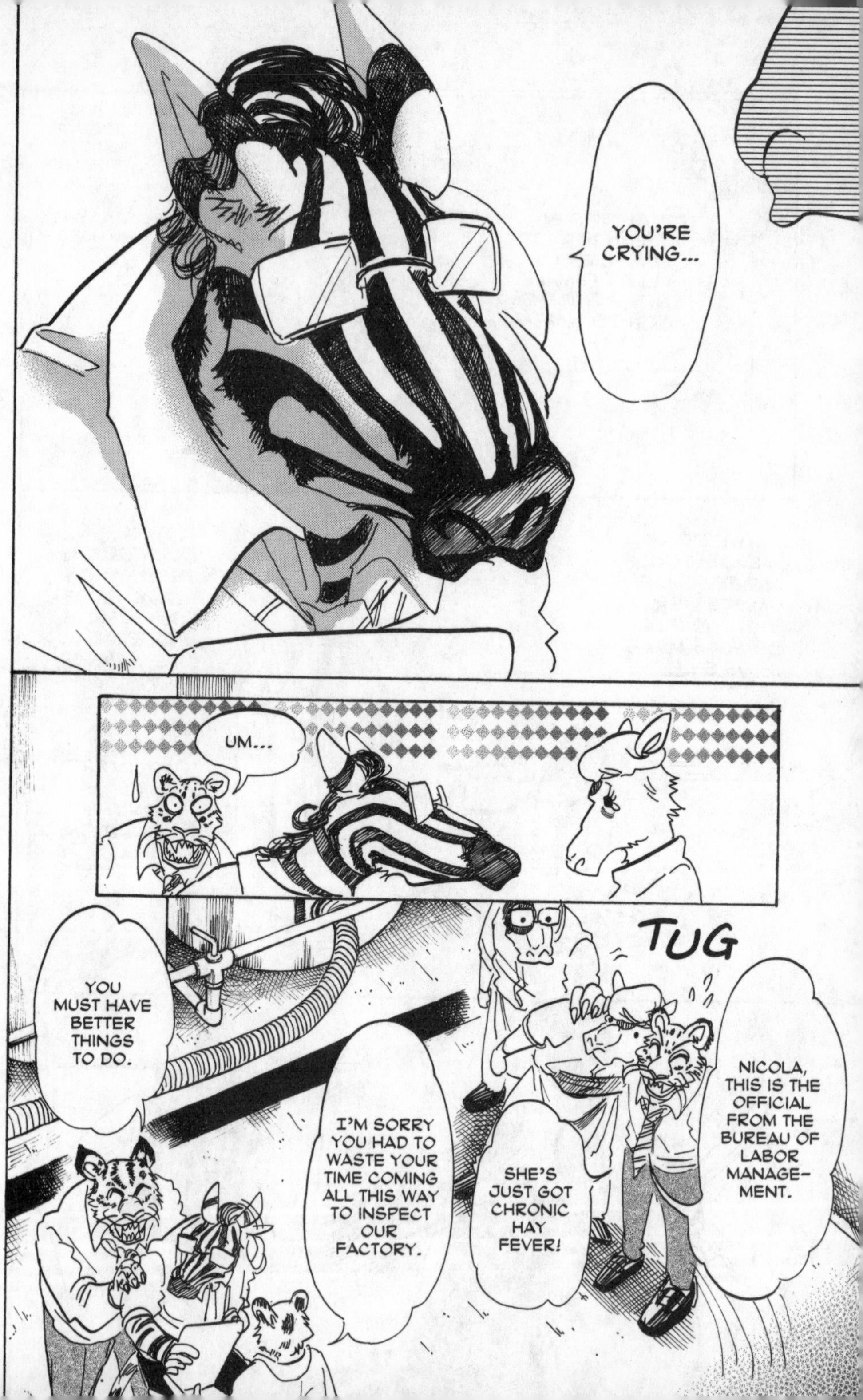
YOU'RE CRYING...
UM...
TUG
NICOLA, THIS IS THE OFFICIAL FROM THE BUREAU OF LABOR MANAGEMENT.
SHE'S JUST GOT CHRONIC HAY FEVER!
I'M SORRY YOU HAD TO WASTE YOUR TIME COMING ALL THIS WAY TO INSPECT OUR FACTORY.
YOU MUST HAVE BETTER THINGS TO DO.

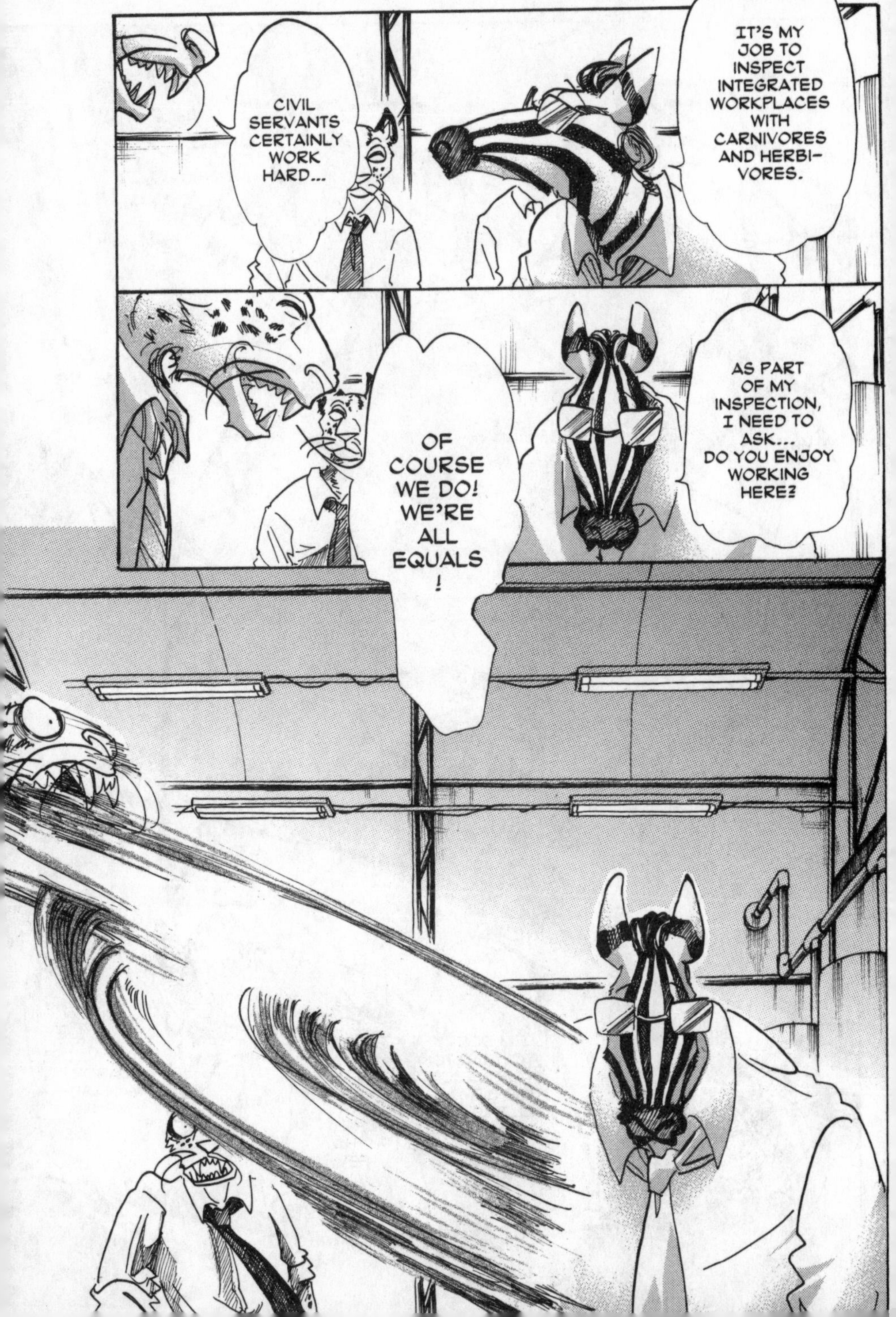
IT'S MY JOB TO INSPECT INTEGRATED WORKPLACES WITH CARNIVORES AND HERBI- VORES.
CIVIL SERVANTS CERTAINLY WORK HARD...
AS PART OF MY INSPECTION, I NEED TO ASK... DO YOU ENJOY WORKING HERE?
OF COURSE WE DO! WE'RE ALL EQUALS !

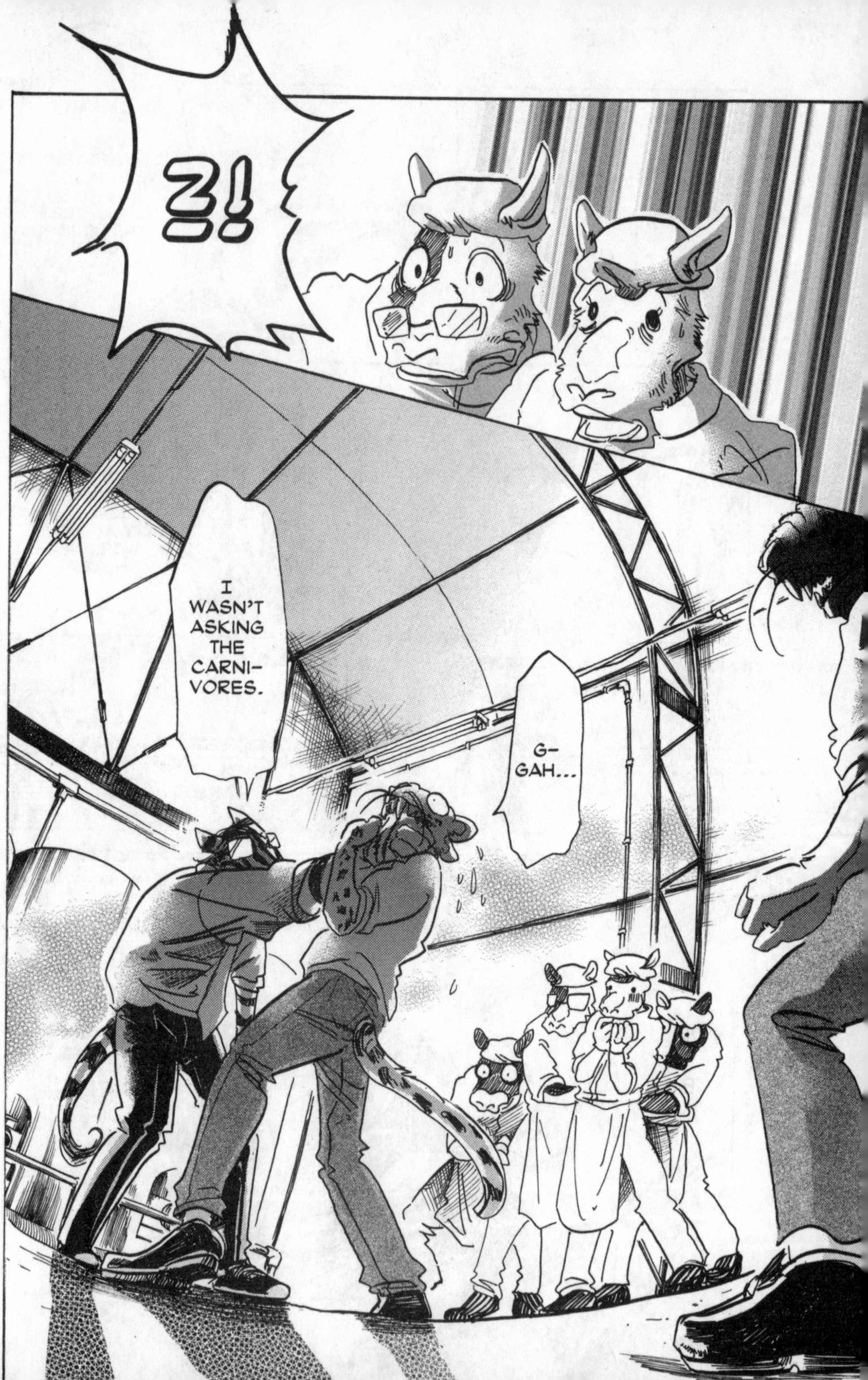
Z!
G-GAH...
I WASN'T ASKING THE CARNIVORES.

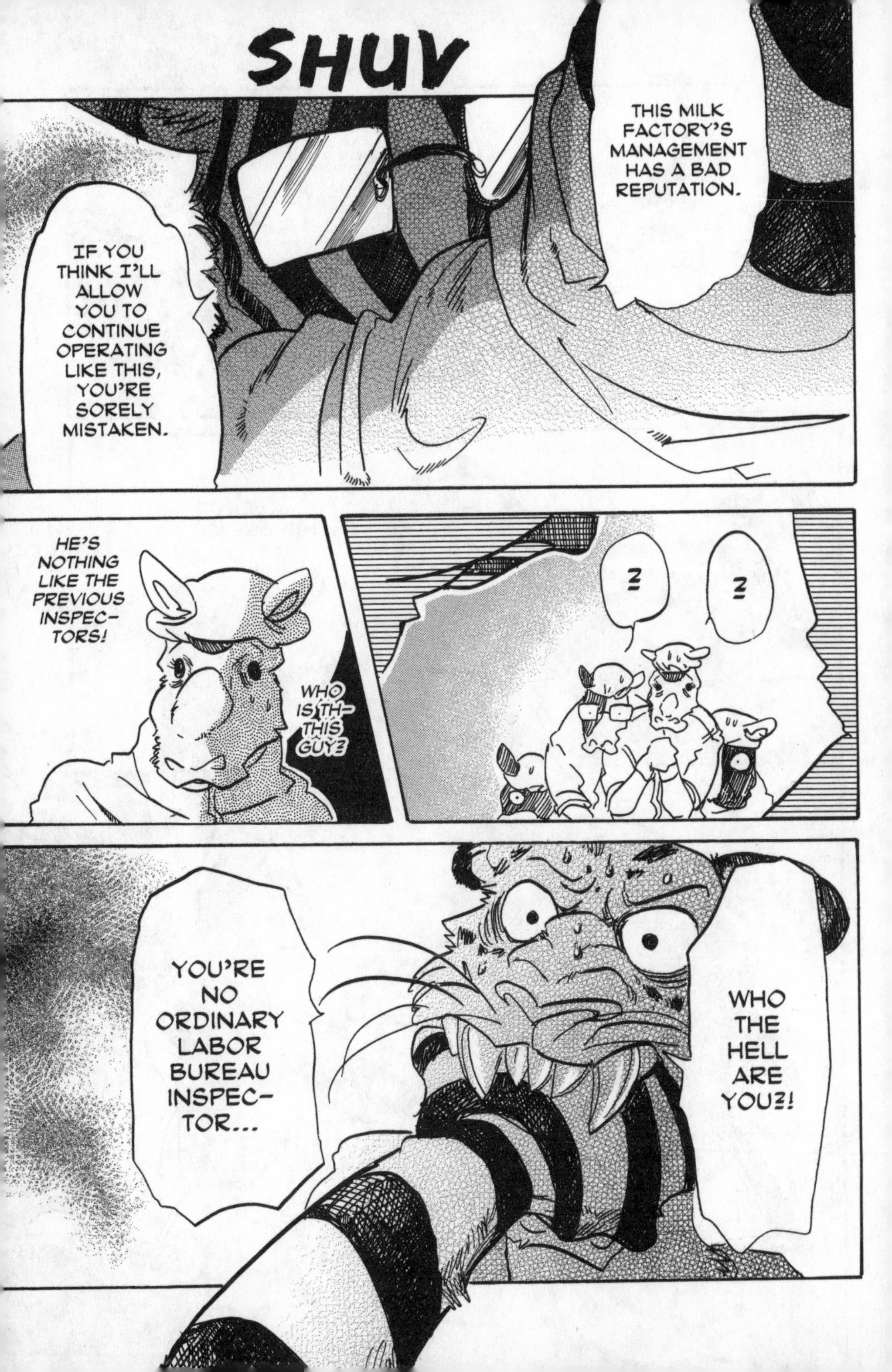
SHUV
THIS MILK FACTORY'S MANAGEMENT HAS A BAD REPUTATION.
IF YOU THINK I'LL ALLOW YOU TO CONTINUE OPERATING LIKE THIS, YOU'RE SORELY MISTAKEN.
?
?
HE'S NOTHING LIKE THE PREVIOUS INSPEC-TORS!
WHO IS TH-THIS GUY?
WHO THE HELL ARE YOU?!
YOU'RE NO ORDINARY LABOR BUREAU INSPEC-TOR...

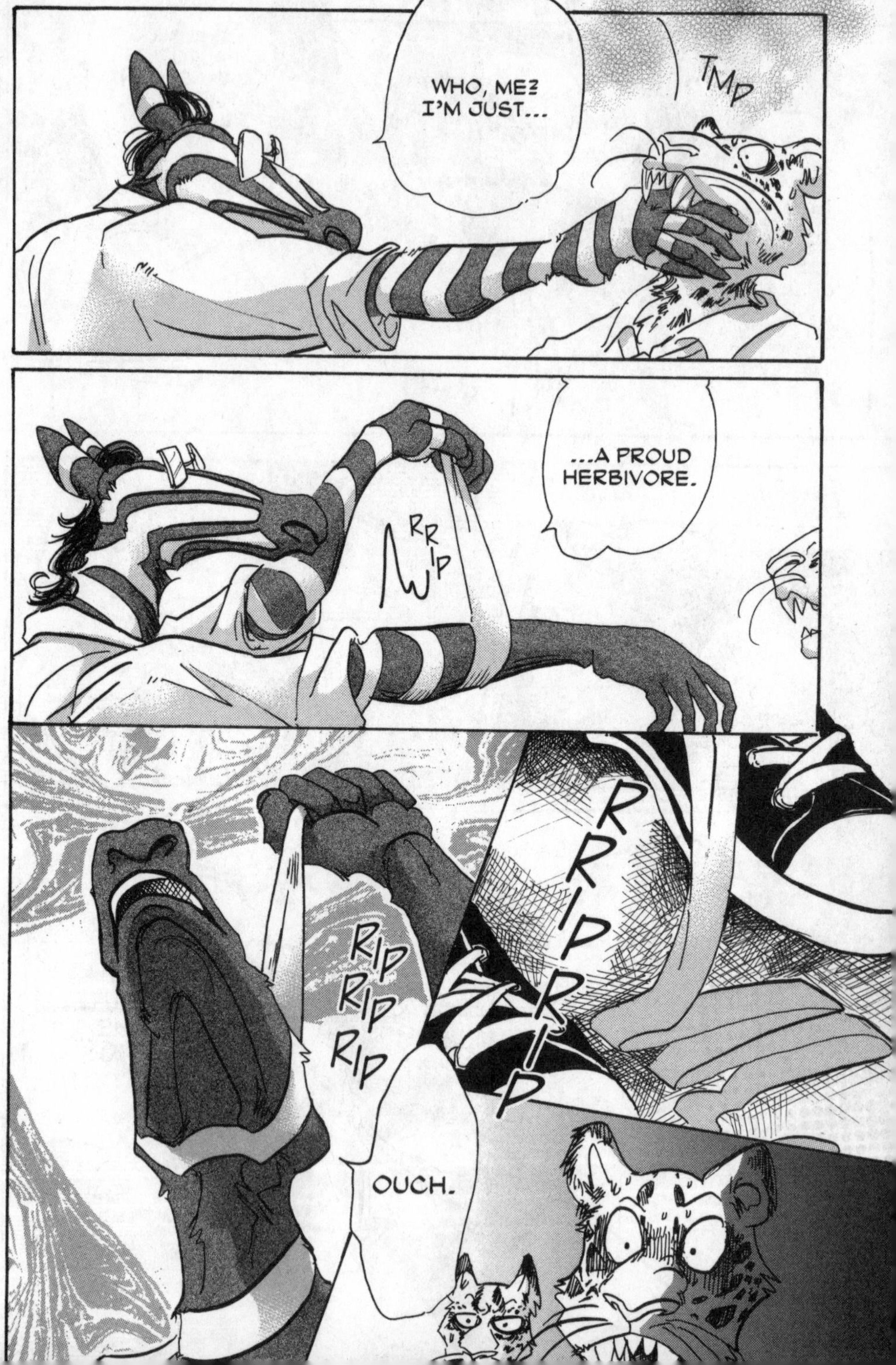
TMP
WHO, ME? I'M JUST...
...A PROUD HERBIVORE.
RRIP
RRIPRIP
RIP RIP RIP
OUCH.

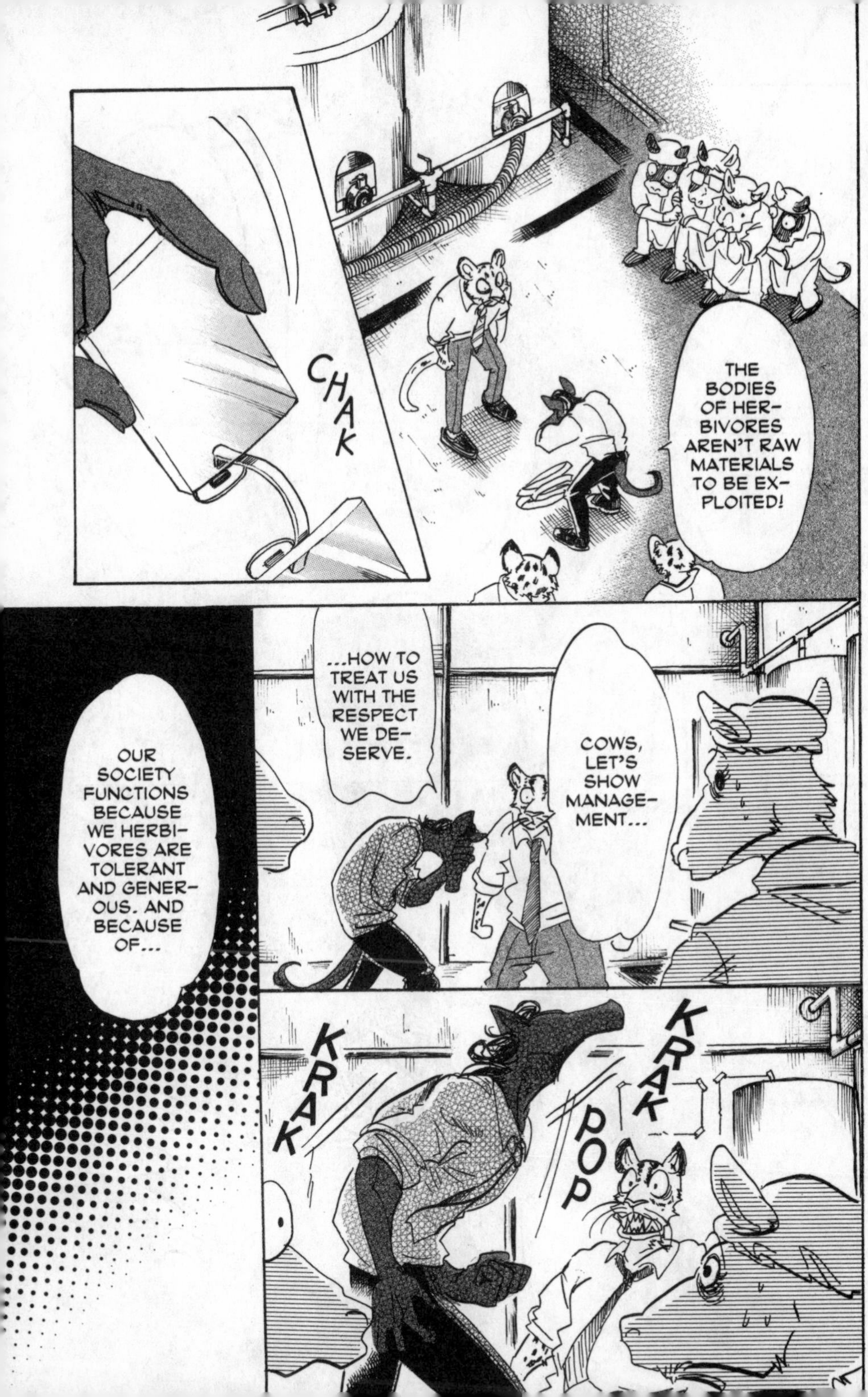
THE BODIES OF HERBIVORES AREN'T RAW MATERIALS TO BE EXPLOITED!
CHAK
COWS, LET'S SHOW MANAGEMENT...
...HOW TO TREAT US WITH THE RESPECT WE DESERVE.
KRAK
POP
KRAK
OUR SOCIETY FUNCTIONS BECAUSE WE HERBIVORES ARE TOLERANT AND GENEROUS. AND BECAUSE OF...

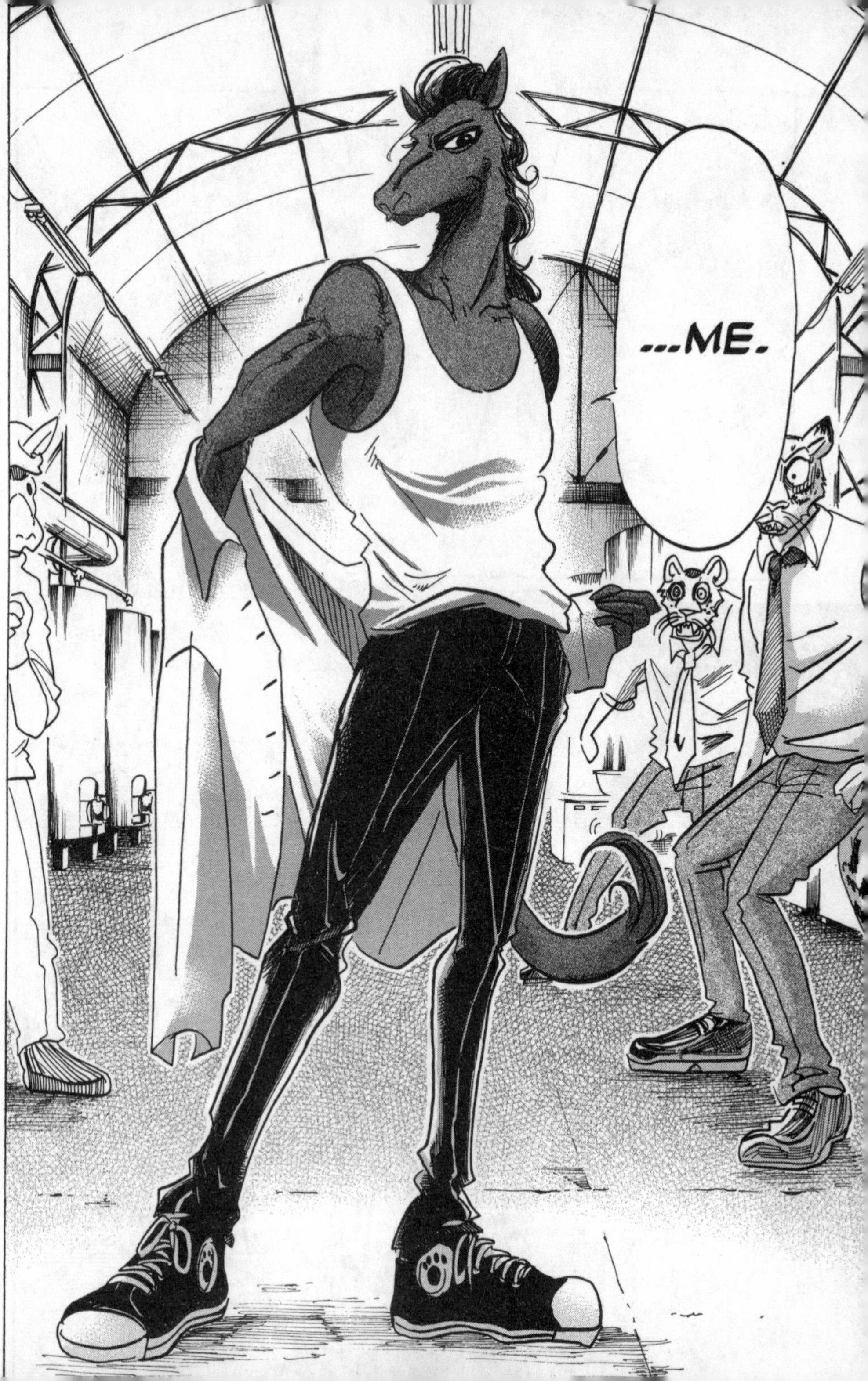
...ME.

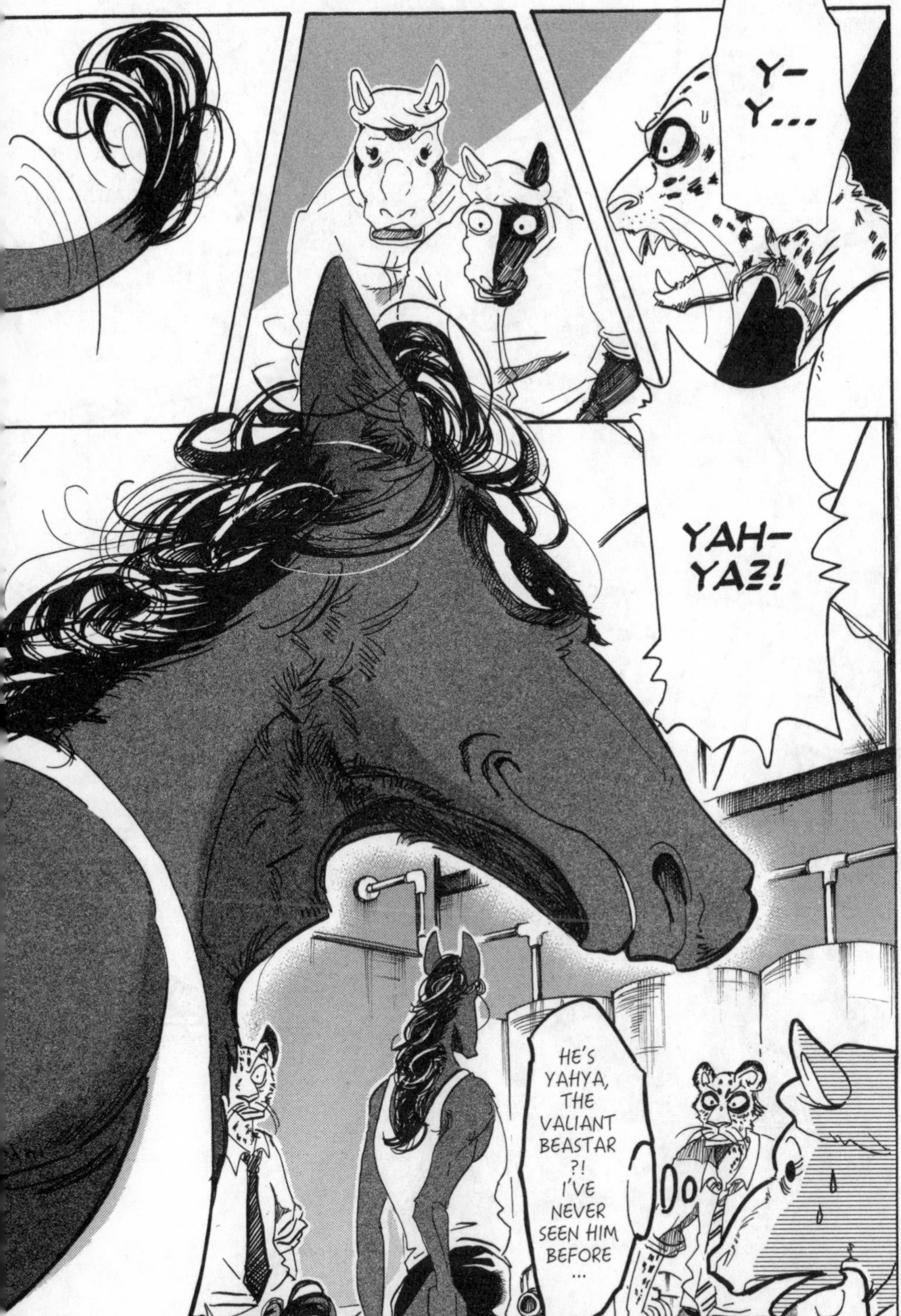
Y- Y...
YAH- YA?!
HE'S YAHYA, THE VALIANT BEASTAR ?! I'VE NEVER SEEN HIM BEFORE ...

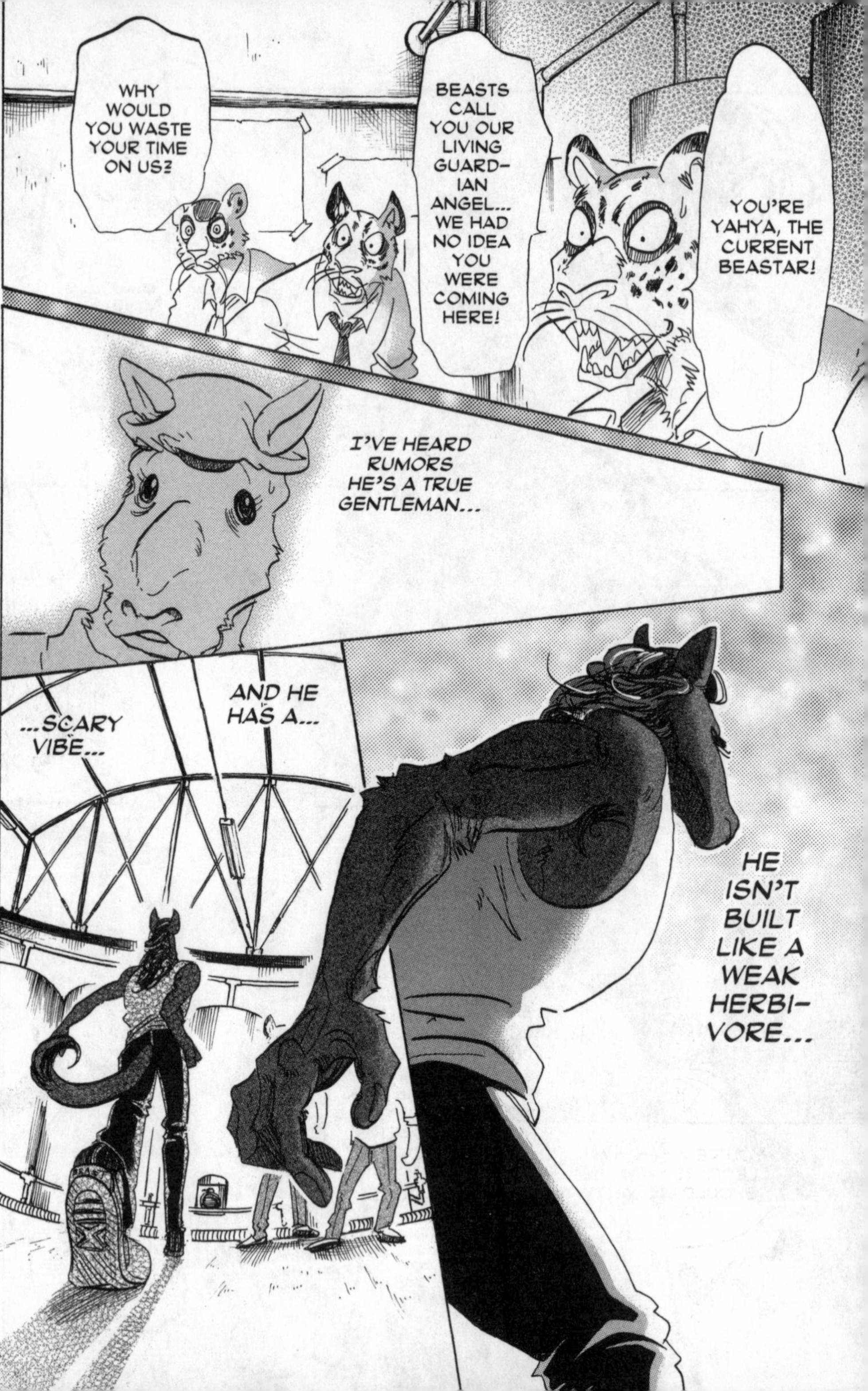
YOU'RE YAHYA, THE CURRENT BEASTAR!
BEASTS CALL YOU OUR LIVING GUARD-IAN ANGEL... WE HAD NO IDEA YOU WERE COMING HERE!
WHY WOULD YOU WASTE YOUR TIME ON US?
I'VE HEARD RUMORS HE'S A TRUE GENTLEMAN...
HE ISN'T BUILT LIKE A WEAK HERBI-VORE...
AND HE HAS A...
...SCARY VIBE...

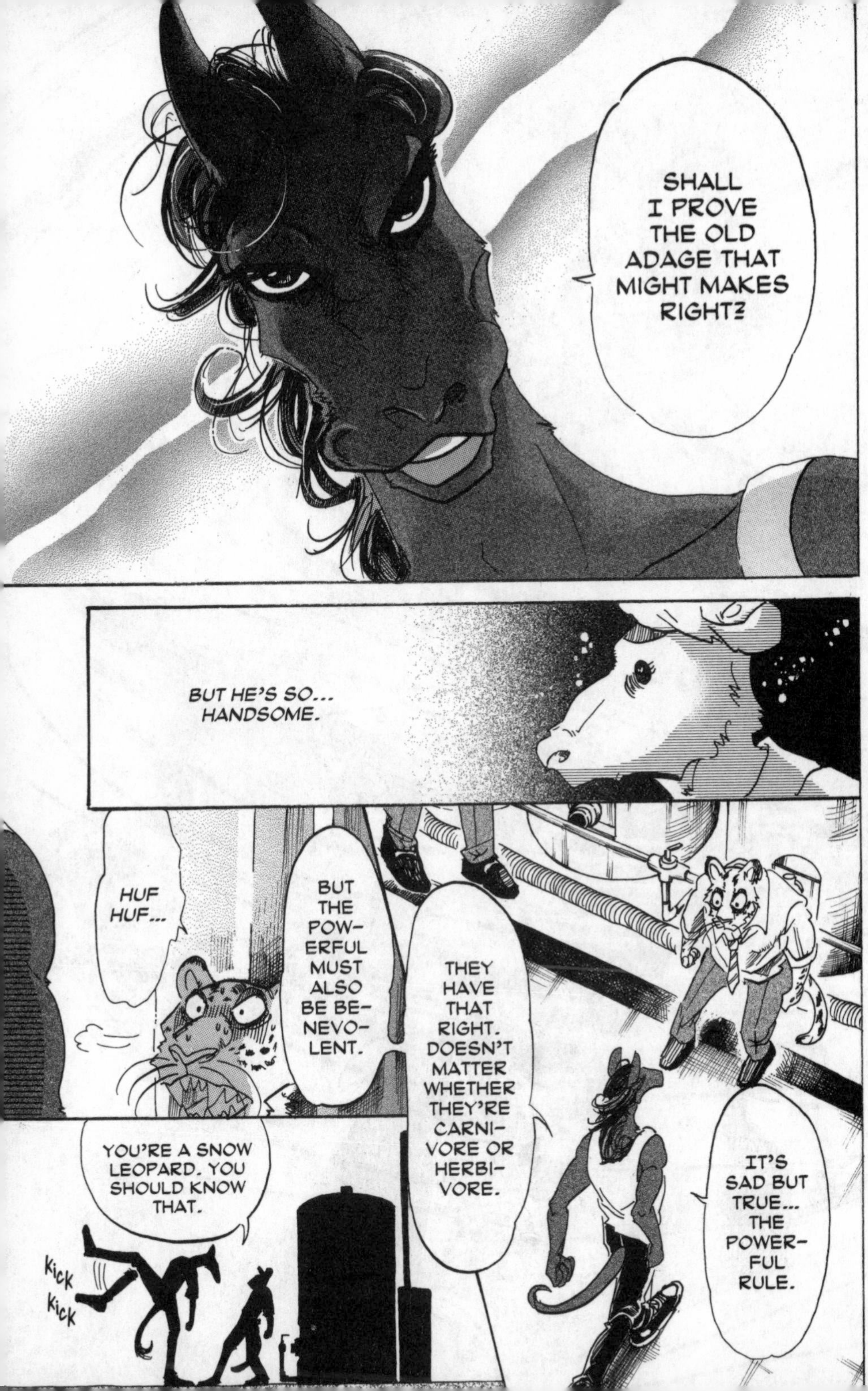
SHALL I PROVE THE OLD ADAGE THAT MIGHT MAKES RIGHT?
BUT HE'S SO... HANDSOME.
IT'S SAD BUT TRUE... THE POWER-FUL RULE.
THEY HAVE THAT RIGHT. DOESN'T MATTER WHETHER THEY'RE CARNI-VORE OR HERBI-VORE.
BUT THE POW-ERFUL MUST ALSO BE BE-NEVO-LENT.
HUF HUF...
YOU'RE A SNOW LEOPARD. YOU SHOULD KNOW THAT.
Kick Kick

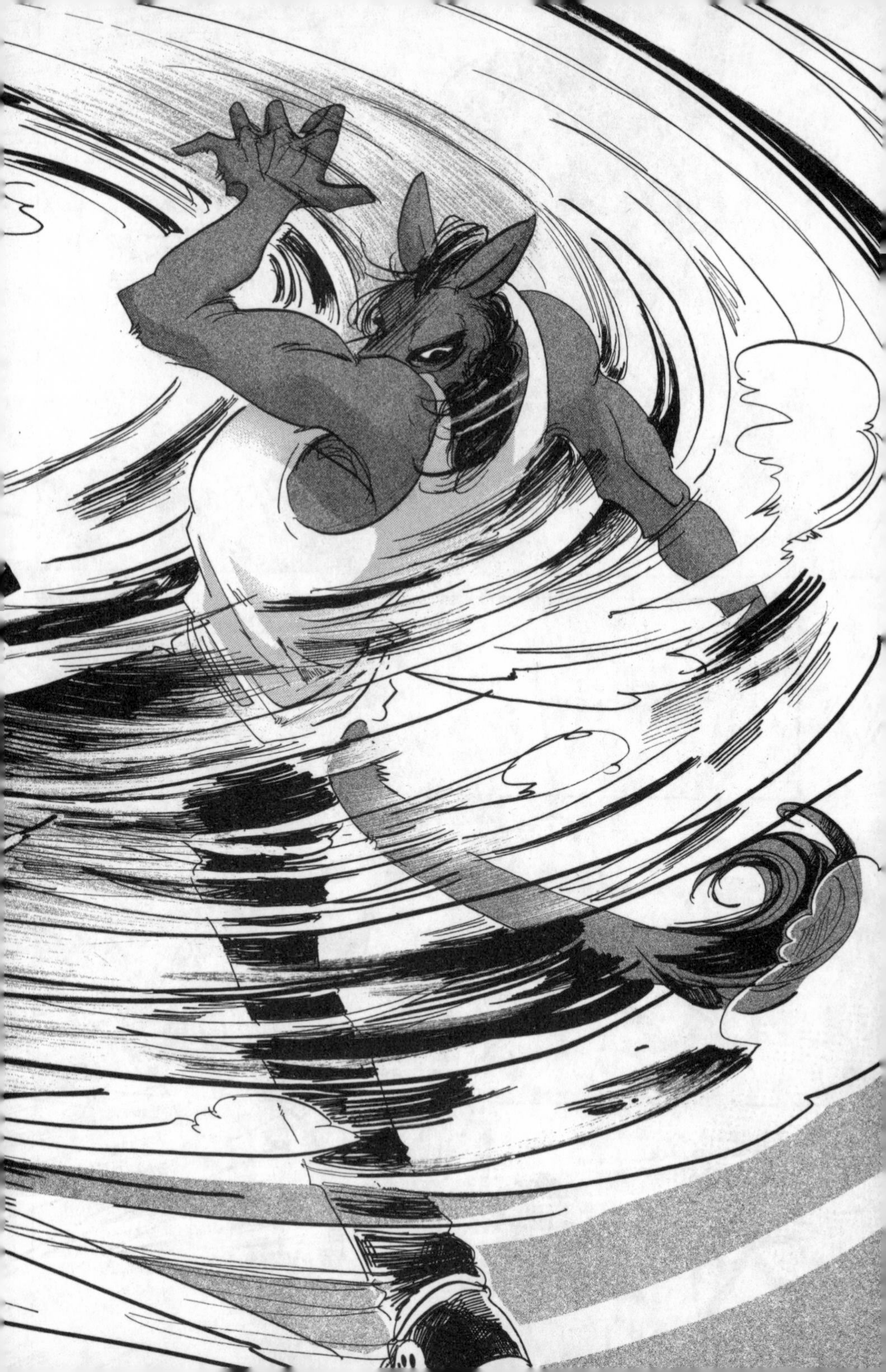

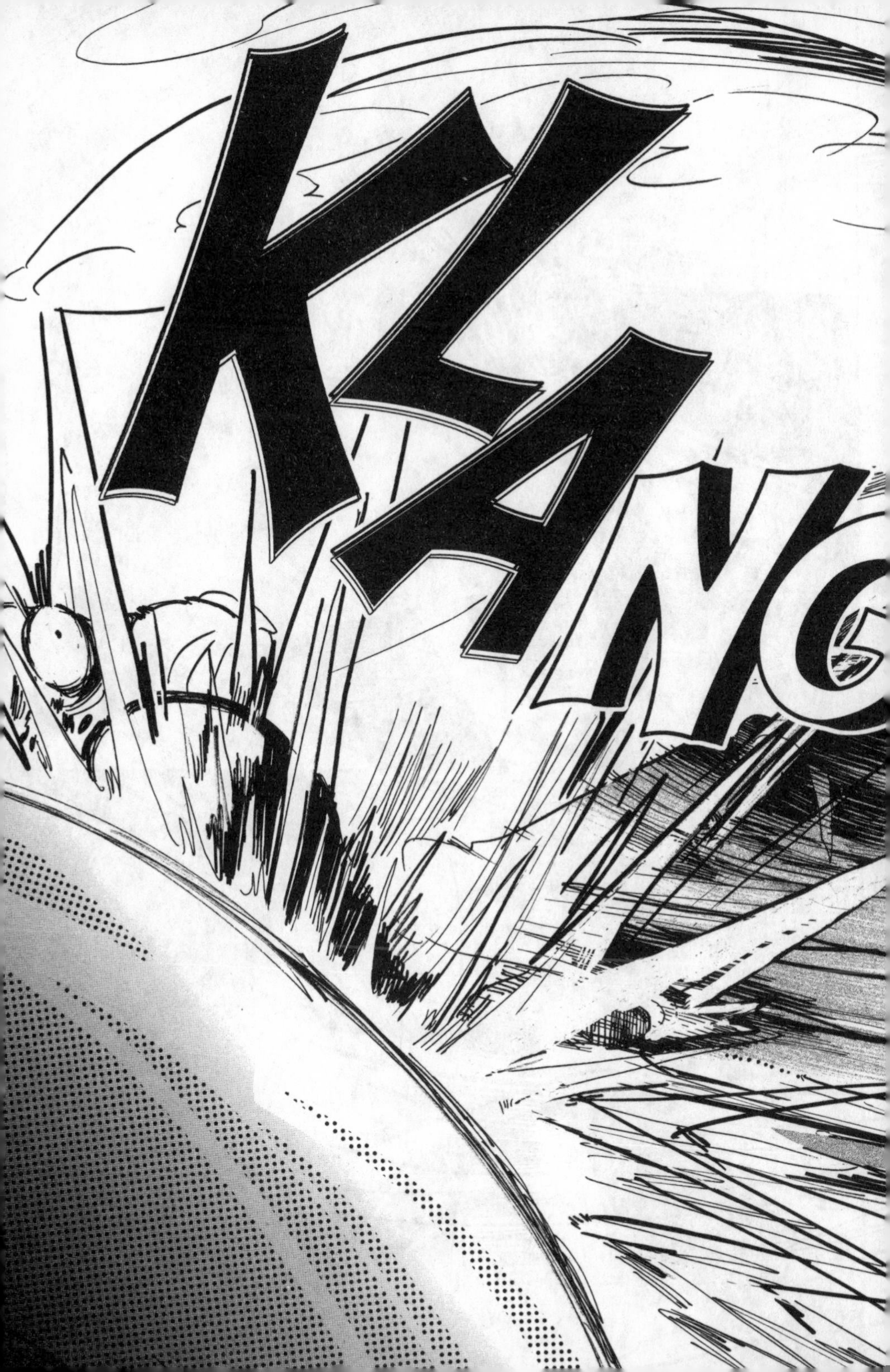
KLANG

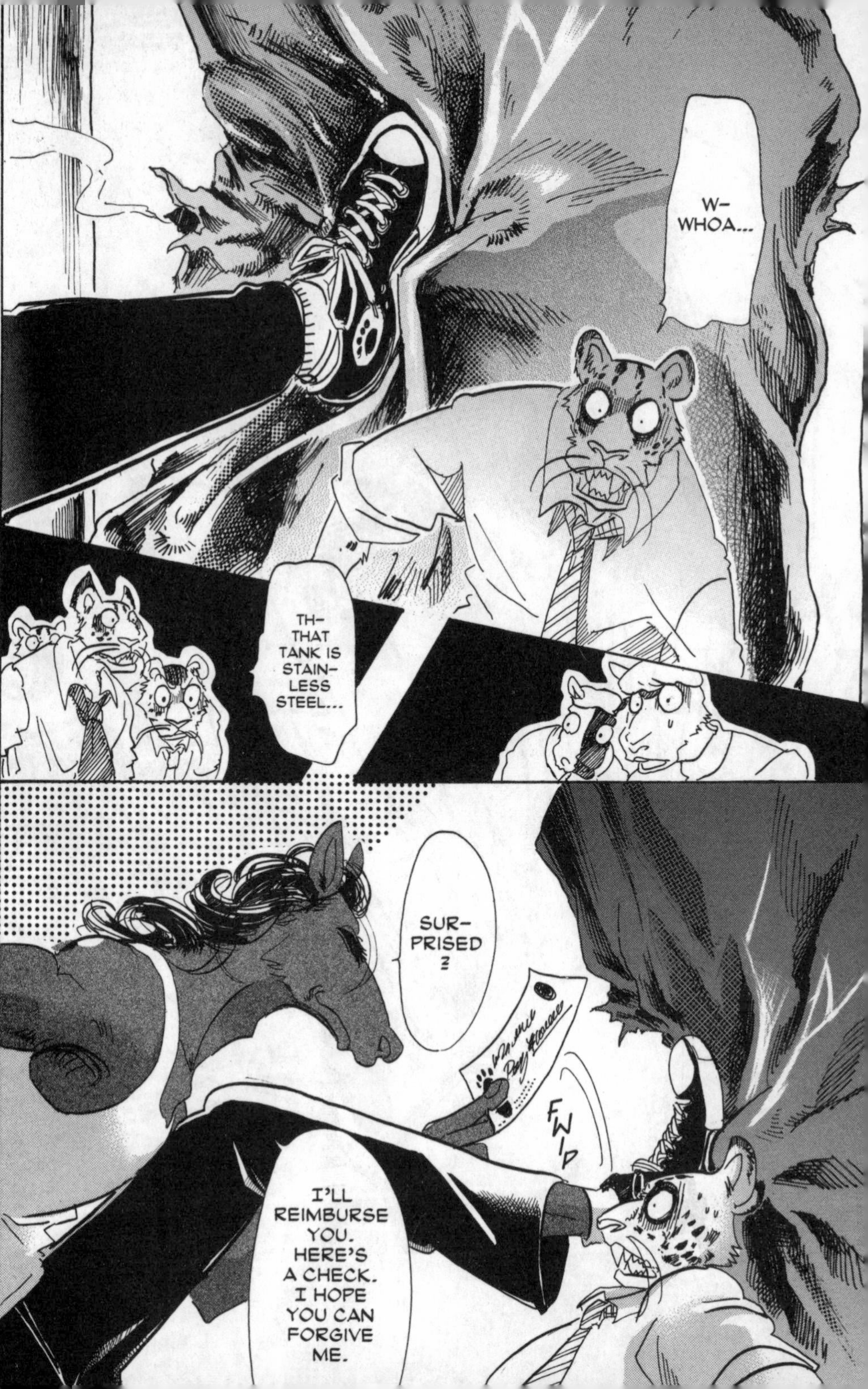
W-WHOA...
TH-THAT TANK IS STAINLESS STEEL...
SURPRISED?
FWIP
I'LL REIMBURSE YOU. HERE'S A CHECK. I HOPE YOU CAN FORGIVE ME.

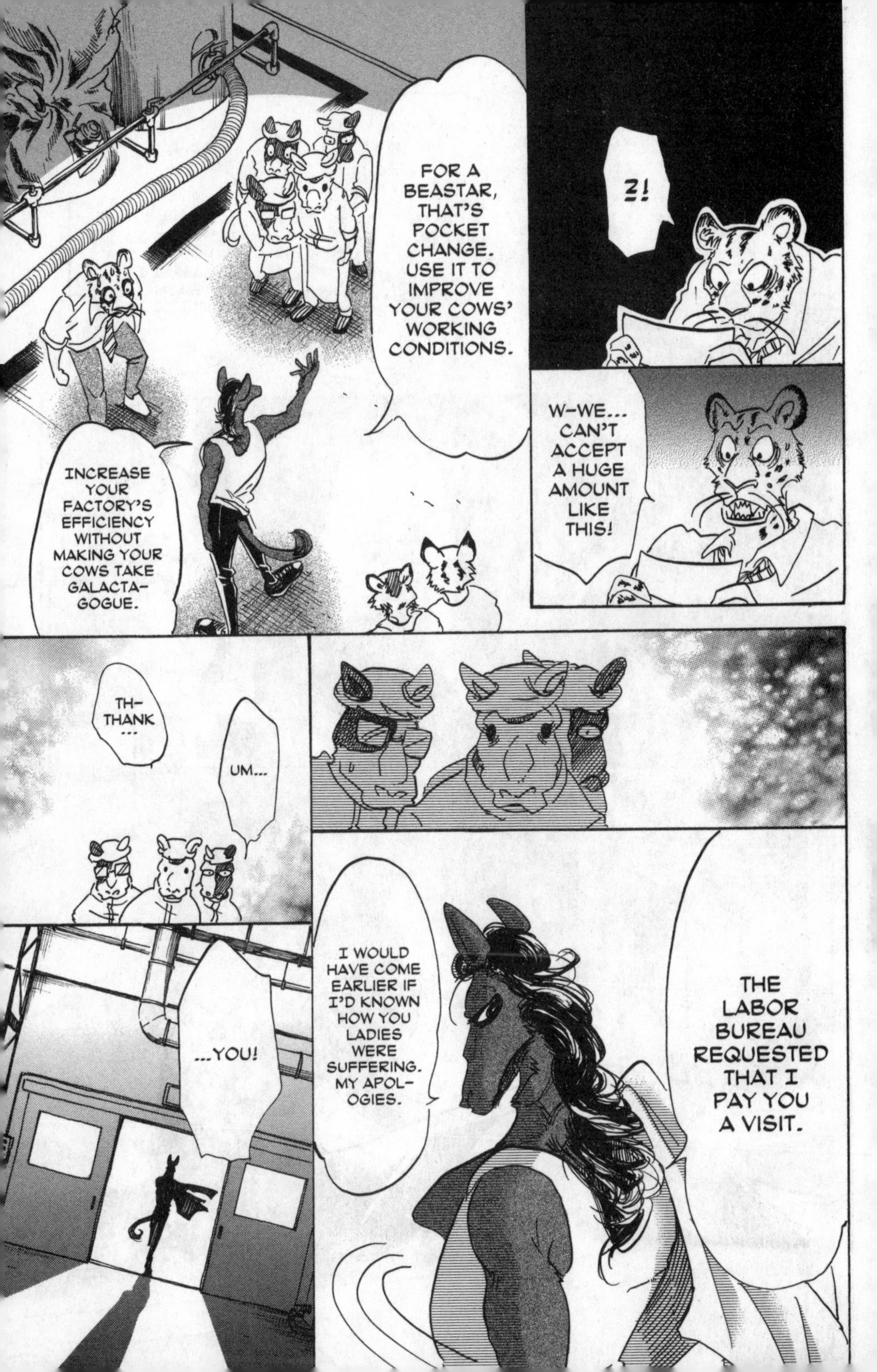
?!
W-WE... CAN'T ACCEPT A HUGE AMOUNT LIKE THIS!
FOR A BEASTAR, THAT'S POCKET CHANGE. USE IT TO IMPROVE YOUR COWS' WORKING CONDITIONS.
INCREASE YOUR FACTORY'S EFFICIENCY WITHOUT MAKING YOUR COWS TAKE GALACTA-GOGUE.
TH-THANK...
UM...
THE LABOR BUREAU REQUESTED THAT I PAY YOU A VISIT.
I WOULD HAVE COME EARLIER IF I'D KNOWN HOW YOU LADIES WERE SUFFERING. MY APOLO-GIES.
...YOU!

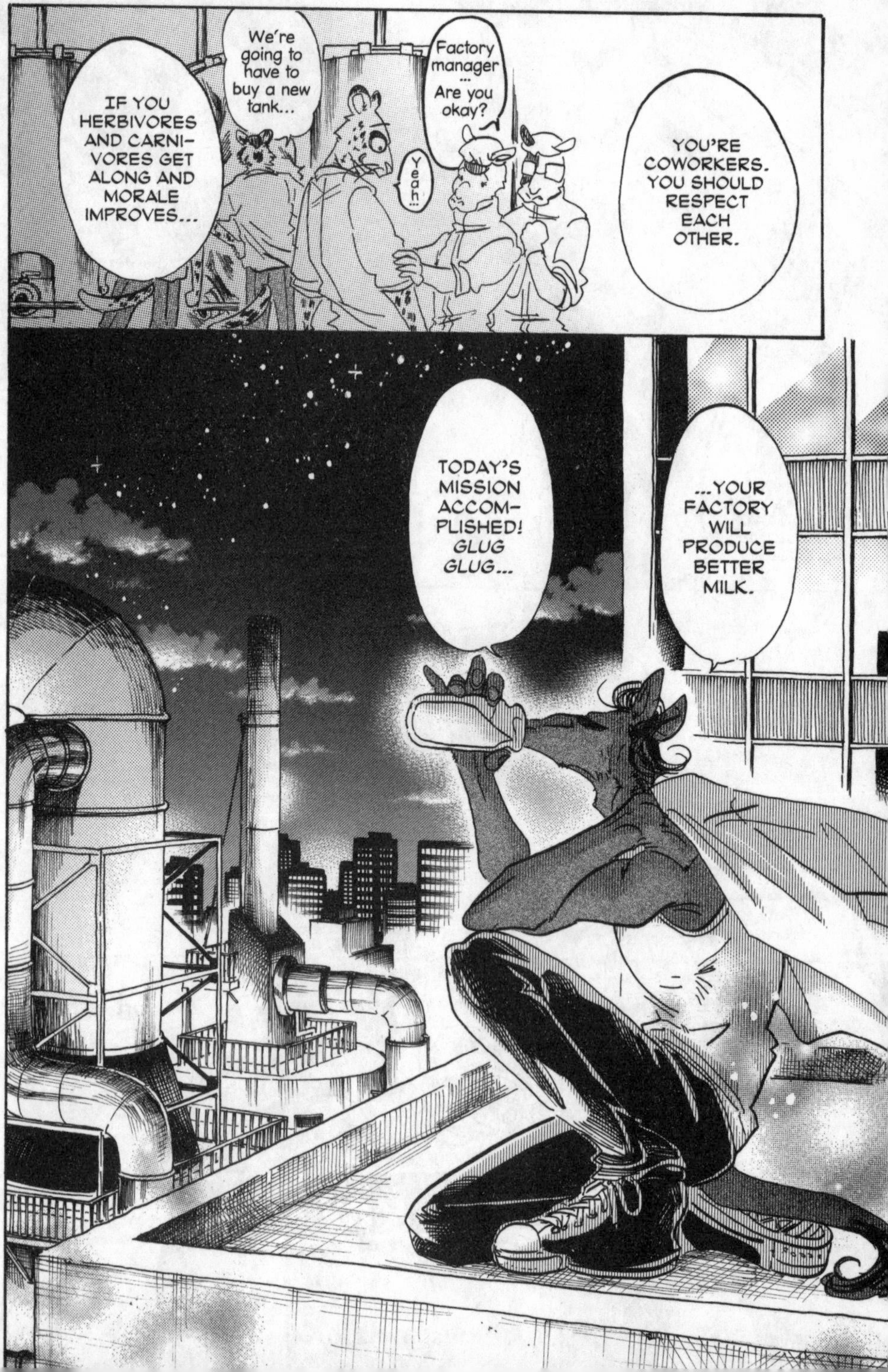
YOU'RE COWORKERS. YOU SHOULD RESPECT EACH OTHER.
Factory manager ... Are you okay?
Yeah...
We're going to have to buy a new tank...
IF YOU HERBIVORES AND CARNIVORES GET ALONG AND MORALE IMPROVES...
...YOUR FACTORY WILL PRODUCE BETTER MILK.
TODAY'S MISSION ACCOMPLISHED! GLUG GLUG...

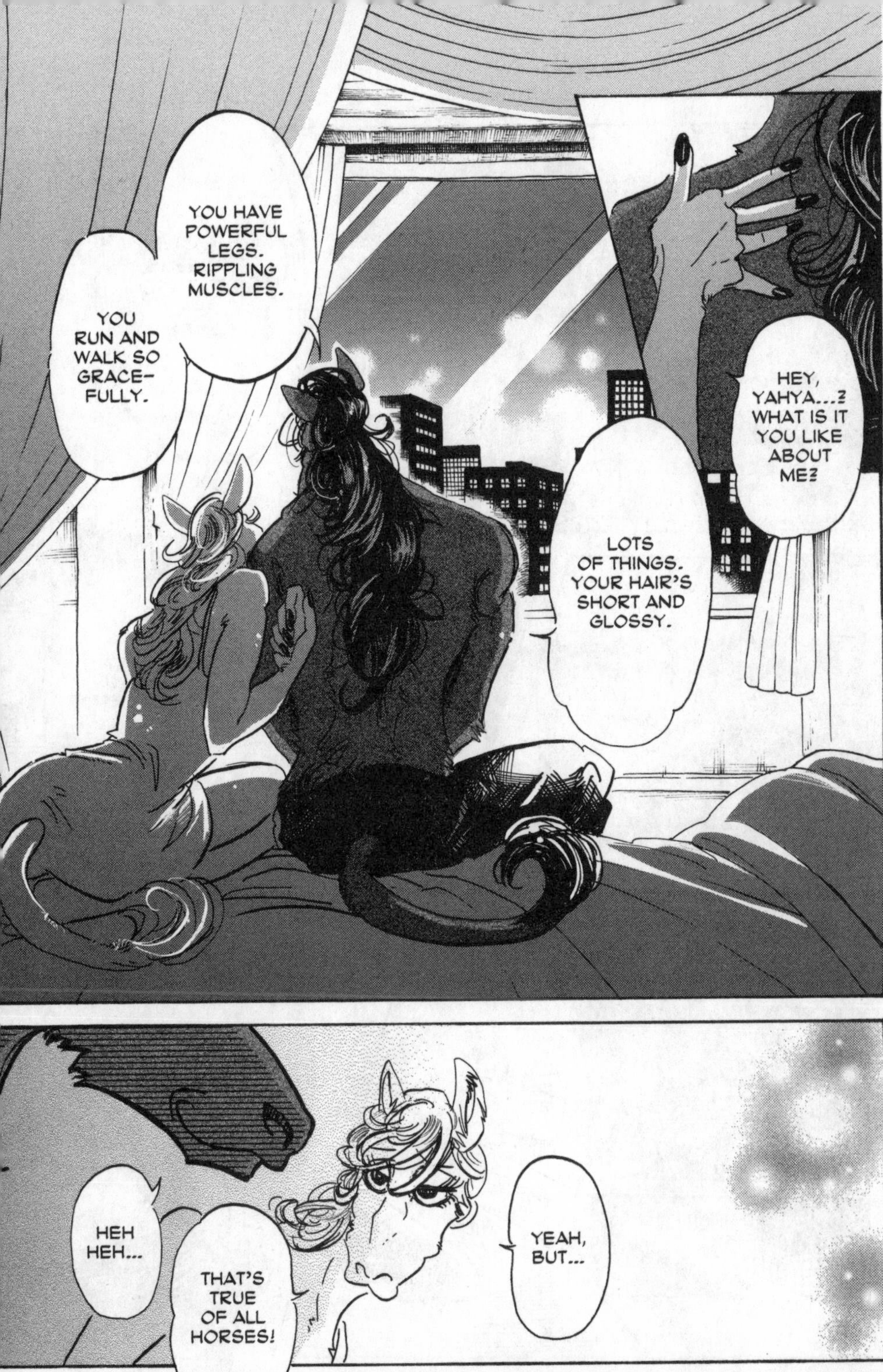
HEY, YAHYA...? WHAT IS IT YOU LIKE ABOUT ME?
LOTS OF THINGS. YOUR HAIR'S SHORT AND GLOSSY.
YOU HAVE POWERFUL LEGS. RIPPLING MUSCLES.
YOU RUN AND WALK SO GRACE-FULLY.
YEAH, BUT...
THAT'S TRUE OF ALL HORSES!
HEH HEH...

Chapter 103: Rainfall After Seeds Are Sown

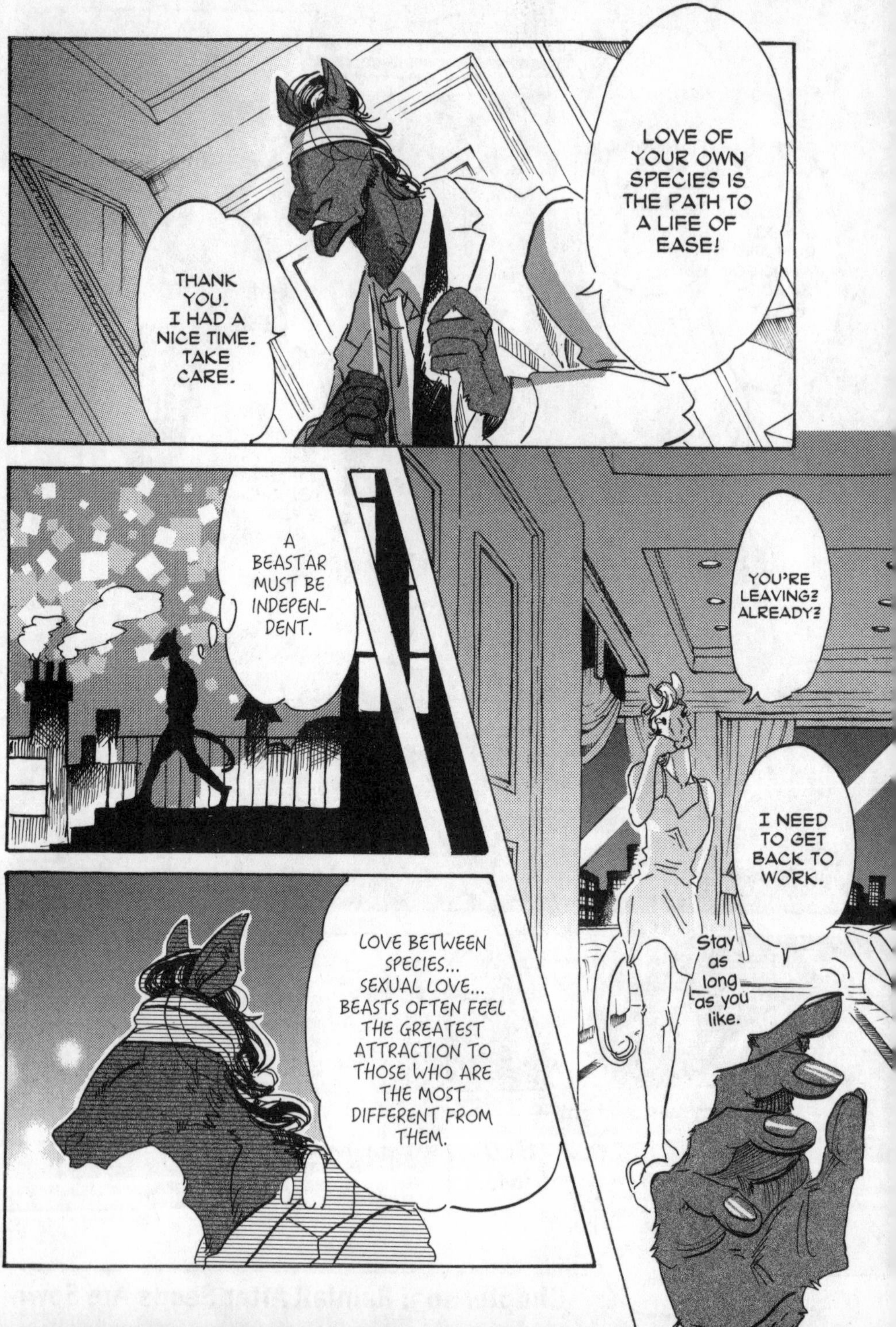
LOVE OF YOUR OWN SPECIES IS THE PATH TO A LIFE OF EASE!
THANK YOU. I HAD A NICE TIME. TAKE CARE.
YOU'RE LEAVING? ALREADY?
I NEED TO GET BACK TO WORK.
Stay as long as you like.
A BEASTAR MUST BE INDEPENDENT.
LOVE BETWEEN SPECIES... SEXUAL LOVE... BEASTS OFTEN FEEL THE GREATEST ATTRACTION TO THOSE WHO ARE THE MOST DIFFERENT FROM THEM.

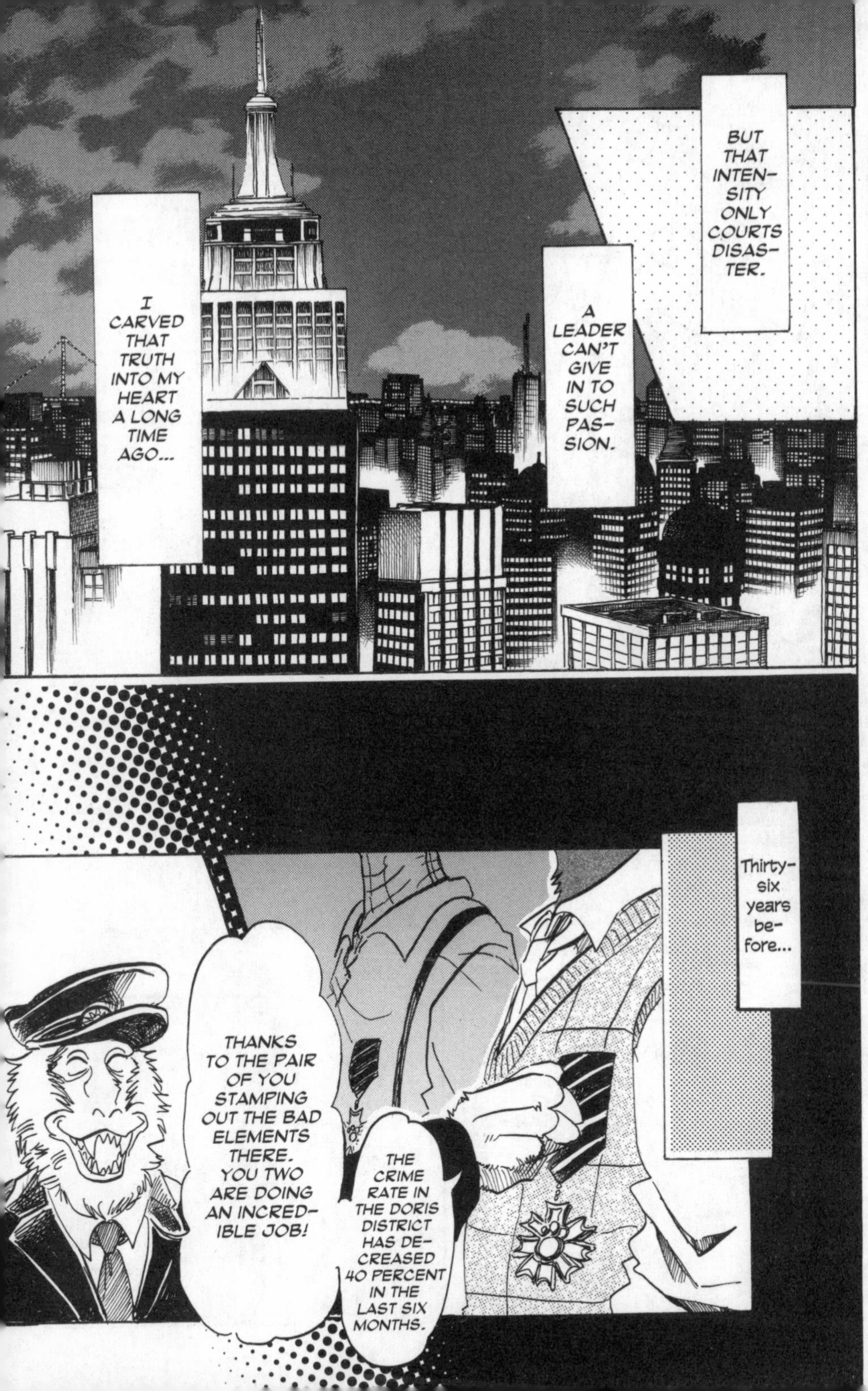
BUT THAT INTEN-SITY ONLY COURTS DISAS-TER.
A LEADER CAN'T GIVE IN TO SUCH PAS-SION.
I CARVED THAT TRUTH INTO MY HEART A LONG TIME AGO...
Thirty-six years be-fore...
THE CRIME RATE IN THE DORIS DISTRICT HAS DE-CREASED 40 PERCENT IN THE LAST SIX MONTHS.
THANKS TO THE PAIR OF YOU STAMPING OUT THE BAD ELEMENTS THERE. YOU TWO ARE DOING AN INCRED-IBLE JOB!

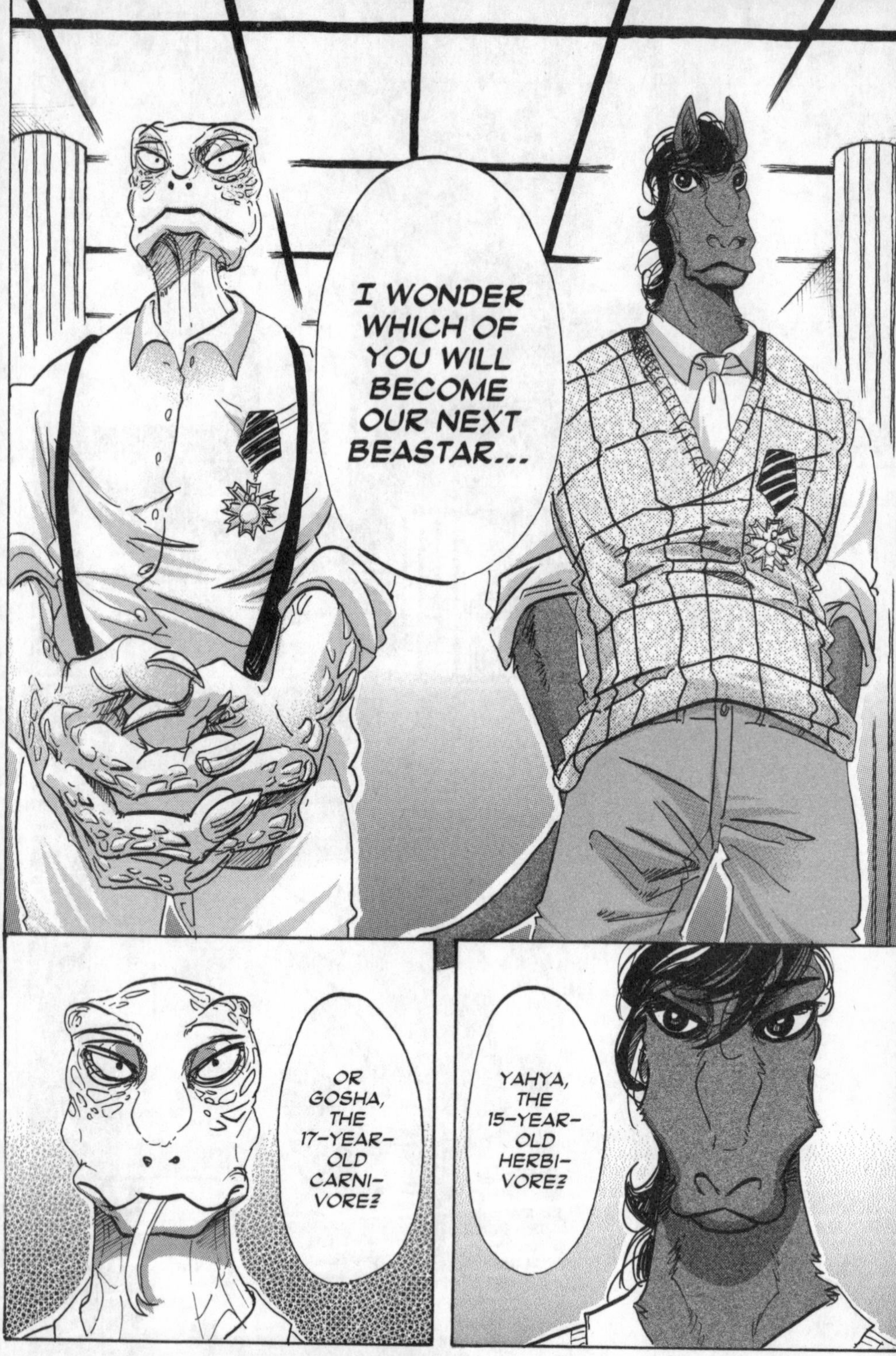
I WONDER WHICH OF YOU WILL BECOME OUR NEXT BEASTAR...
YAHYA, THE 15-YEAR-OLD HERBIVORE?
OR GOSHA, THE 17-YEAR-OLD CARNIVORE?

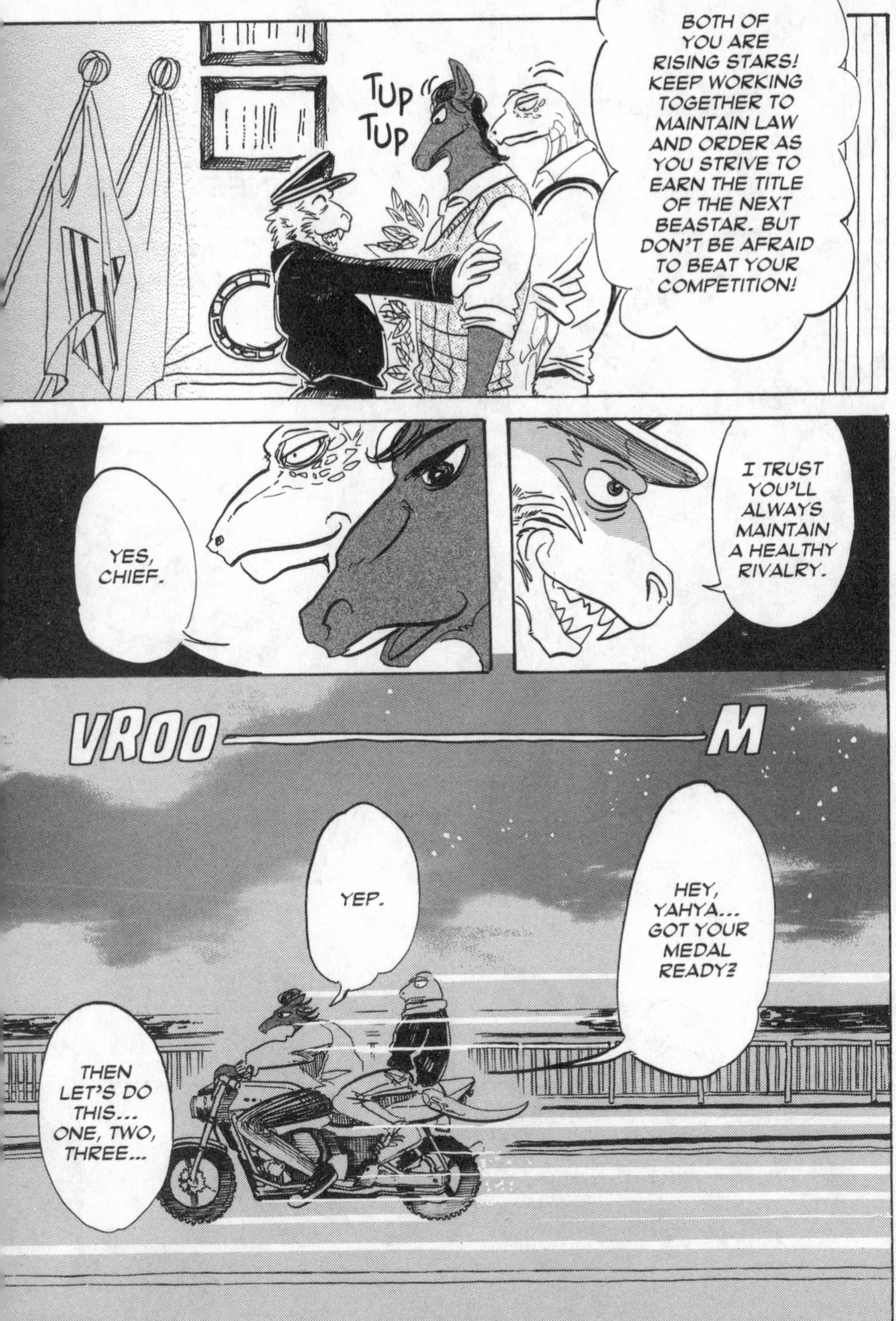
BOTH OF YOU ARE RISING STARS! KEEP WORKING TOGETHER TO MAINTAIN LAW AND ORDER AS YOU STRIVE TO EARN THE TITLE OF THE NEXT BEASTAR. BUT DON'T BE AFRAID TO BEAT YOUR COMPETITION!
TUP TUP
I TRUST YOU'LL ALWAYS MAINTAIN A HEALTHY RIVALRY.
YES, CHIEF.
VROO——M
HEY, YAHYA... GOT YOUR MEDAL READY?
YEP.
THEN LET'S DO THIS... ONE, TWO, THREE...

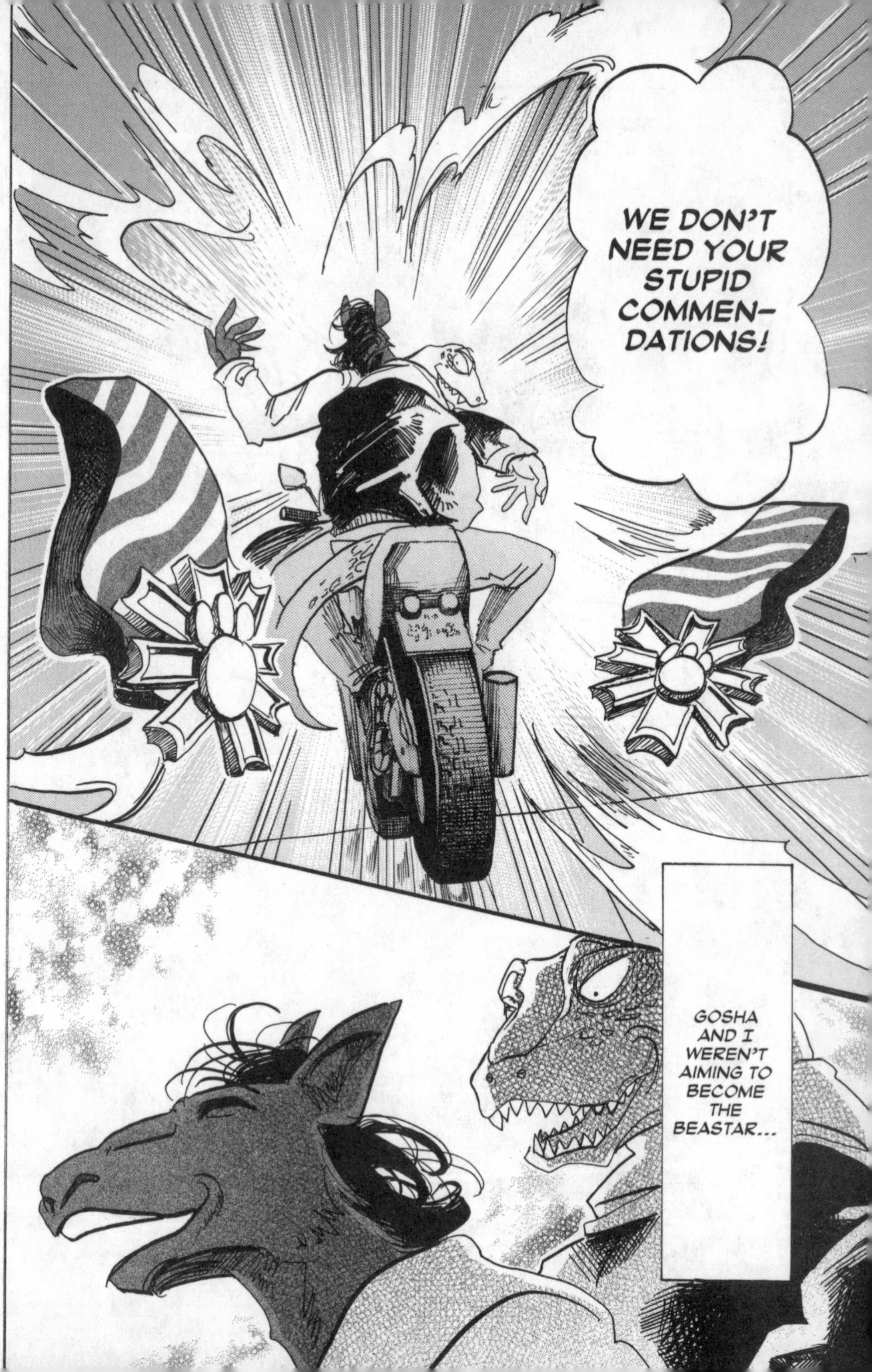
WE DON'T NEED YOUR STUPID COMMEN-DATIONS!
GOSHA AND I WEREN'T AIMING TO BECOME THE BEASTAR...

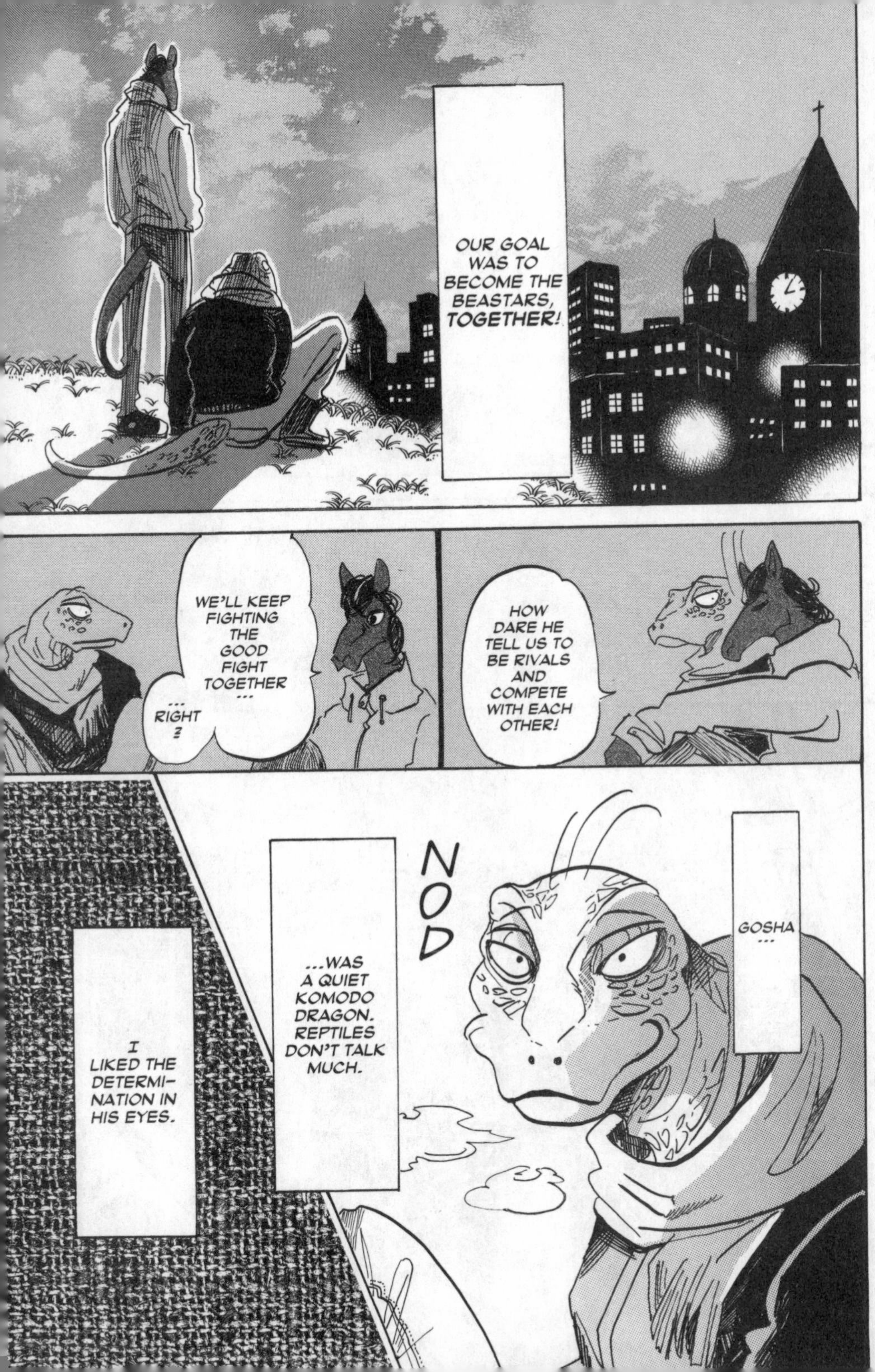
OUR GOAL WAS TO BECOME THE BEASTARS, TOGETHER!
HOW DARE HE TELL US TO BE RIVALS AND COMPETE WITH EACH OTHER!
WE'LL KEEP FIGHTING THE GOOD FIGHT TOGETHER... ...RIGHT?
GOSHA...
NOD
...WAS A QUIET KOMODO DRAGON. REPTILES DON'T TALK MUCH.
I LIKED THE DETERMINATION IN HIS EYES.

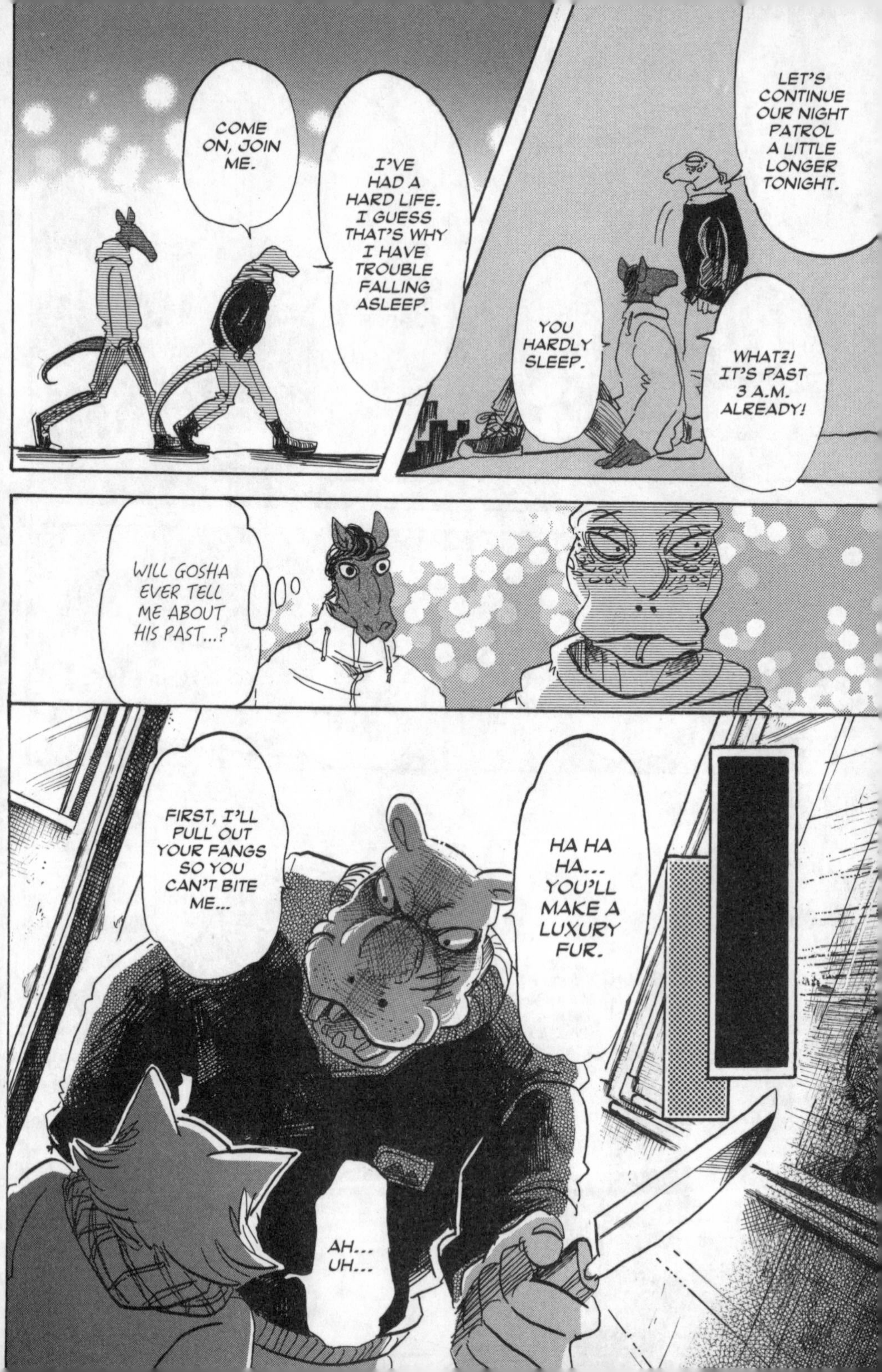
LET'S CONTINUE OUR NIGHT PATROL A LITTLE LONGER TONIGHT.
WHAT?! IT'S PAST 3 A.M. ALREADY!
YOU HARDLY SLEEP.
I'VE HAD A HARD LIFE. I GUESS THAT'S WHY I HAVE TROUBLE FALLING ASLEEP.
COME ON, JOIN ME.
WILL GOSHA EVER TELL ME ABOUT HIS PAST...?
HA HA HA... YOU'LL MAKE A LUXURY FUR.
FIRST, I'LL PULL OUT YOUR FANGS SO YOU CAN'T BITE ME...
AH... UH...

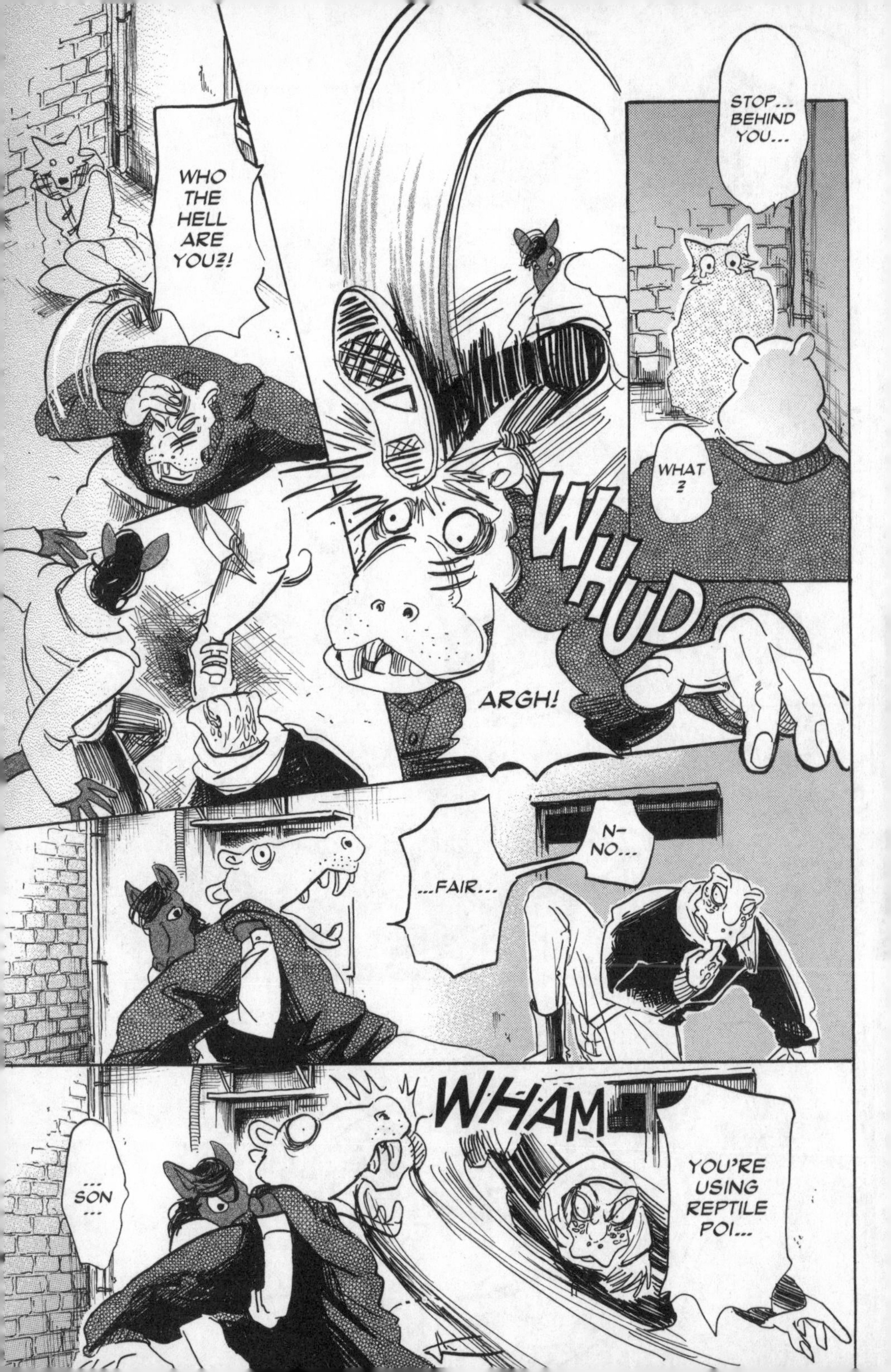
STOP... BEHIND YOU...
WHAT?
WHO THE HELL ARE YOU?!
WHUD
ARGH!
N-NO...
...FAIR...
YOU'RE USING REPTILE POI...
WHAM
...SON...

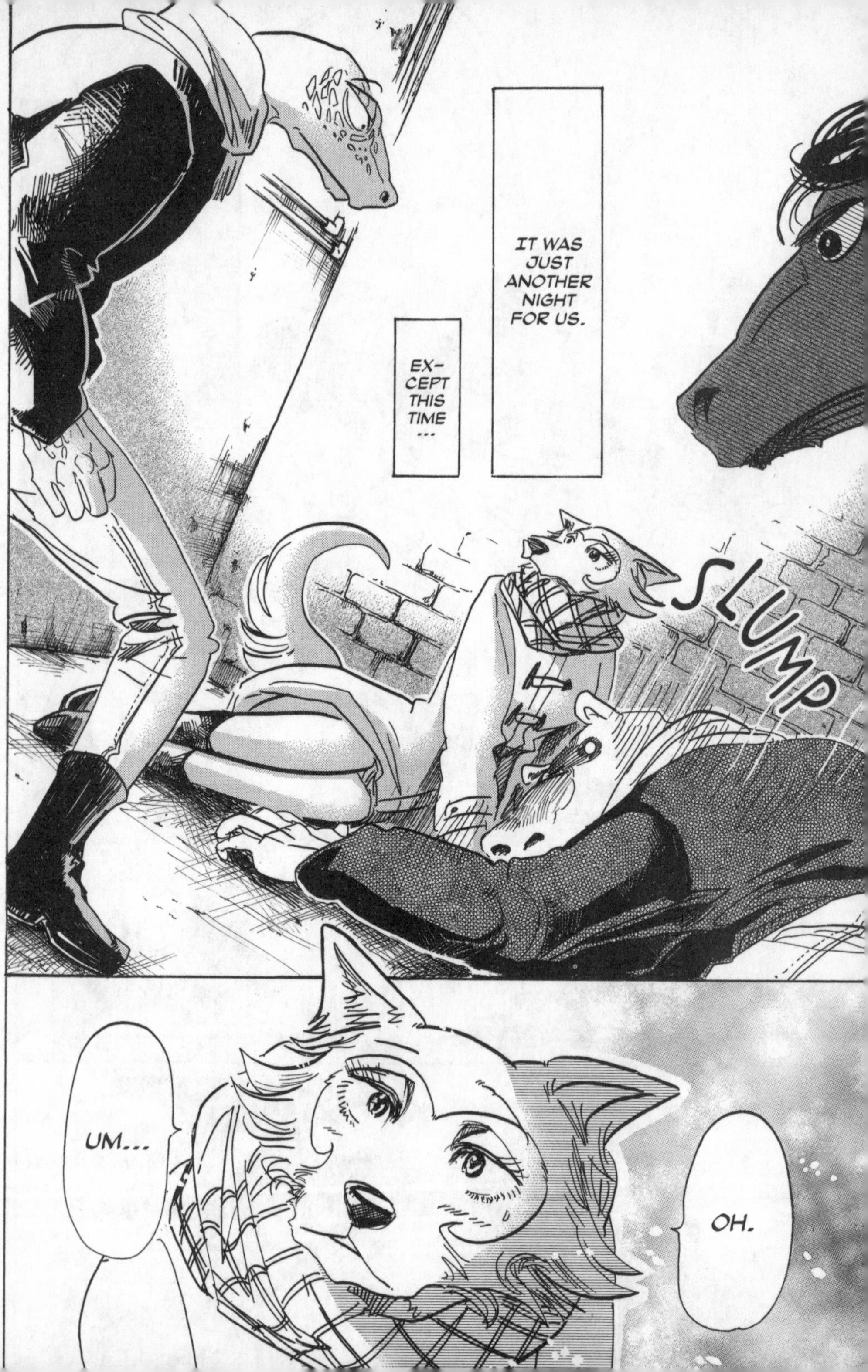
IT WAS JUST ANOTHER NIGHT FOR US.
EX-CEPT THIS TIME ...
SLUMP
OH.
UM...

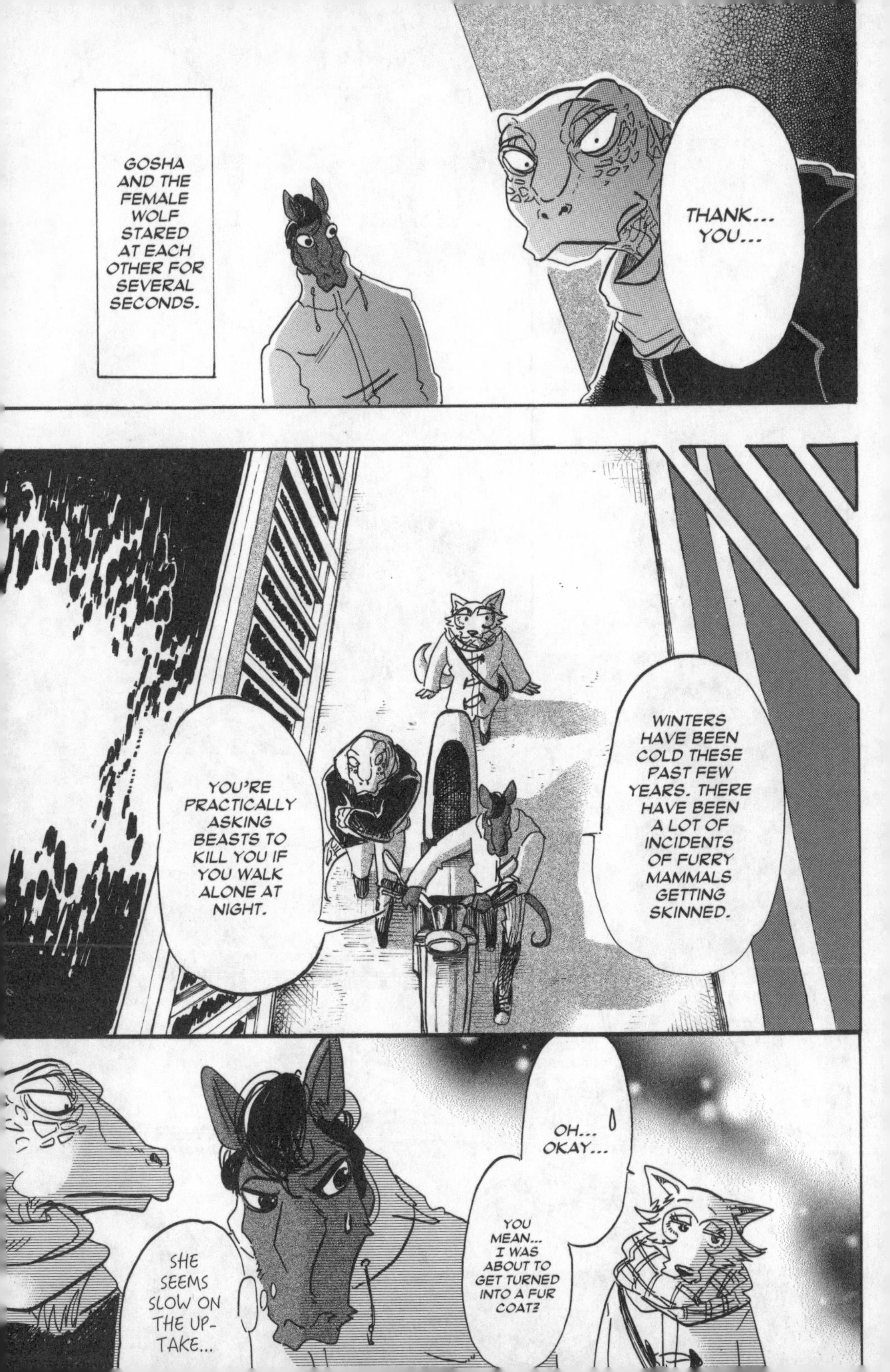
THANK... YOU...
GOSHA AND THE FEMALE WOLF STARED AT EACH OTHER FOR SEVERAL SECONDS.
WINTERS HAVE BEEN COLD THESE PAST FEW YEARS. THERE HAVE BEEN A LOT OF INCIDENTS OF FURRY MAMMALS GETTING SKINNED.
YOU'RE PRACTICALLY ASKING BEASTS TO KILL YOU IF YOU WALK ALONE AT NIGHT.
OH... OKAY...
YOU MEAN... I WAS ABOUT TO GET TURNED INTO A FUR COAT?
SHE SEEMS SLOW ON THE UP-TAKE...

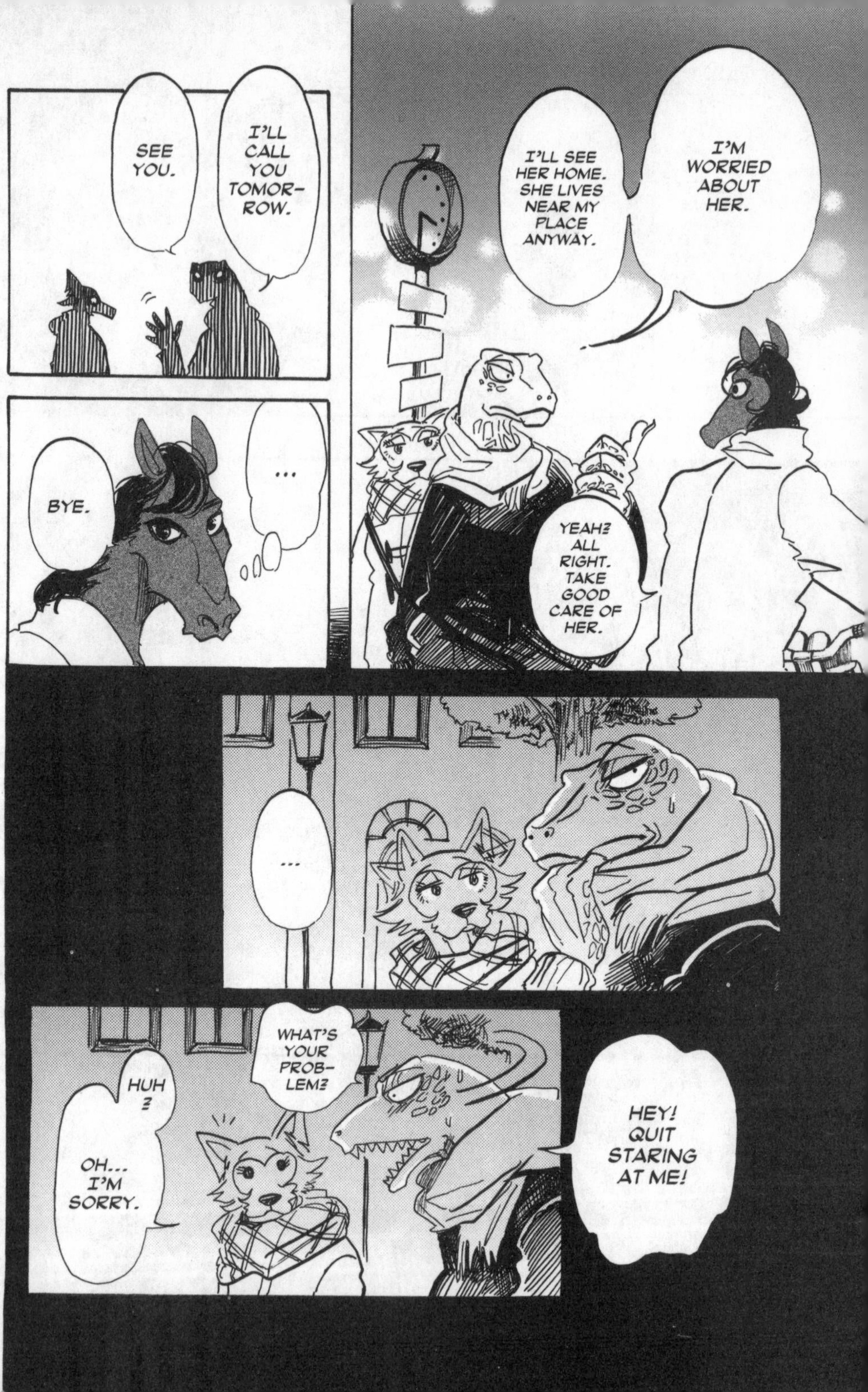
I'M WORRIED ABOUT HER.
I'LL SEE HER HOME. SHE LIVES NEAR MY PLACE ANYWAY.
YEAH? ALL RIGHT. TAKE GOOD CARE OF HER.
I'LL CALL YOU TOMORROW.
SEE YOU.
...
BYE.
...
HEY! QUIT STARING AT ME!
WHAT'S YOUR PROBLEM?
HUH?
OH... I'M SORRY.

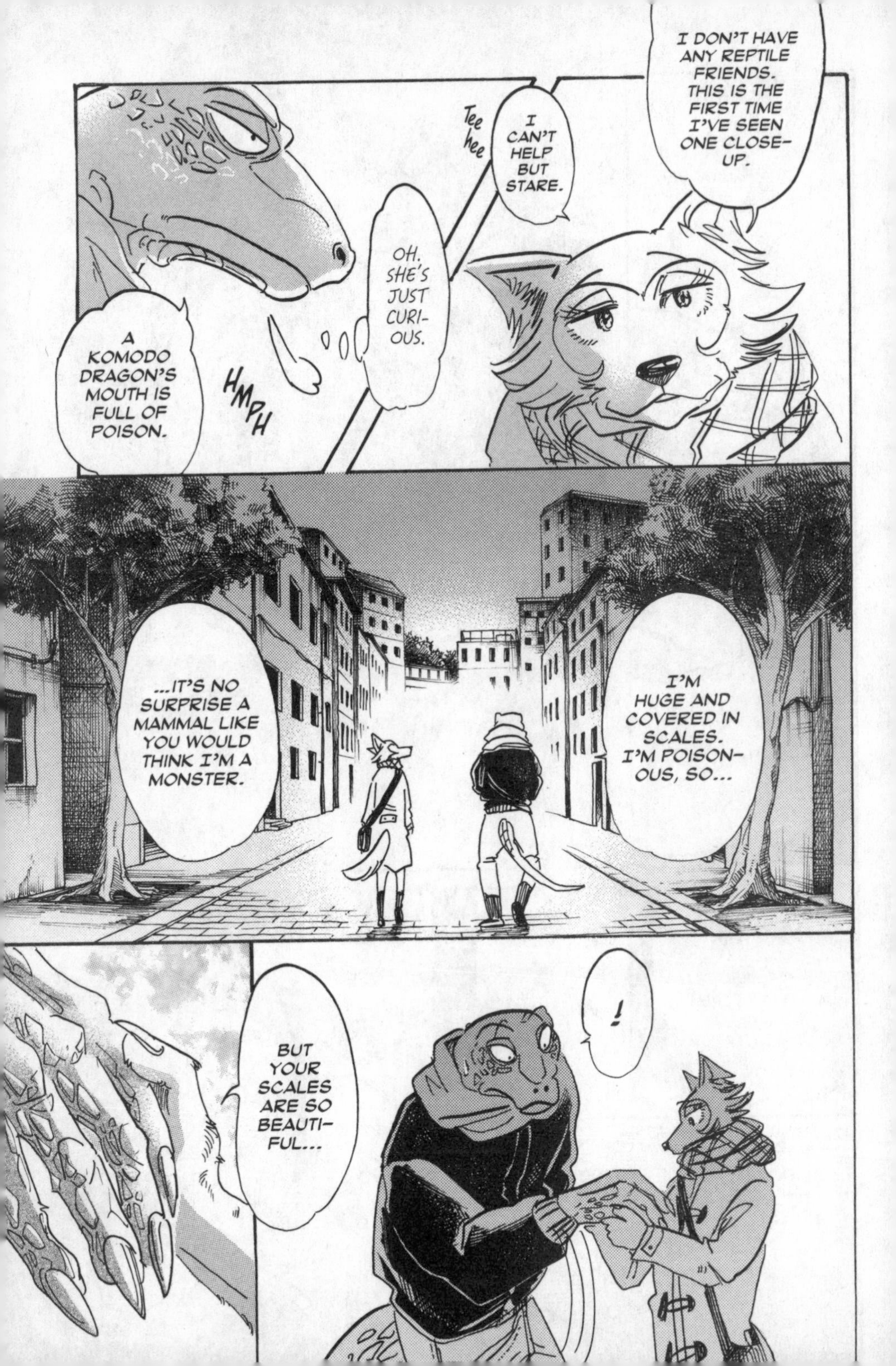
I DON'T HAVE ANY REPTILE FRIENDS. THIS IS THE FIRST TIME I'VE SEEN ONE CLOSE-UP.
Tee hee
I CAN'T HELP BUT STARE.
OH. SHE'S JUST CURIOUS.
HMPH
A KOMODO DRAGON'S MOUTH IS FULL OF POISON.
I'M HUGE AND COVERED IN SCALES. I'M POISONOUS, SO...
...IT'S NO SURPRISE A MAMMAL LIKE YOU WOULD THINK I'M A MONSTER.
!
BUT YOUR SCALES ARE SO BEAUTIFUL...

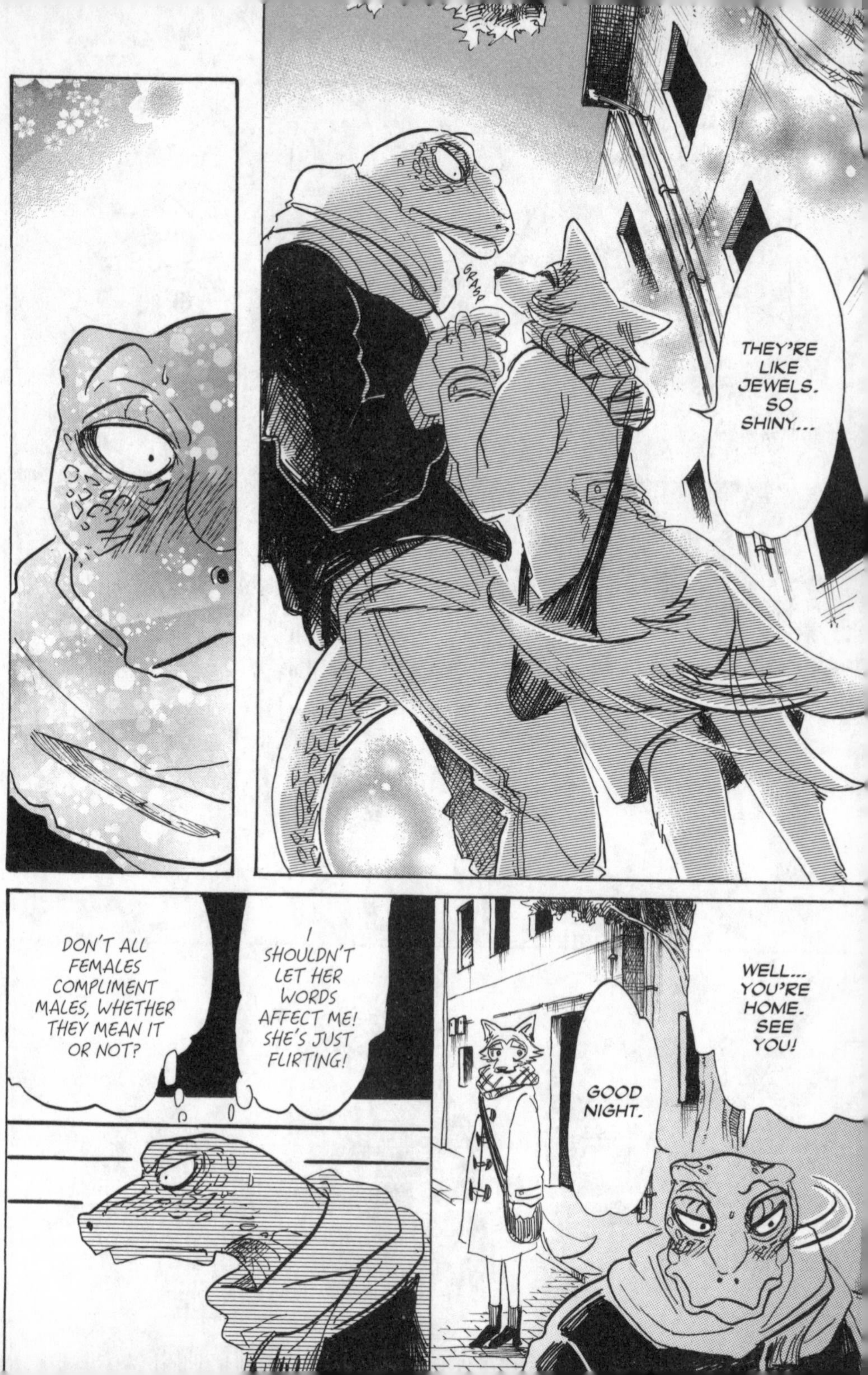
GRASP
THEY'RE LIKE JEWELS. SO SHINY...
WELL... YOU'RE HOME. SEE YOU!
GOOD NIGHT.
I SHOULDN'T LET HER WORDS AFFECT ME! SHE'S JUST FLIRTING!
DON'T ALL FEMALES COMPLIMENT MALES, WHETHER THEY MEAN IT OR NOT?

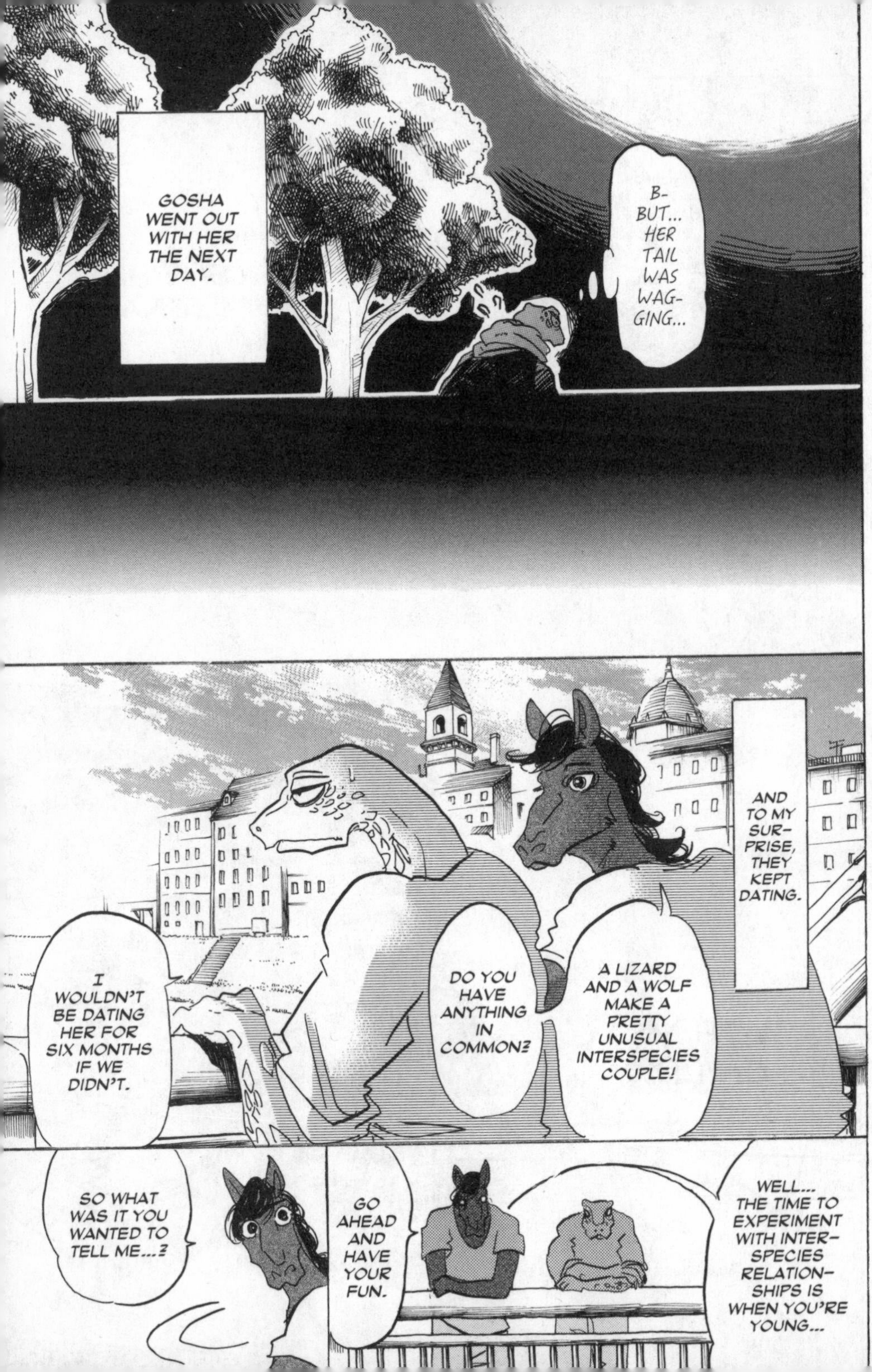
B-BUT... HER TAIL WAS WAGGING...
GOSHA WENT OUT WITH HER THE NEXT DAY.
AND TO MY SURPRISE, THEY KEPT DATING.
A LIZARD AND A WOLF MAKE A PRETTY UNUSUAL INTERSPECIES COUPLE!
DO YOU HAVE ANYTHING IN COMMON?
I WOULDN'T BE DATING HER FOR SIX MONTHS IF WE DIDN'T.
WELL... THE TIME TO EXPERIMENT WITH INTERSPECIES RELATIONSHIPS IS WHEN YOU'RE YOUNG...
GO AHEAD AND HAVE YOUR FUN.
SO WHAT WAS IT YOU WANTED TO TELL ME...?

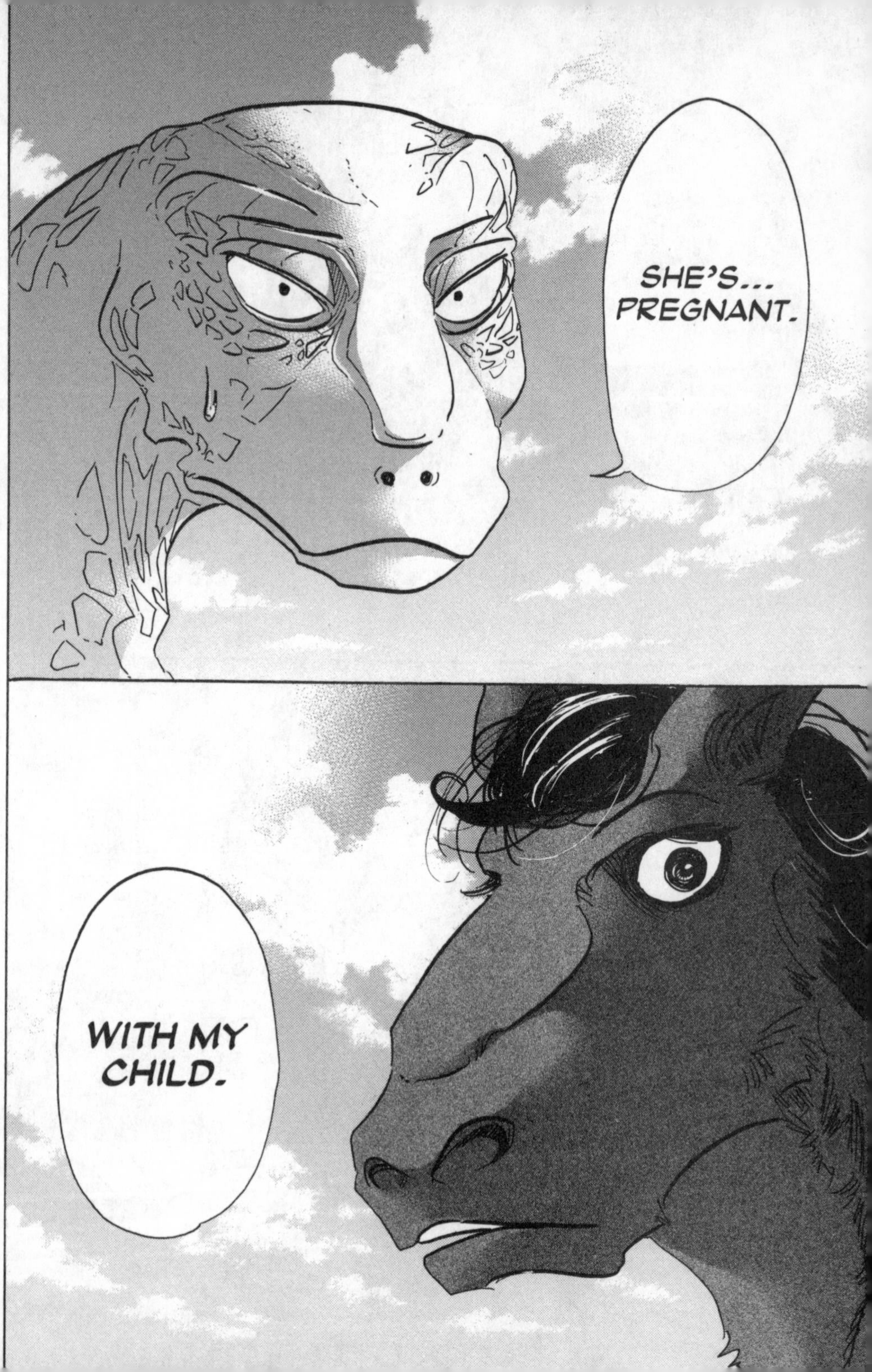
SHE'S... PREGNANT.
WITH MY CHILD.

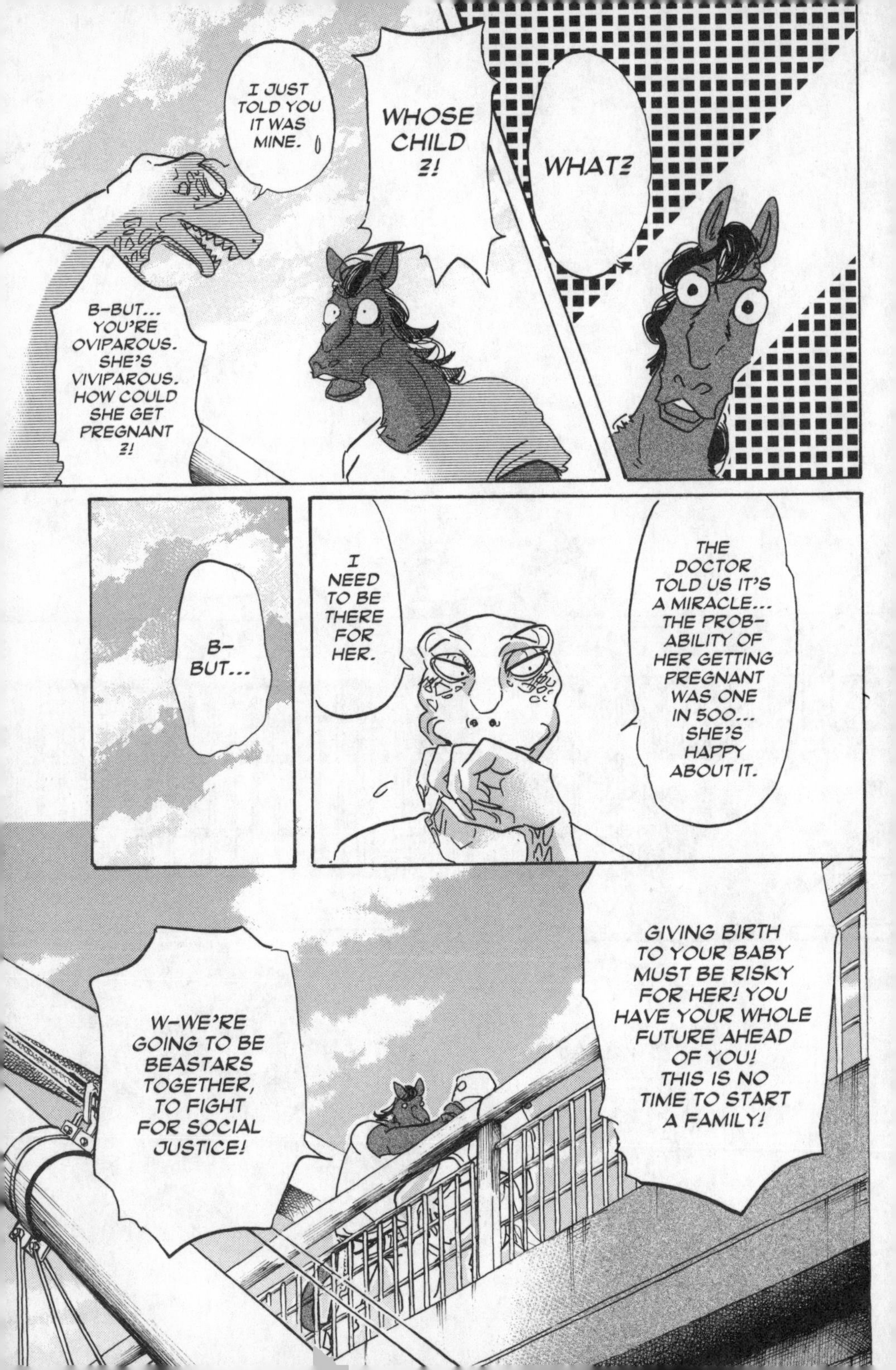
WHAT?
WHOSE CHILD ?!
I JUST TOLD YOU IT WAS MINE.
B-BUT... YOU'RE OVIPAROUS. SHE'S VIVIPAROUS. HOW COULD SHE GET PREGNANT ?!
THE DOCTOR TOLD US IT'S A MIRACLE... THE PROB-ABILITY OF HER GETTING PREGNANT WAS ONE IN 500... SHE'S HAPPY ABOUT IT.
I NEED TO BE THERE FOR HER.
B- BUT...
GIVING BIRTH TO YOUR BABY MUST BE RISKY FOR HER! YOU HAVE YOUR WHOLE FUTURE AHEAD OF YOU! THIS IS NO TIME TO START A FAMILY!
W-WE'RE GOING TO BE BEASTARS TOGETHER, TO FIGHT FOR SOCIAL JUSTICE!

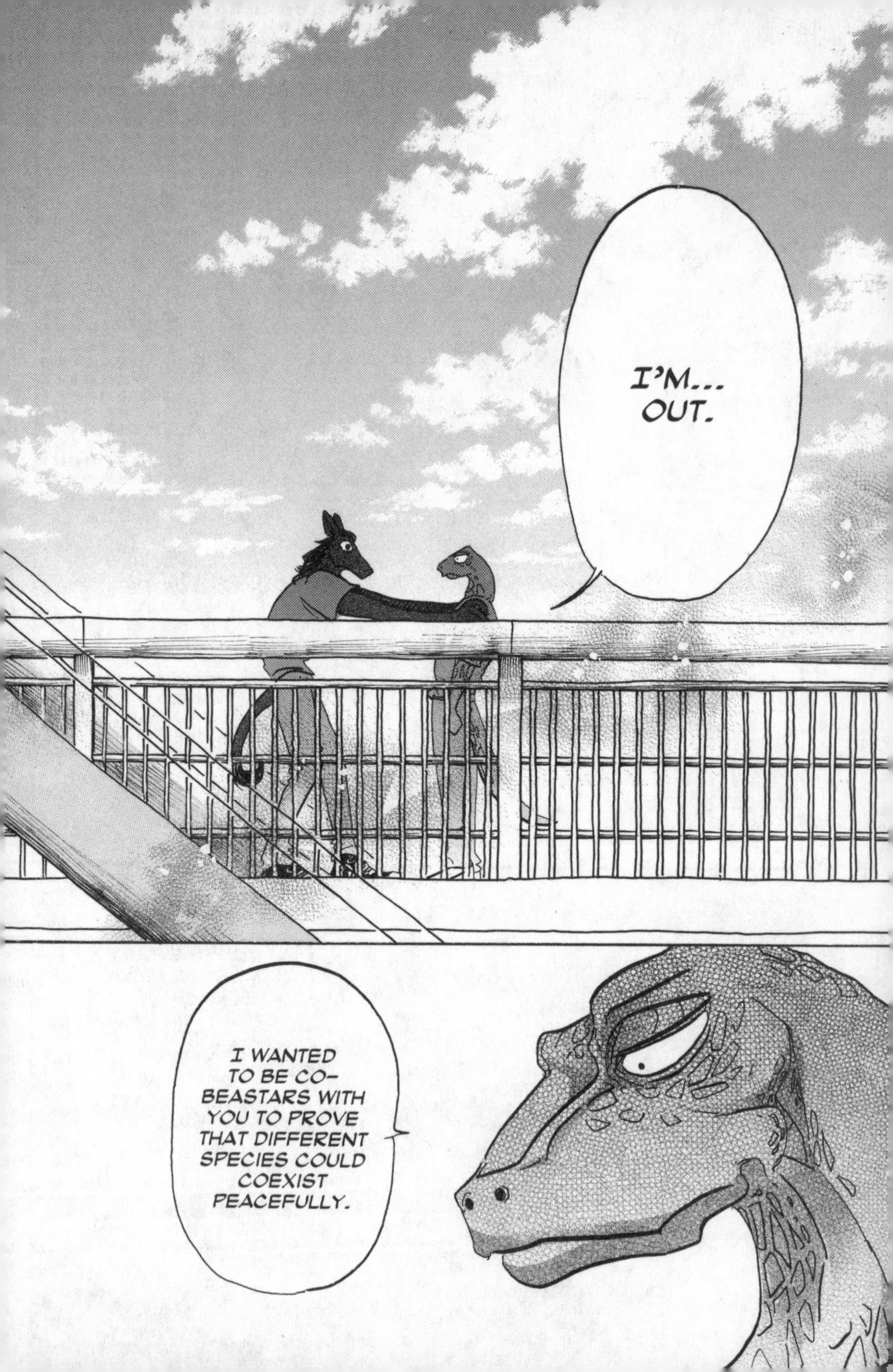
I'M... OUT.
I WANTED TO BE CO-BEASTARS WITH YOU TO PROVE THAT DIFFERENT SPECIES COULD COEXIST PEACEFULLY.

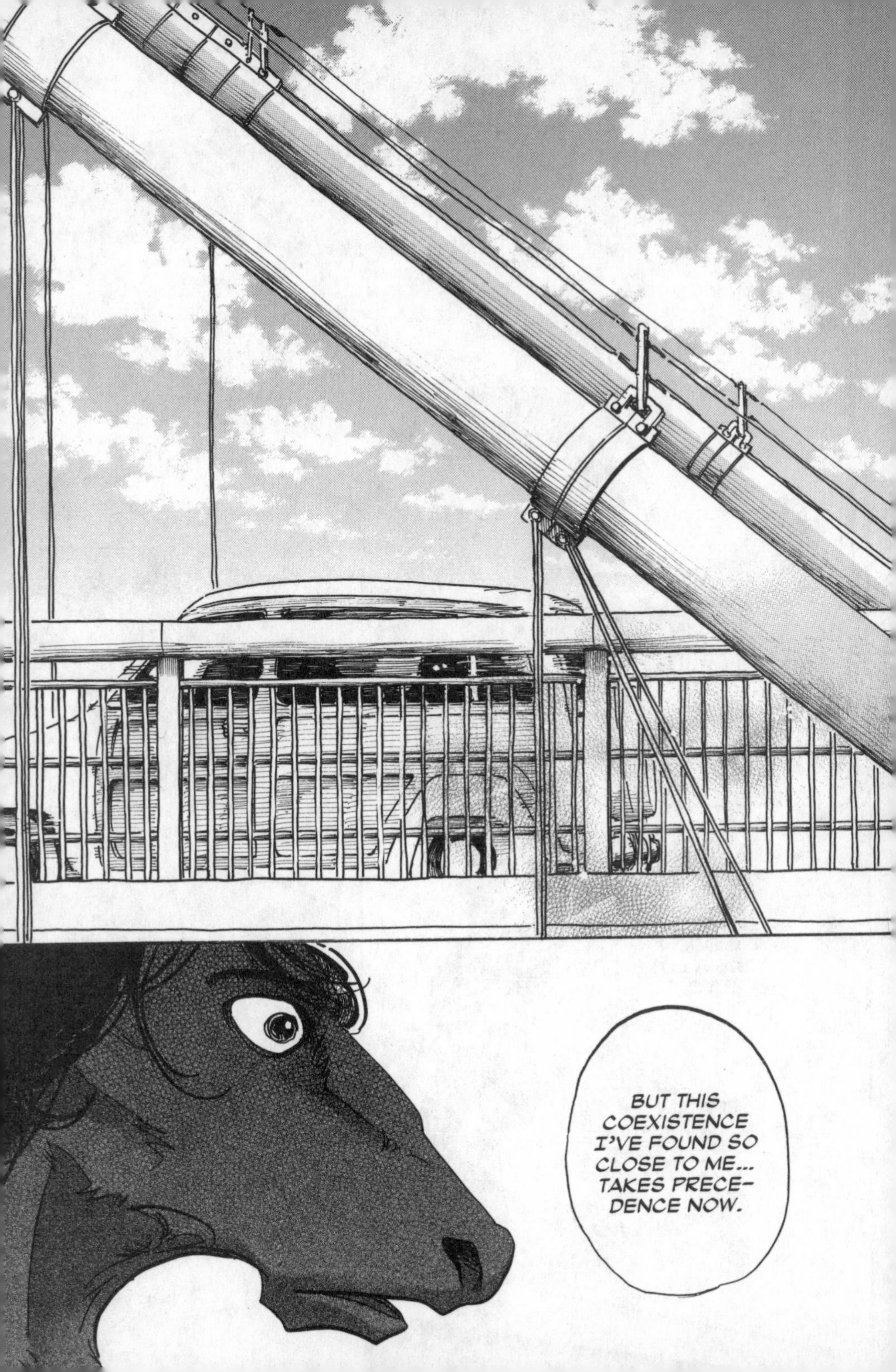
BUT THIS COEXISTENCE I'VE FOUND SO CLOSE TO ME... TAKES PRECE-DENCE NOW.

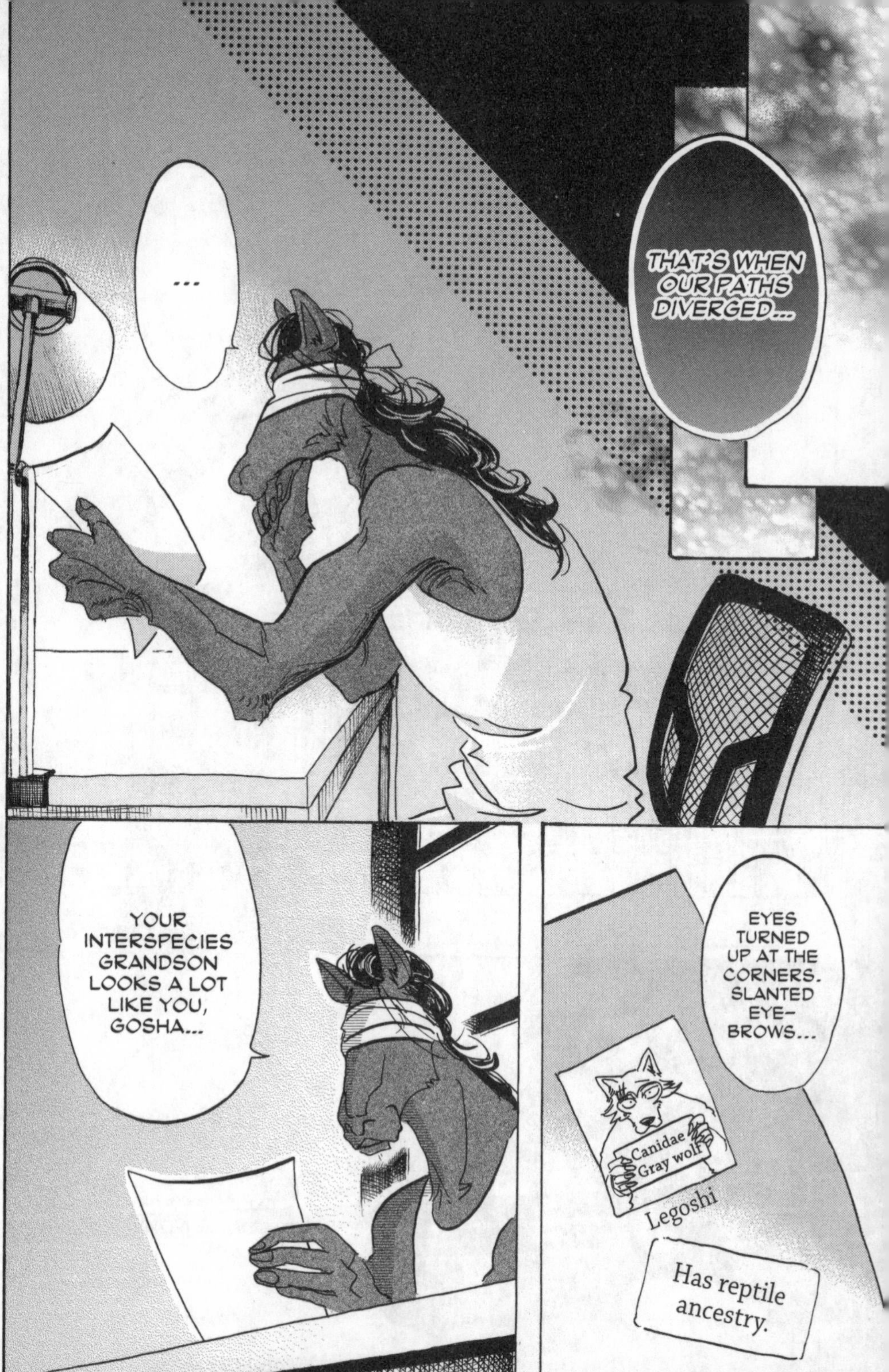
THAT'S WHEN OUR PATHS DIVERGED...
...
EYES TURNED UP AT THE CORNERS. SLANTED EYE-BROWS...
Canidae Gray wolf
Legoshi
Has reptile ancestry.
YOUR INTERSPECIES GRANDSON LOOKS A LOT LIKE YOU, GOSHA...

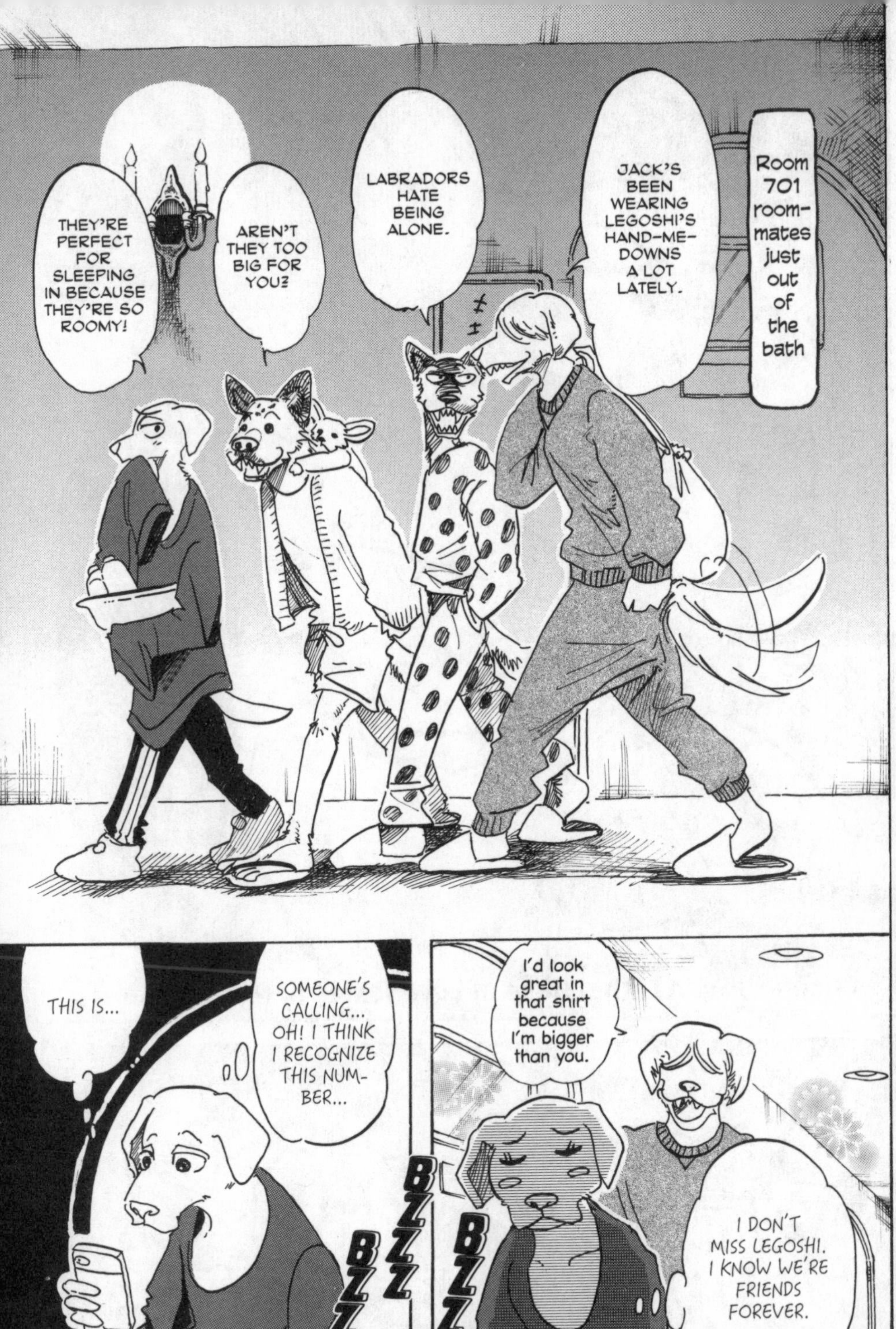
Room 701 room-mates just out of the bath
JACK'S BEEN WEARING LEGOSHI'S HAND-ME-DOWNS A LOT LATELY.
LABRADORS HATE BEING ALONE.
AREN'T THEY TOO BIG FOR YOU?
THEY'RE PERFECT FOR SLEEPING IN BECAUSE THEY'RE SO ROOMY!
I'd look great in that shirt because I'm bigger than you.
I DON'T MISS LEGOSHI. I KNOW WE'RE FRIENDS FOREVER.
BZZZ BZZZ
SOMEONE'S CALLING... OH! I THINK I RECOGNIZE THIS NUM-BER...
THIS IS...
BZZZ BZZZ

Chapter 104: A Lethal Dose of Love Tastes of Marmalade

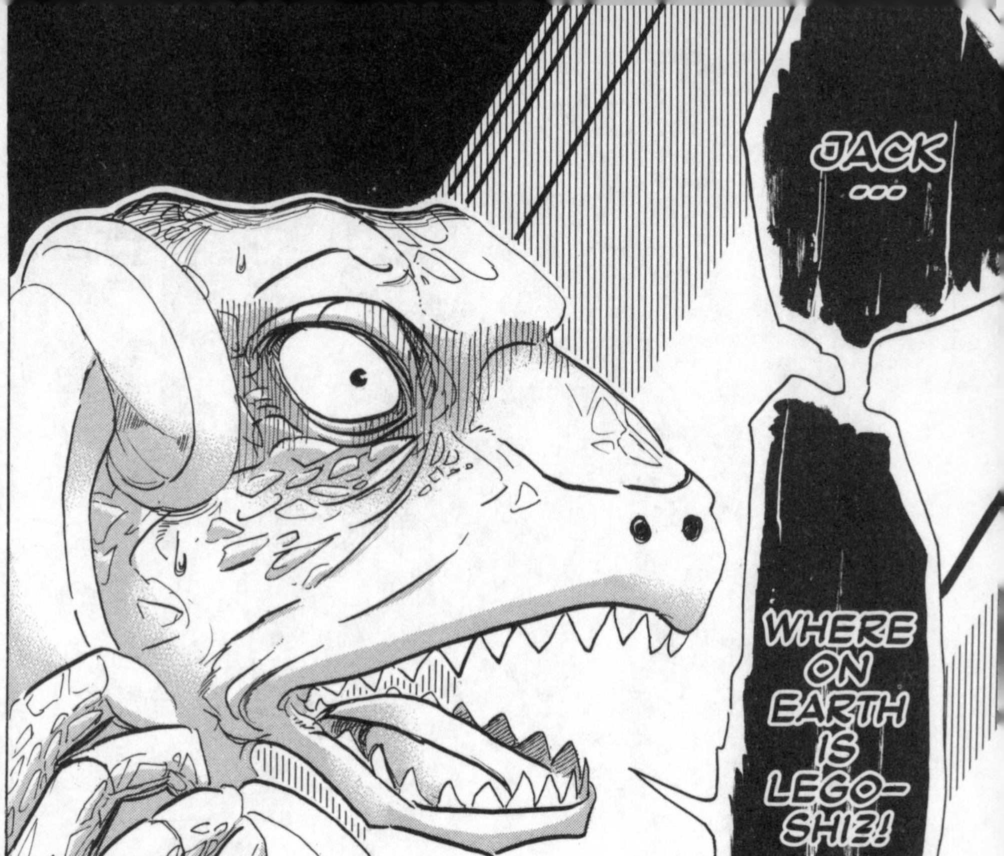
JACK...
WHERE ON EARTH IS LEGOSHI?!

Chapter 104: A Lethal Dose of Love Tastes of Marmalade

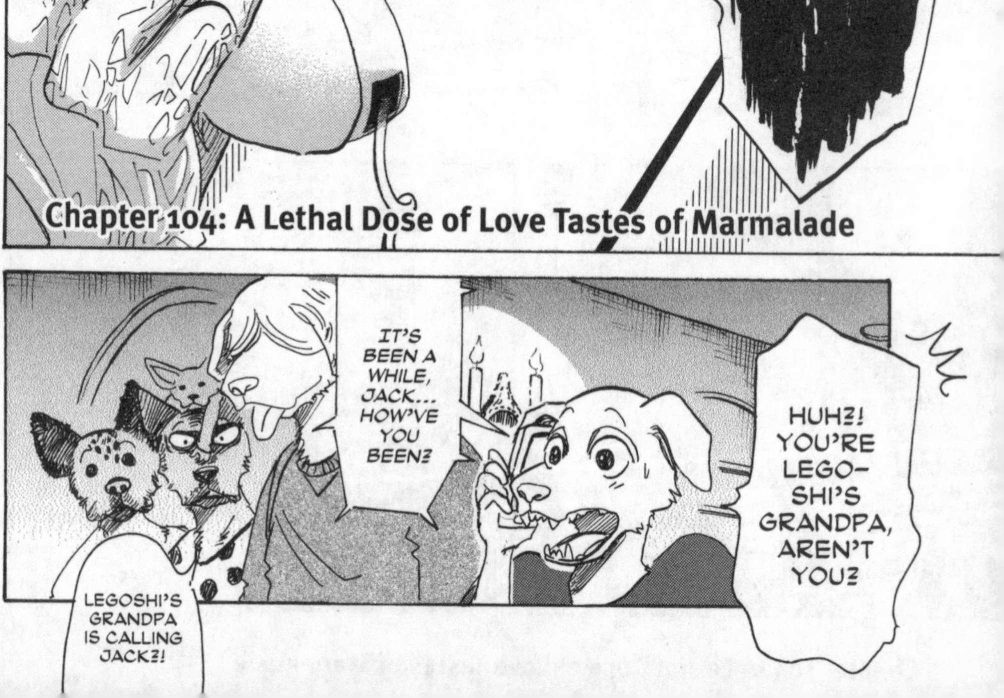
HUH?! YOU'RE LEGOSHI'S GRANDPA, AREN'T YOU?
IT'S BEEN A WHILE, JACK... HOW'VE YOU BEEN?
LEGOSHI'S GRANDPA IS CALLING JACK?!

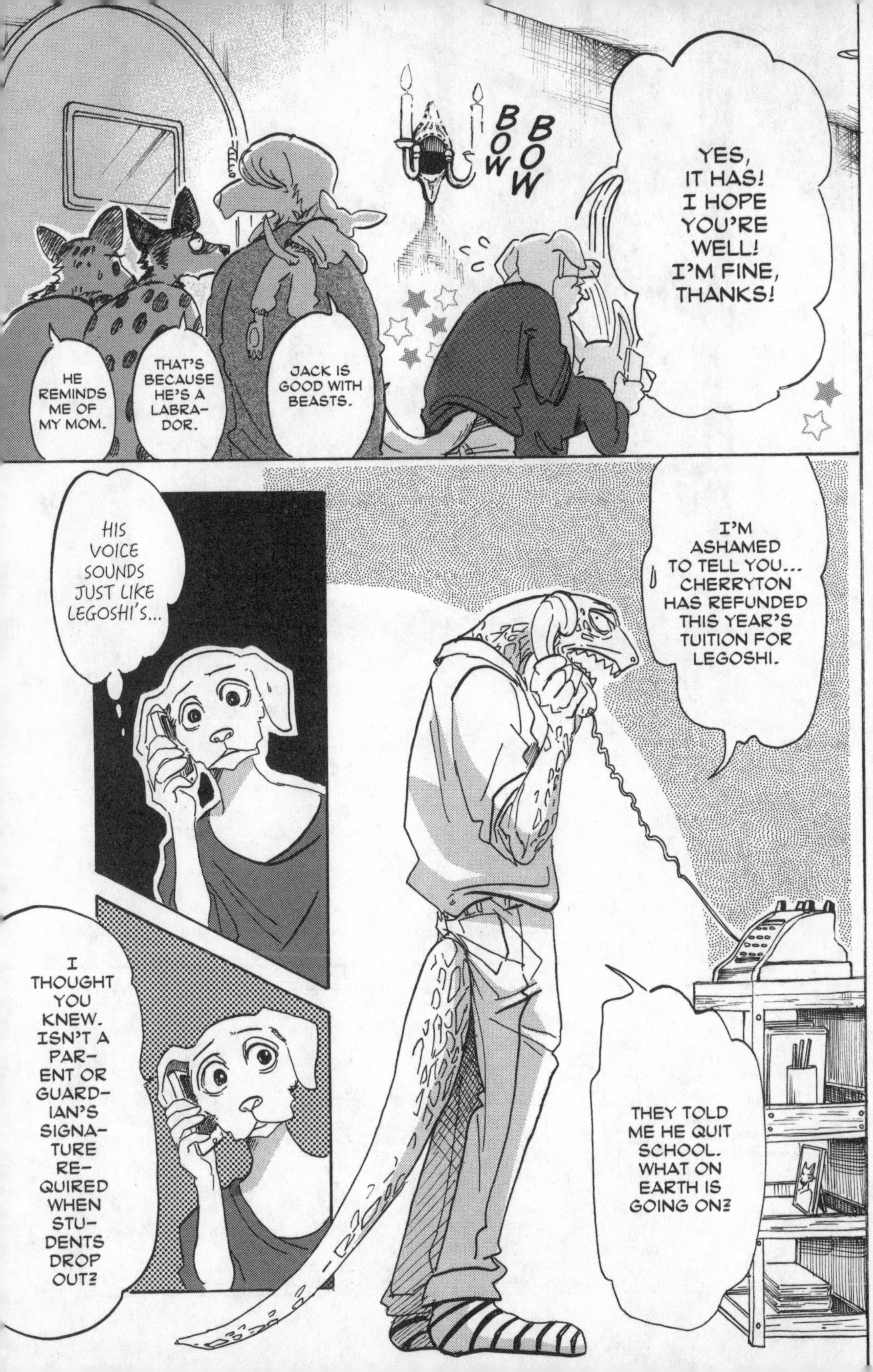
YES, IT HAS! I HOPE YOU'RE WELL! I'M FINE, THANKS!
BOW BOW
JACK IS GOOD WITH BEASTS.
THAT'S BECAUSE HE'S A LABRA-DOR.
HE REMINDS ME OF MY MOM.
I'M ASHAMED TO TELL YOU... CHERRYTON HAS REFUNDED THIS YEAR'S TUITION FOR LEGOSHI.
THEY TOLD ME HE QUIT SCHOOL. WHAT ON EARTH IS GOING ON?
HIS VOICE SOUNDS JUST LIKE LEGOSHI'S...
I THOUGHT YOU KNEW. ISN'T A PAR-ENT OR GUARD-IAN'S SIGNA-TURE RE-QUIRED WHEN STU-DENTS DROP OUT?

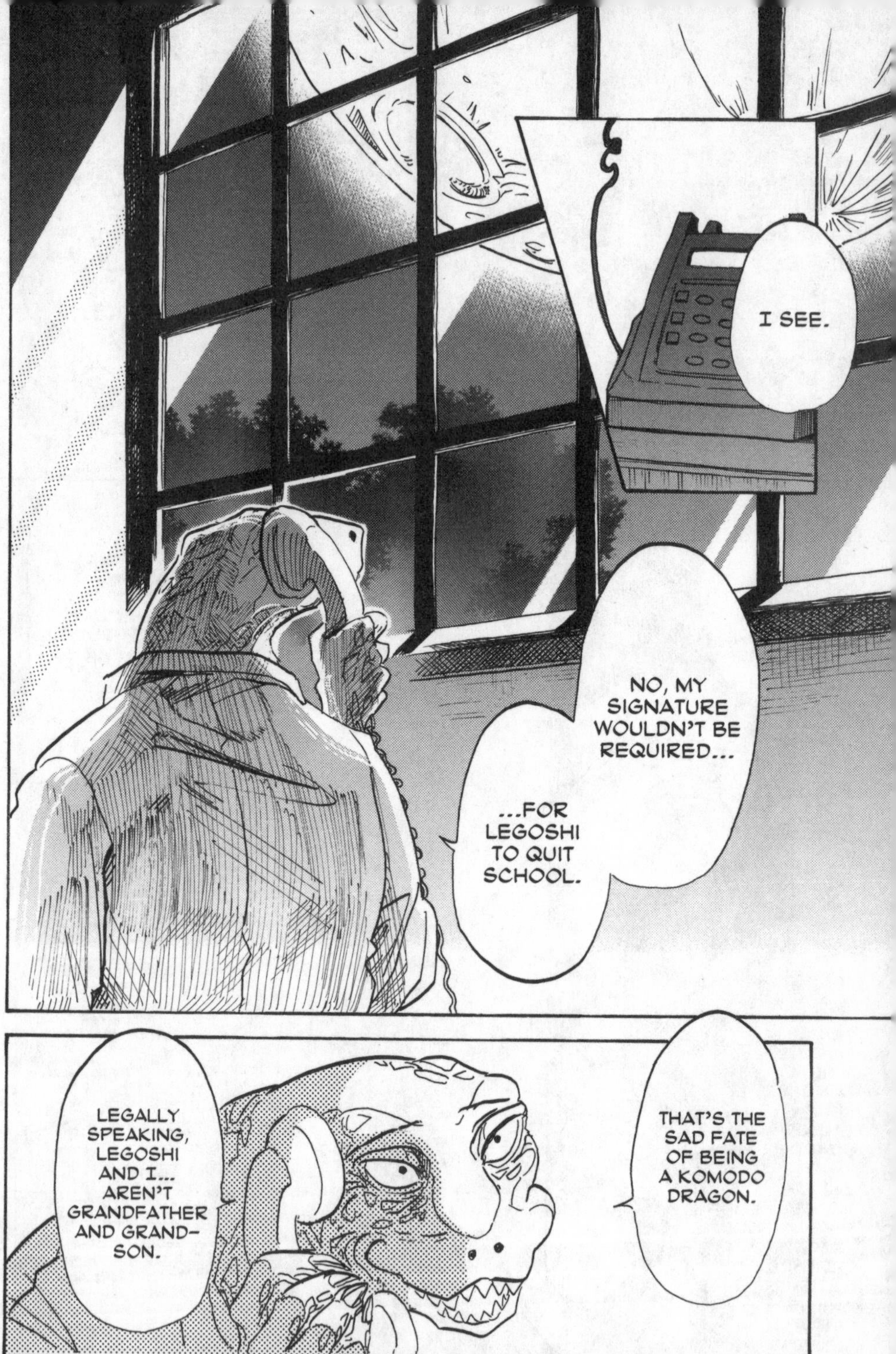
I SEE.
NO, MY SIGNATURE WOULDN'T BE REQUIRED...
...FOR LEGOSHI TO QUIT SCHOOL.
THAT'S THE SAD FATE OF BEING A KOMODO DRAGON.
LEGALLY SPEAKING, LEGOSHI AND I... AREN'T GRANDFATHER AND GRAND-SON.

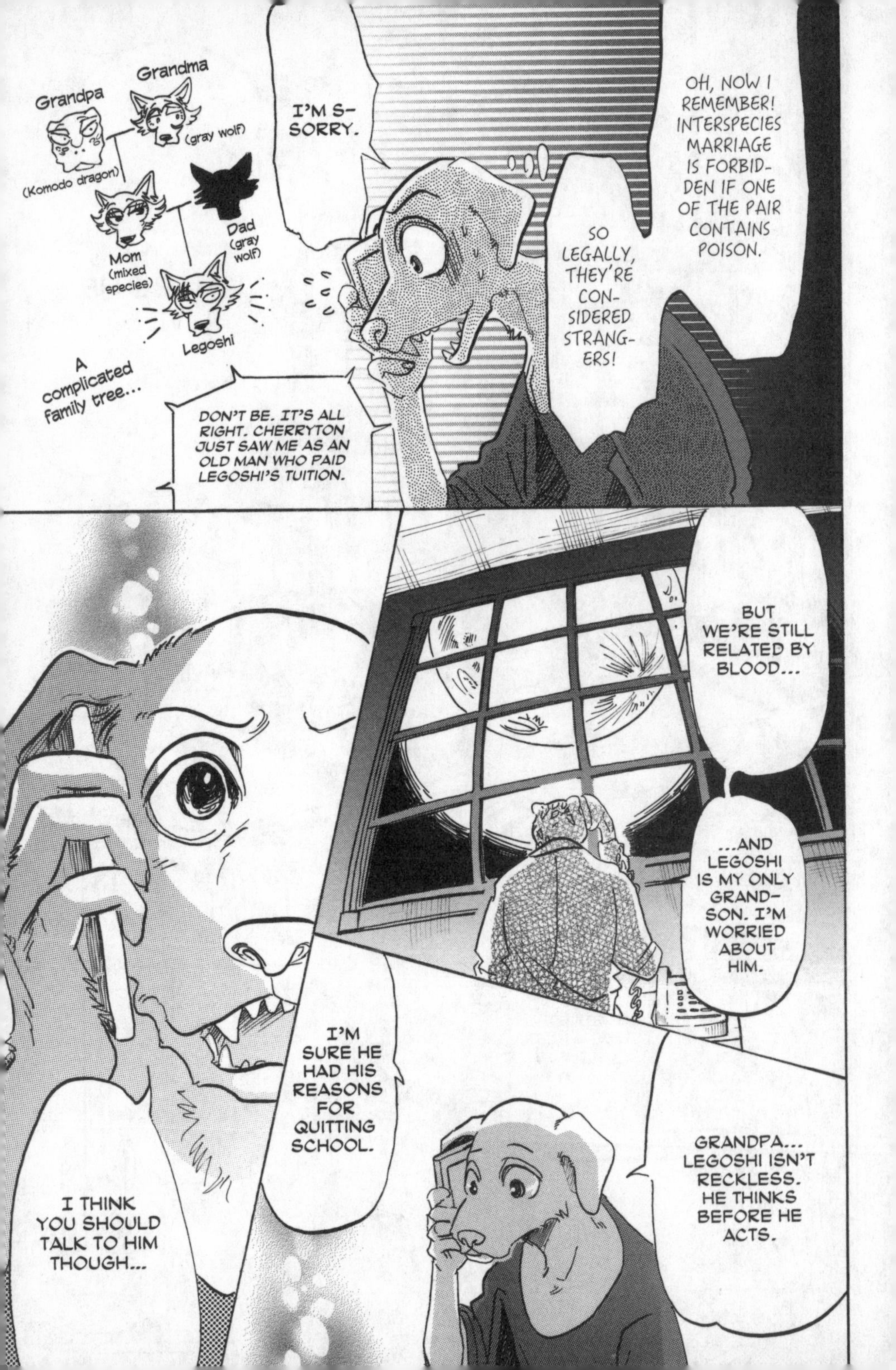
OH, NOW I REMEMBER! INTERSPECIES MARRIAGE IS FORBIDDEN IF ONE OF THE PAIR CONTAINS POISON.
SO LEGALLY, THEY'RE CONSIDERED STRANGERS!
I'M S-SORRY.
DON'T BE. IT'S ALL RIGHT. CHERRYTON JUST SAW ME AS AN OLD MAN WHO PAID LEGOSHI'S TUITION.
Grandma
Grandpa
(gray wolf)
(Komodo dragon)
Mom (mixed species)
Dad (gray wolf)
Legoshi
A complicated family tree...
BUT WE'RE STILL RELATED BY BLOOD...
...AND LEGOSHI IS MY ONLY GRANDSON. I'M WORRIED ABOUT HIM.
GRANDPA... LEGOSHI ISN'T RECKLESS. HE THINKS BEFORE HE ACTS.
I'M SURE HE HAD HIS REASONS FOR QUITTING SCHOOL.
I THINK YOU SHOULD TALK TO HIM THOUGH...

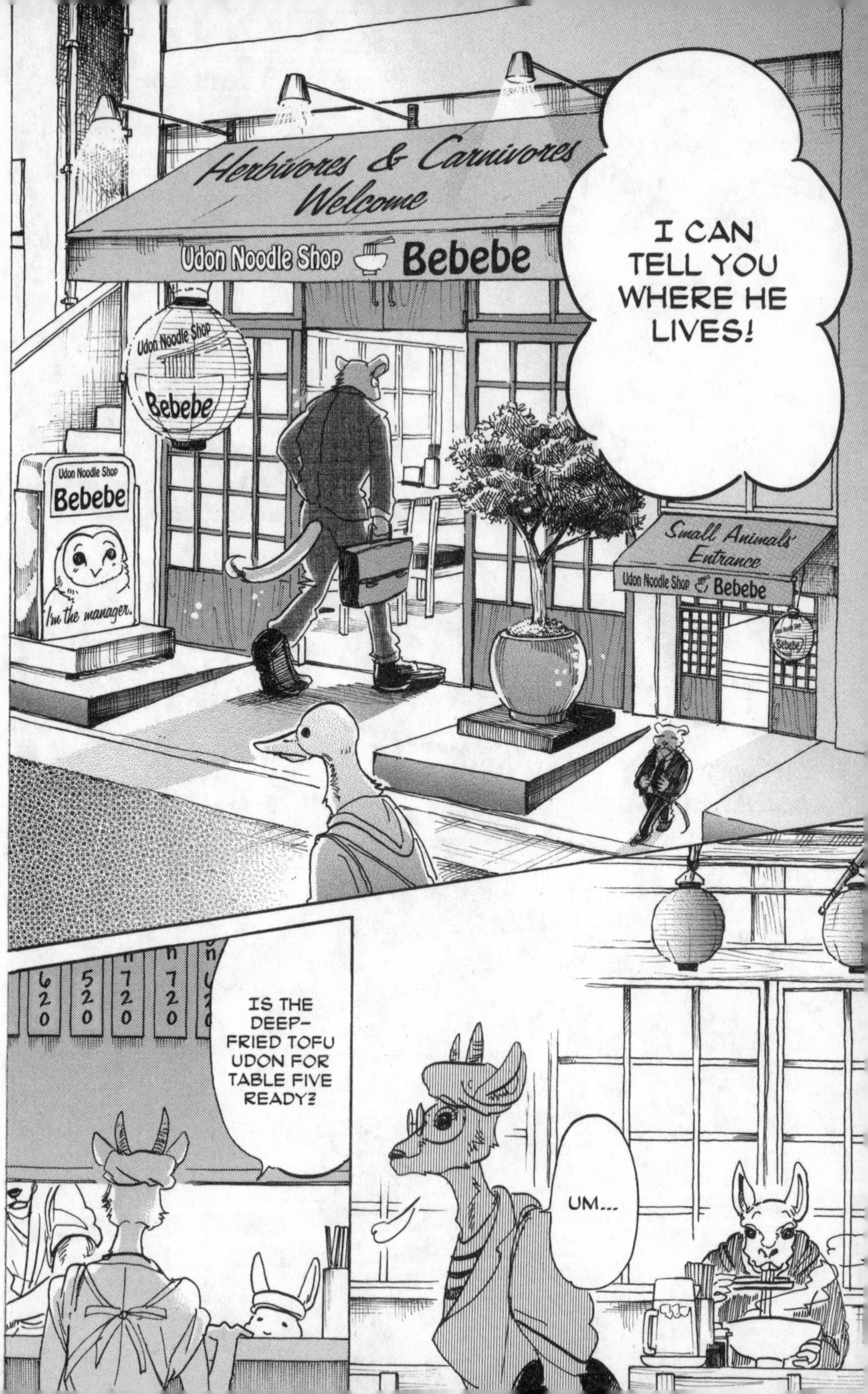
Herbivores & Carnivores Welcome
Udon Noodle Shop Bebebe
Udon Noodle Shop Bebebe
Udon Noodle Shop Bebebe
I'm the manager.
Small Animals' Entrance
Udon Noodle Shop Bebebe
I CAN TELL YOU WHERE HE LIVES!
620
520
720
720
IS THE DEEP-FRIED TOFU UDON FOR TABLE FIVE READY?
UM...

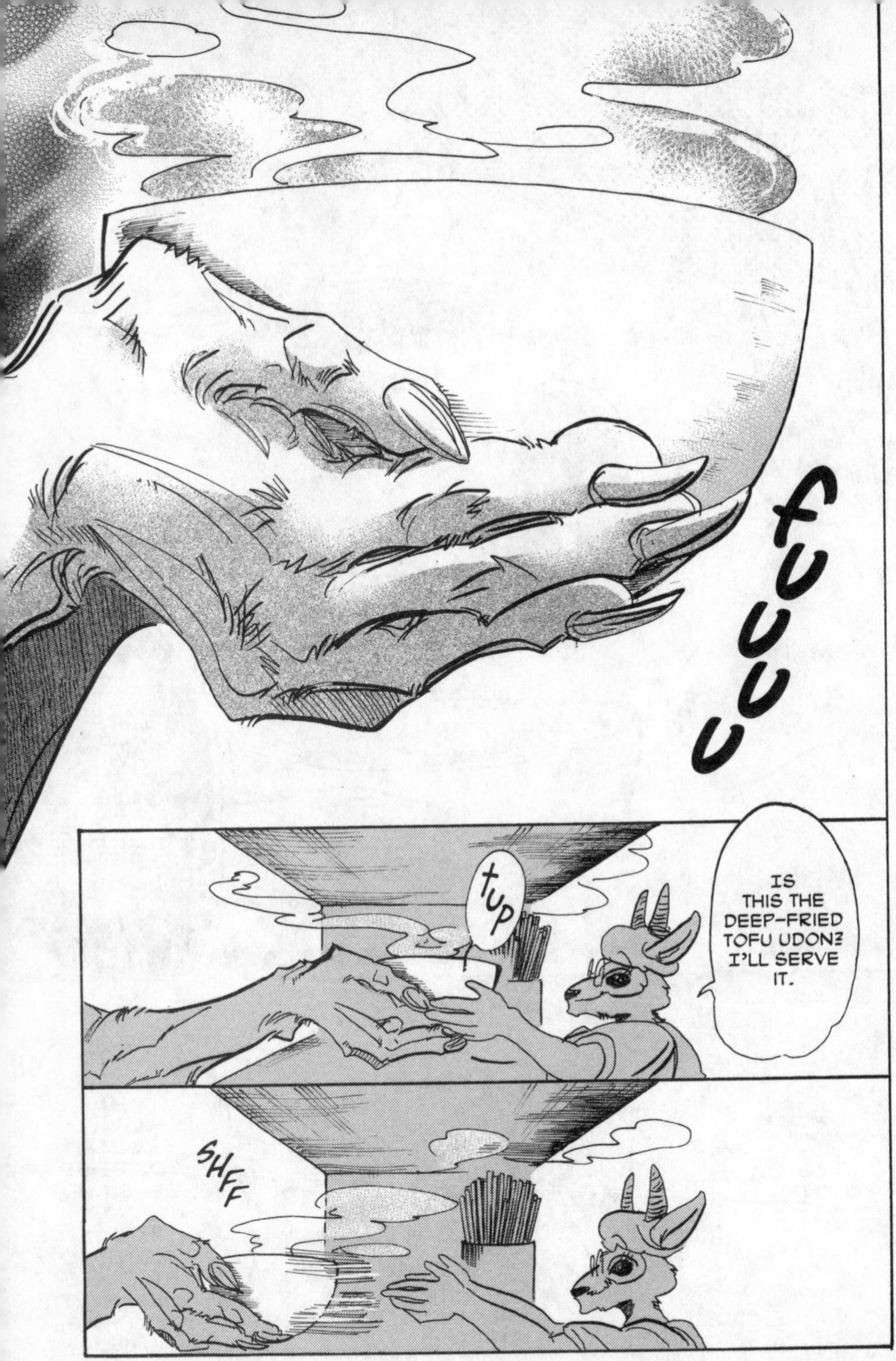
fuuuu
IS THIS THE DEEP-FRIED TOFU UDON? I'LL SERVE IT.
tup
SHFF

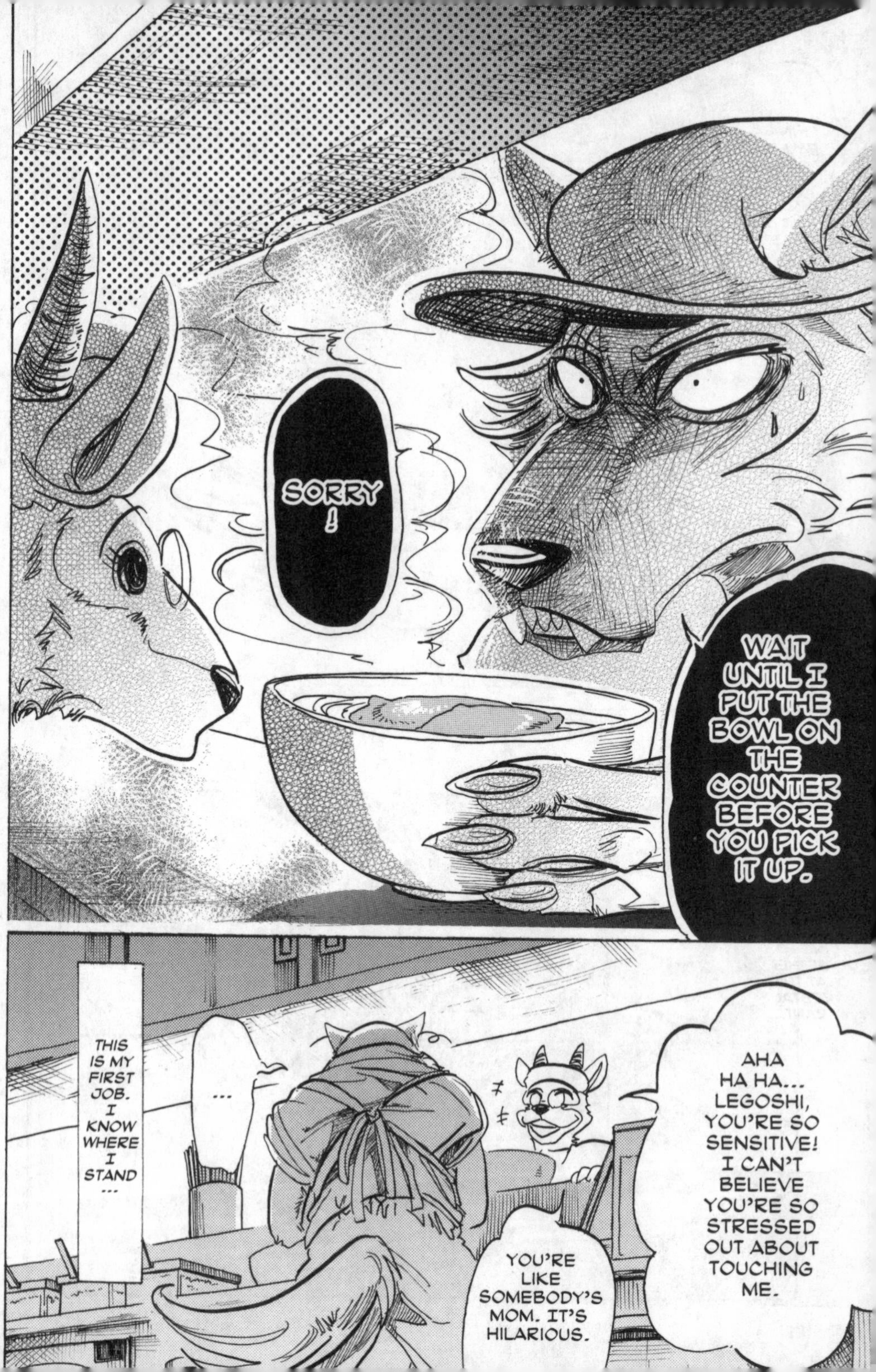
WAIT UNTIL I PUT THE BOWL ON THE COUNTER BEFORE YOU PICK IT UP.
SORRY!
AHA HA HA... LEGOSHI, YOU'RE SO SENSITIVE! I CAN'T BELIEVE YOU'RE SO STRESSED OUT ABOUT TOUCHING ME.
YOU'RE LIKE SOMEBODY'S MOM. IT'S HILARIOUS.
...
THIS IS MY FIRST JOB. I KNOW WHERE I STAND...

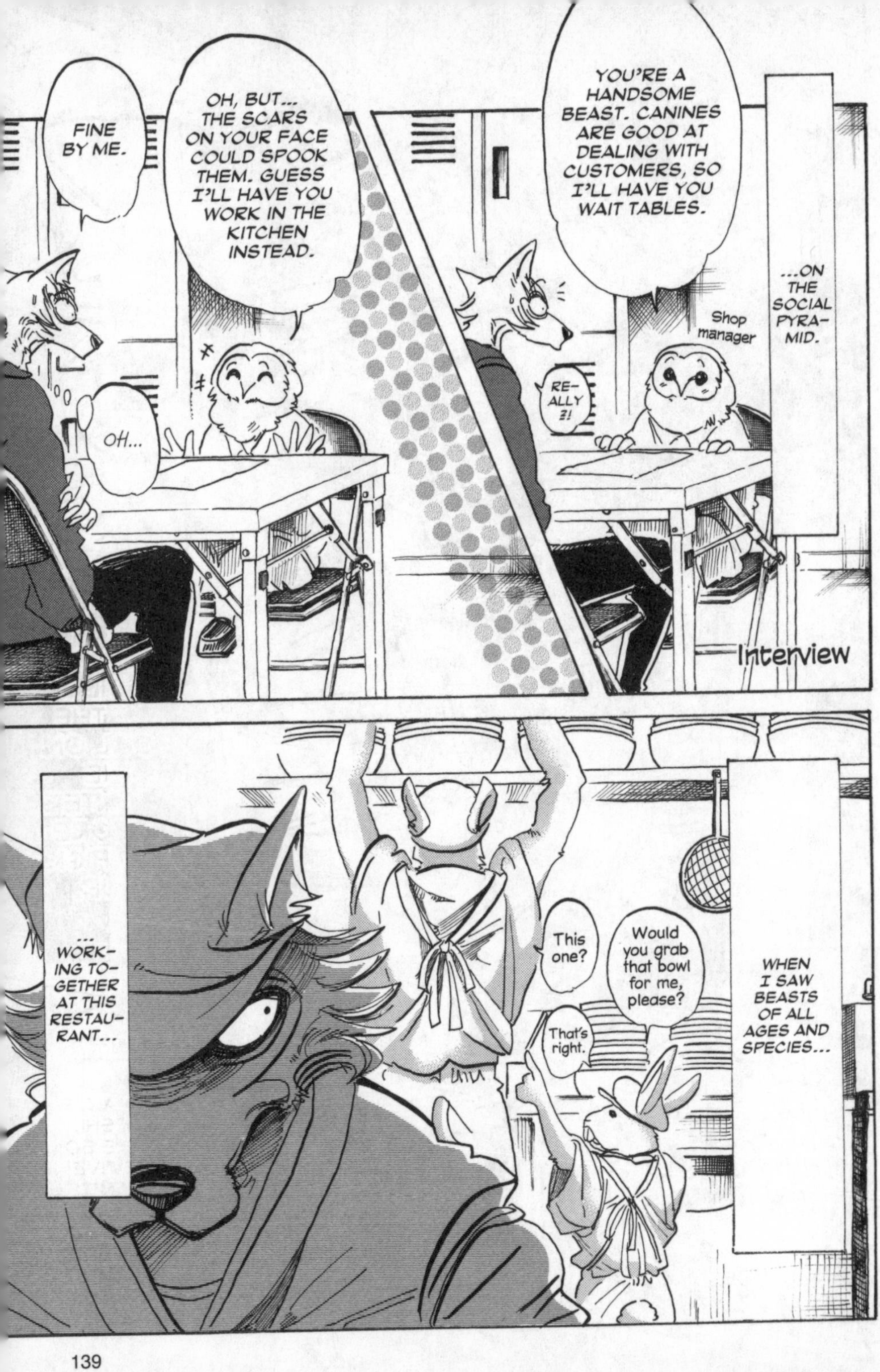
...ON THE SOCIAL PYRAMID.
YOU'RE A HANDSOME BEAST. CANINES ARE GOOD AT DEALING WITH CUSTOMERS, SO I'LL HAVE YOU WAIT TABLES.
Shop manager
REALLY?!
Interview
OH, BUT... THE SCARS ON YOUR FACE COULD SPOOK THEM. GUESS I'LL HAVE YOU WORK IN THE KITCHEN INSTEAD.
FINE BY ME.
OH...
WHEN I SAW BEASTS OF ALL AGES AND SPECIES...
Would you grab that bowl for me, please?
This one?
That's right.
...WORKING TOGETHER AT THIS RESTAURANT...

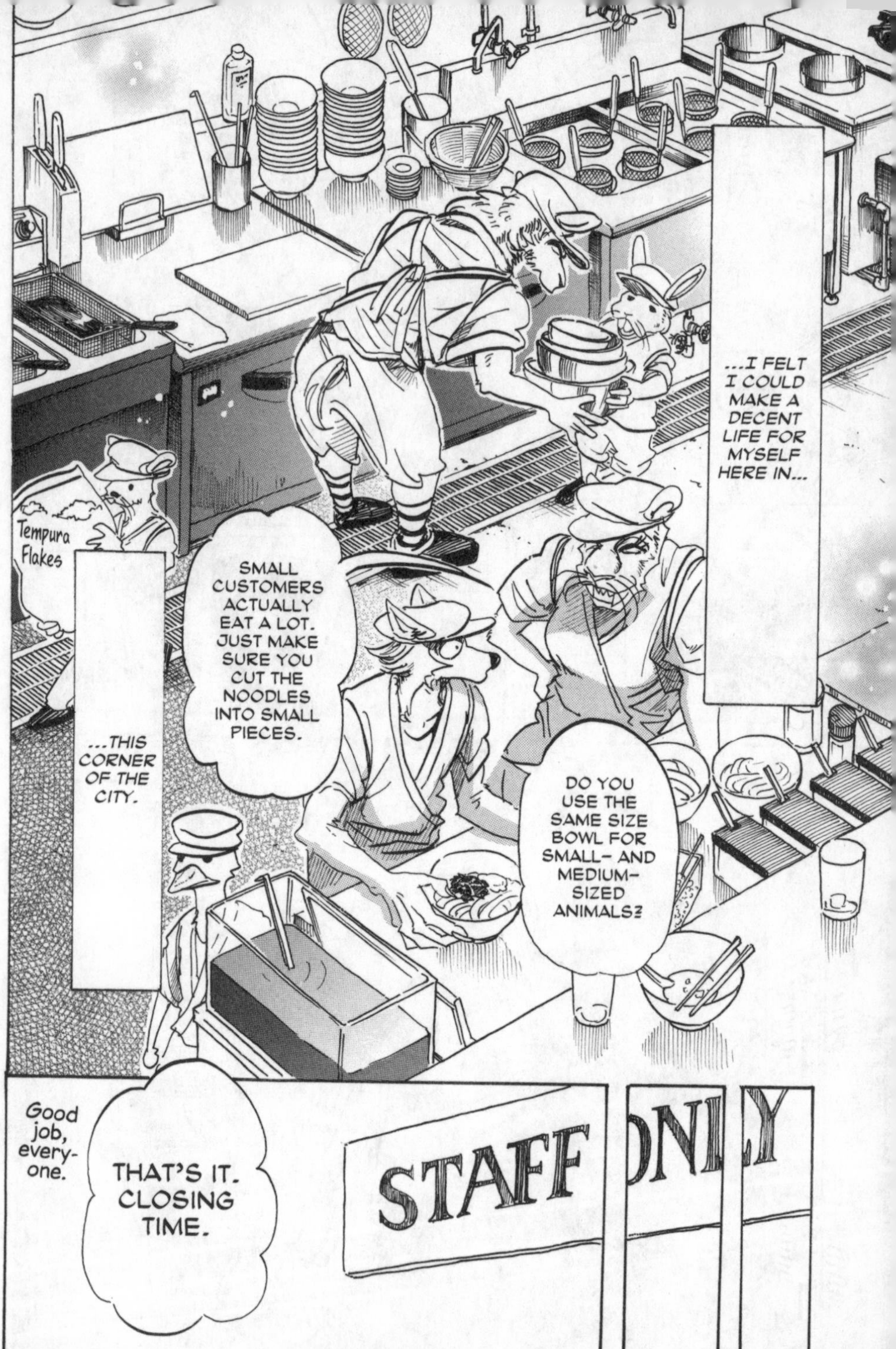
...I FELT I COULD MAKE A DECENT LIFE FOR MYSELF HERE IN...
...THIS CORNER OF THE CITY.
DO YOU USE THE SAME SIZE BOWL FOR SMALL- AND MEDIUM-SIZED ANIMALS?
SMALL CUSTOMERS ACTUALLY EAT A LOT. JUST MAKE SURE YOU CUT THE NOODLES INTO SMALL PIECES.
Tempura Flakes
STAFF ONLY
THAT'S IT. CLOSING TIME.
Good job, every-one.

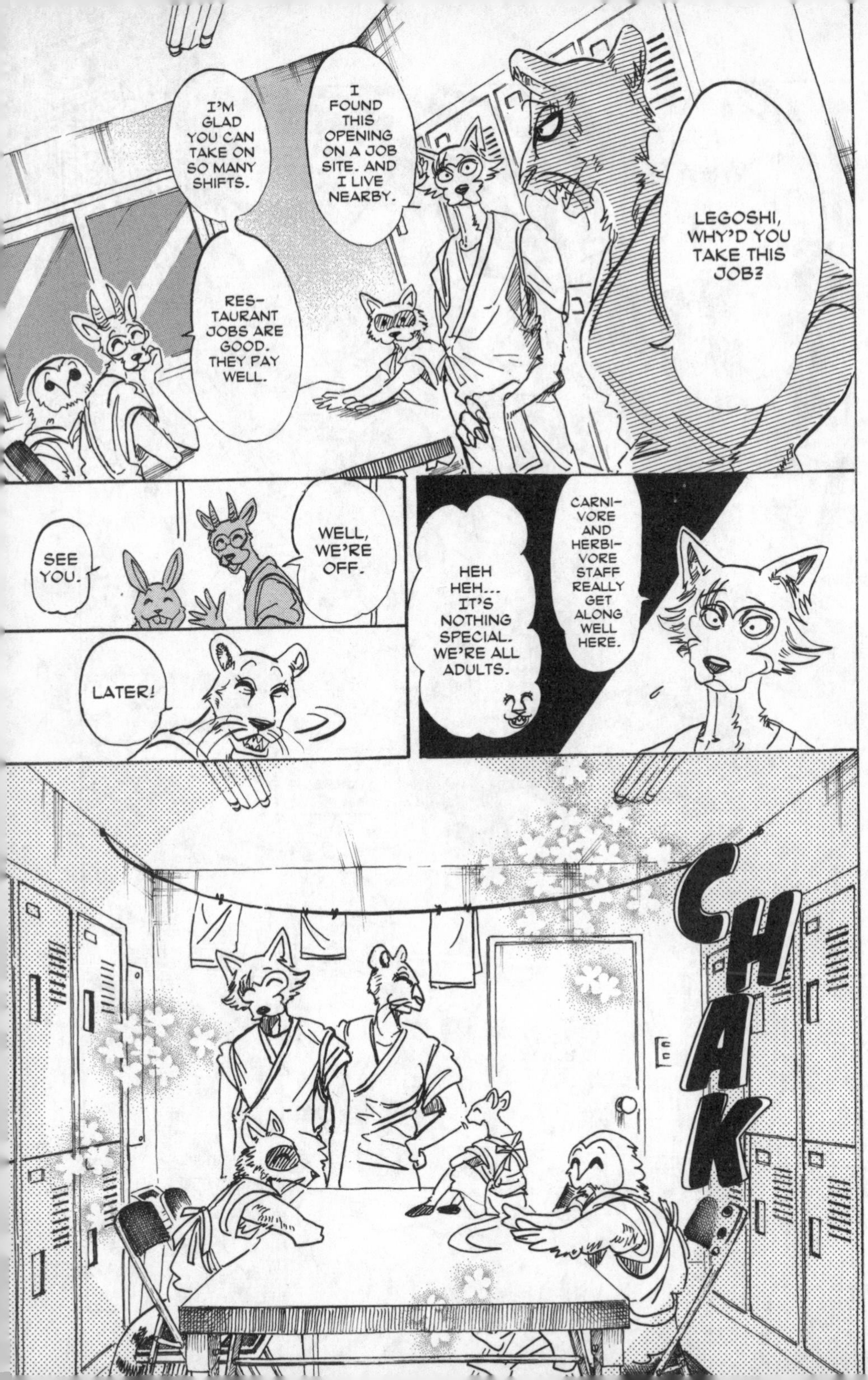
LEGOSHI, WHY'D YOU TAKE THIS JOB?
I FOUND THIS OPENING ON A JOB SITE. AND I LIVE NEARBY.
I'M GLAD YOU CAN TAKE ON SO MANY SHIFTS.
RES-TAURANT JOBS ARE GOOD. THEY PAY WELL.
CARNI-VORE AND HERBI-VORE STAFF REALLY GET ALONG WELL HERE.
HEH HEH... IT'S NOTHING SPECIAL. WE'RE ALL ADULTS.
WELL, WE'RE OFF.
SEE YOU.
LATER!
CHAK

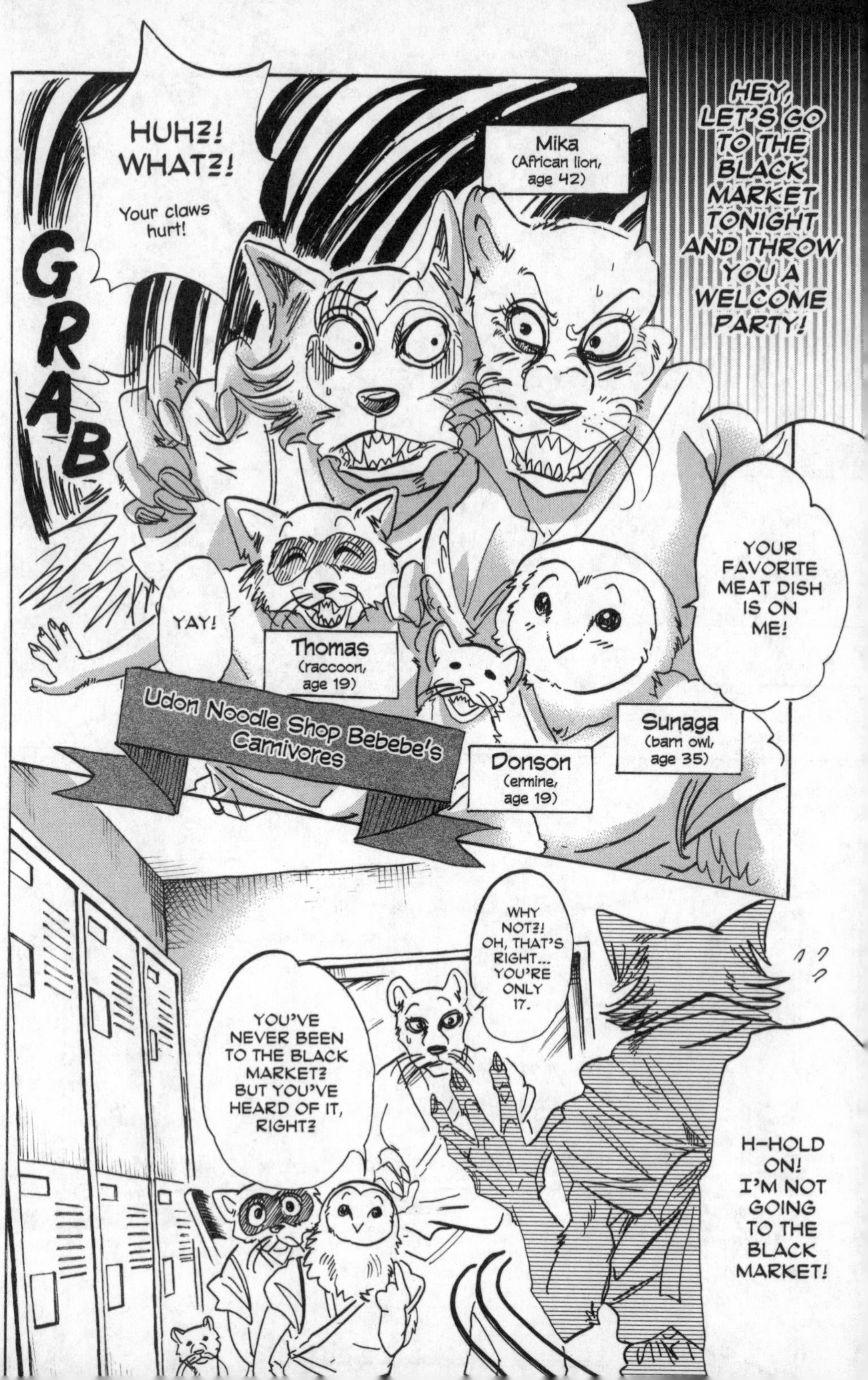

HEY, LET'S GO TO THE BLACK MARKET TONIGHT AND THROW YOU A WELCOME PARTY!
Mika (African lion, age 42)
HUH?! WHAT?!
Your claws hurt!
GRAB
YOUR FAVORITE MEAT DISH IS ON ME!
Sunaga (barn owl, age 35)
Donson (ermine, age 19)
Thomas (raccoon, age 19)
YAY!
Udon Noodle Shop Bebebe's Carnivores
H-HOLD ON! I'M NOT GOING TO THE BLACK MARKET!
WHY NOT?! OH, THAT'S RIGHT... YOU'RE ONLY 17.
YOU'VE NEVER BEEN TO THE BLACK MARKET? BUT YOU'VE HEARD OF IT, RIGHT?

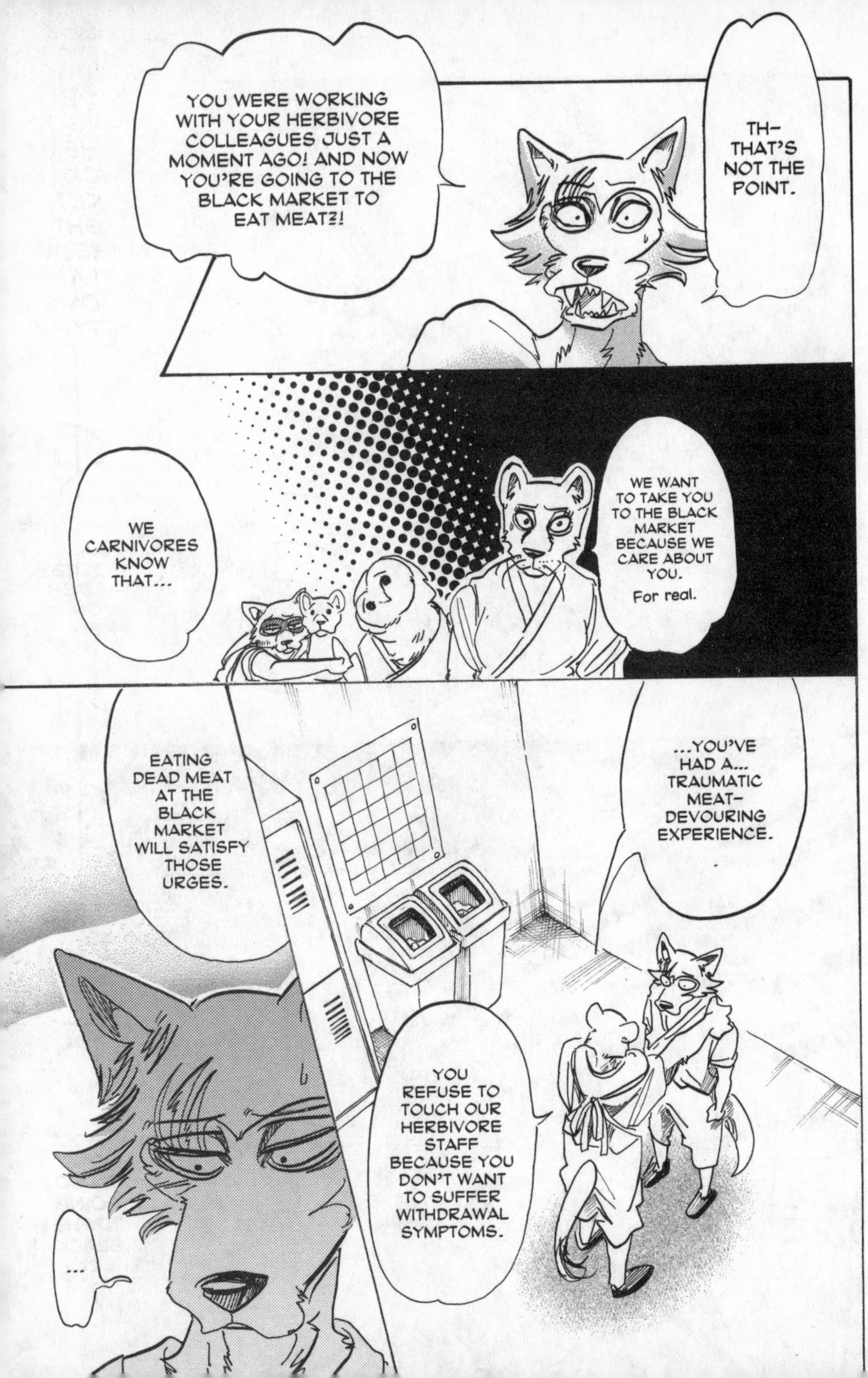
TH— THAT'S NOT THE POINT.
YOU WERE WORKING WITH YOUR HERBIVORE COLLEAGUES JUST A MOMENT AGO! AND NOW YOU'RE GOING TO THE BLACK MARKET TO EAT MEAT?!
WE WANT TO TAKE YOU TO THE BLACK MARKET BECAUSE WE CARE ABOUT YOU.
For real.
WE CARNIVORES KNOW THAT...
...YOU'VE HAD A... TRAUMATIC MEAT-DEVOURING EXPERIENCE.
YOU REFUSE TO TOUCH OUR HERBIVORE STAFF BECAUSE YOU DON'T WANT TO SUFFER WITHDRAWAL SYMPTOMS.
EATING DEAD MEAT AT THE BLACK MARKET WILL SATISFY THOSE URGES.
...

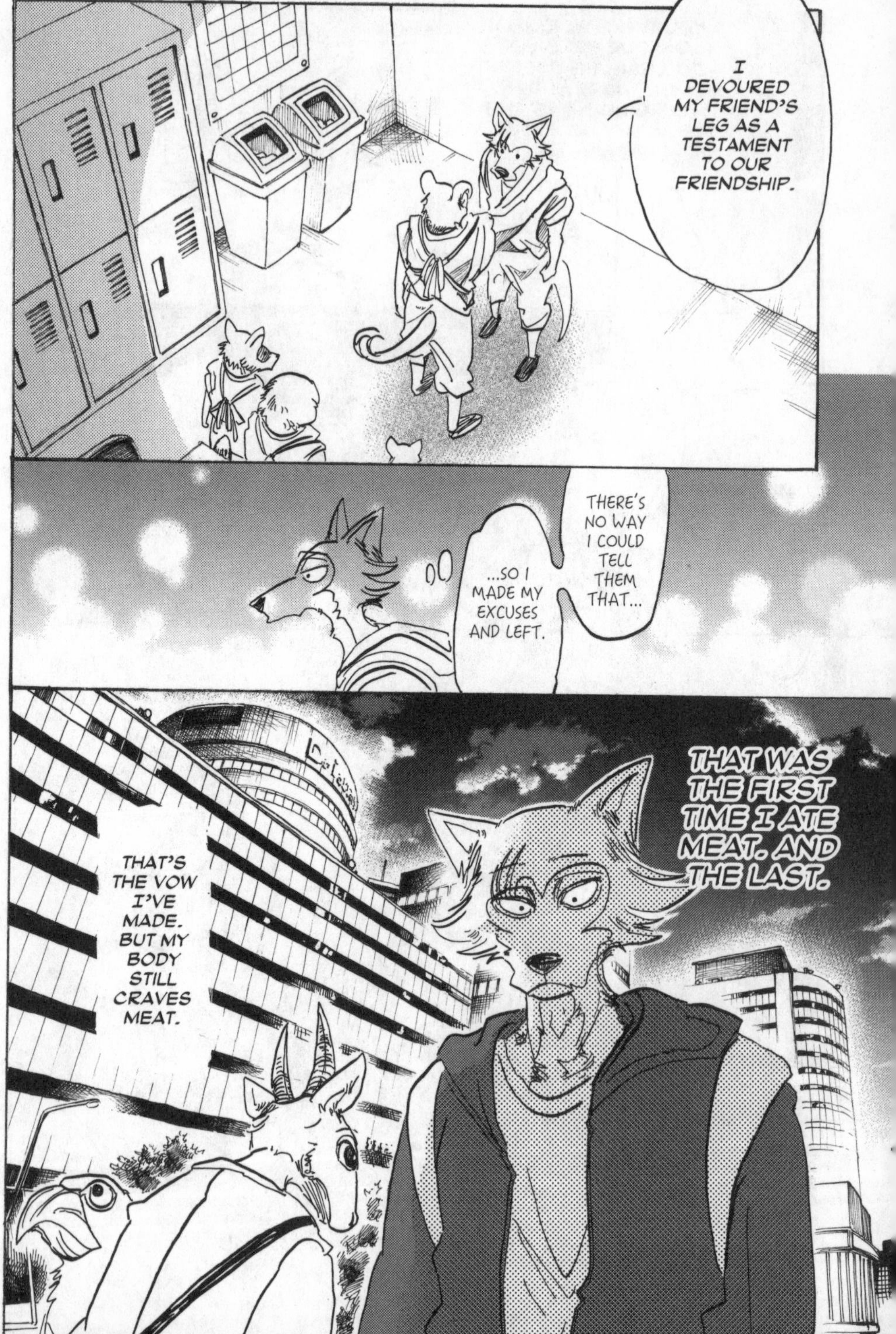
I DEVOURED MY FRIEND'S LEG AS A TESTAMENT TO OUR FRIENDSHIP.
THERE'S NO WAY I COULD TELL THEM THAT...
...SO I MADE MY EXCUSES AND LEFT.
THAT WAS THE FIRST TIME I ATE MEAT. AND THE LAST.
THAT'S THE VOW I'VE MADE. BUT MY BODY STILL CRAVES MEAT.

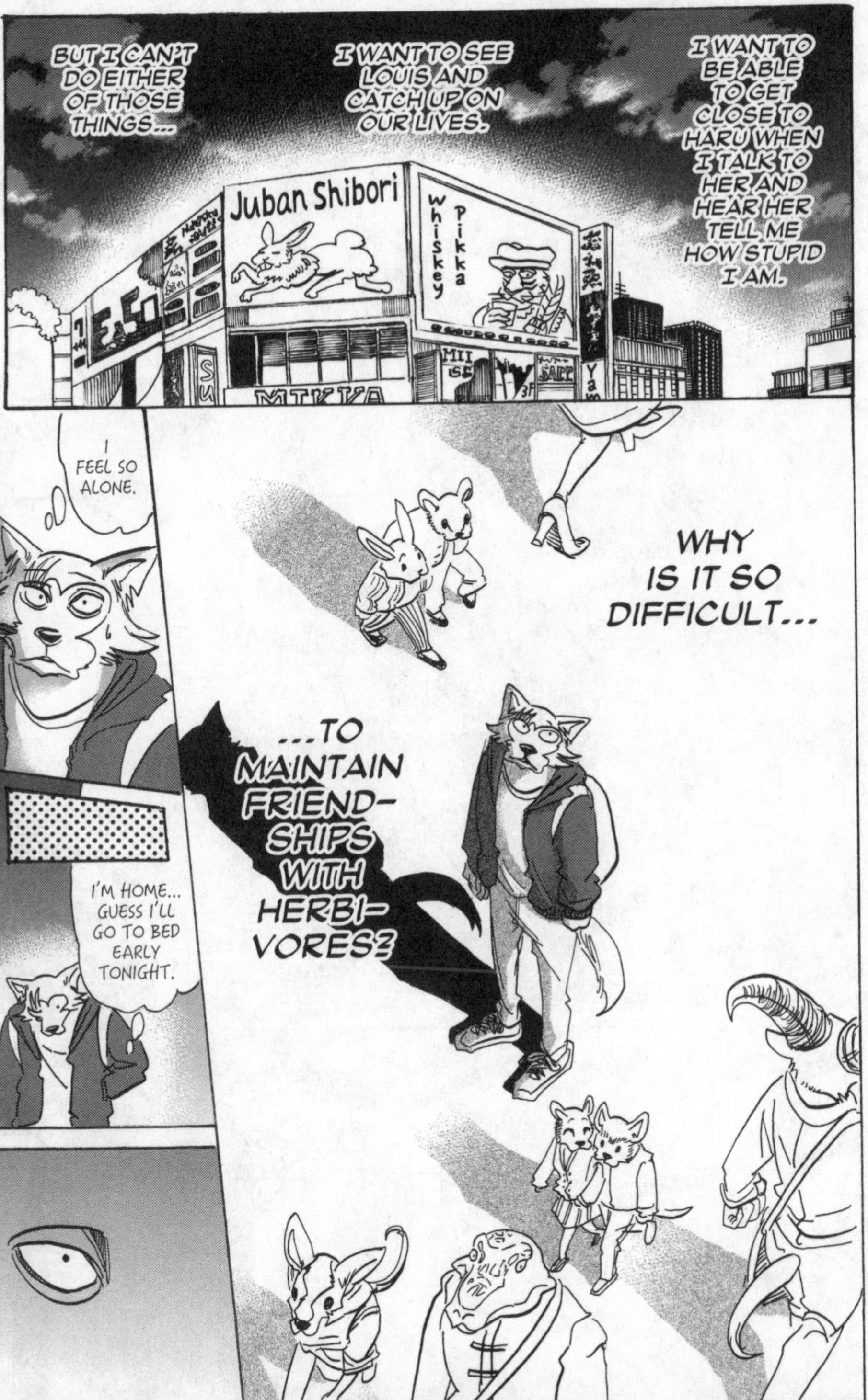
I WANT TO BE ABLE TO GET CLOSE TO HARU WHEN I TALK TO HER AND HEAR HER TELL ME HOW STUPID I AM.
I WANT TO SEE LOUIS AND CATCH UP ON OUR LIVES.
BUT I CAN'T DO EITHER OF THOSE THINGS...
Juban Shibori
Pikka
whiskey
WHY IS IT SO DIFFICULT...
...TO MAINTAIN FRIEND-SHIPS WITH HERBI-VORES?
I FEEL SO ALONE.
I'M HOME... GUESS I'LL GO TO BED EARLY TONIGHT.

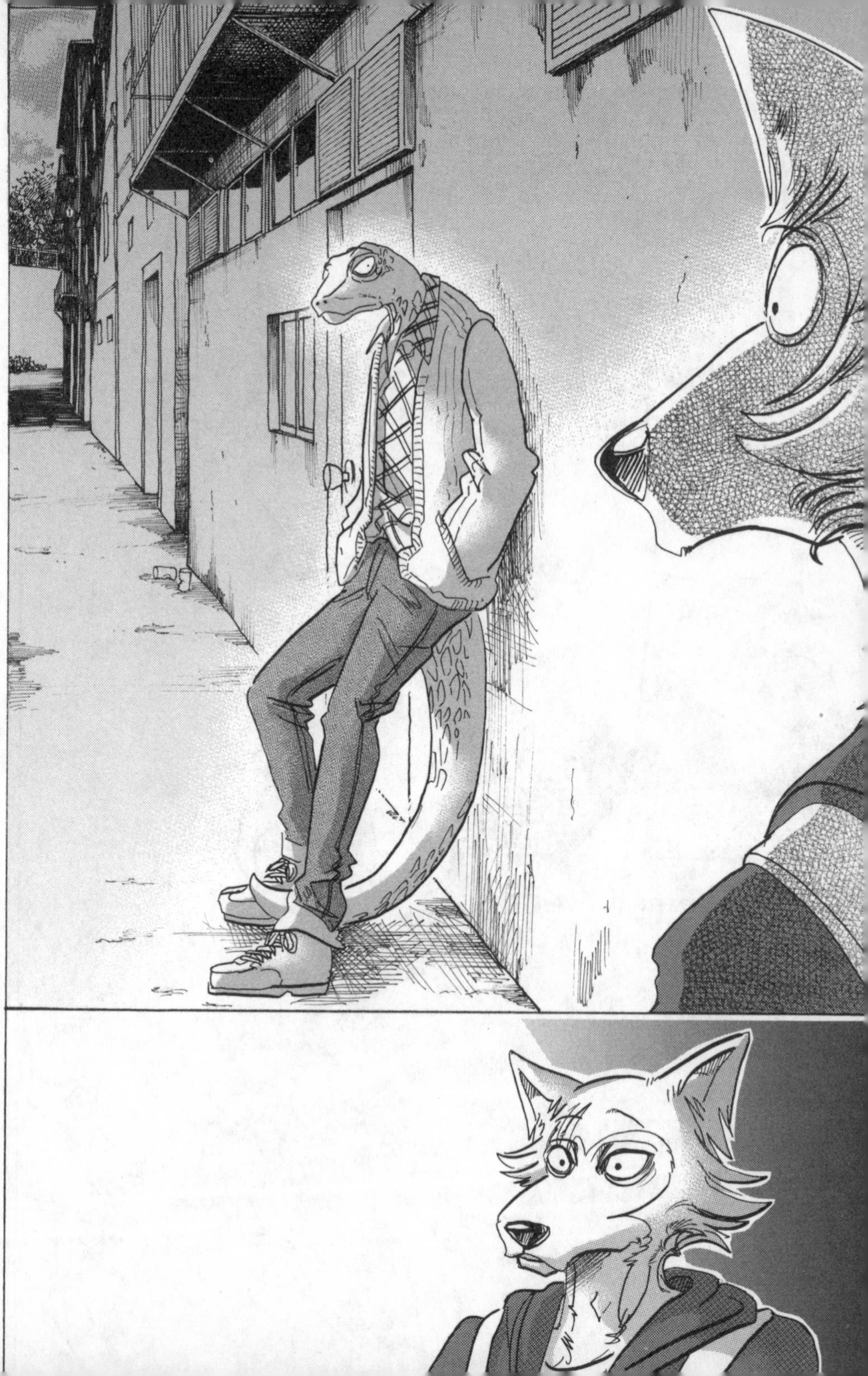

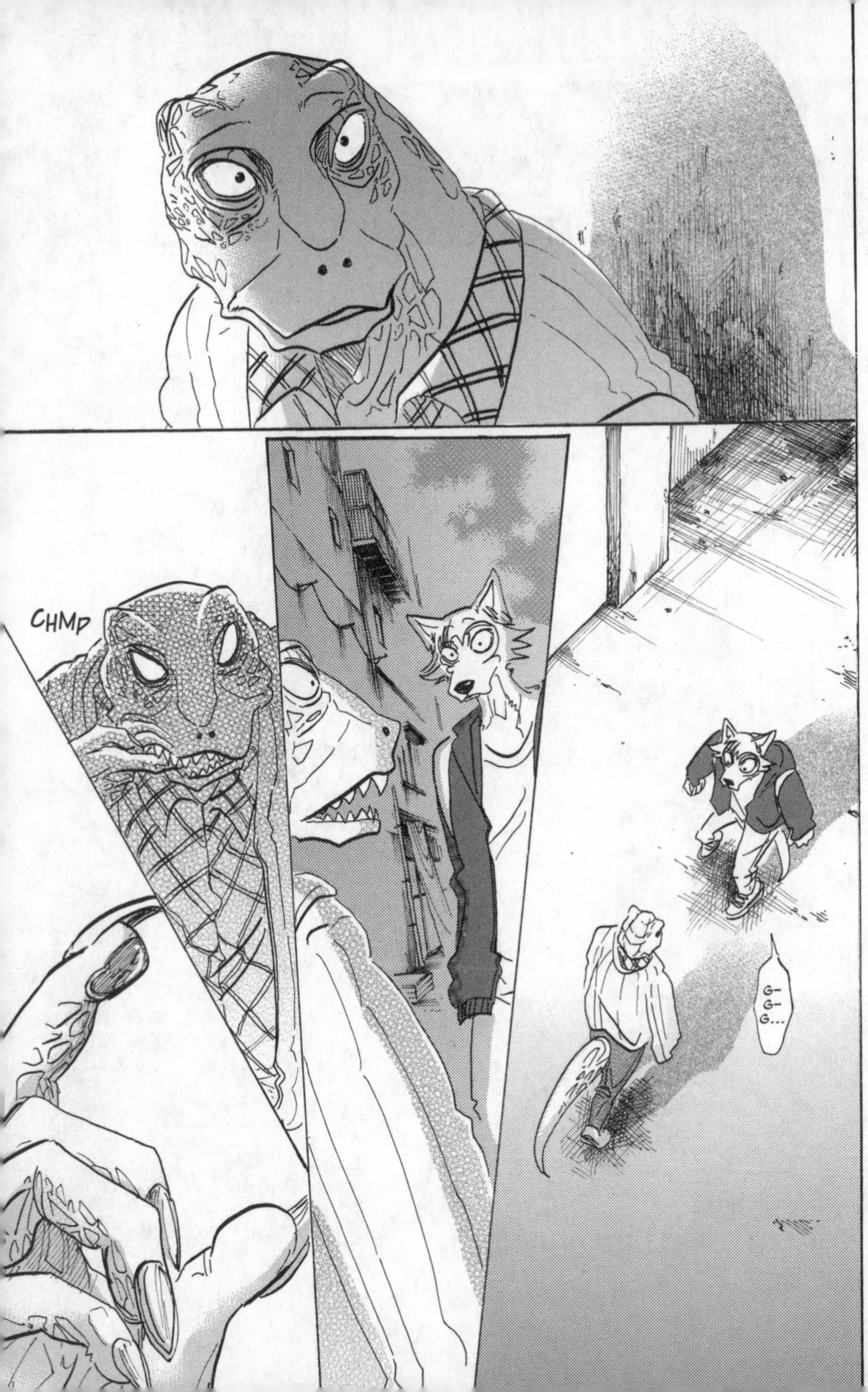

G-
G-
G...
CHMP

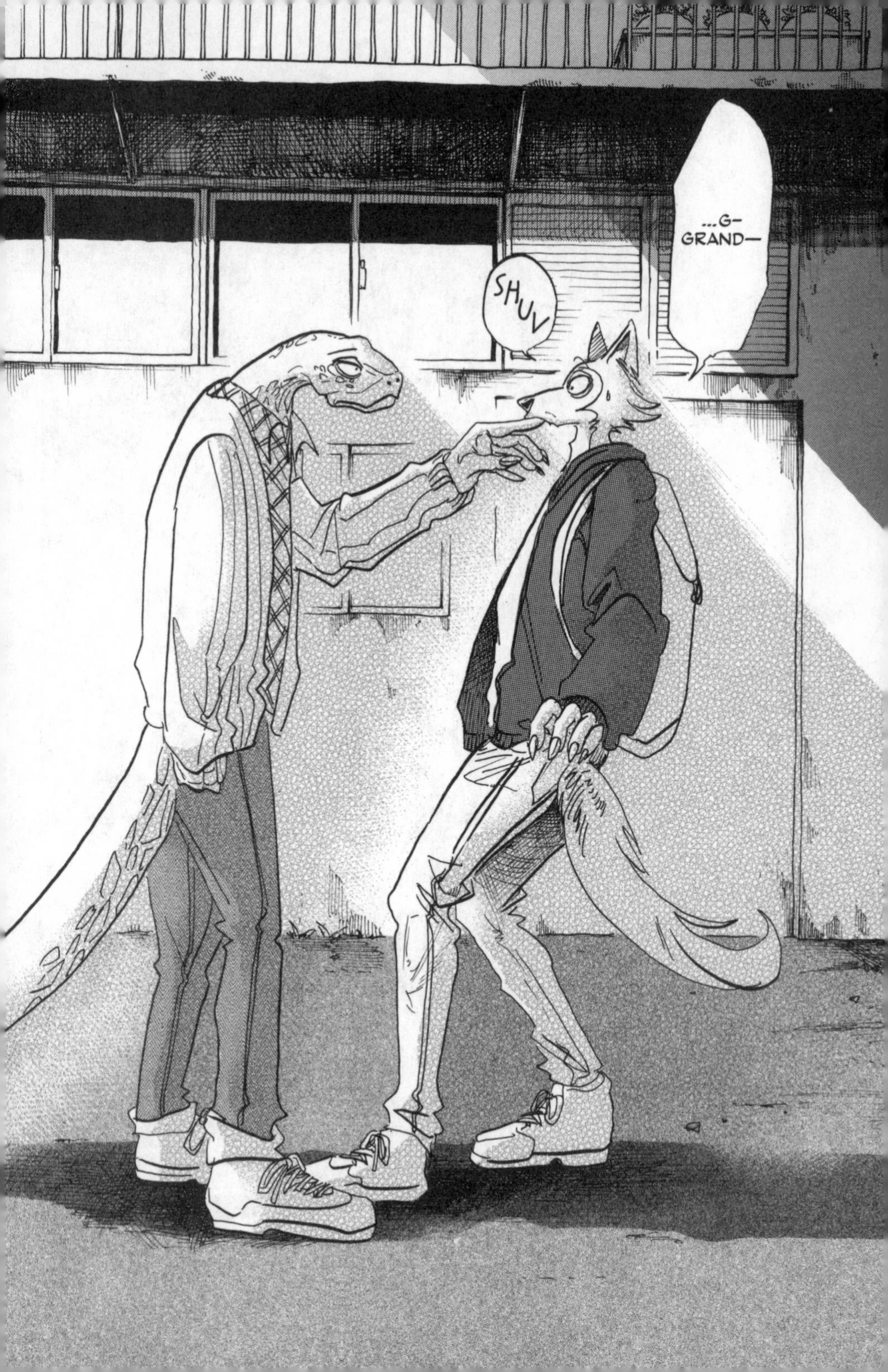
...G-
GRAND—
SHUV

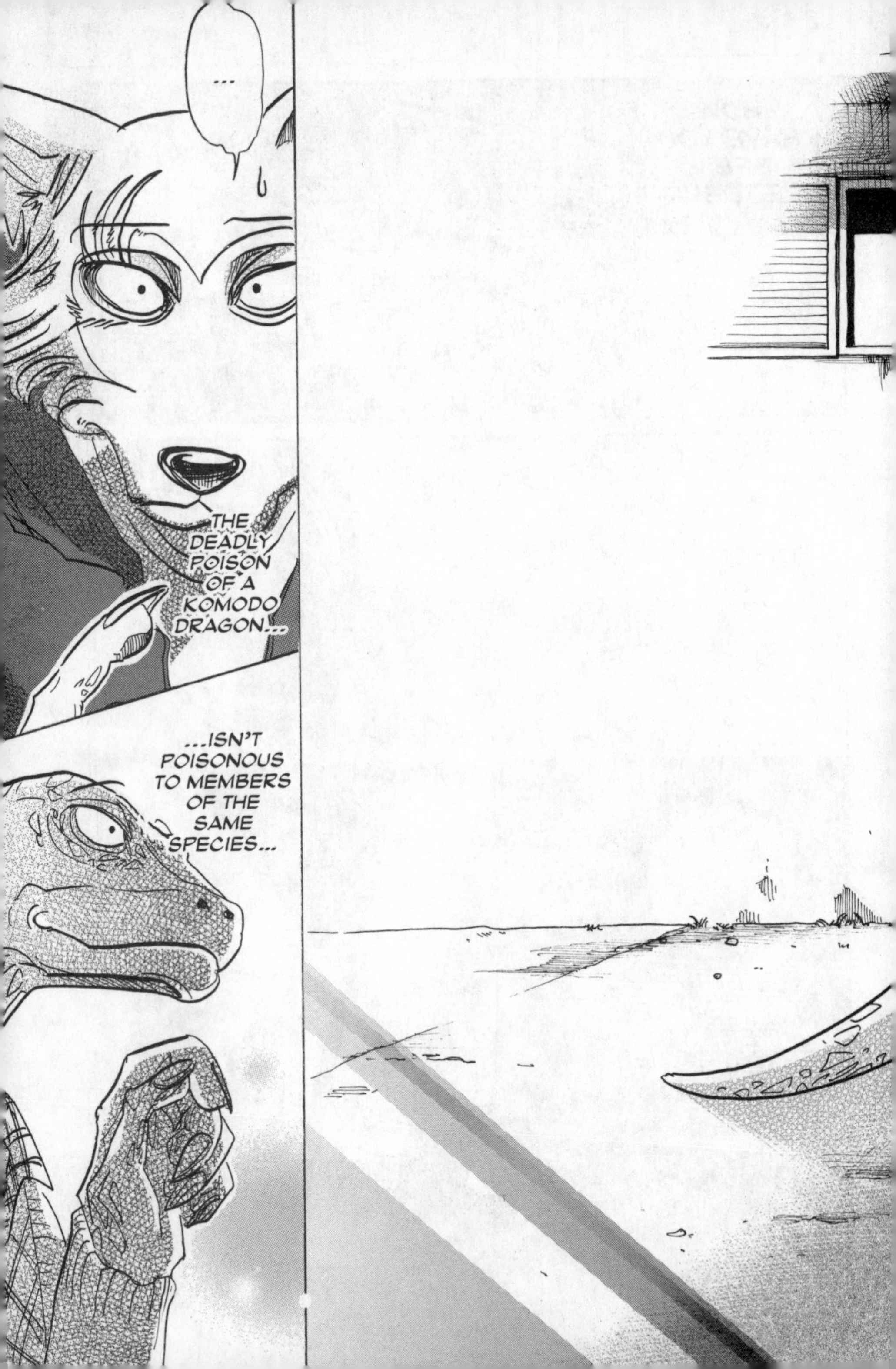
...
THE DEADLY POISON OF A KOMODO DRAGON...
...ISN'T POISONOUS TO MEMBERS OF THE SAME SPECIES...

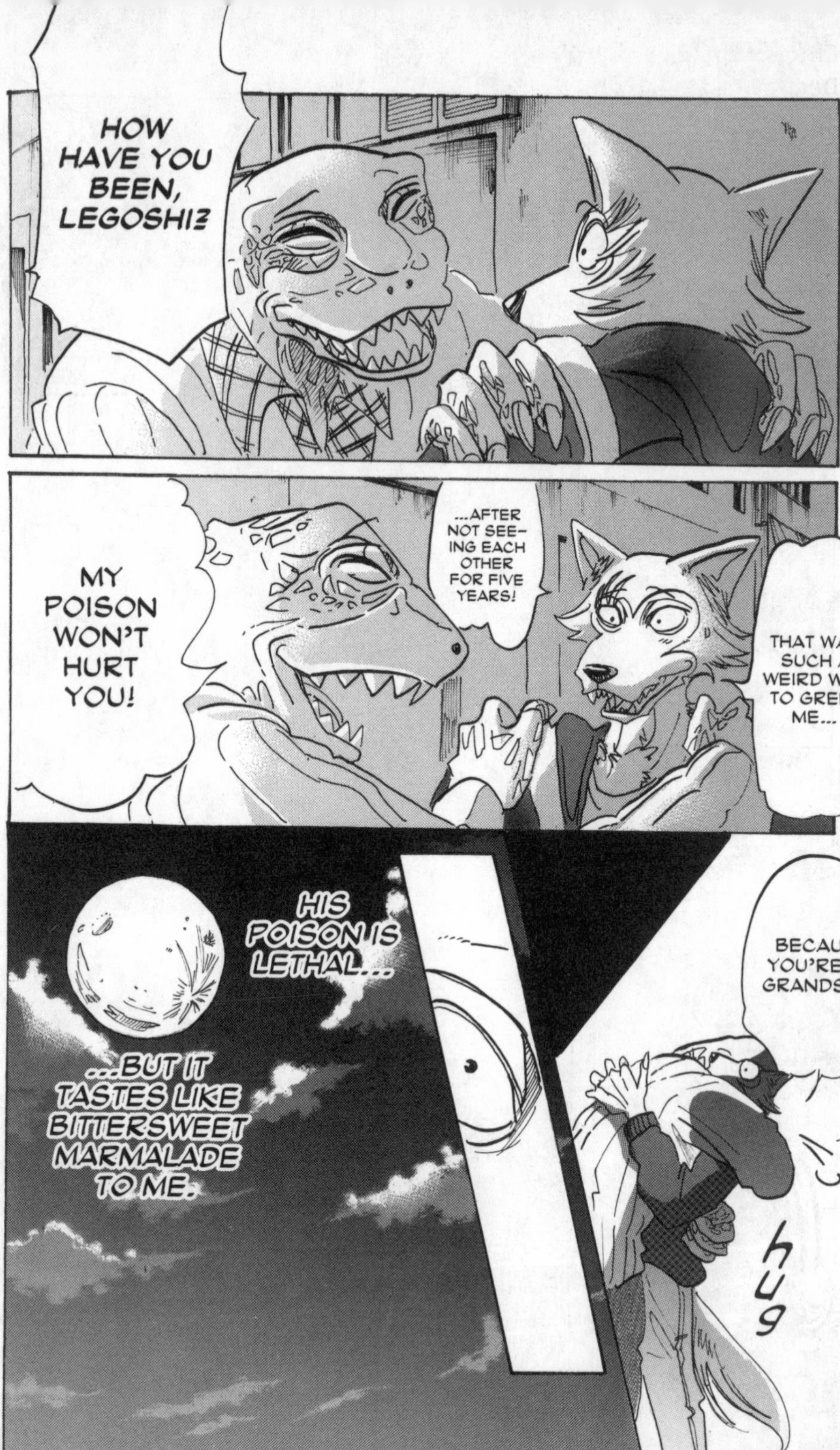
HOW HAVE YOU BEEN, LEGOSHI!?
THAT WAS SUCH A WEIRD WAY TO GREET ME...
...AFTER NOT SEE-ING EACH OTHER FOR FIVE YEARS!
MY POISON WON'T HURT YOU!
BECAUSE YOU'RE MY GRANDSON!
HUG
HIS POISON IS LETHAL...
...BUT IT TASTES LIKE BITTERSWEET MARMALADE TO ME.

Chapter 105: The Man of Destiny Is Devoured

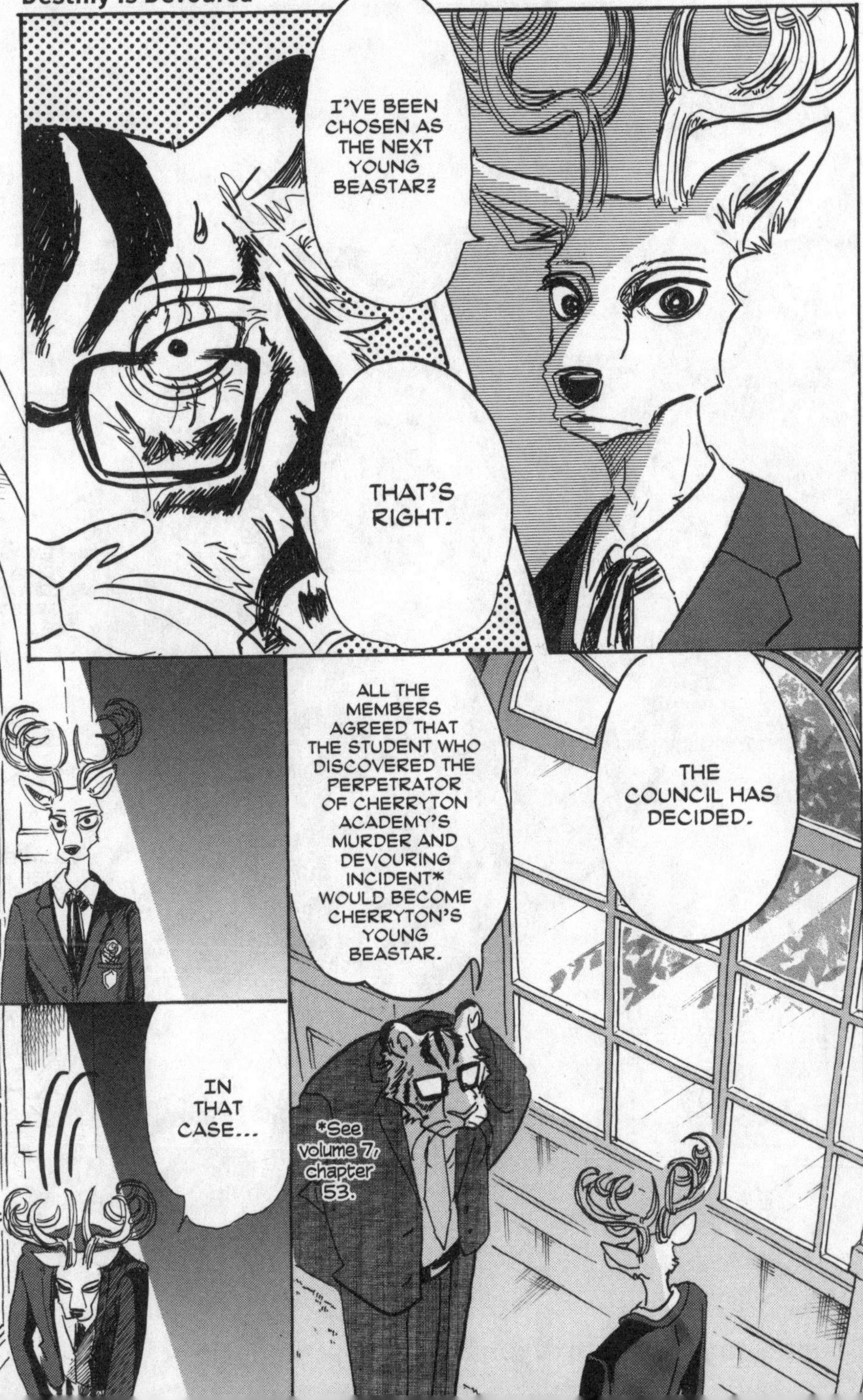
I'VE BEEN CHOSEN AS THE NEXT YOUNG BEASTAR?
THAT'S RIGHT.
THE COUNCIL HAS DECIDED.
ALL THE MEMBERS AGREED THAT THE STUDENT WHO DISCOVERED THE PERPETRATOR OF CHERRYTON ACADEMY'S MURDER AND DEVOURING INCIDENT* WOULD BECOME CHERRYTON'S YOUNG BEASTAR.
*See volume 7, chapter 53.
IN THAT CASE...

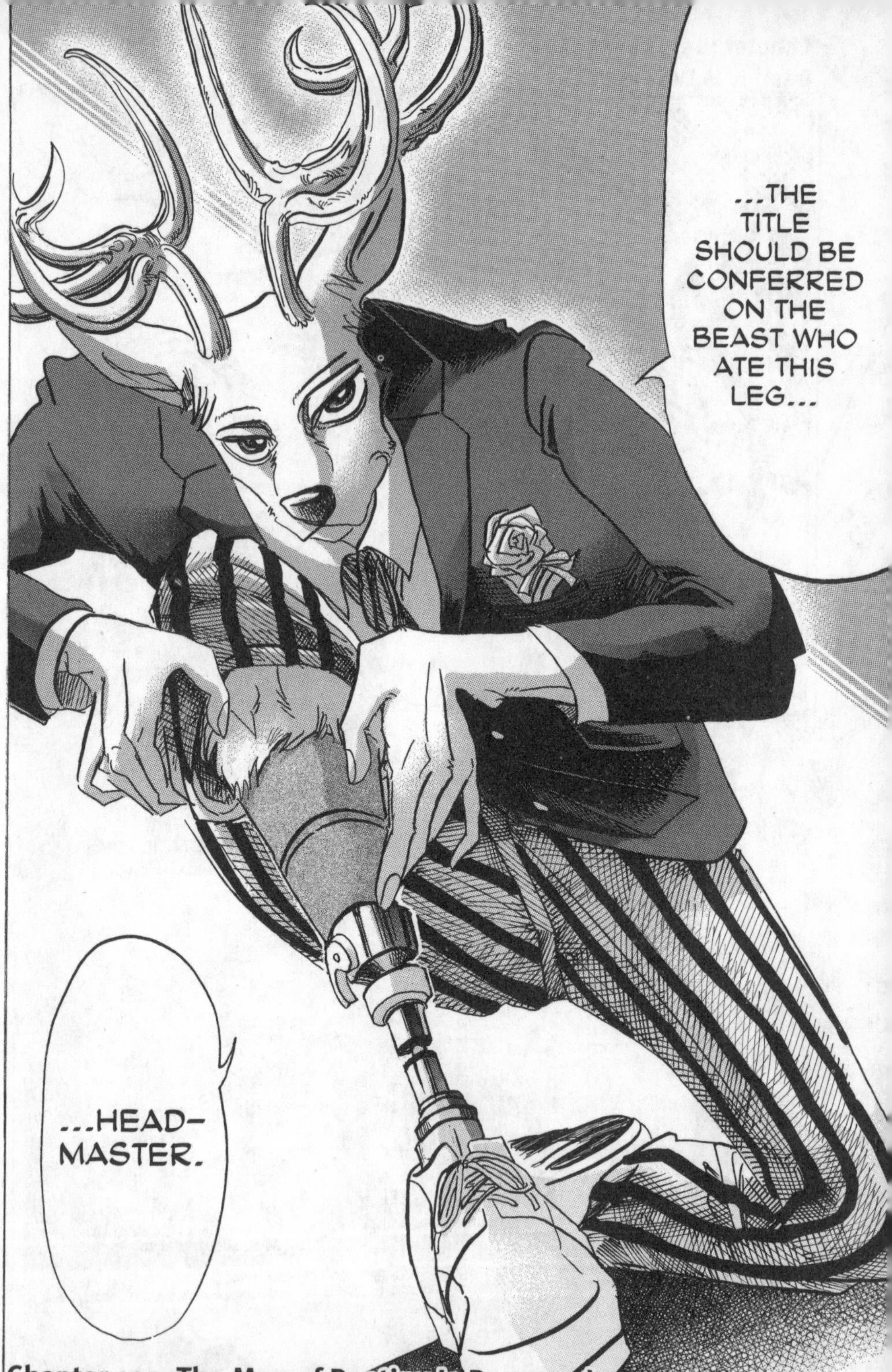
...THE TITLE SHOULD BE CONFERRED ON THE BEAST WHO ATE THIS LEG...
...HEAD-MASTER.

Chapter 105: The Man of Destiny Is Devoured

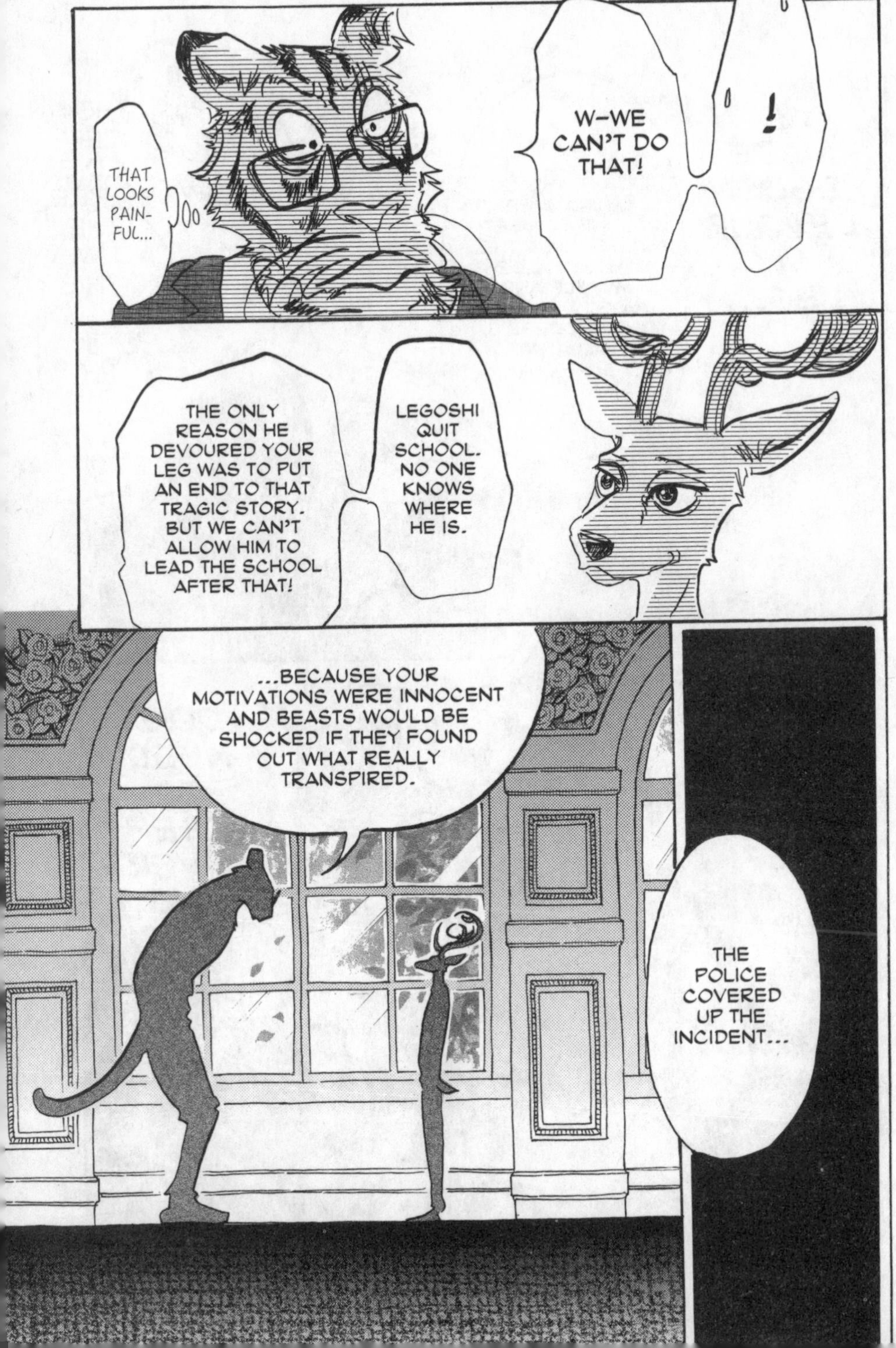
!
W-WE CAN'T DO THAT!
THAT LOOKS PAIN-FUL...
LEGOSHI QUIT SCHOOL. NO ONE KNOWS WHERE HE IS.
THE ONLY REASON HE DEVOURED YOUR LEG WAS TO PUT AN END TO THAT TRAGIC STORY. BUT WE CAN'T ALLOW HIM TO LEAD THE SCHOOL AFTER THAT!
THE POLICE COVERED UP THE INCIDENT...
...BECAUSE YOUR MOTIVATIONS WERE INNOCENT AND BEASTS WOULD BE SHOCKED IF THEY FOUND OUT WHAT REALLY TRANSPIRED.

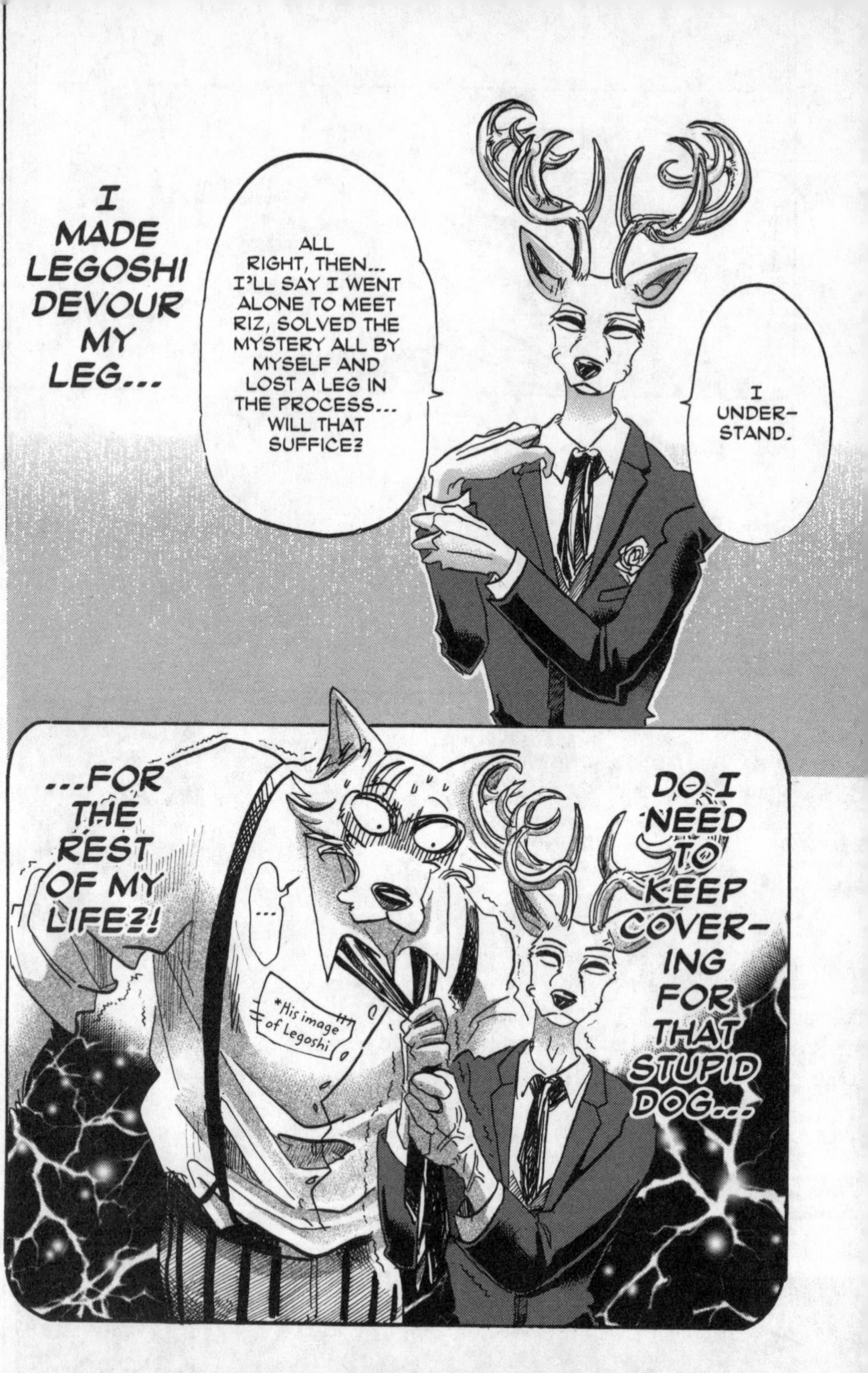
I UNDER-STAND.
ALL RIGHT, THEN... I'LL SAY I WENT ALONE TO MEET RIZ, SOLVED THE MYSTERY ALL BY MYSELF AND LOST A LEG IN THE PROCESS... WILL THAT SUFFICE?
I MADE LEGOSHI DEVOUR MY LEG...
DO I NEED TO KEEP COVER-ING FOR THAT STUPID DOG...
...
*His image of Legoshi
...FOR THE REST OF MY LIFE?!

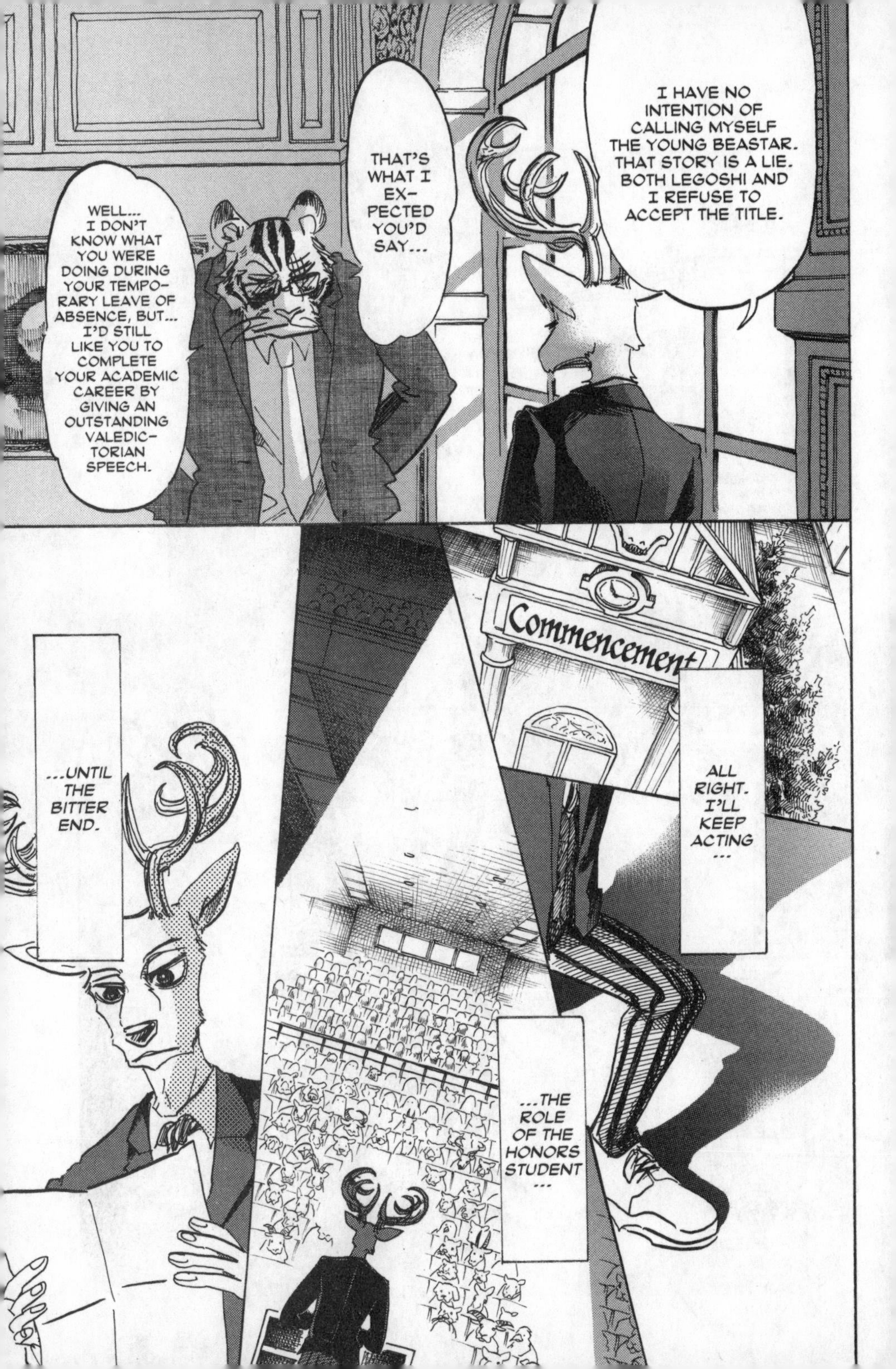
I HAVE NO INTENTION OF CALLING MYSELF THE YOUNG BEASTAR. THAT STORY IS A LIE. BOTH LEGOSHI AND I REFUSE TO ACCEPT THE TITLE.
THAT'S WHAT I EX-PECTED YOU'D SAY...
WELL... I DON'T KNOW WHAT YOU WERE DOING DURING YOUR TEMPO-RARY LEAVE OF ABSENCE, BUT... I'D STILL LIKE YOU TO COMPLETE YOUR ACADEMIC CAREER BY GIVING AN OUTSTANDING VALEDIC-TORIAN SPEECH.
Commencement
ALL RIGHT. I'LL KEEP ACTING ...
...THE ROLE OF THE HONORS STUDENT ...
...UNTIL THE BITTER END.

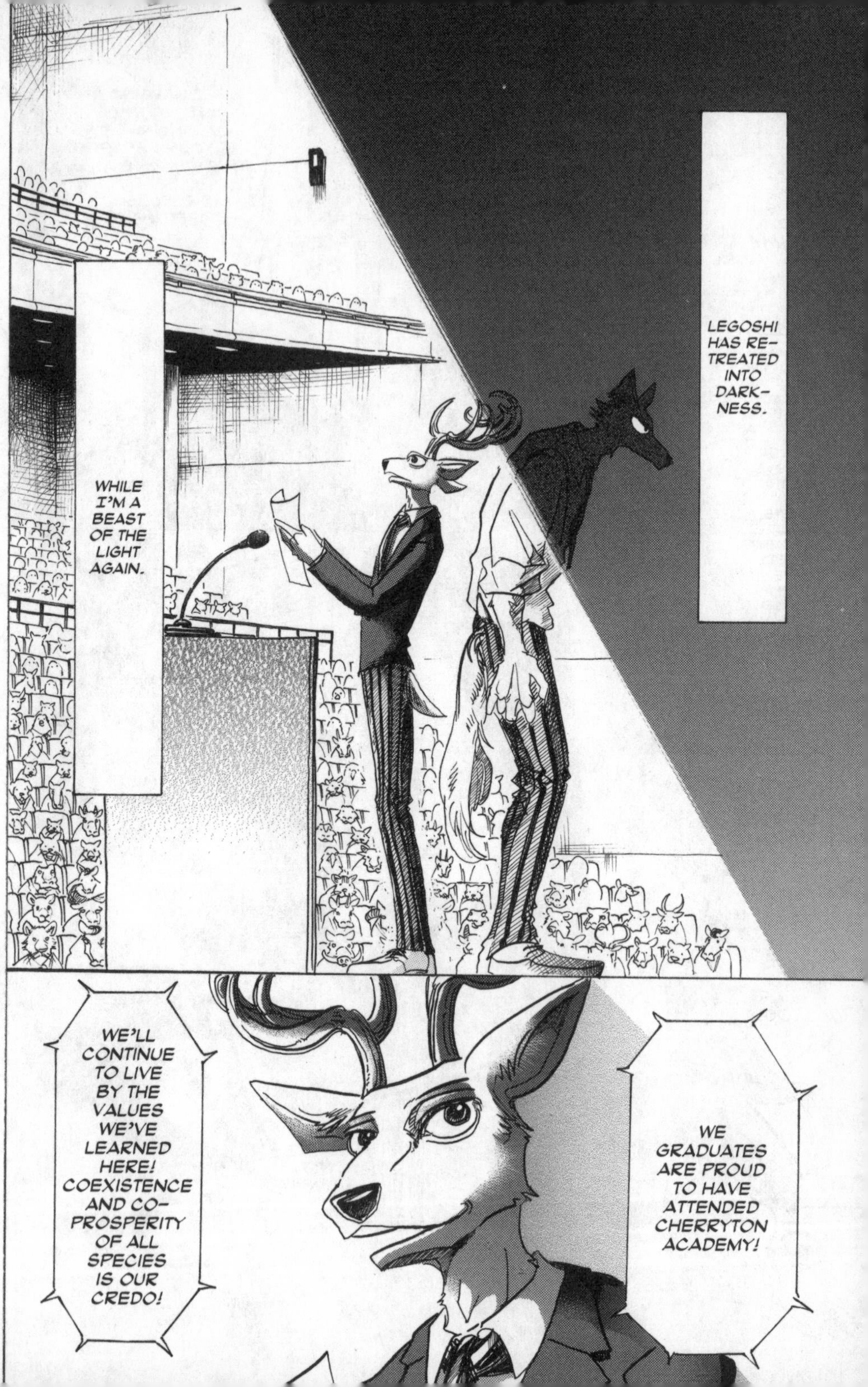
LEGOSHI HAS RETREATED INTO DARKNESS.
WHILE I'M A BEAST OF THE LIGHT AGAIN.
WE GRADUATES ARE PROUD TO HAVE ATTENDED CHERRYTON ACADEMY!
WE'LL CONTINUE TO LIVE BY THE VALUES WE'VE LEARNED HERE! COEXISTENCE AND CO-PROSPERITY OF ALL SPECIES IS OUR CREDO!

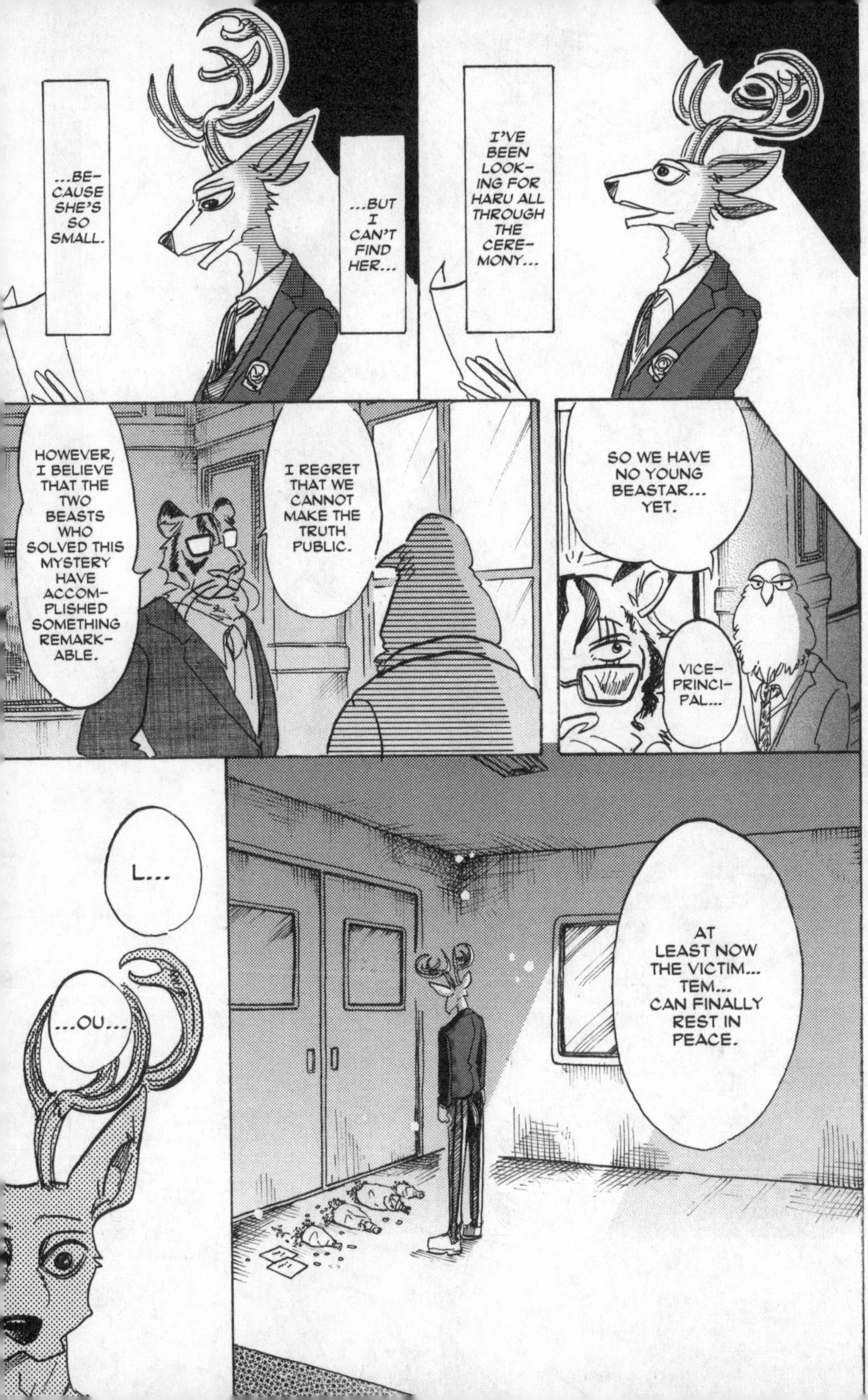
I'VE BEEN LOOKING FOR HARU ALL THROUGH THE CEREMONY...
...BUT I CAN'T FIND HER...
...BECAUSE SHE'S SO SMALL.
SO WE HAVE NO YOUNG BEASTAR... YET.
VICE-PRINCIPAL...
I REGRET THAT WE CANNOT MAKE THE TRUTH PUBLIC.
HOWEVER, I BELIEVE THAT THE TWO BEASTS WHO SOLVED THIS MYSTERY HAVE ACCOMPLISHED SOMETHING REMARKABLE.
AT LEAST NOW THE VICTIM... TEM... CAN FINALLY REST IN PEACE.
L...
...OU...

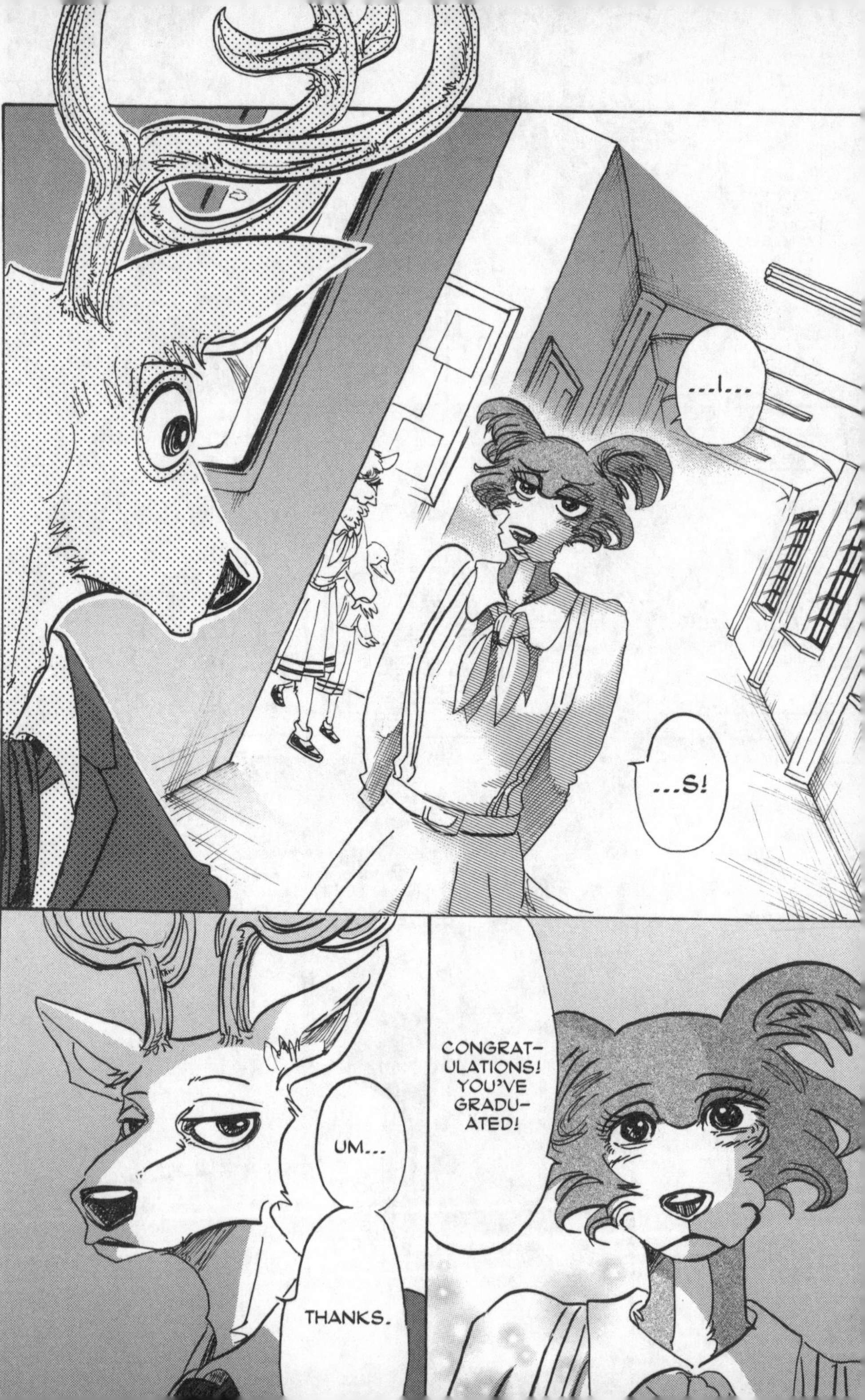
...I...
...S!
CONGRAT-ULATIONS! YOU'VE GRADU-ATED!
UM...
THANKS.

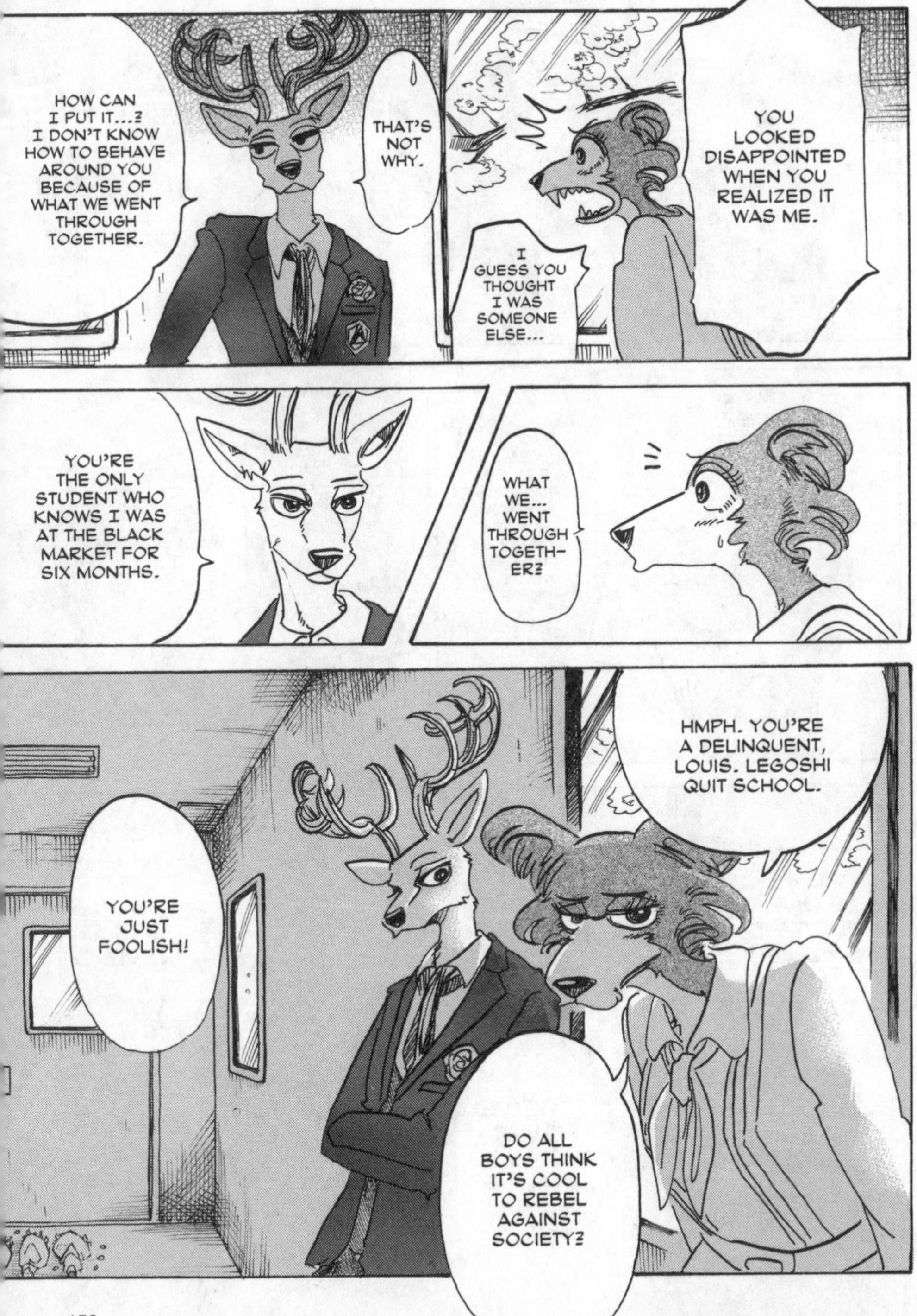
YOU LOOKED DISAPPOINTED WHEN YOU REALIZED IT WAS ME.
I GUESS YOU THOUGHT I WAS SOMEONE ELSE...
THAT'S NOT WHY.
HOW CAN I PUT IT...? I DON'T KNOW HOW TO BEHAVE AROUND YOU BECAUSE OF WHAT WE WENT THROUGH TOGETHER.
WHAT WE... WENT THROUGH TOGETHER?
YOU'RE THE ONLY STUDENT WHO KNOWS I WAS AT THE BLACK MARKET FOR SIX MONTHS.
HMPH. YOU'RE A DELINQUENT, LOUIS. LEGOSHI QUIT SCHOOL.
DO ALL BOYS THINK IT'S COOL TO REBEL AGAINST SOCIETY?
YOU'RE JUST FOOLISH!

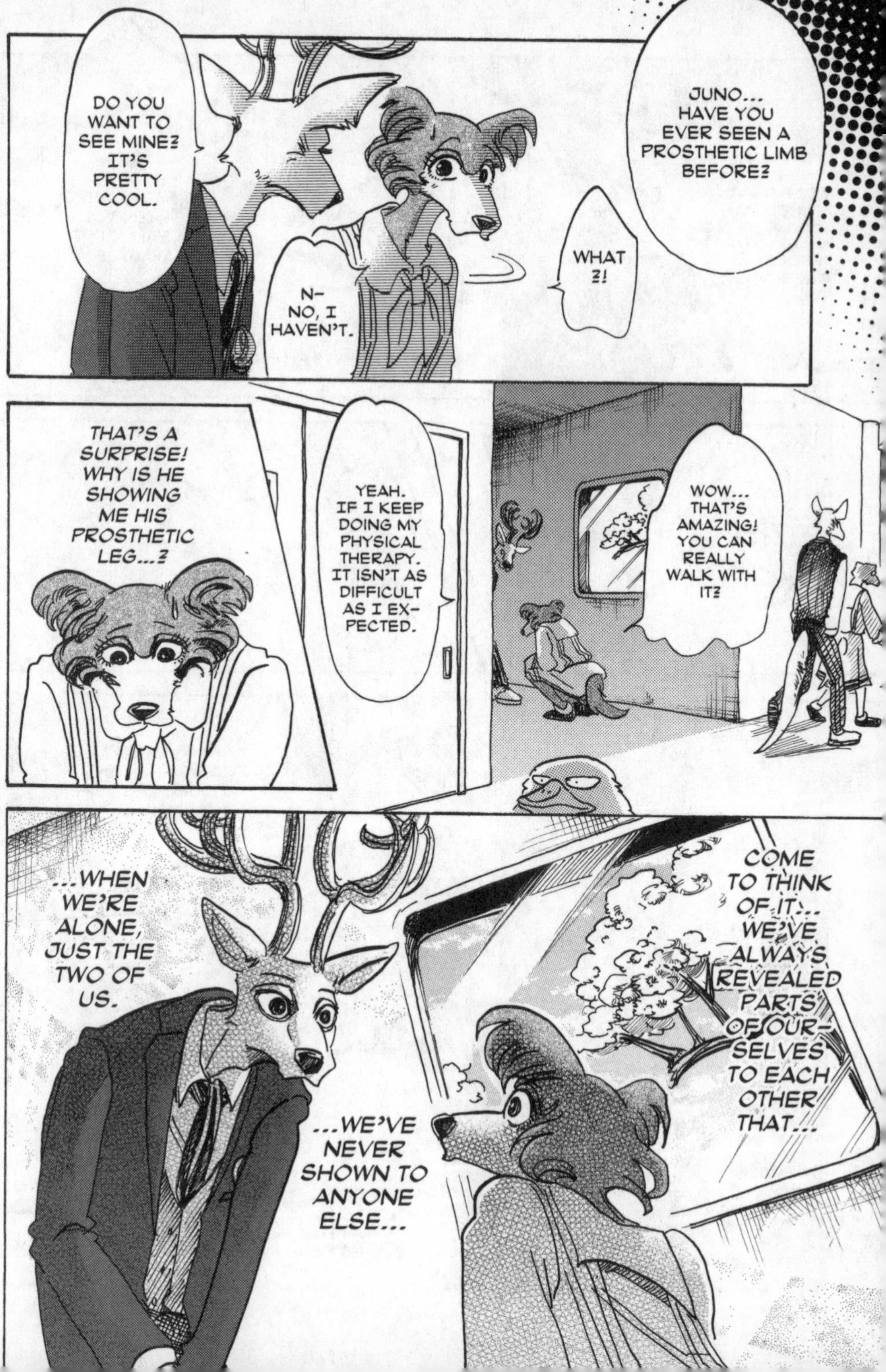
JUNO... HAVE YOU EVER SEEN A PROSTHETIC LIMB BEFORE?
WHAT ?!
N– NO, I HAVEN'T.
DO YOU WANT TO SEE MINE? IT'S PRETTY COOL.
WOW... THAT'S AMAZING! YOU CAN REALLY WALK WITH IT?
YEAH. IF I KEEP DOING MY PHYSICAL THERAPY. IT ISN'T AS DIFFICULT AS I EX-PECTED.
THAT'S A SURPRISE! WHY IS HE SHOWING ME HIS PROSTHETIC LEG...?
COME TO THINK OF IT... WE'VE ALWAYS REVEALED PARTS OF OUR-SELVES TO EACH OTHER THAT...
...WE'VE NEVER SHOWN TO ANYONE ELSE...
...WHEN WE'RE ALONE, JUST THE TWO OF US.

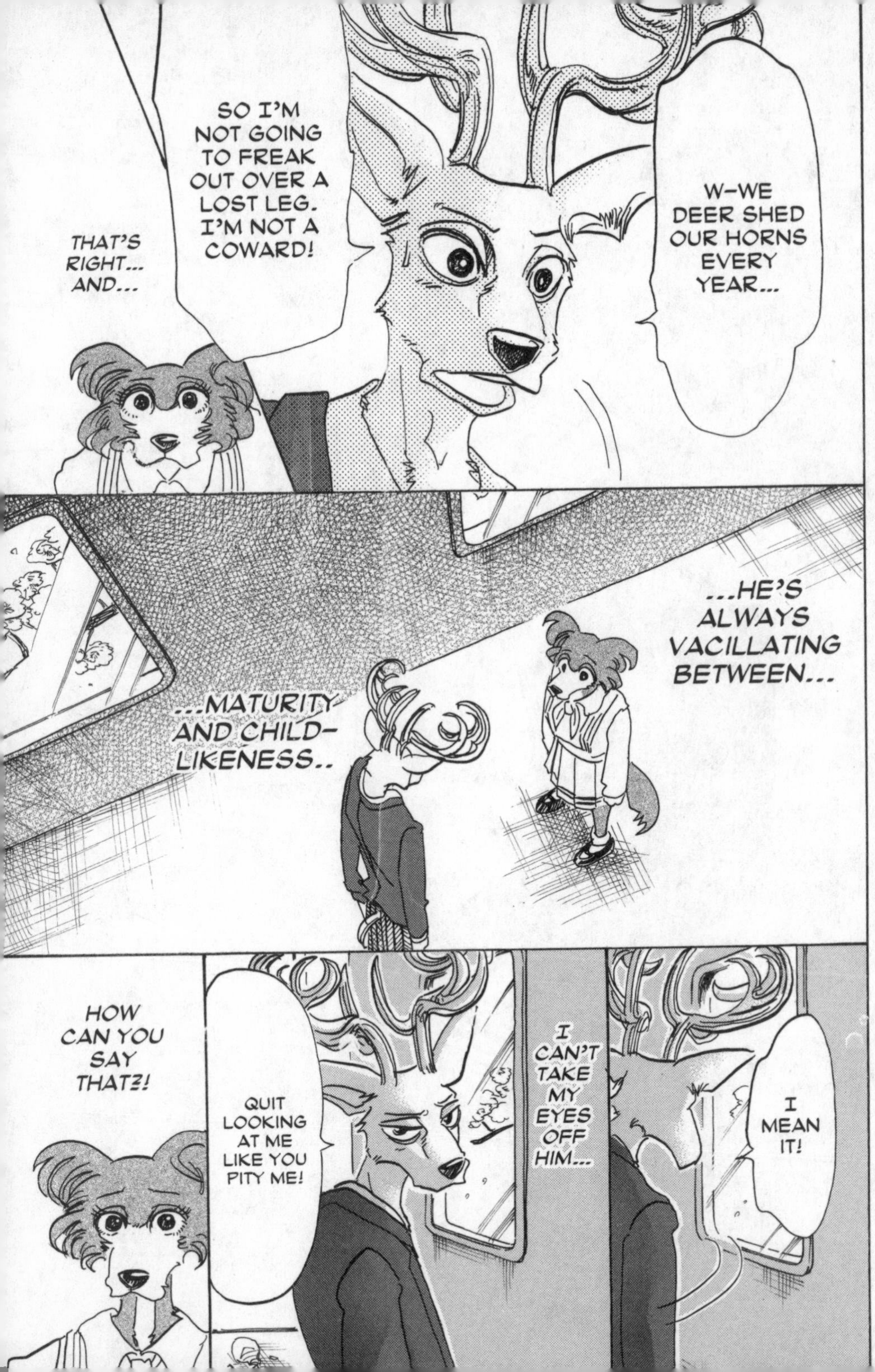
W-WE DEER SHED OUR HORNS EVERY YEAR...
SO I'M NOT GOING TO FREAK OUT OVER A LOST LEG. I'M NOT A COWARD!
THAT'S RIGHT... AND...
...HE'S ALWAYS VACILLATING BETWEEN...
...MATURITY AND CHILD-LIKENESS...
I MEAN IT!
I CAN'T TAKE MY EYES OFF HIM...
QUIT LOOKING AT ME LIKE YOU PITY ME!
HOW CAN YOU SAY THAT?!

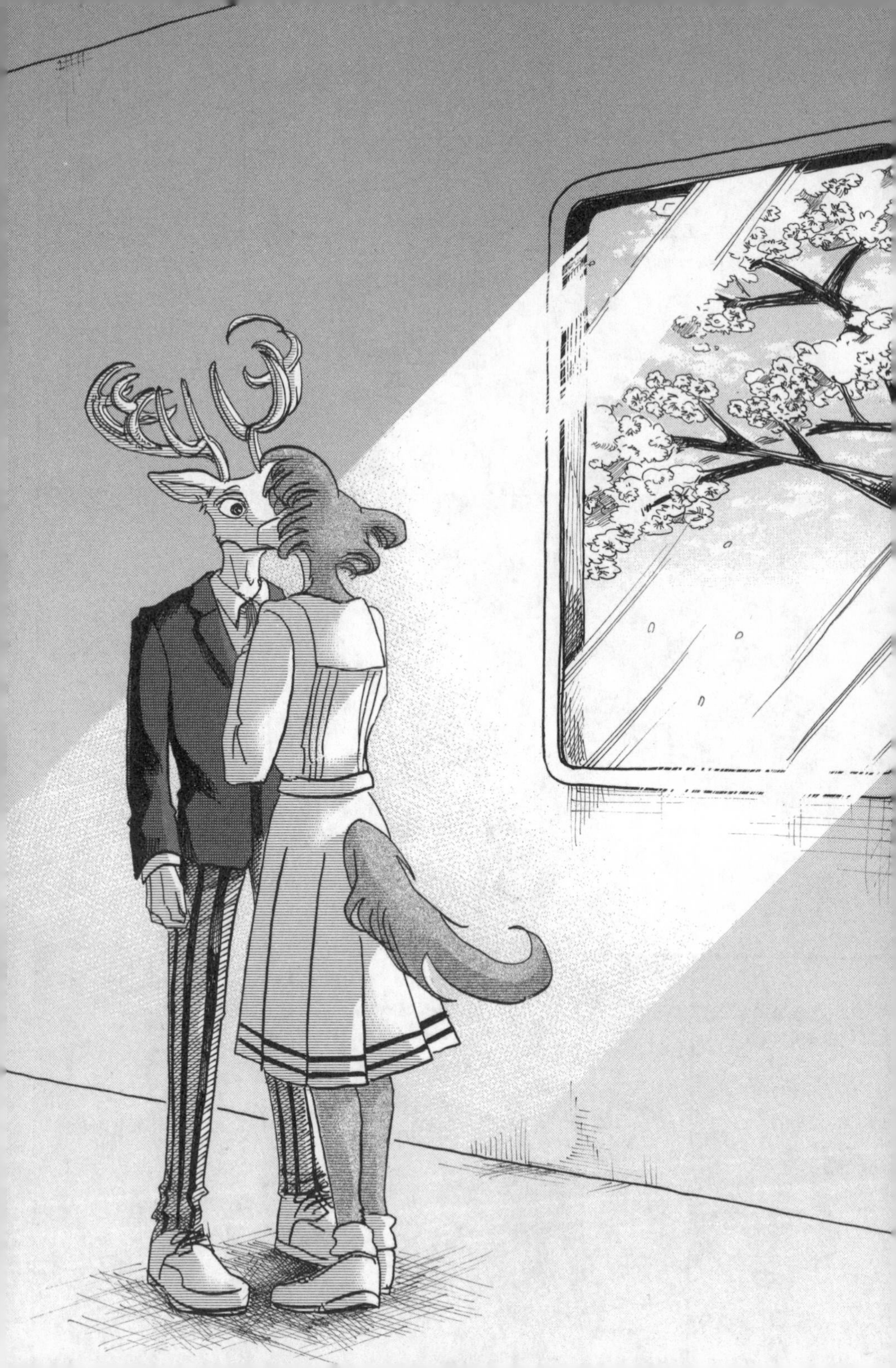

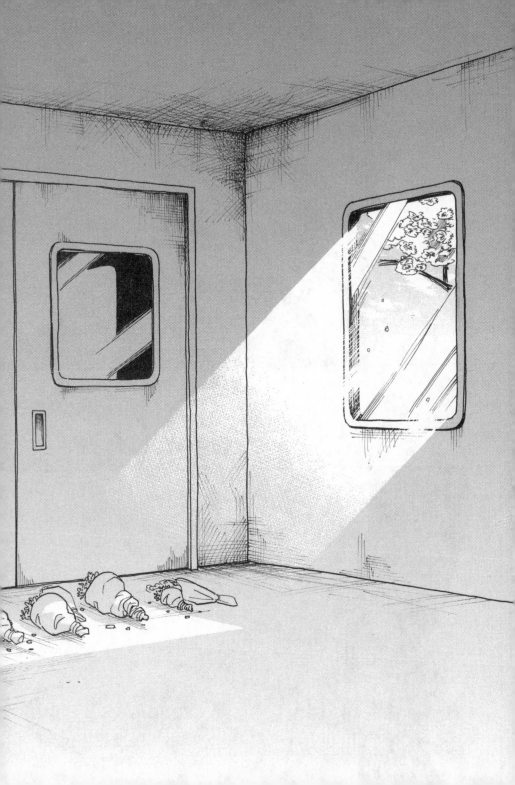

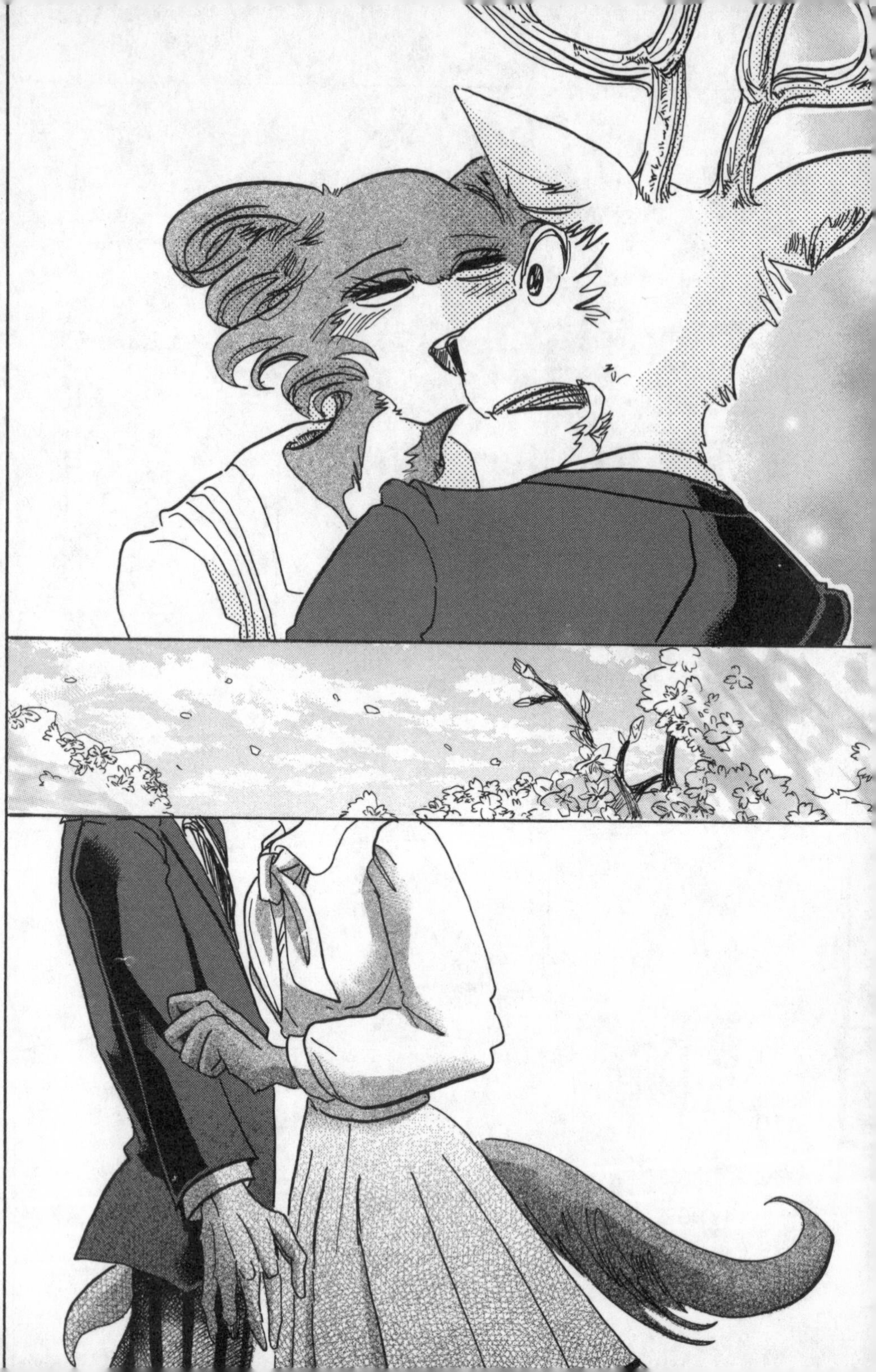

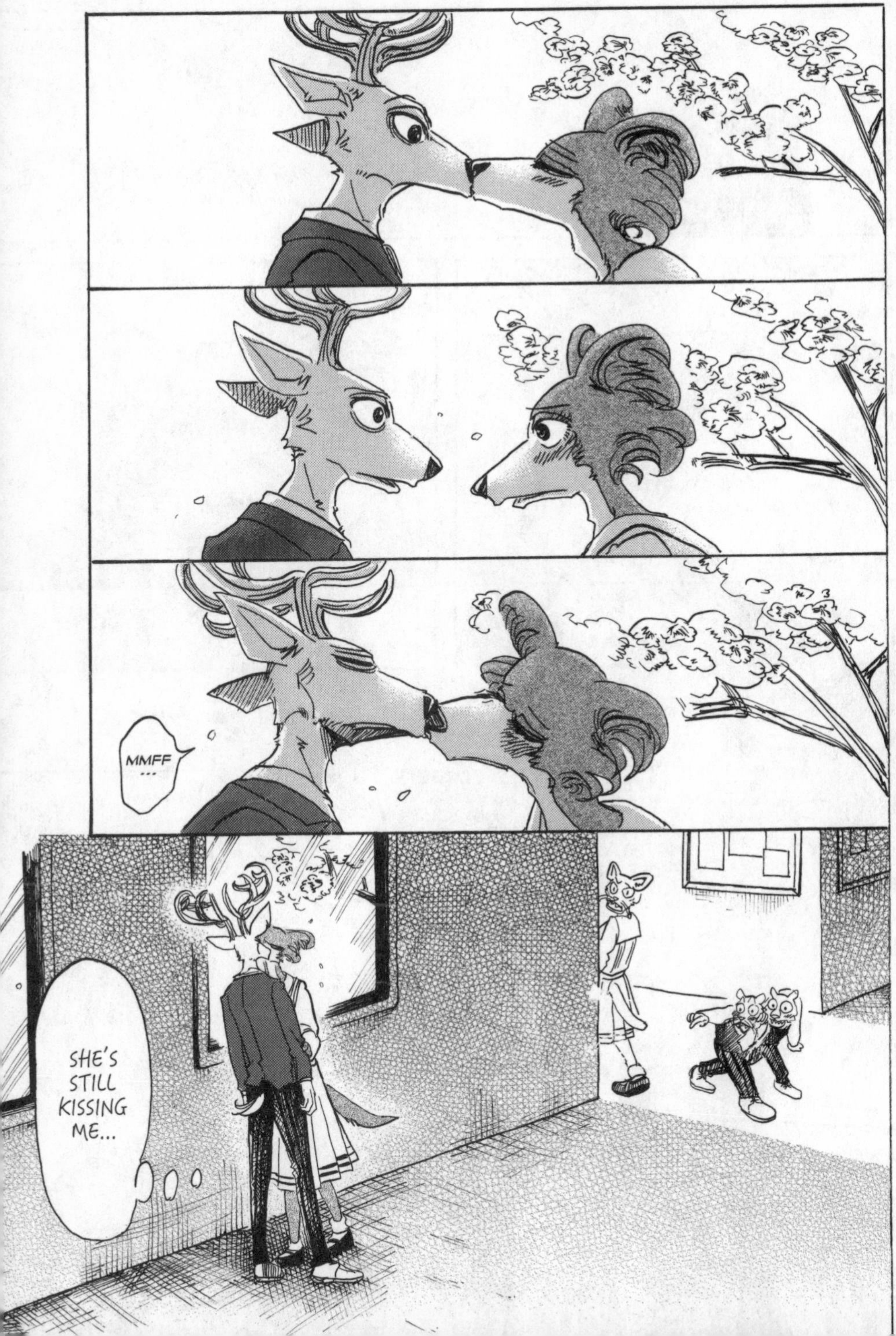
MMFF...
SHE'S STILL KISSING ME...

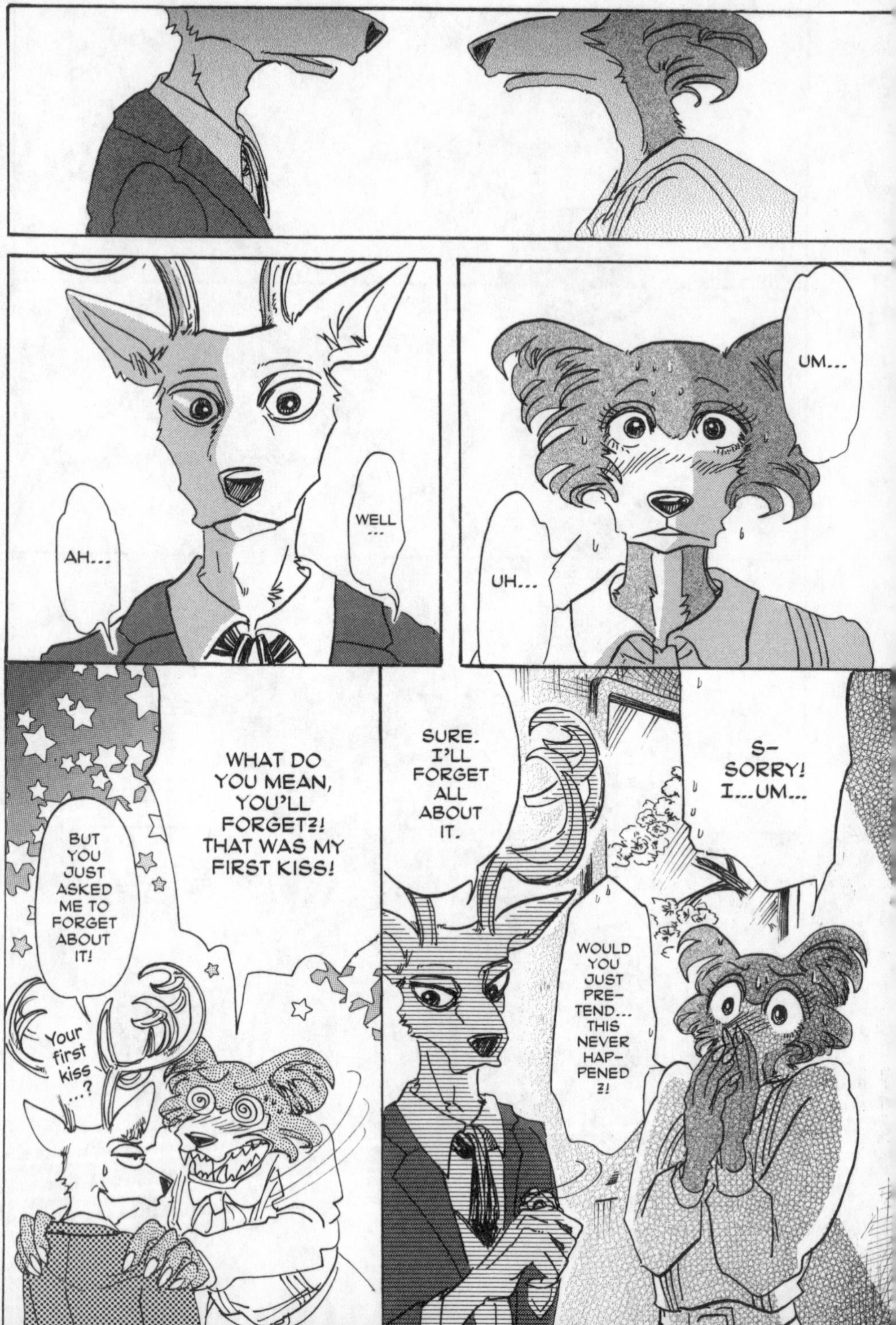
UM...
UH...
WELL ...
AH...
S-SORRY! I...UM...
WOULD YOU JUST PRE-TEND... THIS NEVER HAP-PENED?!
SURE. I'LL FORGET ALL ABOUT IT.
WHAT DO YOU MEAN, YOU'LL FORGET?! THAT WAS MY FIRST KISS!
BUT YOU JUST ASKED ME TO FORGET ABOUT IT!
Your first kiss ...?

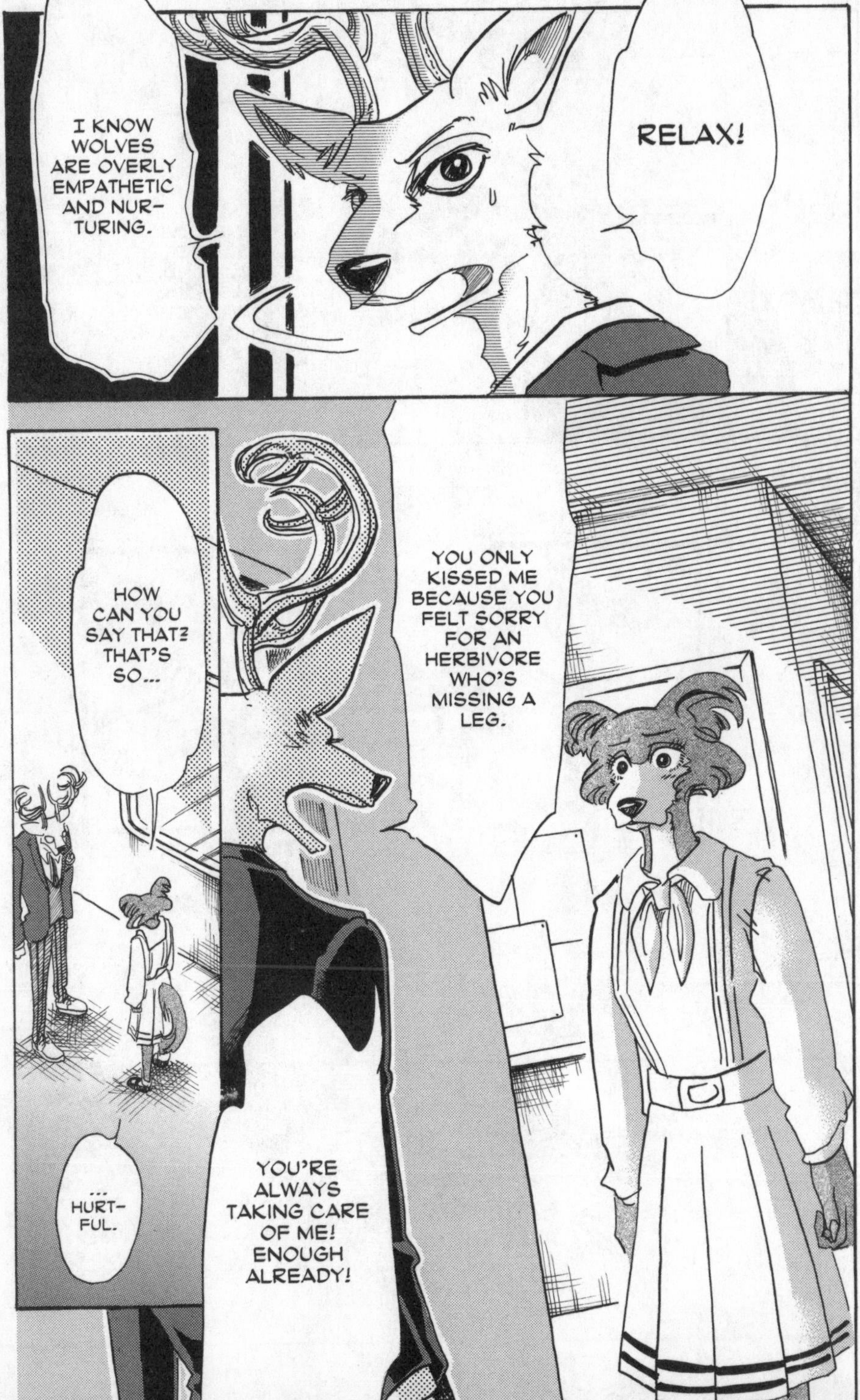
RELAX!
I KNOW WOLVES ARE OVERLY EMPATHETIC AND NUR-TURING.
YOU ONLY KISSED ME BECAUSE YOU FELT SORRY FOR AN HERBIVORE WHO'S MISSING A LEG.
YOU'RE ALWAYS TAKING CARE OF ME! ENOUGH ALREADY!
HOW CAN YOU SAY THAT? THAT'S SO...
... HURT-FUL.

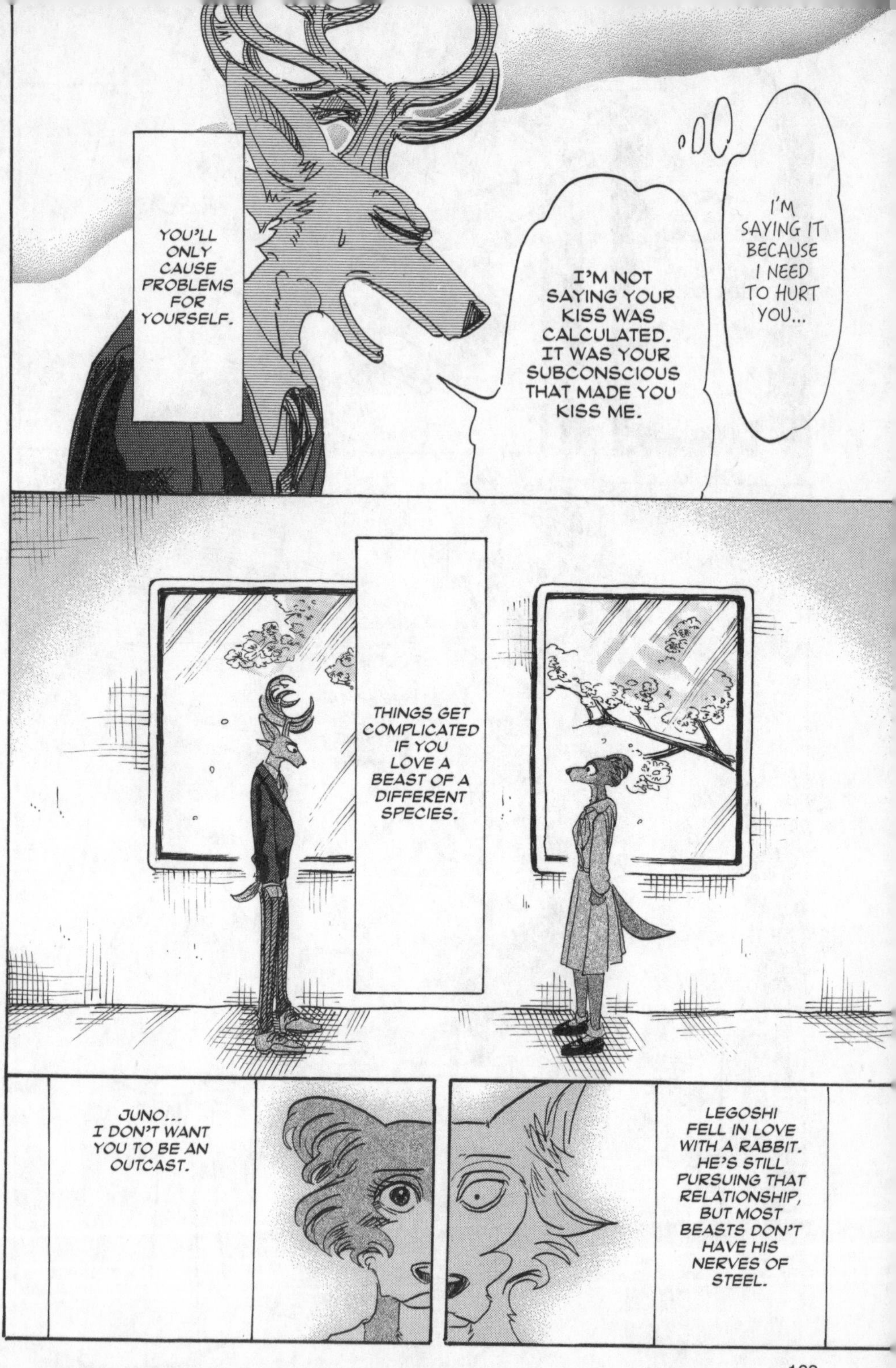
I'M SAYING IT BECAUSE I NEED TO HURT YOU...
I'M NOT SAYING YOUR KISS WAS CALCULATED. IT WAS YOUR SUBCONSCIOUS THAT MADE YOU KISS ME.
YOU'LL ONLY CAUSE PROBLEMS FOR YOURSELF.
THINGS GET COMPLICATED IF YOU LOVE A BEAST OF A DIFFERENT SPECIES.
LEGOSHI FELL IN LOVE WITH A RABBIT. HE'S STILL PURSUING THAT RELATIONSHIP, BUT MOST BEASTS DON'T HAVE HIS NERVES OF STEEL.
JUNO... I DON'T WANT YOU TO BE AN OUTCAST.

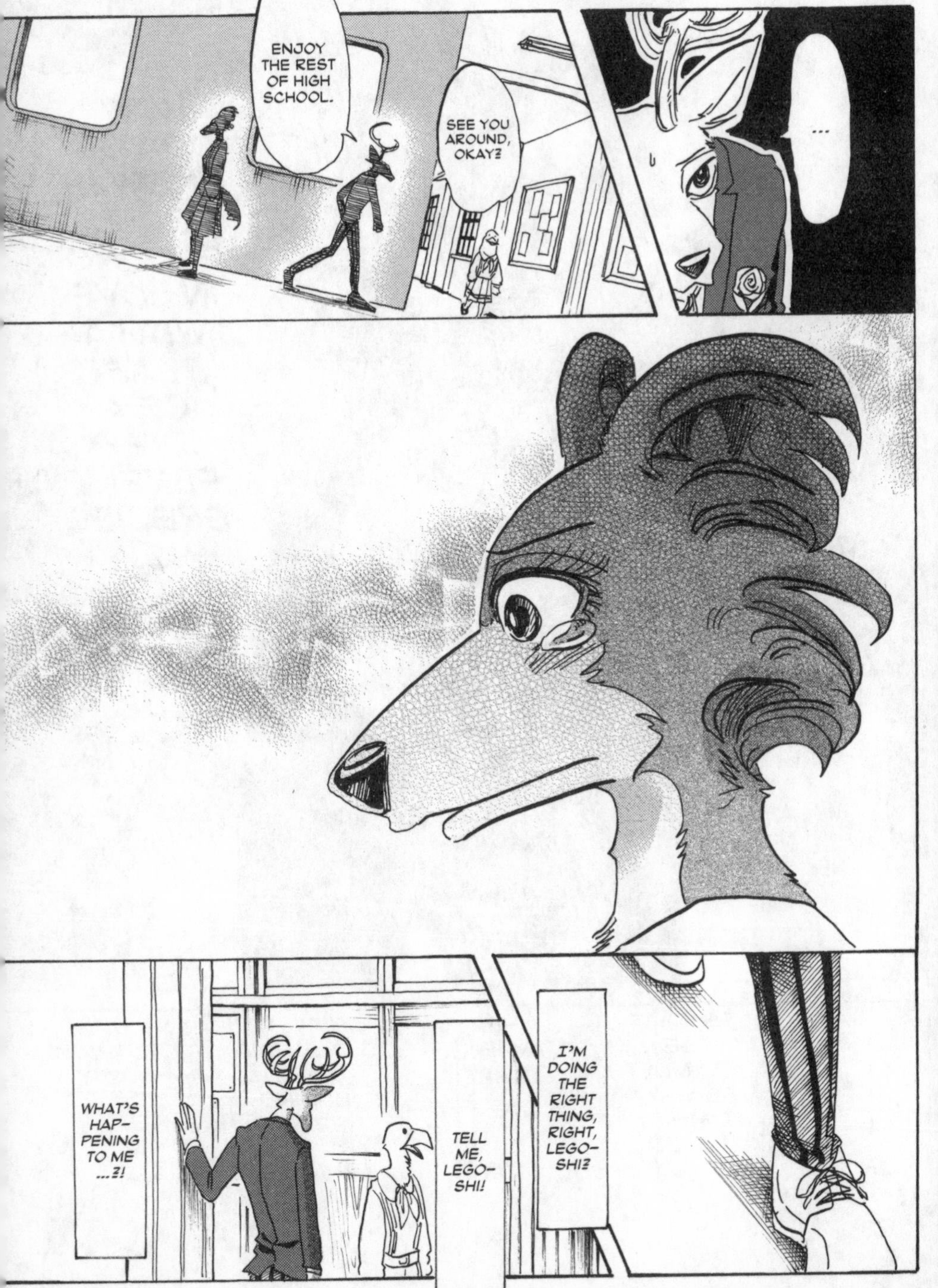
...
SEE YOU AROUND, OKAY?
ENJOY THE REST OF HIGH SCHOOL.
I'M DOING THE RIGHT THING, RIGHT, LEGO-SHI?
TELL ME, LEGO-SHI!
WHAT'S HAP-PENING TO ME ...?!

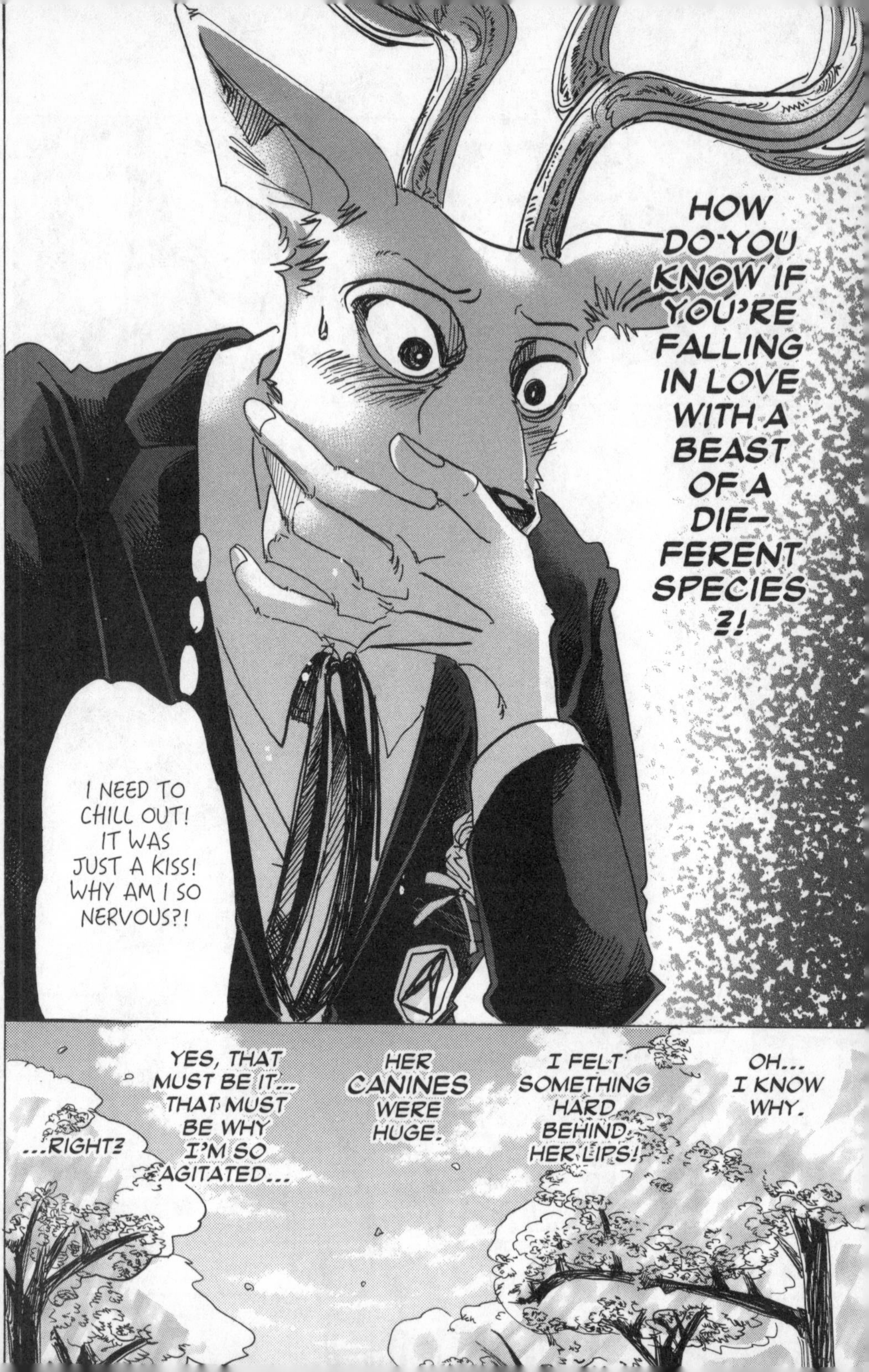
HOW DO YOU KNOW IF YOU'RE FALLING IN LOVE WITH A BEAST OF A DIF-FERENT SPECIES?!
I NEED TO CHILL OUT! IT WAS JUST A KISS! WHY AM I SO NERVOUS?!
OH... I KNOW WHY.
I FELT SOMETHING HARD BEHIND HER LIPS!
HER CANINES WERE HUGE.
YES, THAT MUST BE IT... THAT MUST BE WHY I'M SO AGITATED...
...RIGHT?

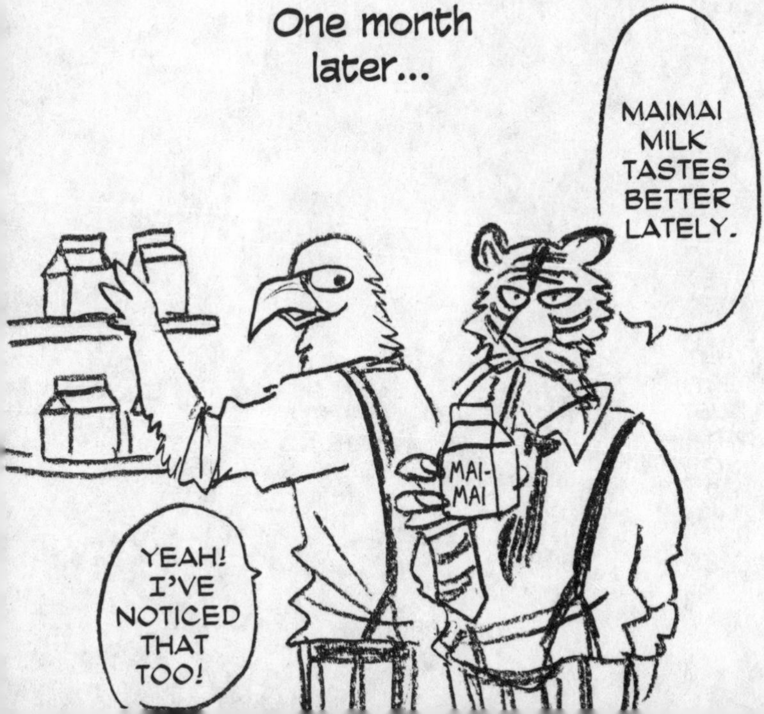
One month later...
MAIMAI MILK TASTES BETTER LATELY.
MAI-MAI
YEAH! I'VE NOTICED THAT TOO!

Chapter 106: Moonlight Reflected in Twinkling Scales

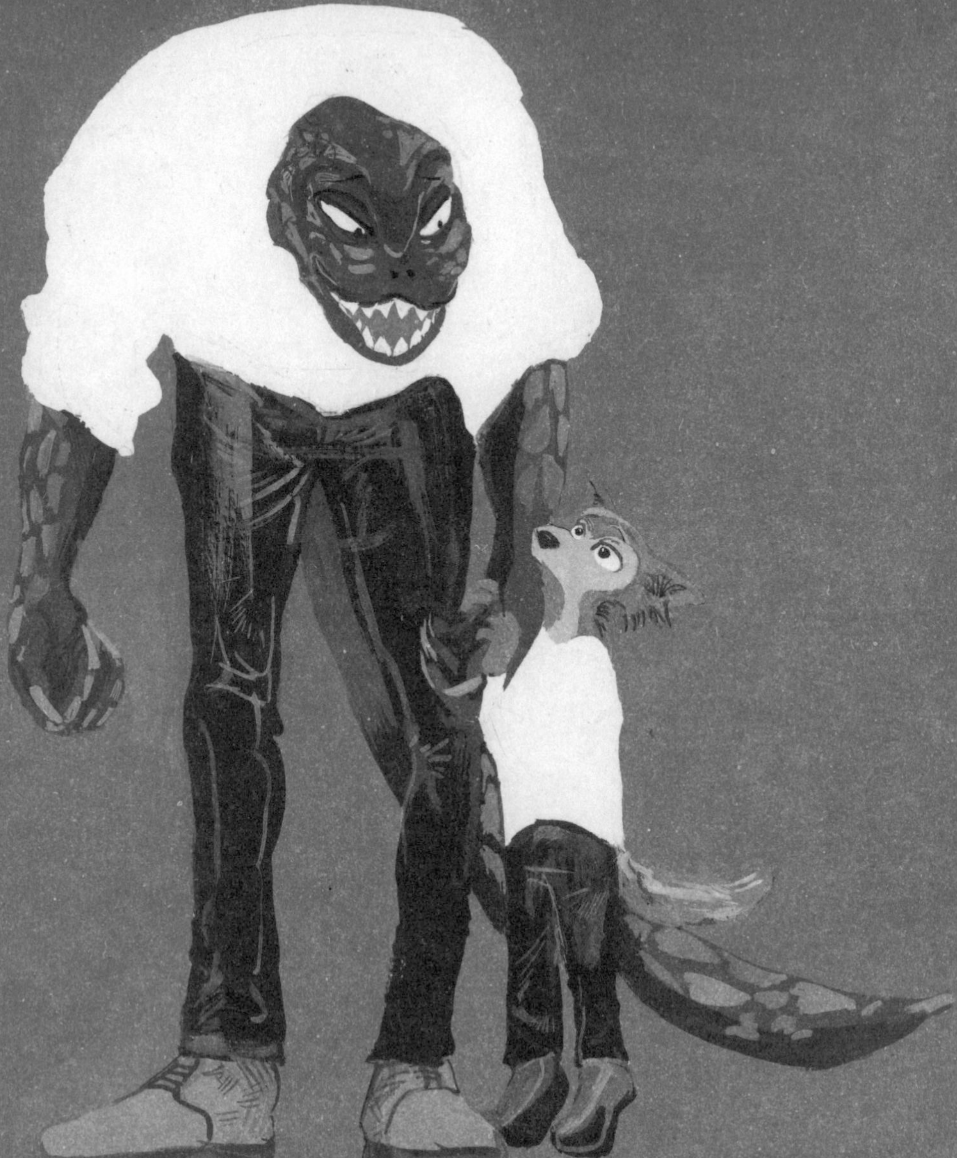

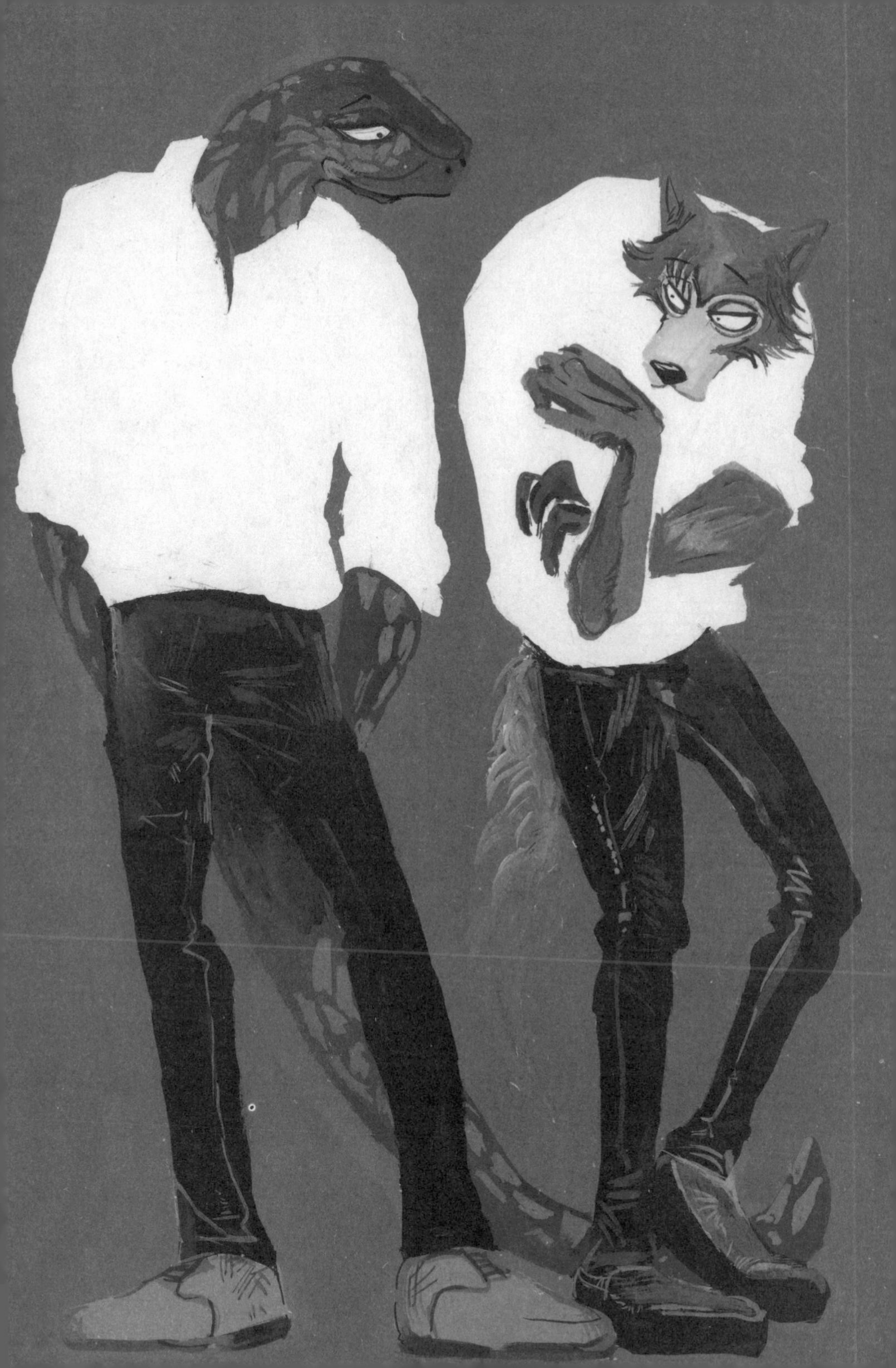

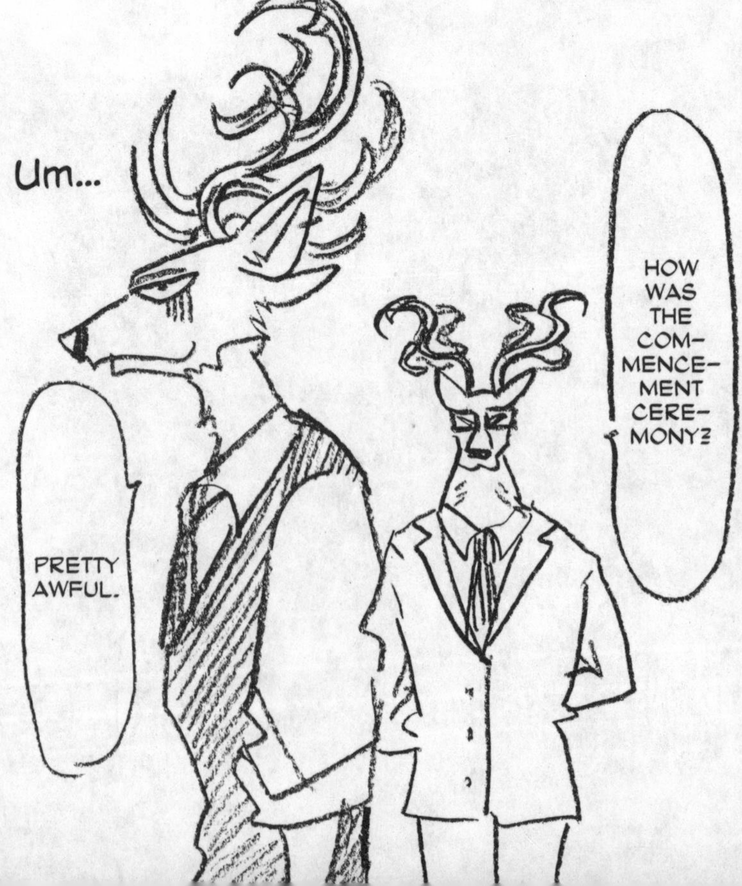
HOW WAS THE COM-MENCE-MENT CERE-MONY?
Um...
PRETTY AWFUL.

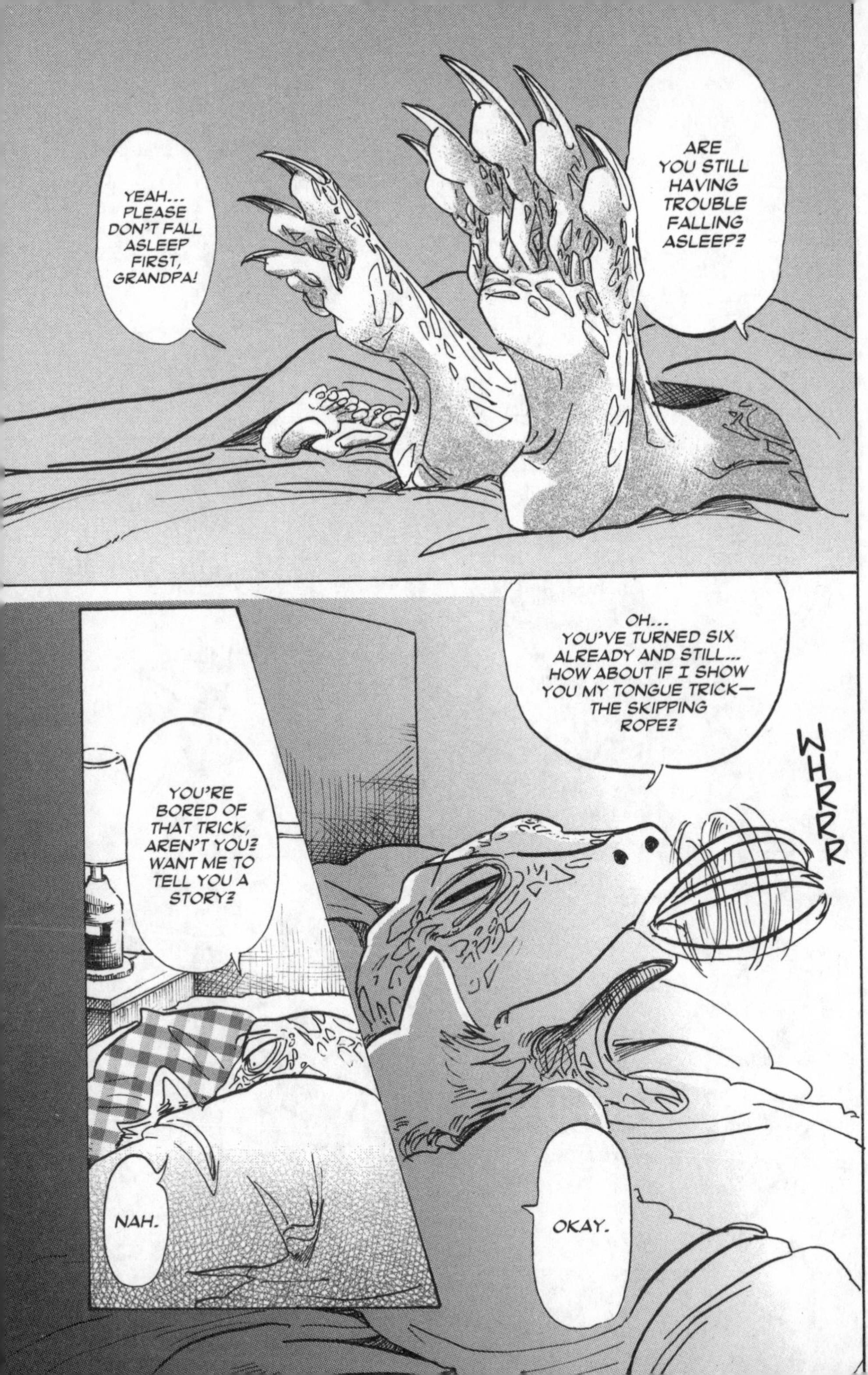
ARE YOU STILL HAVING TROUBLE FALLING ASLEEP?
YEAH... PLEASE DON'T FALL ASLEEP FIRST, GRANDPA!
OH... YOU'VE TURNED SIX ALREADY AND STILL... HOW ABOUT IF I SHOW YOU MY TONGUE TRICK— THE SKIPPING ROPE?
WHRRR
YOU'RE BORED OF THAT TRICK, AREN'T YOU? WANT ME TO TELL YOU A STORY?
NAH.
OKAY.

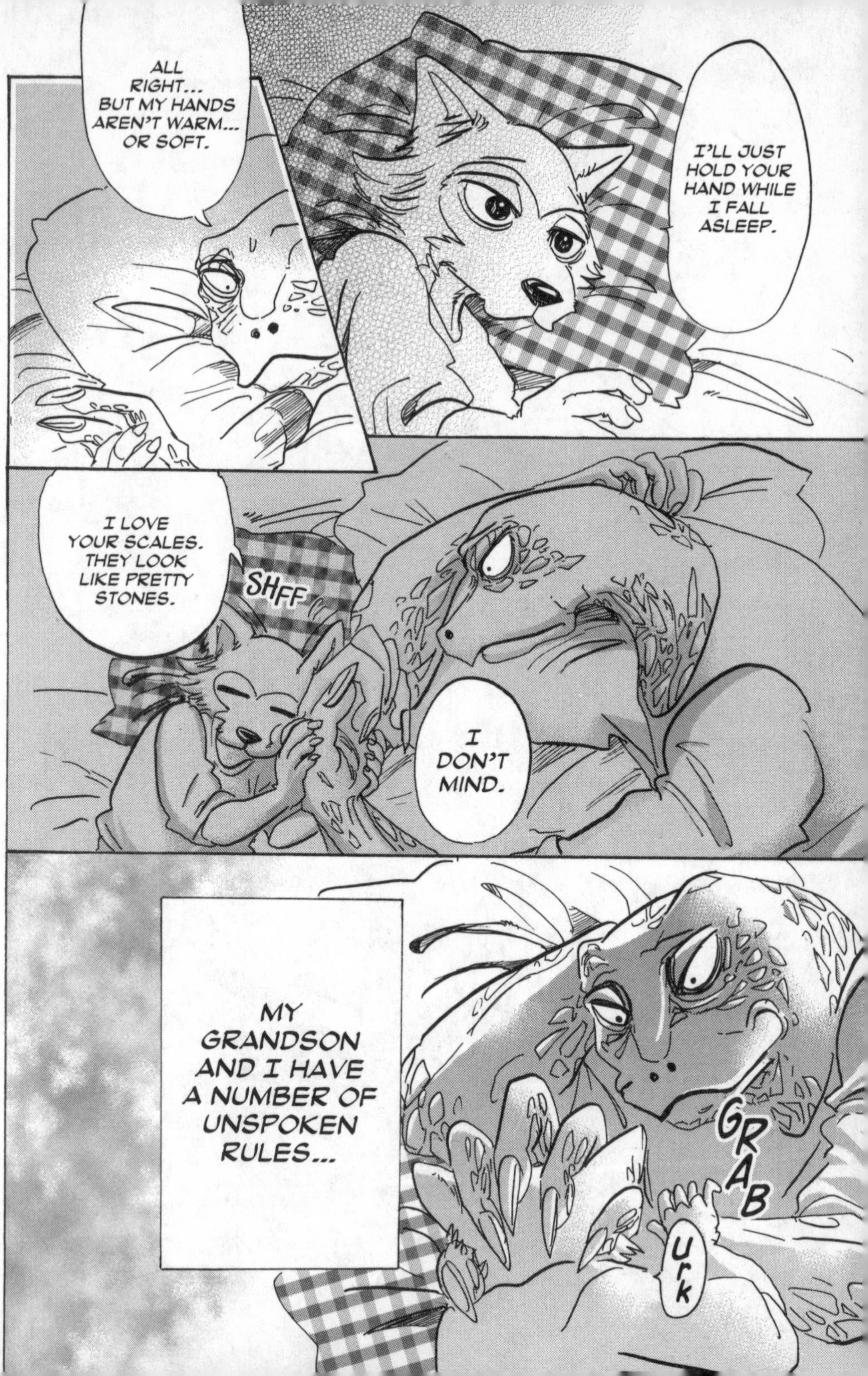
I'LL JUST HOLD YOUR HAND WHILE I FALL ASLEEP.
ALL RIGHT... BUT MY HANDS AREN'T WARM... OR SOFT.
I LOVE YOUR SCALES. THEY LOOK LIKE PRETTY STONES.
SHFF
I DON'T MIND.
MY GRANDSON AND I HAVE A NUMBER OF UNSPOKEN RULES...
GRAB
Urk

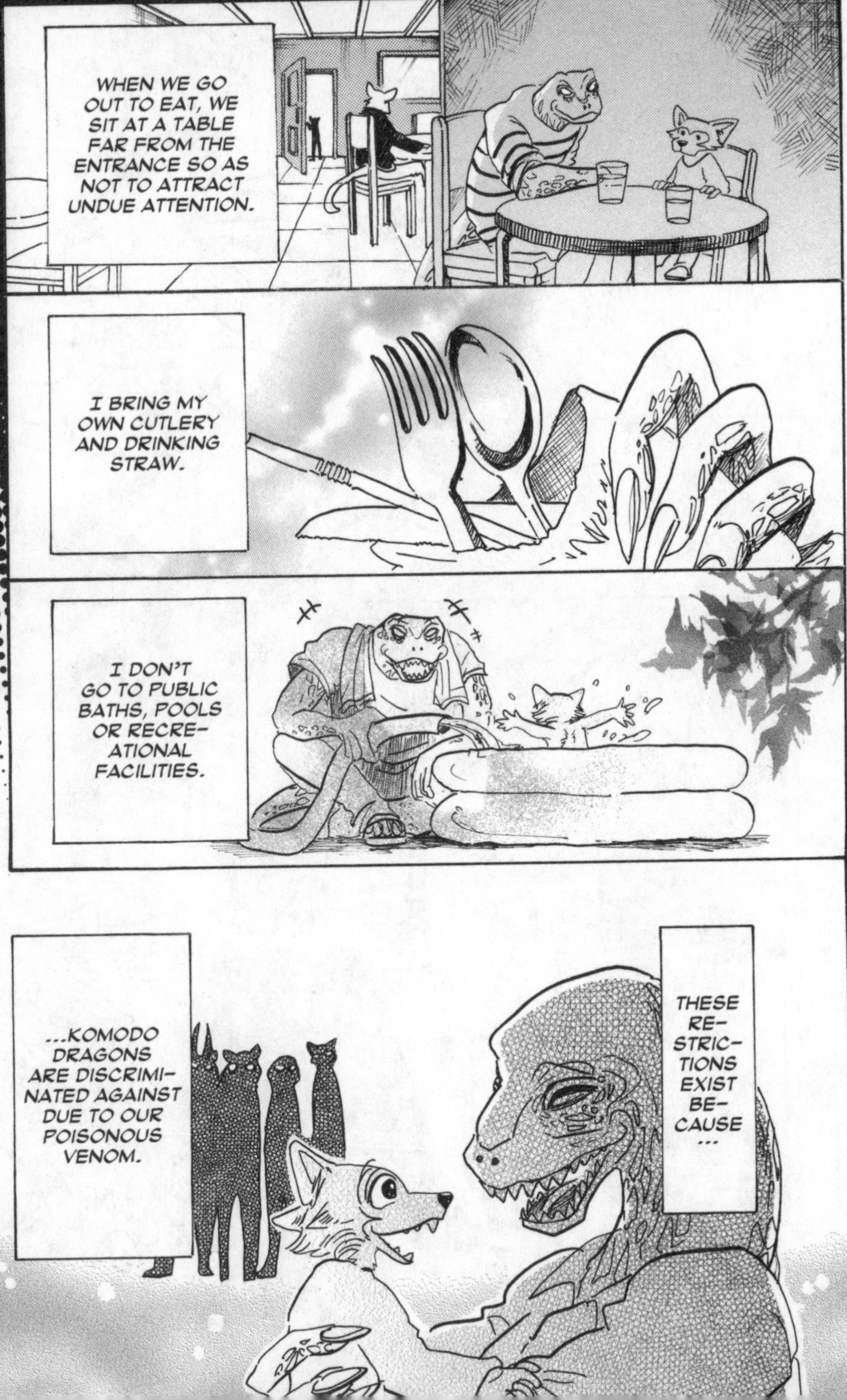
WHEN WE GO OUT TO EAT, WE SIT AT A TABLE FAR FROM THE ENTRANCE SO AS NOT TO ATTRACT UNDUE ATTENTION.
I BRING MY OWN CUTLERY AND DRINKING STRAW.
I DON'T GO TO PUBLIC BATHS, POOLS OR RECRE-ATIONAL FACILITIES.
THESE RE-STRIC-TIONS EXIST BE-CAUSE...
...KOMODO DRAGONS ARE DISCRIMI-NATED AGAINST DUE TO OUR POISONOUS VENOM.

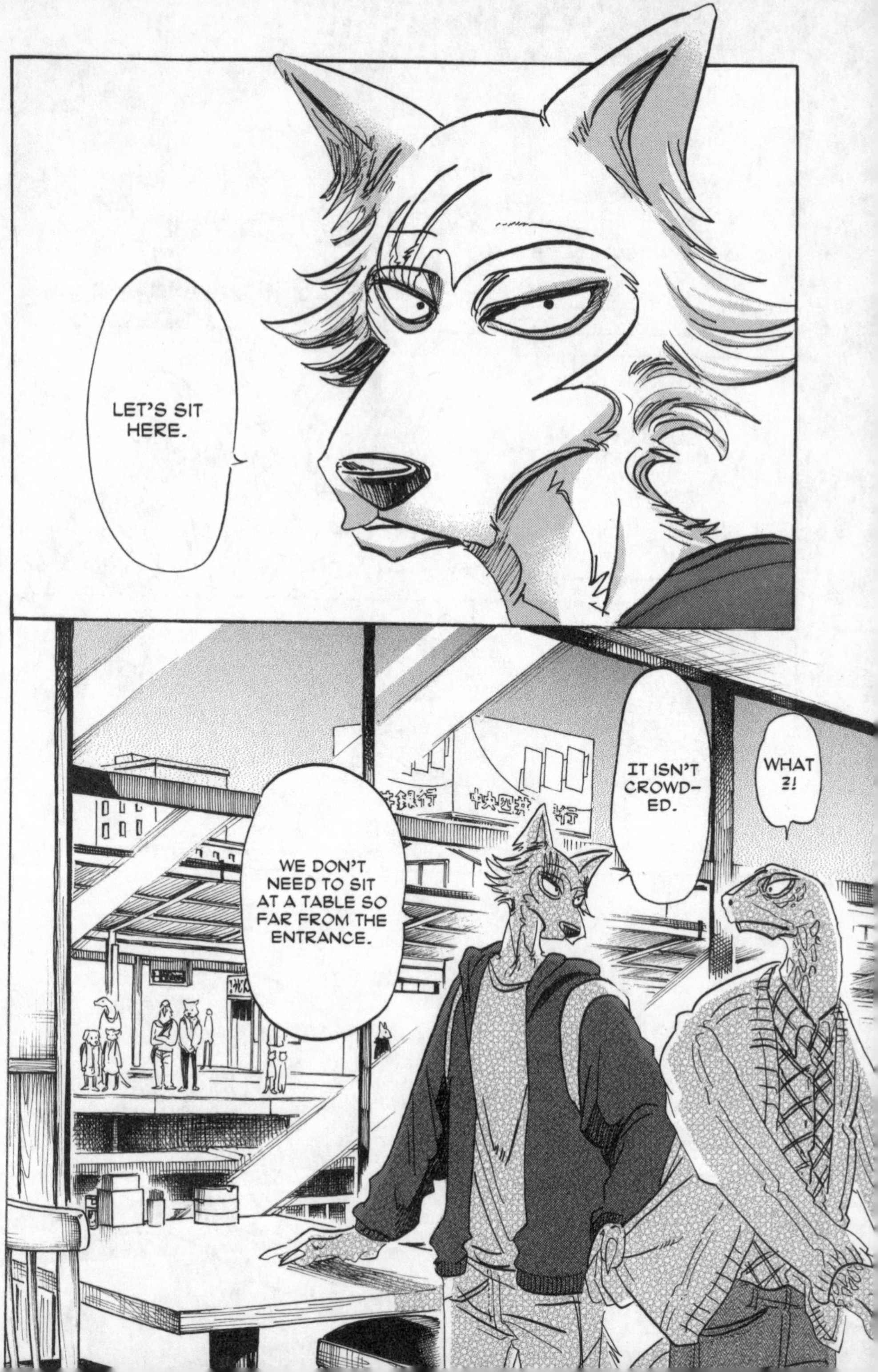
LET'S SIT HERE.
WHAT?!
IT ISN'T CROWDED.
WE DON'T NEED TO SIT AT A TABLE SO FAR FROM THE ENTRANCE.

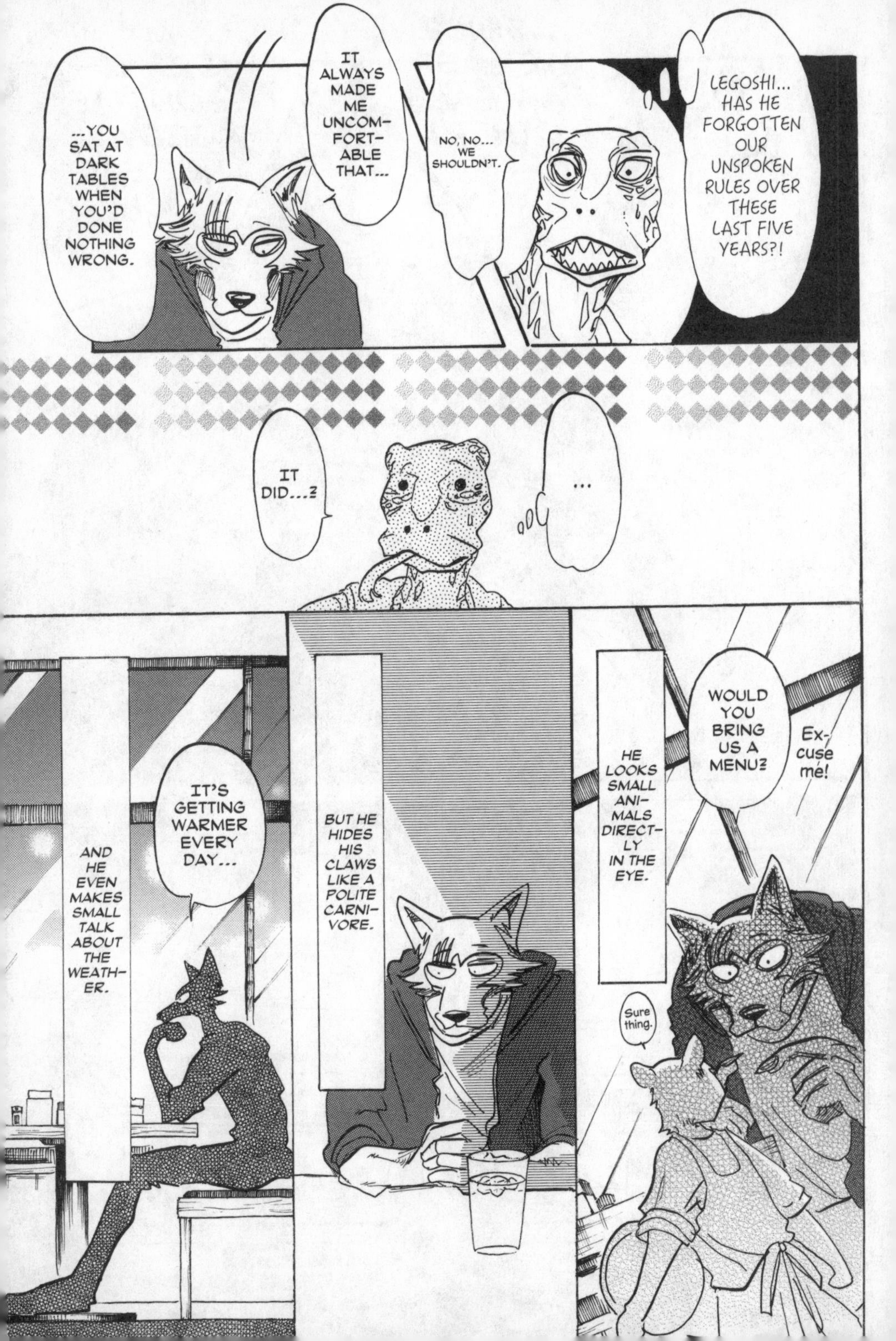
LEGOSHI... HAS HE FORGOTTEN OUR UNSPOKEN RULES OVER THESE LAST FIVE YEARS?!
NO, NO... WE SHOULDN'T.
IT ALWAYS MADE ME UNCOMFORTABLE THAT...
...YOU SAT AT DARK TABLES WHEN YOU'D DONE NOTHING WRONG.
...
IT DID...?
Excuse me!
WOULD YOU BRING US A MENU?
HE LOOKS SMALL ANIMALS DIRECTLY IN THE EYE.
Sure thing.
BUT HE HIDES HIS CLAWS LIKE A POLITE CARNIVORE.
IT'S GETTING WARMER EVERY DAY...
AND HE EVEN MAKES SMALL TALK ABOUT THE WEATHER.

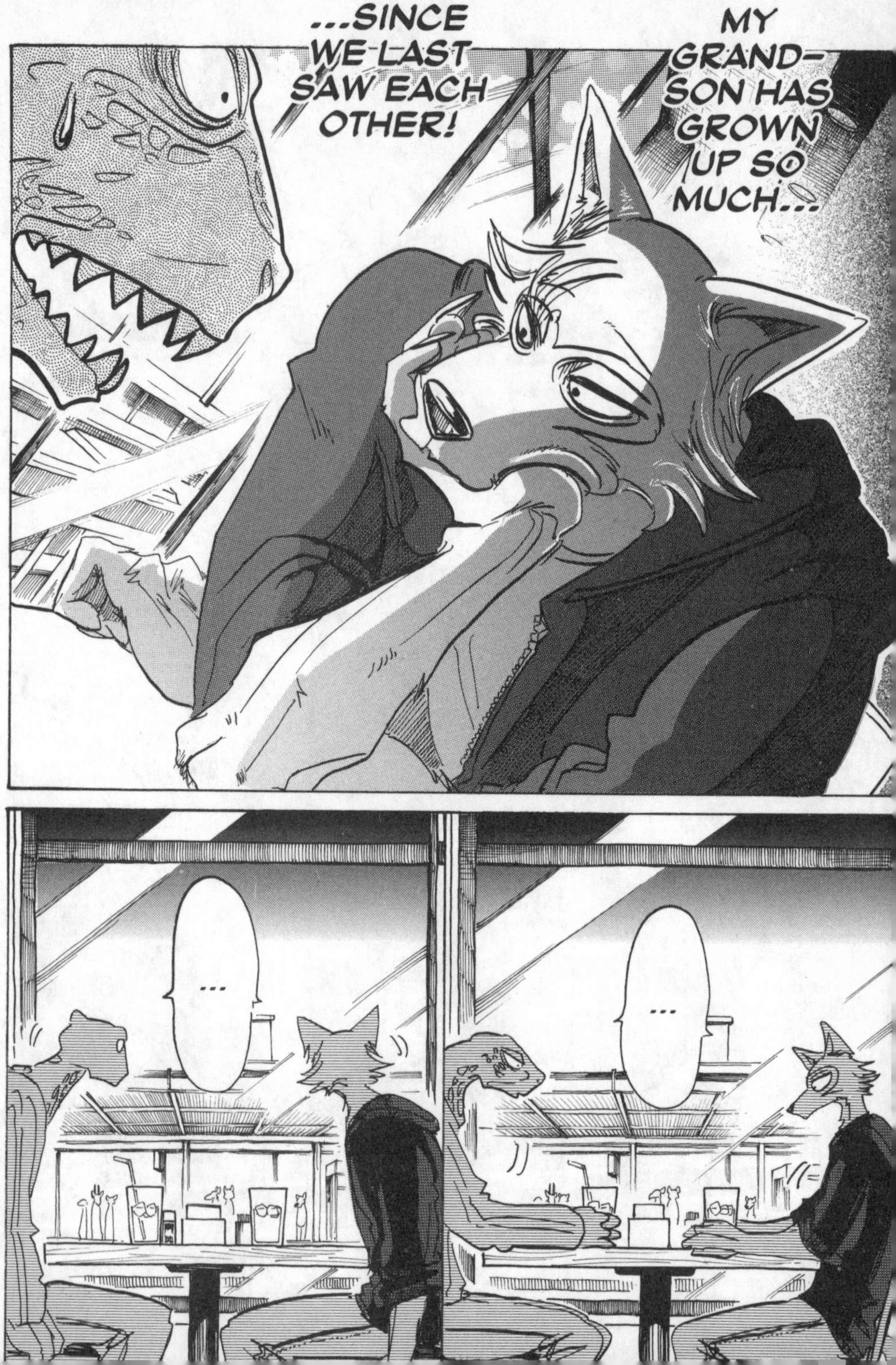
MY GRAND-SON HAS GROWN UP SO MUCH...
...SINCE WE LAST SAW EACH OTHER!
...
...

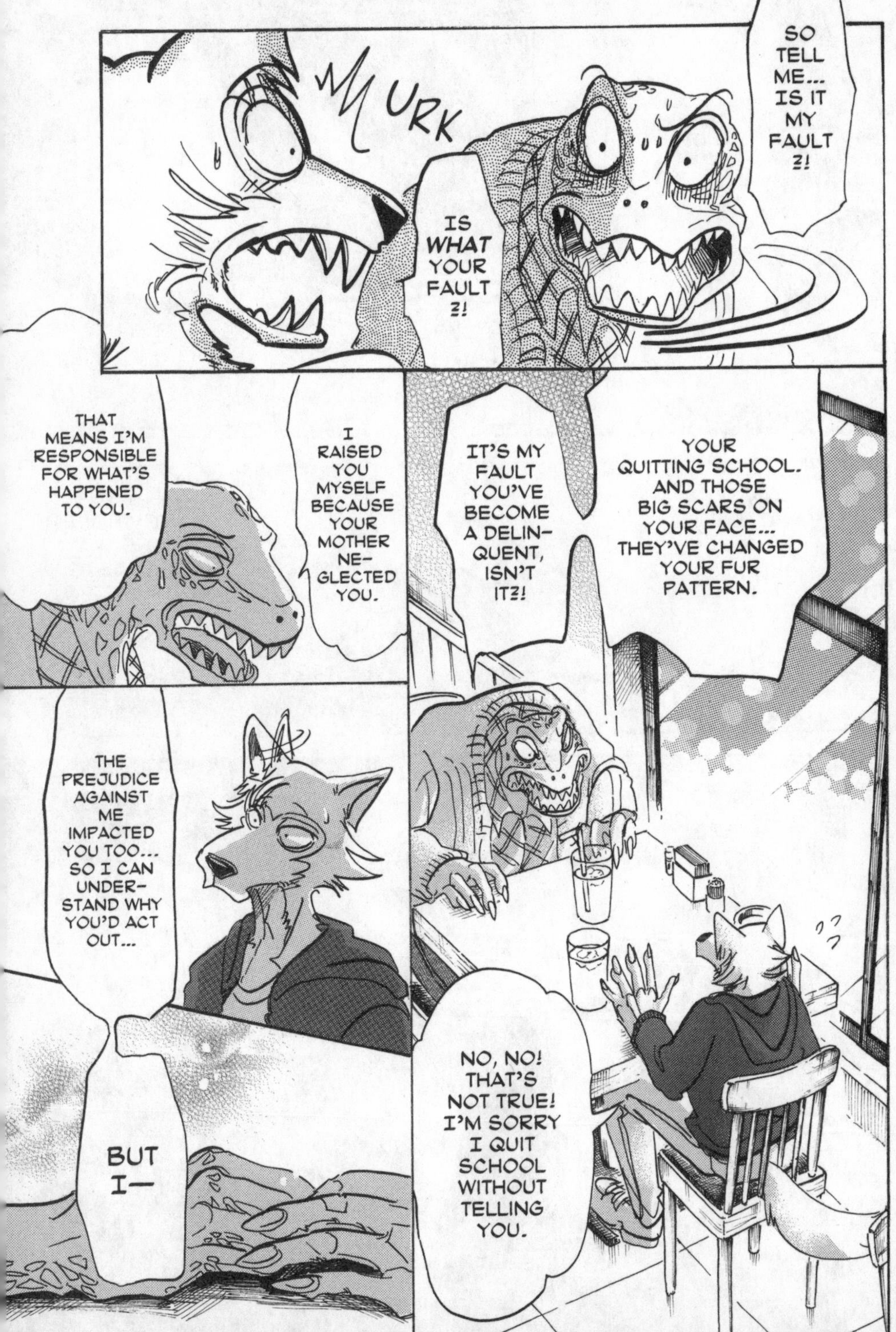
SO TELL ME... IS IT MY FAULT ?!
URK
IS WHAT YOUR FAULT ?!
YOUR QUITTING SCHOOL. AND THOSE BIG SCARS ON YOUR FACE... THEY'VE CHANGED YOUR FUR PATTERN.
IT'S MY FAULT YOU'VE BECOME A DELIN-QUENT, ISN'T IT?!
I RAISED YOU MYSELF BECAUSE YOUR MOTHER NE-GLECTED YOU.
THAT MEANS I'M RESPONSIBLE FOR WHAT'S HAPPENED TO YOU.
NO, NO! THAT'S NOT TRUE! I'M SORRY I QUIT SCHOOL WITHOUT TELLING YOU.
THE PREJUDICE AGAINST ME IMPACTED YOU TOO... SO I CAN UNDER-STAND WHY YOU'D ACT OUT...
BUT I—

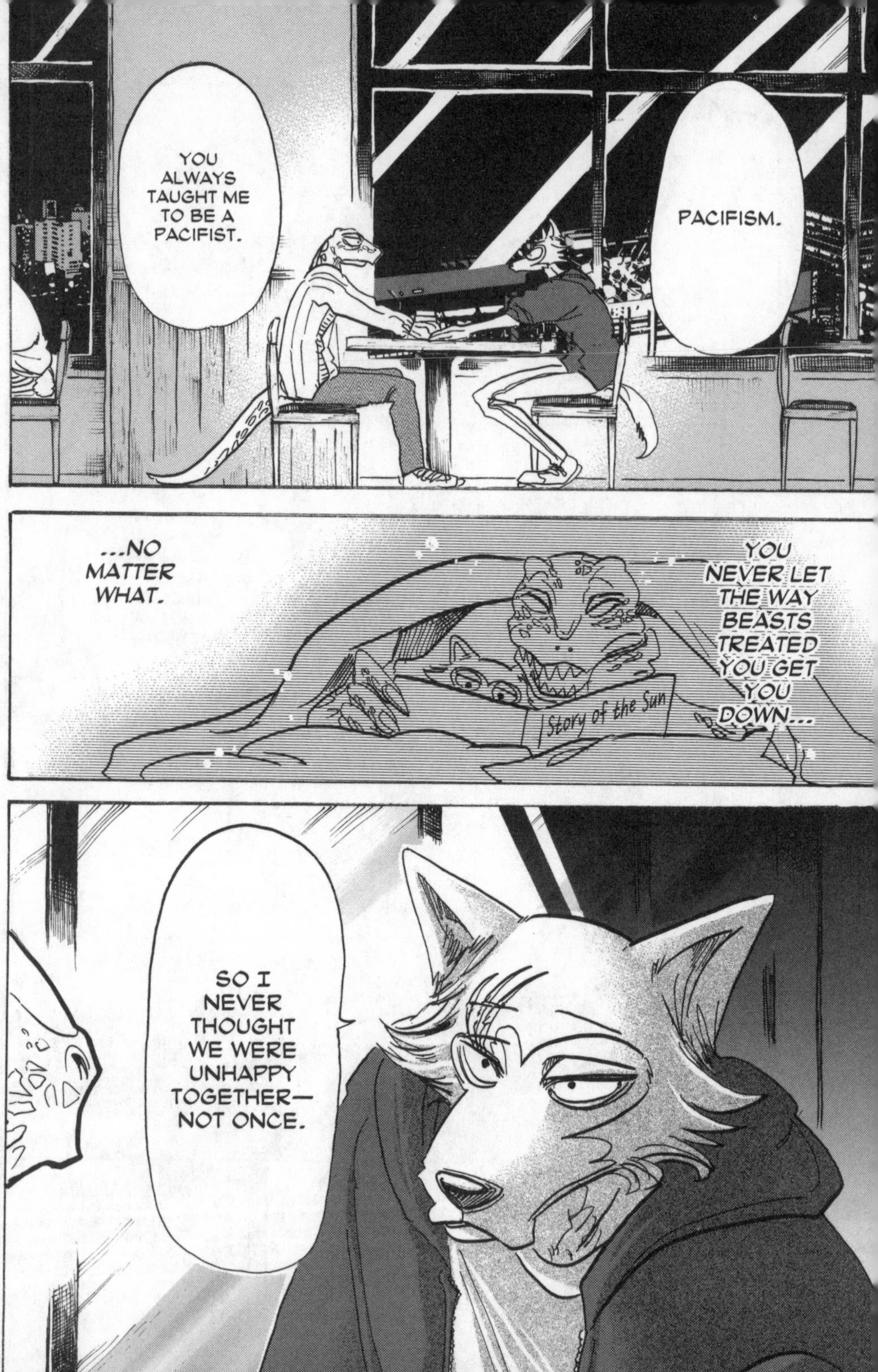
PACIFISM.
YOU ALWAYS TAUGHT ME TO BE A PACIFIST.
YOU NEVER LET THE WAY BEASTS TREATED YOU GET YOU DOWN...
Story of the Sun
...NO MATTER WHAT.
SO I NEVER THOUGHT WE WERE UNHAPPY TOGETHER—NOT ONCE.

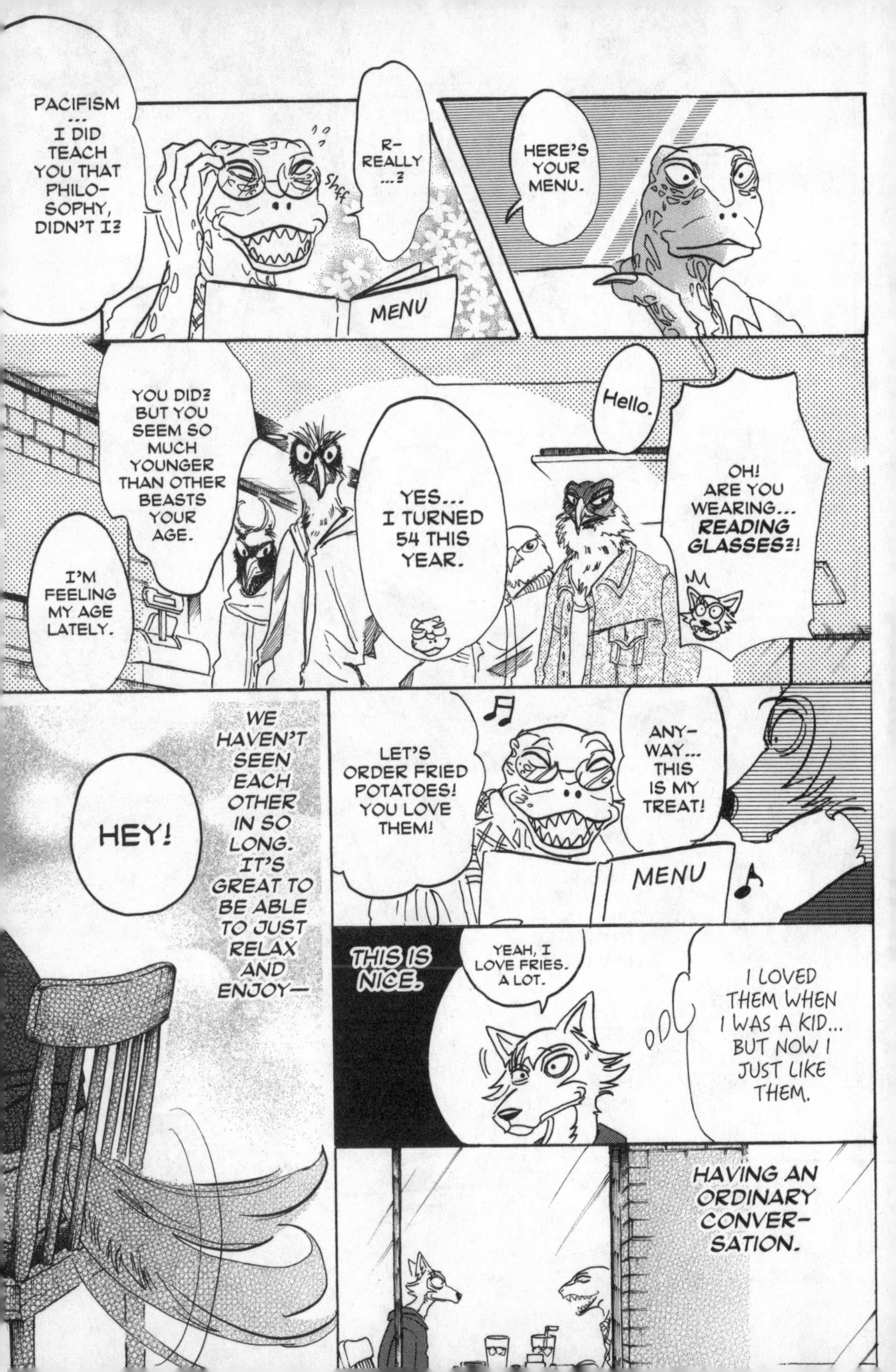
HERE'S YOUR MENU.
R-REALLY...?
Shff
MENU
PACIFISM... I DID TEACH YOU THAT PHILOSOPHY, DIDN'T I?
Hello.
OH! ARE YOU WEARING... READING GLASSES?!
YES... I TURNED 54 THIS YEAR.
YOU DID? BUT YOU SEEM SO MUCH YOUNGER THAN OTHER BEASTS YOUR AGE.
I'M FEELING MY AGE LATELY.
ANY-WAY... THIS IS MY TREAT!
LET'S ORDER FRIED POTATOES! YOU LOVE THEM!
MENU
I LOVED THEM WHEN I WAS A KID... BUT NOW I JUST LIKE THEM.
YEAH, I LOVE FRIES. A LOT.
THIS IS NICE.
HAVING AN ORDINARY CONVERSATION.
WE HAVEN'T SEEN EACH OTHER IN SO LONG. IT'S GREAT TO BE ABLE TO JUST RELAX AND ENJOY—
HEY!

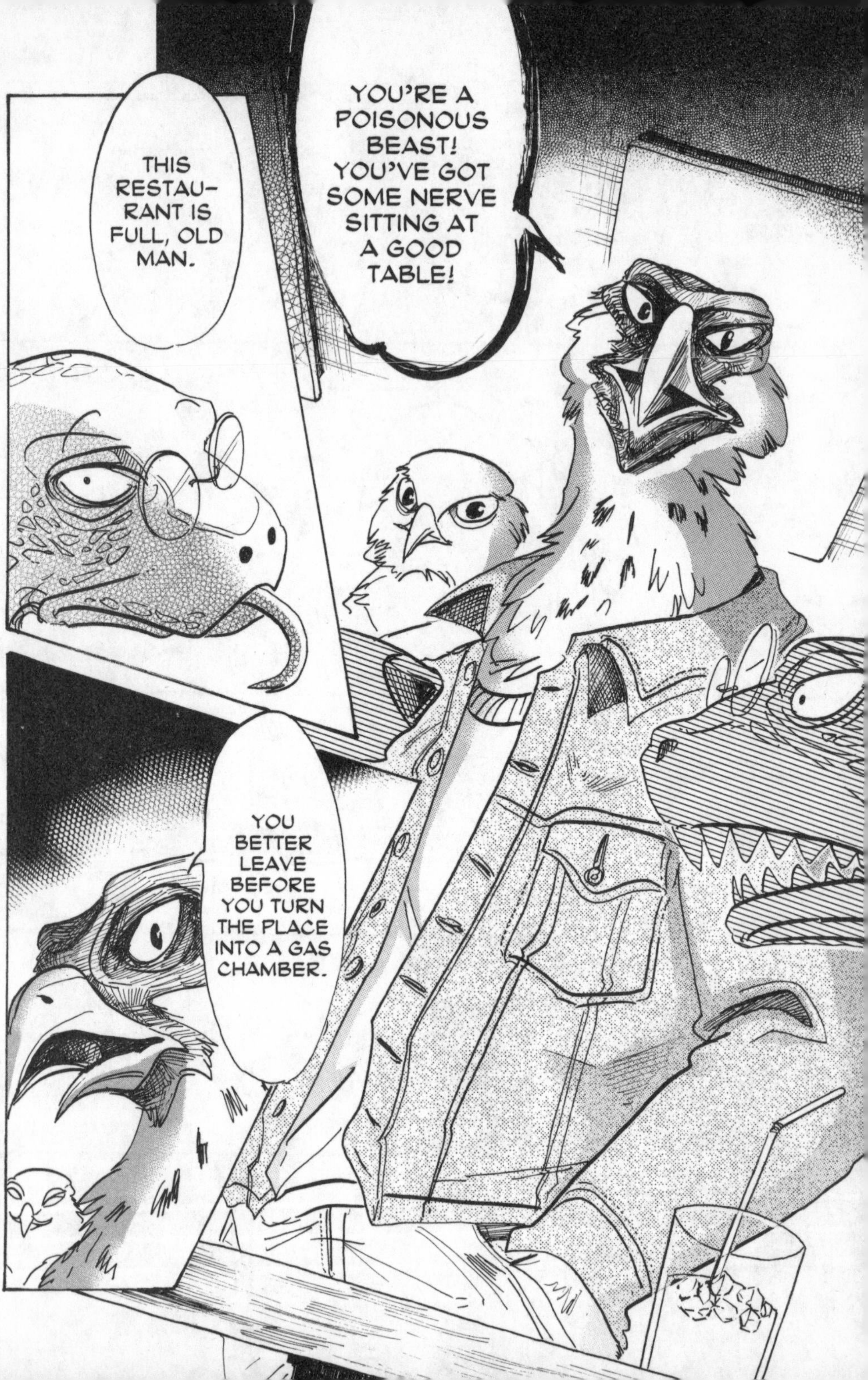
YOU'RE A POISONOUS BEAST! YOU'VE GOT SOME NERVE SITTING AT A GOOD TABLE!
THIS RESTAU-RANT IS FULL, OLD MAN.
YOU BETTER LEAVE BEFORE YOU TURN THE PLACE INTO A GAS CHAMBER.

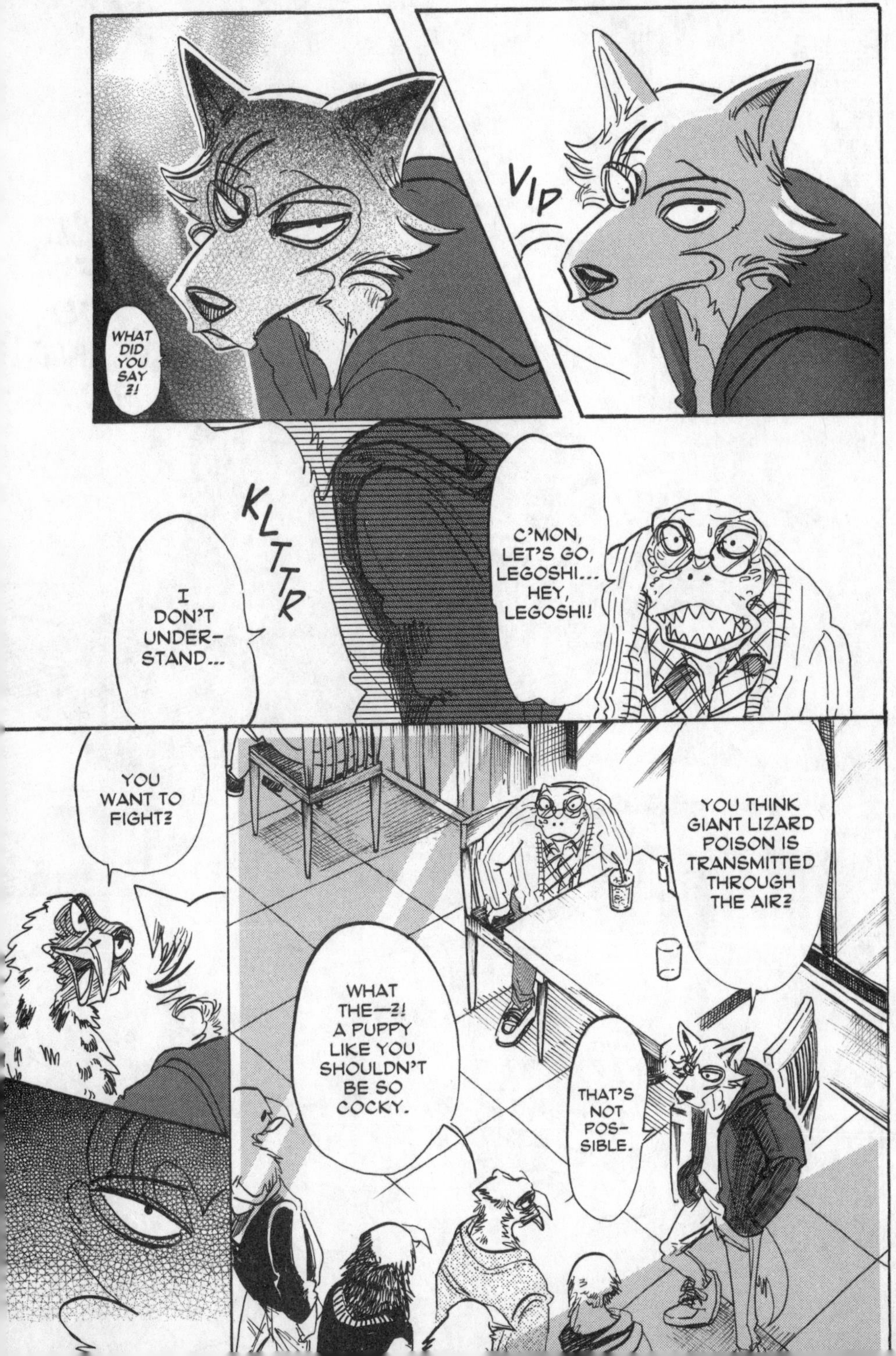
VIP
WHAT DID YOU SAY?!
C'MON, LET'S GO, LEGOSHI... HEY, LEGOSHI!
KLTTR
I DON'T UNDER-STAND...
YOU THINK GIANT LIZARD POISON IS TRANSMITTED THROUGH THE AIR?
THAT'S NOT POS-SIBLE.
WHAT THE—?! A PUPPY LIKE YOU SHOULDN'T BE SO COCKY.
YOU WANT TO FIGHT?

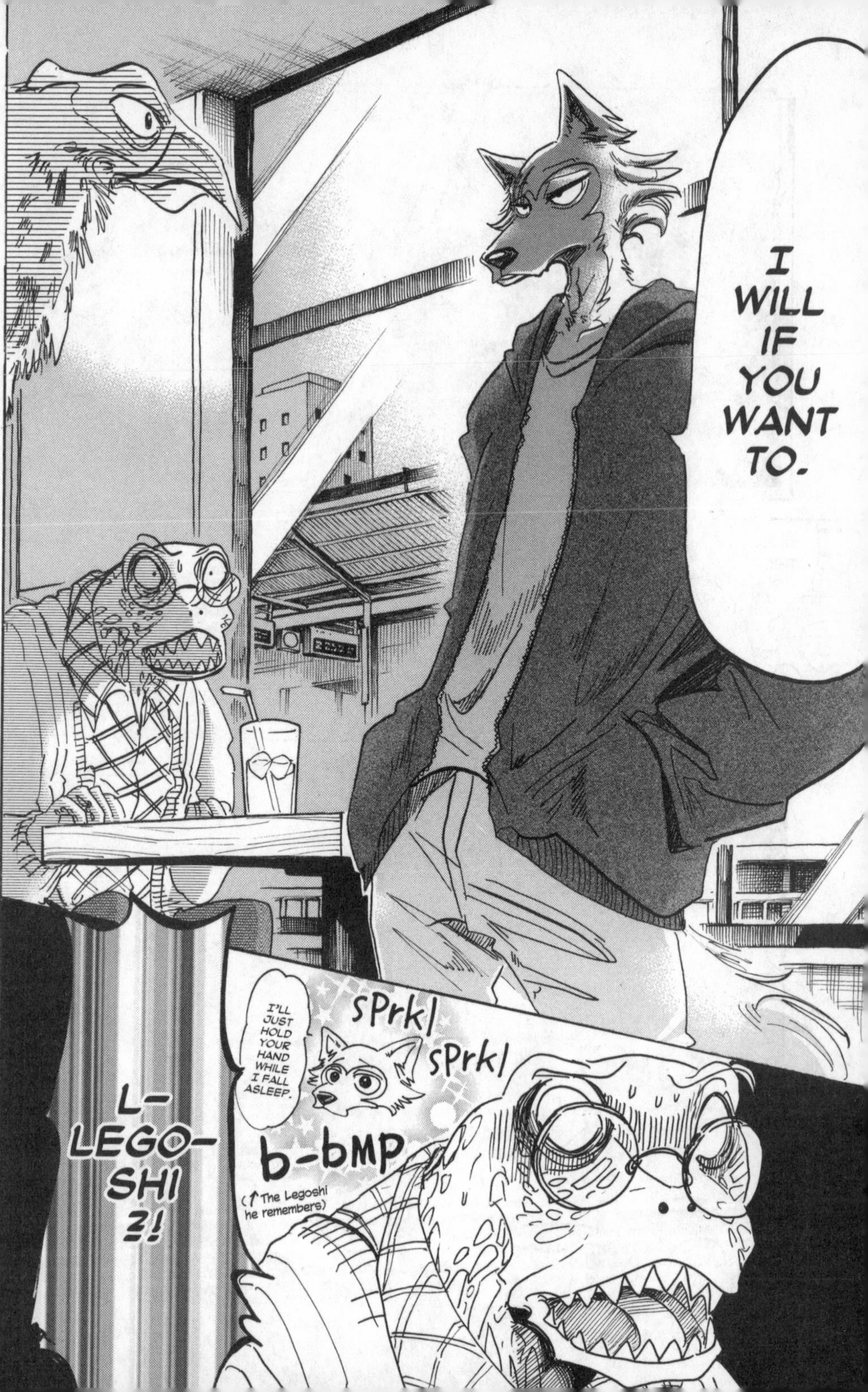
I WILL IF YOU WANT TO.
SPRKL SPRKL
I'LL JUST HOLD YOUR HAND WHILE I FALL ASLEEP.
B-BMP
(↑ The Legoshi he remembers)
L-LEGO-SHI?!

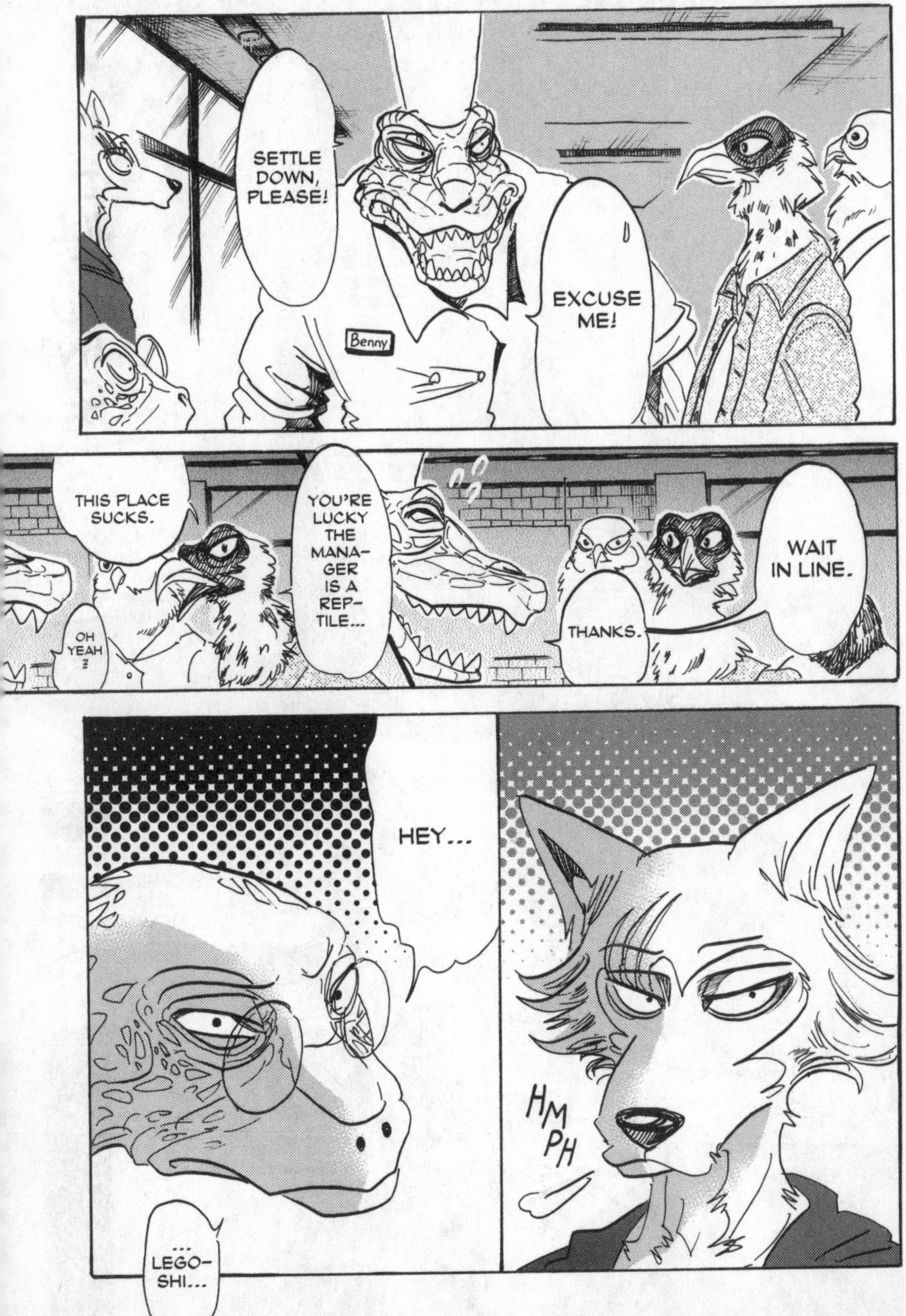
EXCUSE ME!
SETTLE DOWN, PLEASE!
WAIT IN LINE.
THANKS.
YOU'RE LUCKY THE MANA-GER IS A REP-TILE...
THIS PLACE SUCKS.
OH YEAH?
HMPH
HEY...
...LEGO-SHI...

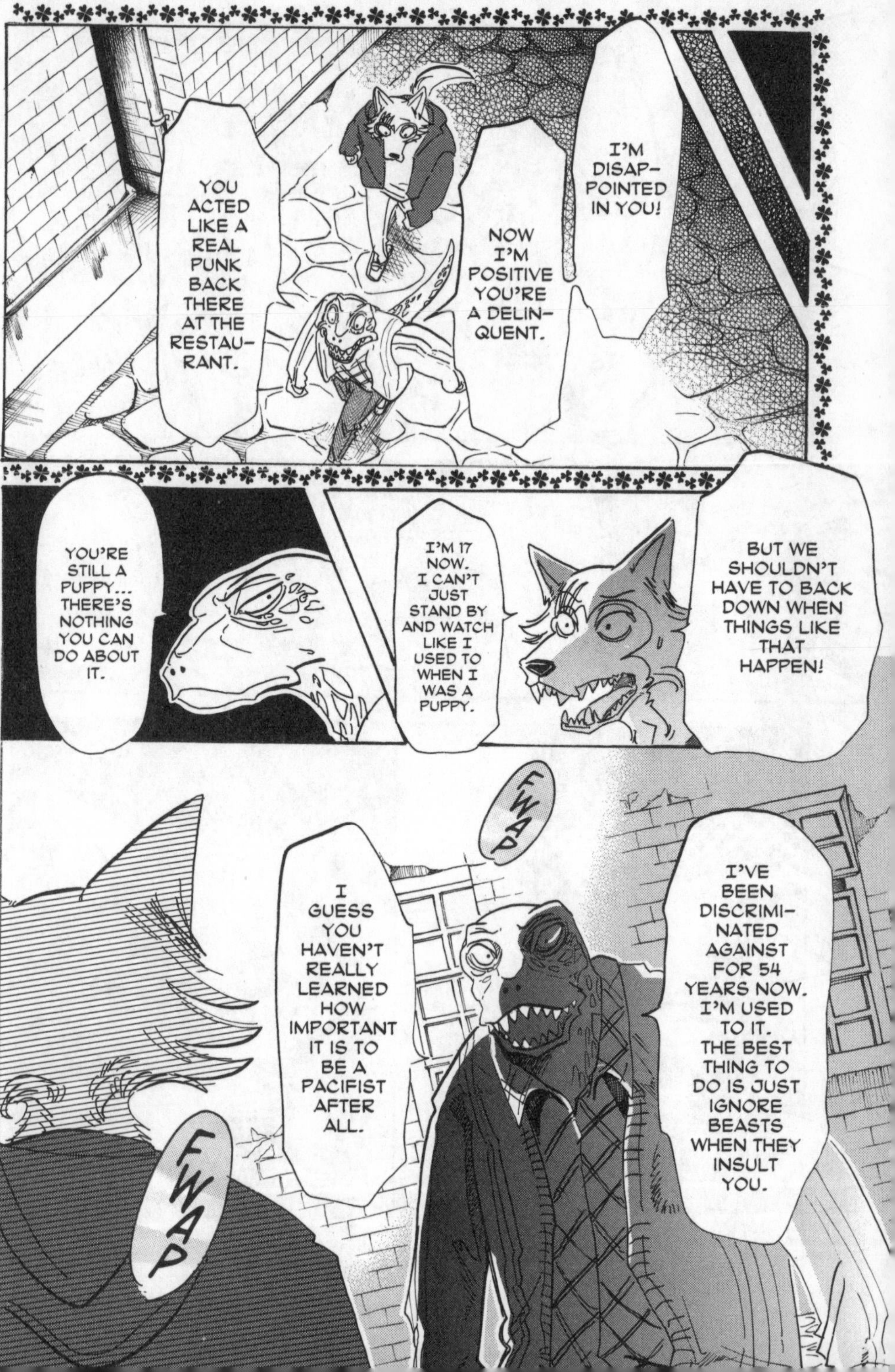
I'M DISAPPOINTED IN YOU!
NOW I'M POSITIVE YOU'RE A DELINQUENT.
YOU ACTED LIKE A REAL PUNK BACK THERE AT THE RESTAURANT.
BUT WE SHOULDN'T HAVE TO BACK DOWN WHEN THINGS LIKE THAT HAPPEN!
I'M 17 NOW. I CAN'T JUST STAND BY AND WATCH LIKE I USED TO WHEN I WAS A PUPPY.
YOU'RE STILL A PUPPY... THERE'S NOTHING YOU CAN DO ABOUT IT.
I'VE BEEN DISCRIMINATED AGAINST FOR 54 YEARS NOW. I'M USED TO IT. THE BEST THING TO DO IS JUST IGNORE BEASTS WHEN THEY INSULT YOU.
FWAP
I GUESS YOU HAVEN'T REALLY LEARNED HOW IMPORTANT IT IS TO BE A PACIFIST AFTER ALL.
FWAP

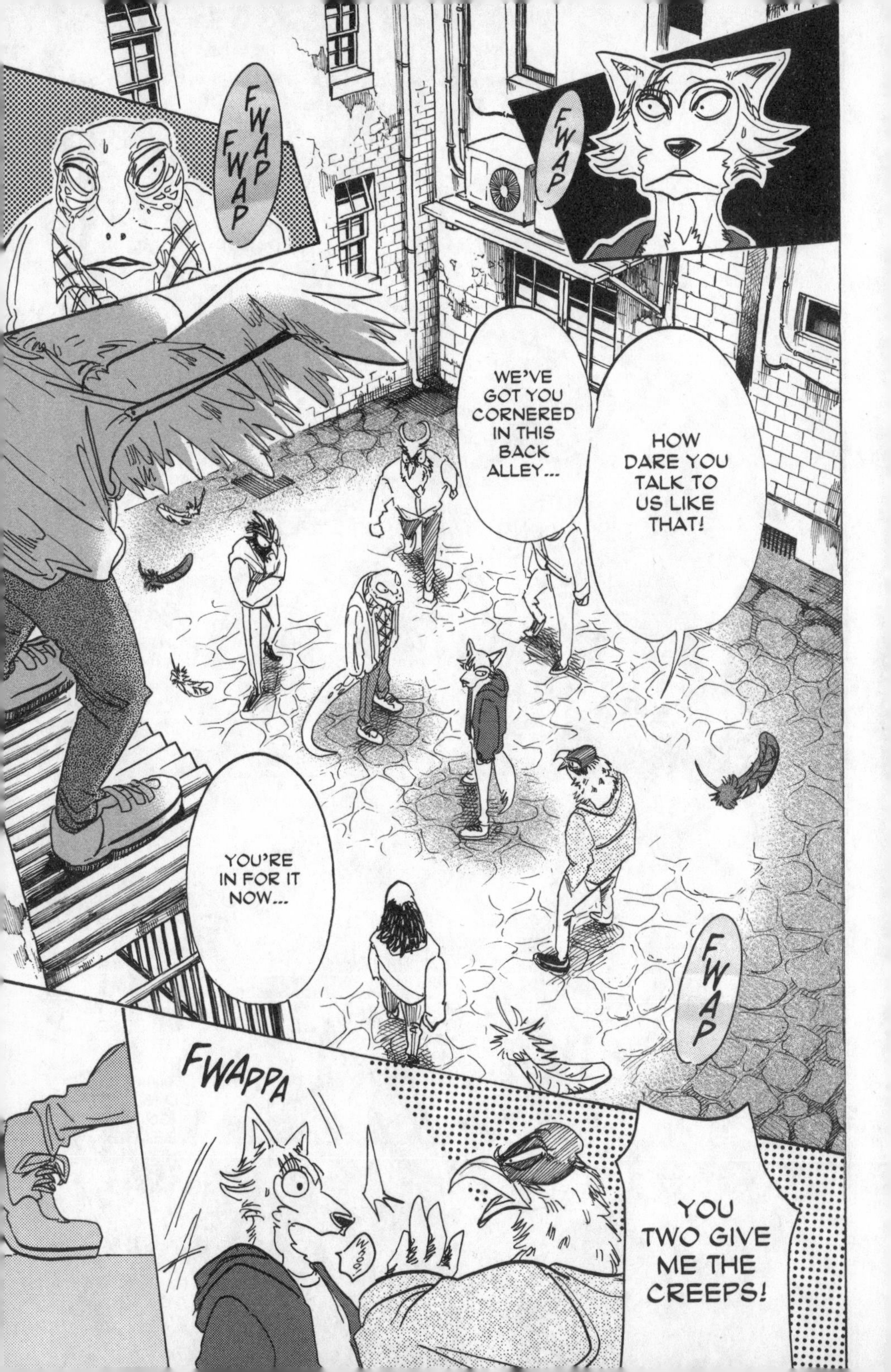
FWAP
FWAP FWAP
HOW DARE YOU TALK TO US LIKE THAT!
WE'VE GOT YOU CORNERED IN THIS BACK ALLEY...
FWAP
YOU'RE IN FOR IT NOW...
FWAPPA
YOU TWO GIVE ME THE CREEPS!

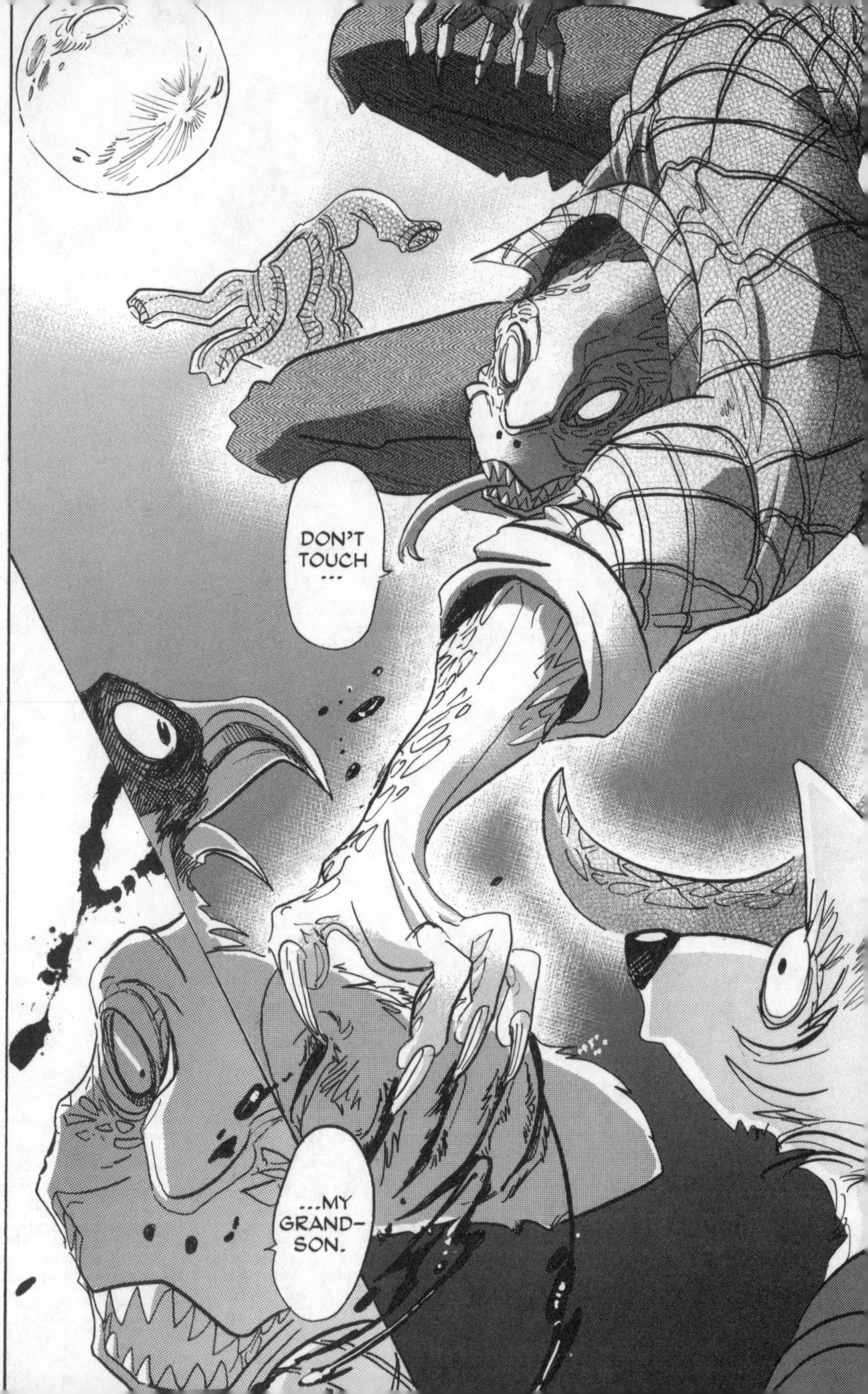
DON'T TOUCH ...
...MY GRANDSON.

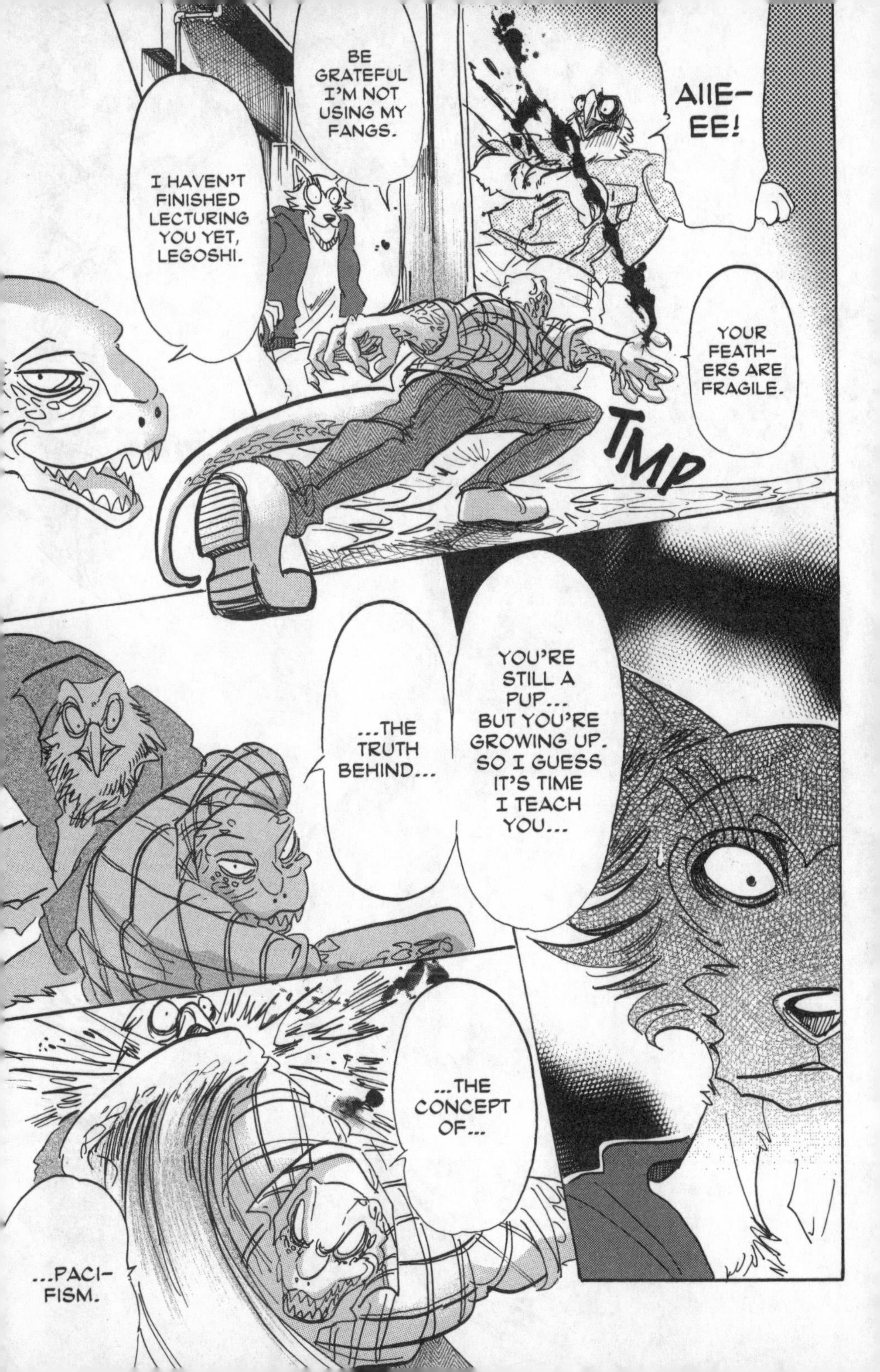
AIIE-EE!
BE GRATEFUL I'M NOT USING MY FANGS.
I HAVEN'T FINISHED LECTURING YOU YET, LEGOSHI.
YOUR FEATH-ERS ARE FRAGILE.
TMP
YOU'RE STILL A PUP... BUT YOU'RE GROWING UP. SO I GUESS IT'S TIME I TEACH YOU...
...THE TRUTH BEHIND...
...THE CONCEPT OF...
...PACI-FISM.

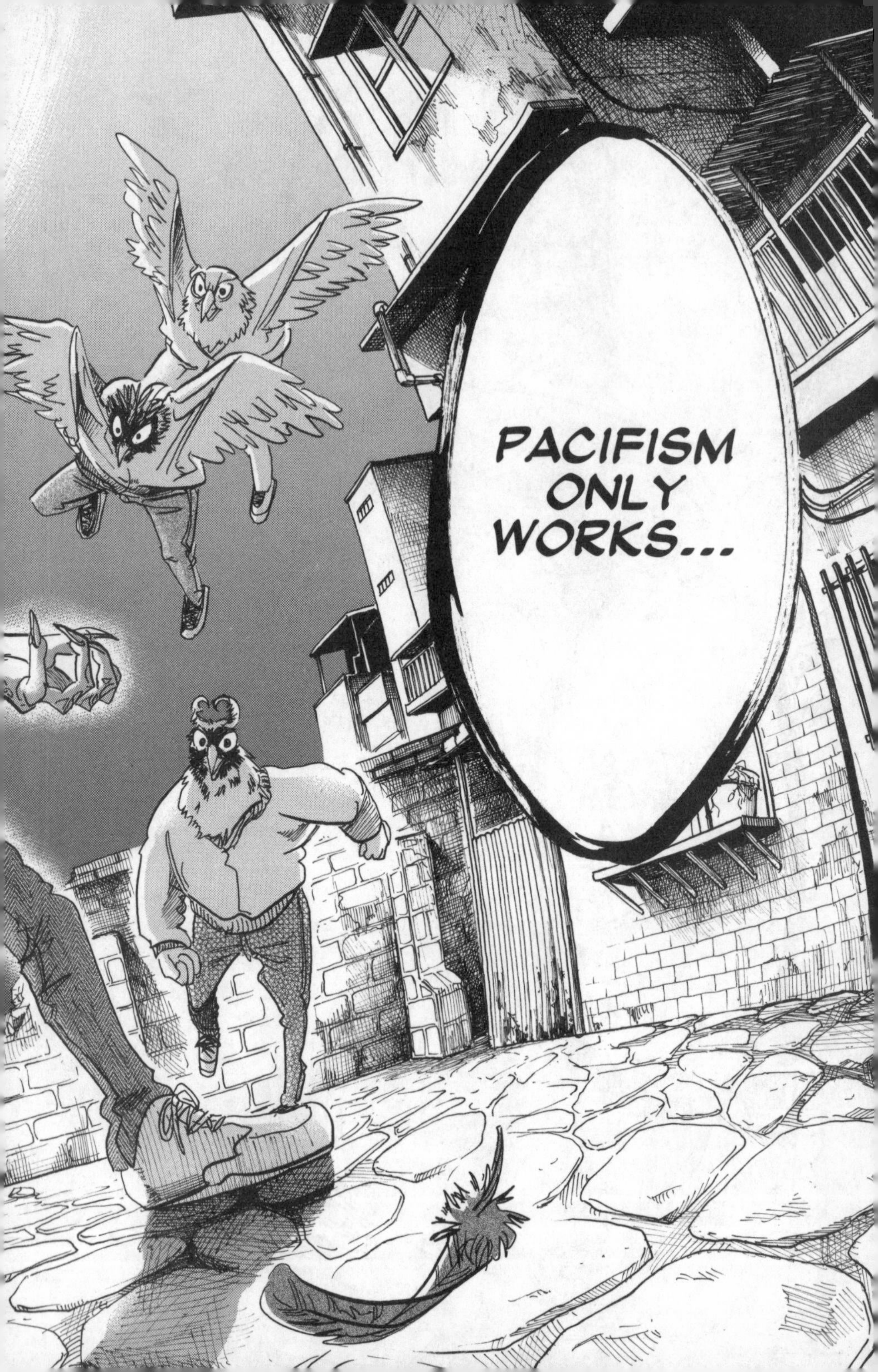
PACIFISM ONLY WORKS...

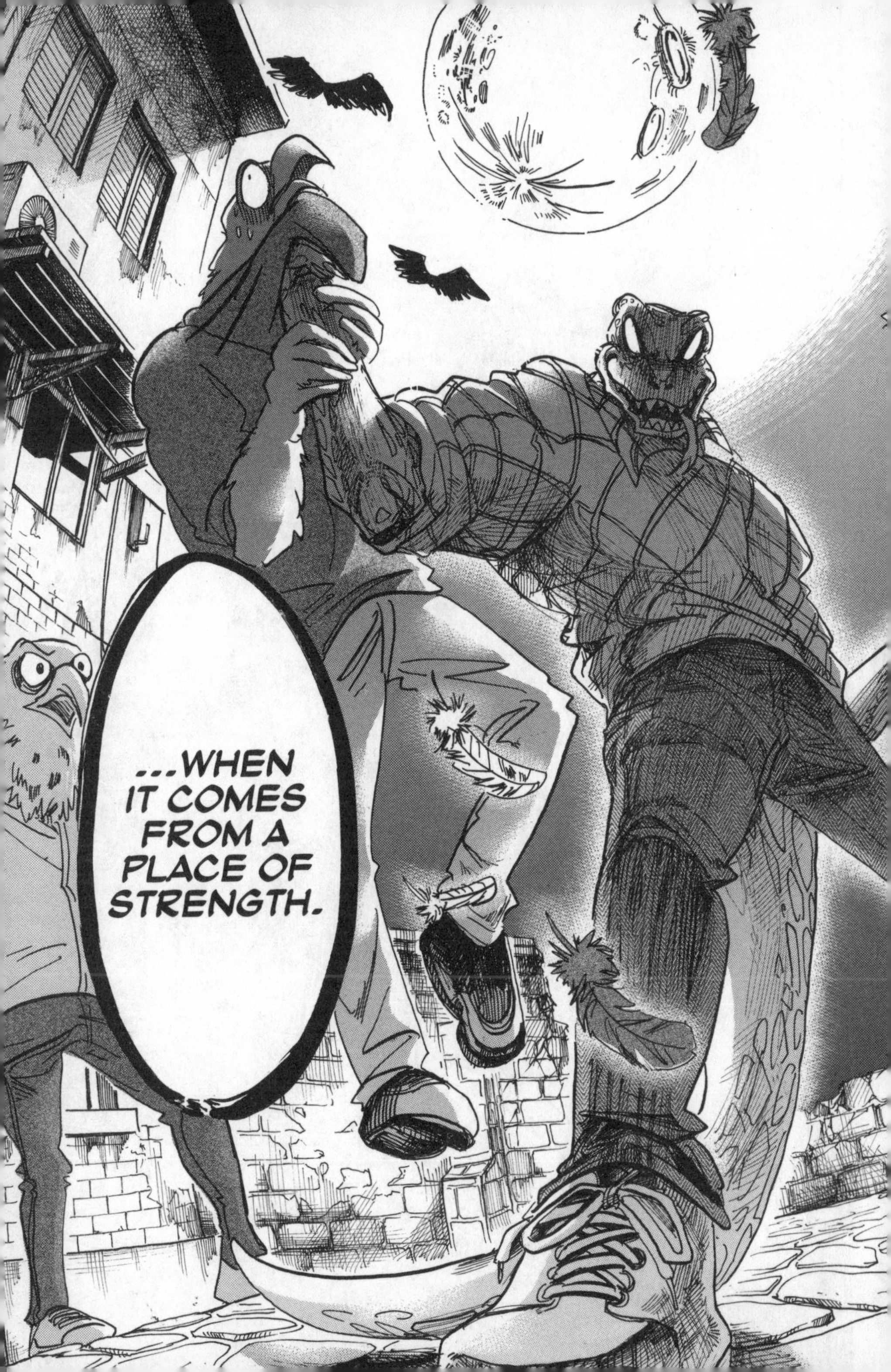
...WHEN IT COMES FROM A PLACE OF STRENGTH.

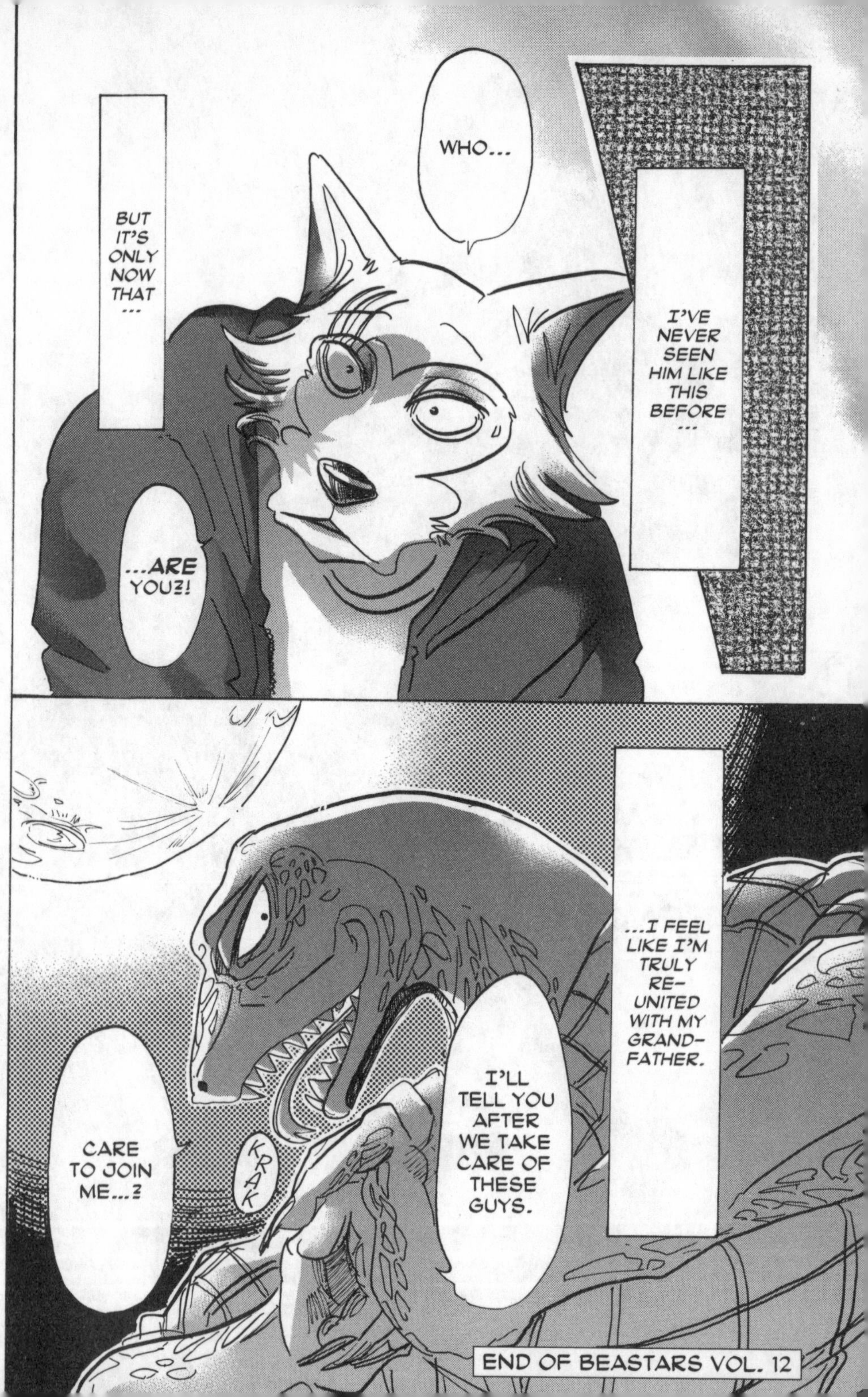
I'VE NEVER SEEN HIM LIKE THIS BEFORE...
WHO...
...ARE YOU?!
BUT IT'S ONLY NOW THAT...
...I FEEL LIKE I'M TRULY RE-UNITED WITH MY GRAND-FATHER.
I'LL TELL YOU AFTER WE TAKE CARE OF THESE GUYS.
KRAK
CARE TO JOIN ME...?
END OF BEASTARS VOL. 12

To be continued...

Housing in the World of BEASTARS

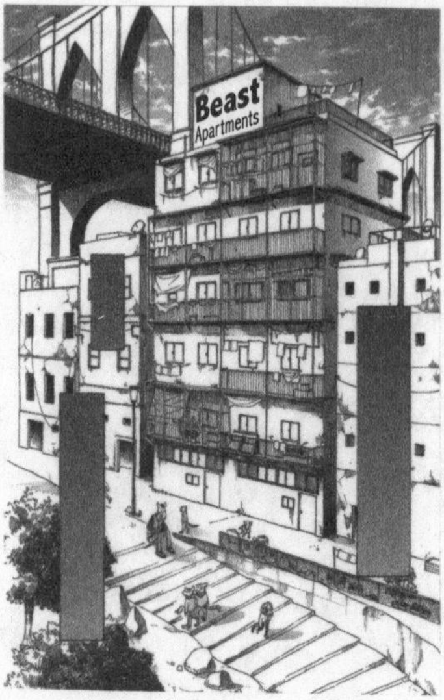
Beast Apartments

←

Legoshi moved into Beast Apartments after dropping out of school. It's an old apartment building, so the rent is cheap. Good properties are places that are...

- Limited in terms of the species allowed (herbivores only, carnivores only)
- Located far from the black market

These two qualities are highly prized.

Both carnivores and herbivores live in Beast Apartments. Legoshi, a beast with a criminal record, is permitted to live here, which goes to show that it is a dangerous apartment complex without strict rules and regulations.

In other words, you wouldn't want your kids to live here.

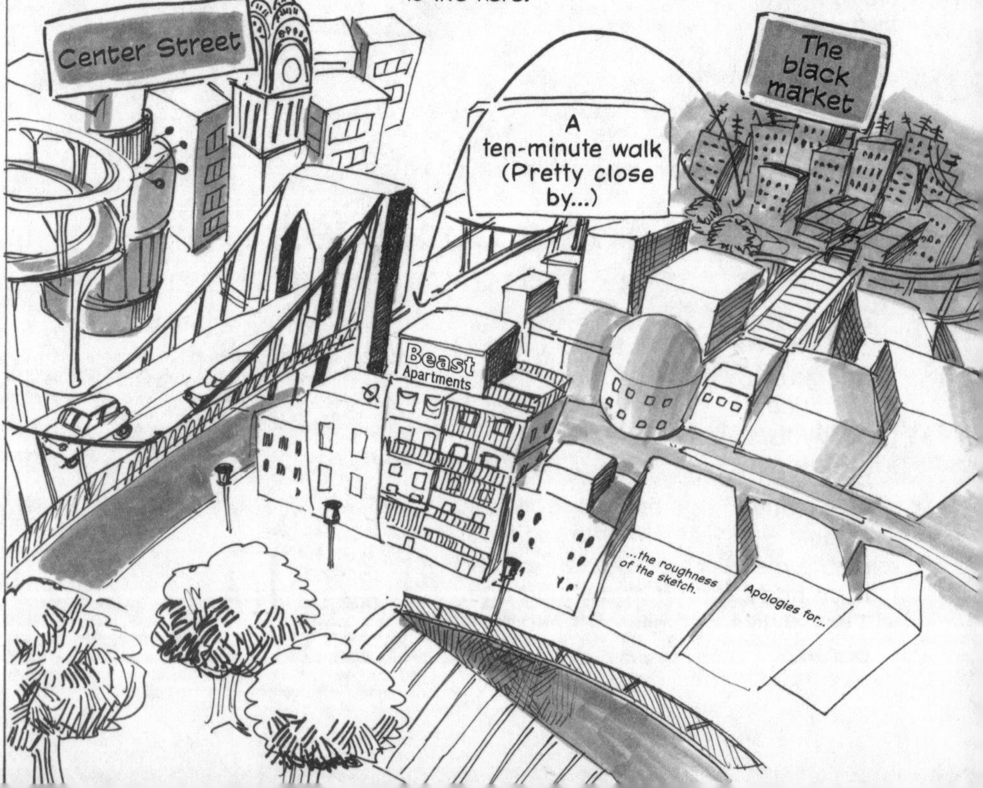
The black market
A ten-minute walk (Pretty close by...)
Center Street
Beast Apartments
Apologies for...
...the roughness of the sketch.

Warning: Serious Spoilers

Safari Times

Since 2016.

The relationship between the (current) Beastar Yahya and Legoshi's grandfather revealed!

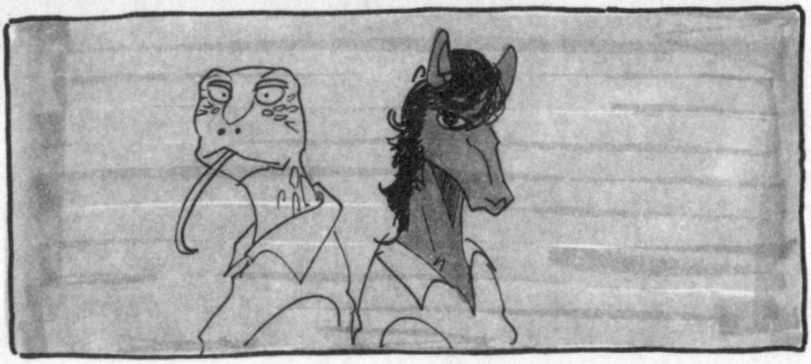

Plus another piece of new information! Yahya, the current Beastar (male horse) and Gosha, Legoshi's grandfather (male Komodo dragon), were once close friends who have gone their separate ways. (You can read about them starting in chapter 103!)

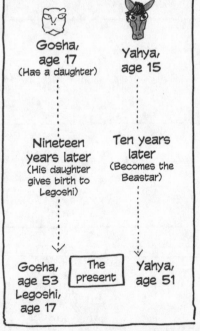

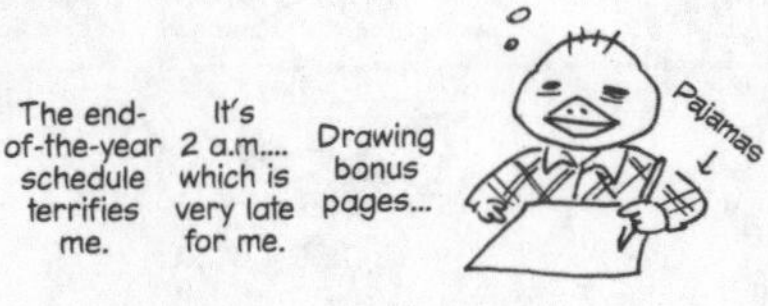

The end-of-the-year schedule terrifies me.
It's 2 a.m.... which is very late for me.
Drawing bonus pages...
Pajamas

Gosha, age 17
(Has a daughter)
Yahya, age 15
Nineteen years later
(His daughter gives birth to Legoshi)
Ten years later
(Becomes the Beastar)
Gosha, age 53
Legoshi, age 17
The present
Yahya, age 51

This diagram explains when certain events occurred. →

"Don't I have the skills to make this clear to my readers through the manga?!" That's what I ask myself, but I need to fill this bonus page, so I'll lay it out explicitly here.

Gosha's daughter (Legoshi's beautiful mother) has only appeared in volume 9, chapter 73, so far. Most of the members of Legoshi's family have had children at a young age. They're like a family of teenage parents.

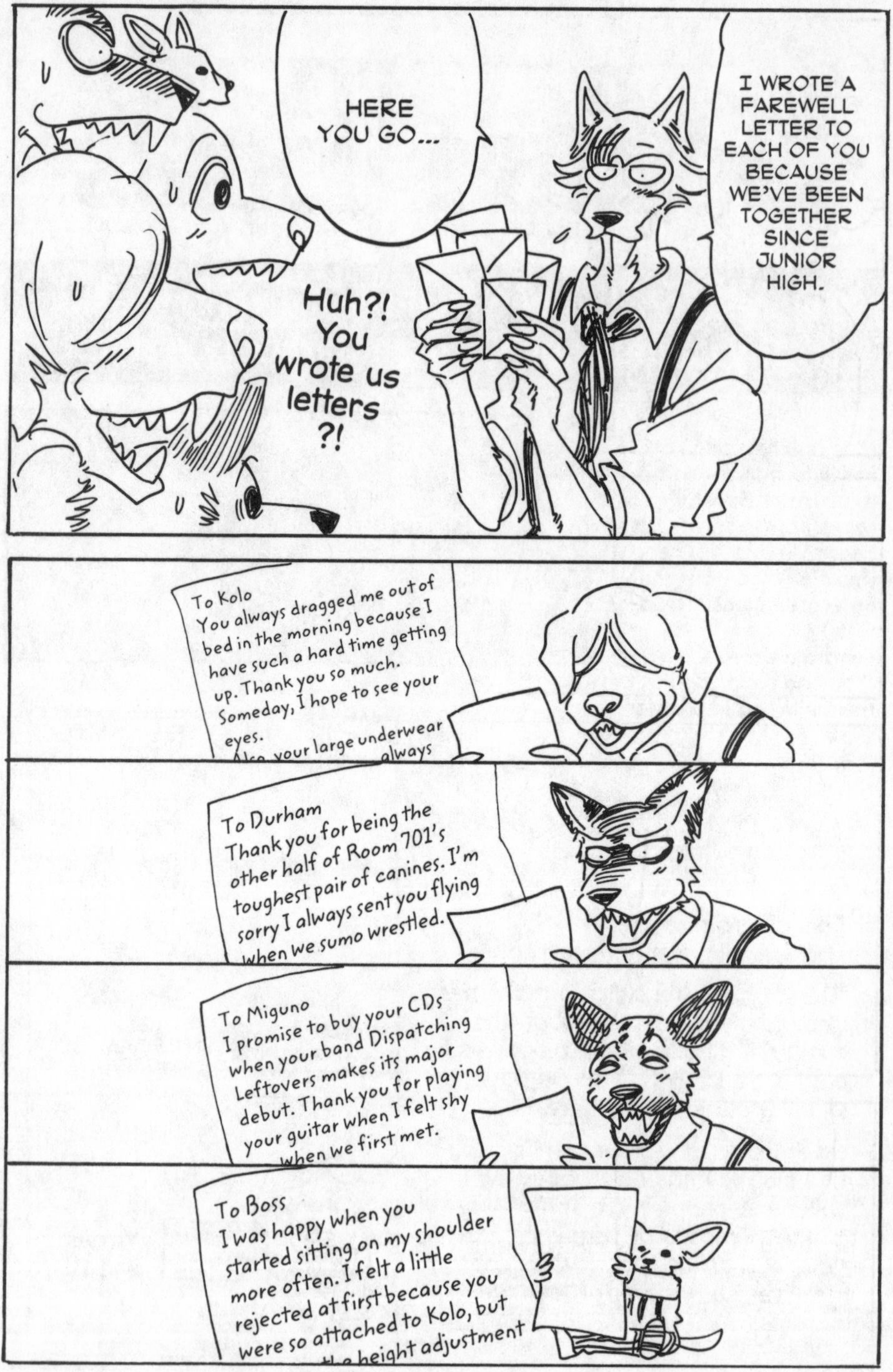
I WROTE A FAREWELL LETTER TO EACH OF YOU BECAUSE WE'VE BEEN TOGETHER SINCE JUNIOR HIGH.
HERE YOU GO...
Huh?! You wrote us letters?!
To Kolo
You always dragged me out of bed in the morning because I have such a hard time getting up. Thank you so much. Someday, I hope to see your eyes.
your large underwear always
To Durham
Thank you for being the other half of Room 701's toughest pair of canines. I'm sorry I always sent you flying when we sumo wrestled.
To Miguno
I promise to buy your CDs when your band Dispatching Leftovers makes its major debut. Thank you for playing your guitar when I felt shy when we first met.
To Boss
I was happy when you started sitting on my shoulder more often. I felt a little rejected at first because you were so attached to Kolo, but
height adjustment

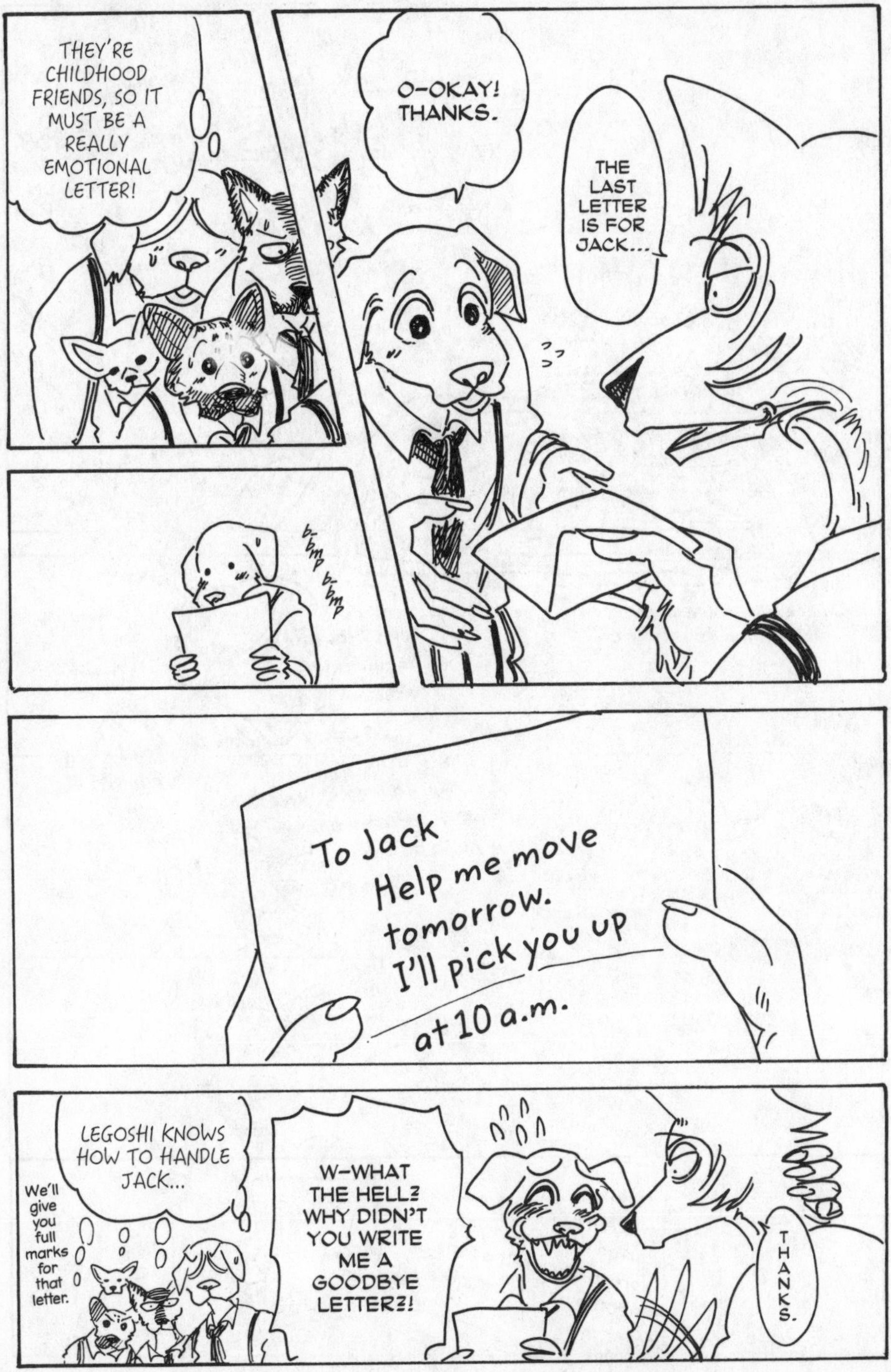
THE LAST LETTER IS FOR JACK...
O-OKAY! THANKS.
THEY'RE CHILDHOOD FRIENDS, SO IT MUST BE A REALLY EMOTIONAL LETTER!
b-bmp b-bmp
To Jack
Help me move tomorrow.
I'll pick you up at 10 a.m.
THANKS.
W-WHAT THE HELL?! WHY DIDN'T YOU WRITE ME A GOODBYE LETTER?!
LEGOSHI KNOWS HOW TO HANDLE JACK...
We'll give you full marks for that letter.

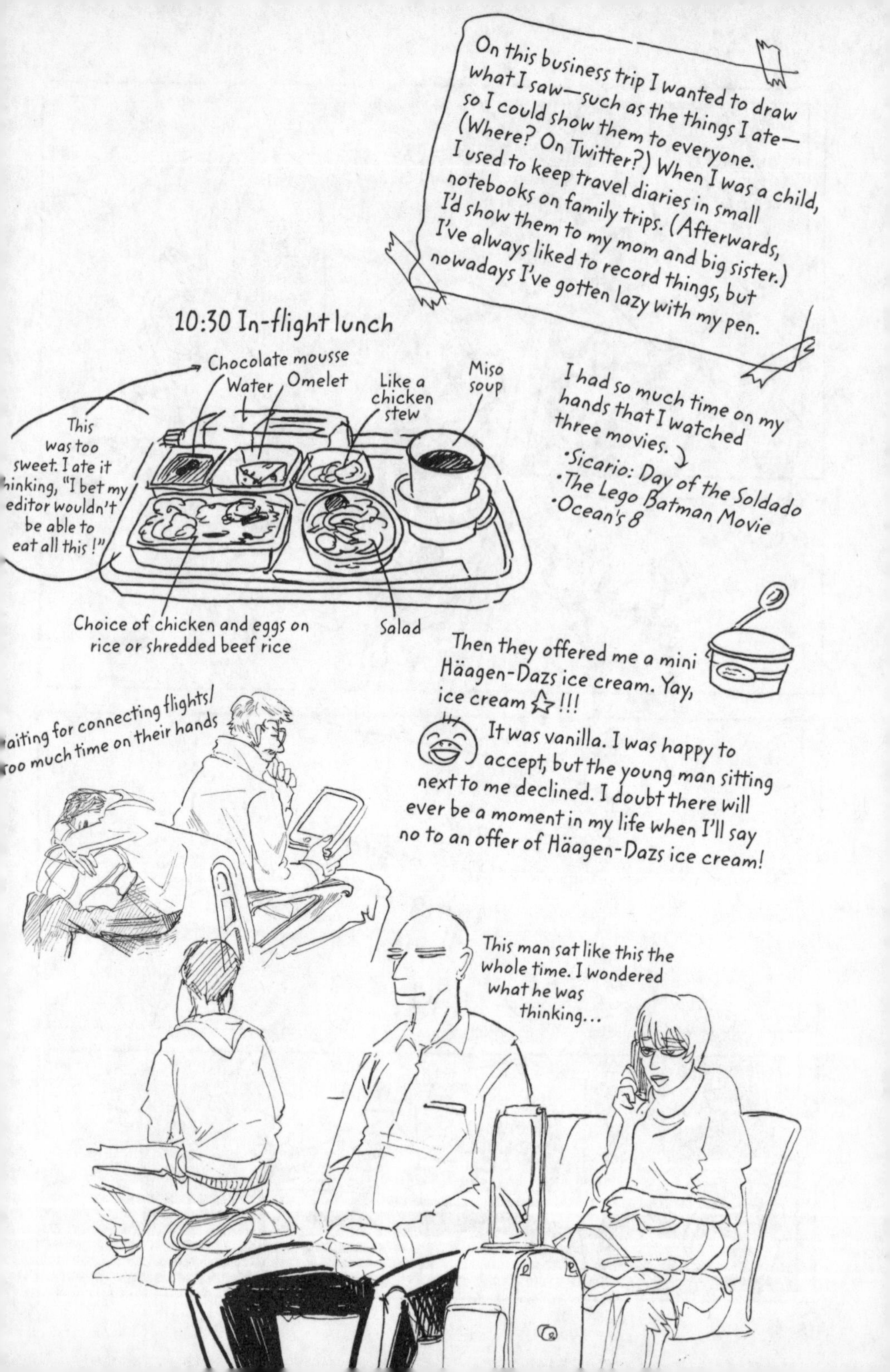
On this business trip I wanted to draw what I saw—such as the things I ate—so I could show them to everyone. (Where? On Twitter?) When I was a child, I used to keep travel diaries in small notebooks on family trips. (Afterwards, I'd show them to my mom and big sister.) I've always liked to record things, but nowadays I've gotten lazy with my pen.
10:30 In-flight lunch
Chocolate mousse
Water
Omelet
Like a chicken stew
Miso soup
This was too sweet. I ate it hinking, "I bet my editor wouldn't be able to eat all this!"
Choice of chicken and eggs on rice or shredded beef rice
Salad
I had so much time on my hands that I watched three movies.
·Sicario: Day of the Soldado
·The Lego Batman Movie
·Ocean's 8
Then they offered me a mini Häagen-Dazs ice cream. Yay, ice cream ☆!!!
It was vanilla. I was happy to accept, but the young man sitting next to me declined. I doubt there will ever be a moment in my life when I'll say no to an offer of Häagen-Dazs ice cream!
aiting for connecting flights/
oo much time on their hands
This man sat like this the whole time. I wondered what he was thinking...

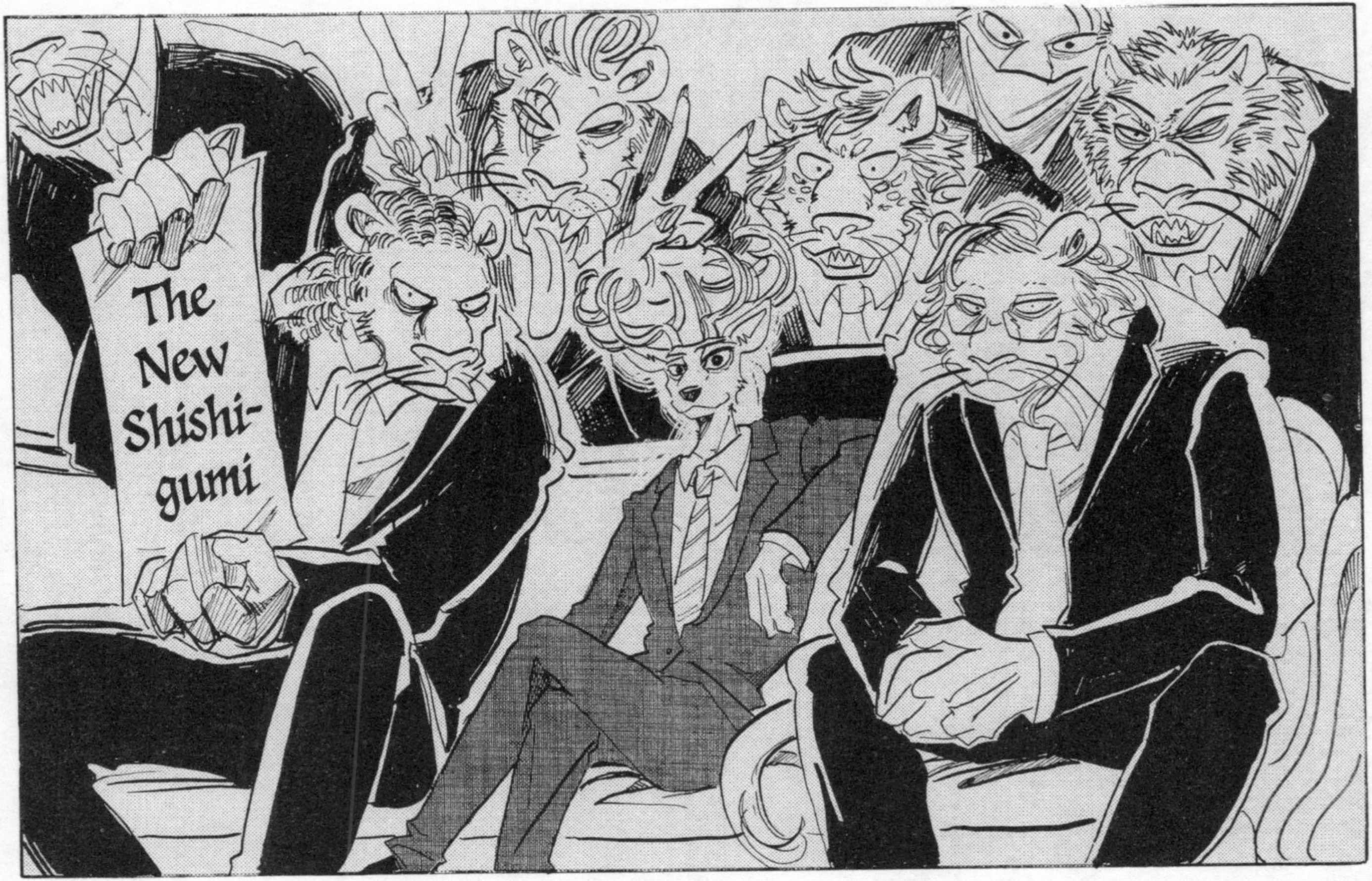
The New Shishi-gumi

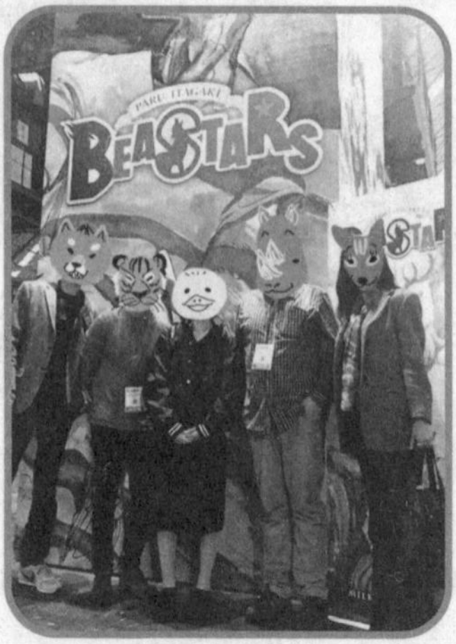
PARU ITAGAKI
BEASTARS

I THINK EVERY EMOTION IS AMPLIFIED THREEFOLD AT NIGHT. THAT'S WHY THINGS ALWAYS HAPPEN AFTER DARK IN *BEASTARS*. (THIS PHOTO WAS TAKEN AT AN EVENT IN SPAIN. THE SKETCHES I DREW ON THAT TRIP ARE ON THE PRECEDING PAGES.)

PARU ITAGAKI

Paru Itagaki began her professional career as a manga author in 2016 with the short story collection **BEAST COMPLEX. BEASTARS** is her first serialization. **BEASTARS** has won multiple awards in Japan, including the prestigious 2018 Manga Taisho Award.

BEASTARS

VOL. 12
VIZ Signature Edition

Story & Art by
Paru Itagaki

Translation/Tomo Kimura
English Adaptation/Annette Roman
Touch-Up Art & Lettering/Susan Daigle-Leach
Cover & Interior Design/Yukiko Whitley
Editor/Annette Roman

BEASTARS Volume 12
© 2019 PARU ITAGAKI
All rights reserved.
First published in 2019 by Akita Publishing Co., Ltd., Tokyo
English translation rights arranged with Akita Publishing Co., Ltd., through
Tuttle-Mori Agency, Inc., Tokyo

Printed in Canada

Published by VIZ Media, LLC
P.O. Box 77010
San Francisco, CA 94107

10 9 8 7 6 5 4 3 2 1
First printing, May 2021

viz.com   vizsignature.com

COMING IN VOLUME 13...

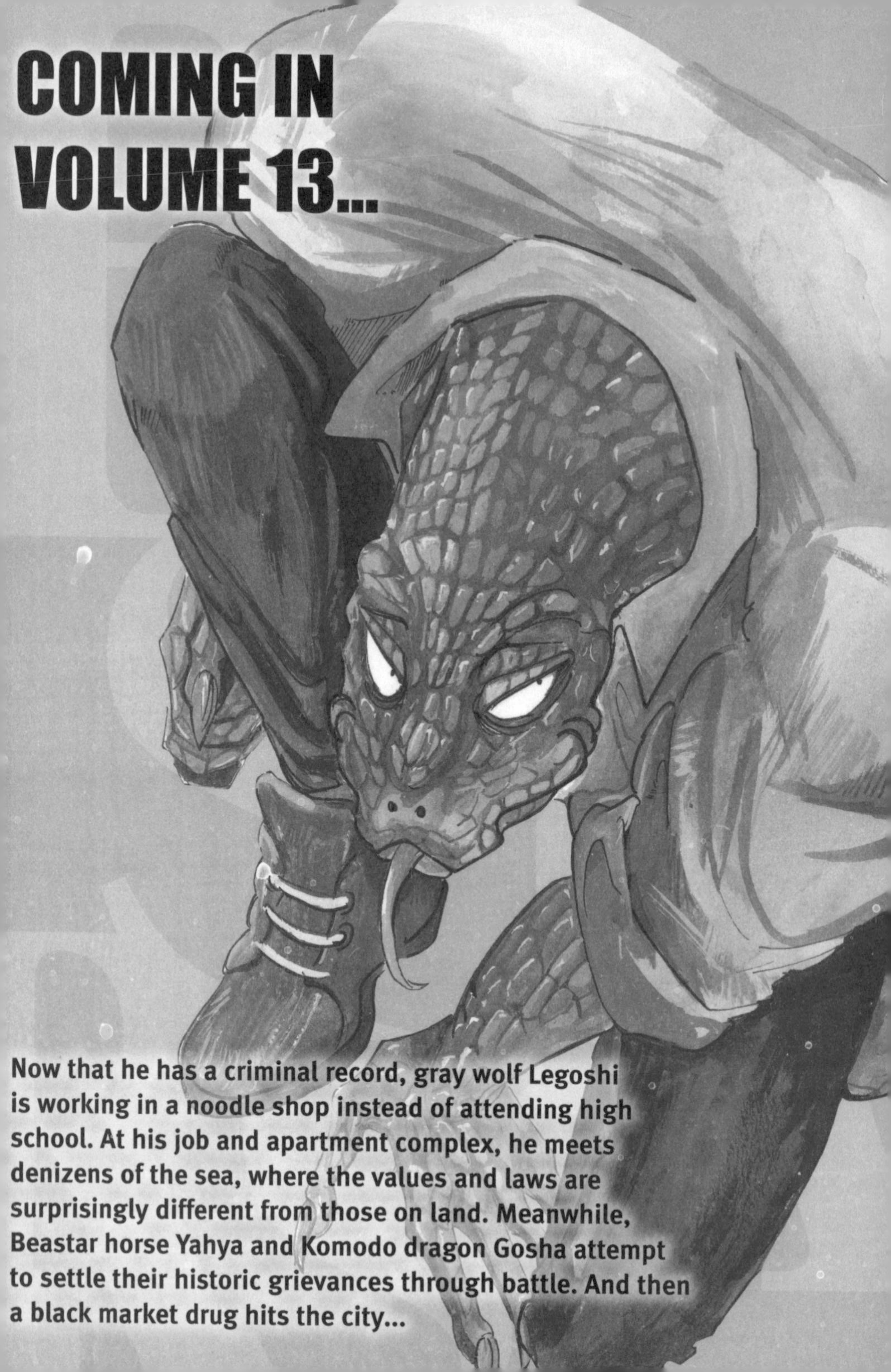

Now that he has a criminal record, gray wolf Legoshi is working in a noodle shop instead of attending high school. At his job and apartment complex, he meets denizens of the sea, where the values and laws are surprisingly different from those on land. Meanwhile, Beastar horse Yahya and Komodo dragon Gosha attempt to settle their historic grievances through battle. And then a black market drug hits the city...

Cats of the Louvre

by TAIYO MATSUMOTO

A surreal tale of the secret world of the cats of the Louvre,
told by Eisner Award winner Taiyo Matsumoto.

The world-renowned Louvre museum in Paris contains more than
just the most famous works of art in history. At night, within its
darkened galleries, an unseen and surreal world comes alive—
a world witnessed only by the small family of cats that lives in
the attic. Until now…

Translated by *Tekkonkinkreet* film director Michael Arias.

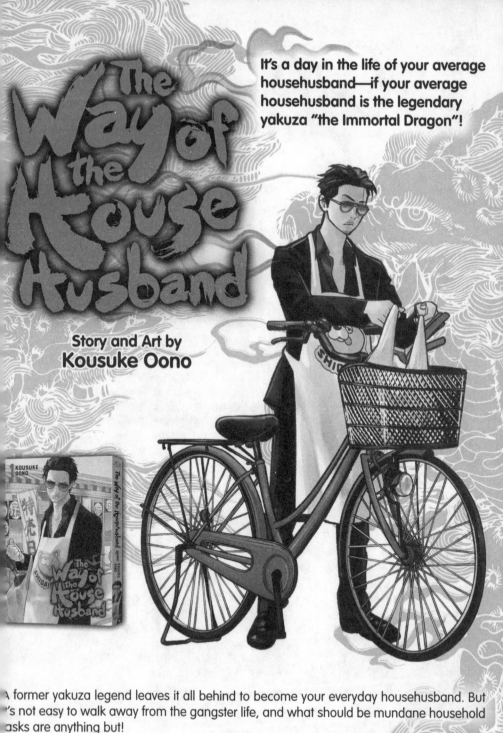

It's a day in the life of your average househusband—if your average househusband is the legendary yakuza "the Immortal Dragon"!

The Way of the House Husband

Story and Art by
Kousuke Oono

A former yakuza legend leaves it all behind to become your everyday househusband. But 's not easy to walk away from the gangster life, and what should be mundane household asks are anything but!

This is the last page.

**BEASTARS reads from right to left
to preserve the orientation of the
original Japanese artwork.**